DATE DUE			
MAY 1 2 1998			
APR 2 8 1998			
APR 2 8 1998			
MAR 1 9 1998			

DEMCO 38-297

Foreign Trade Regimes and Economic Development:

A Special Conference Series on Foreign Trade Regimes and Economic Development

VOLUME IV

NATIONAL BUREAU OF ECONOMIC RESEARCH
New York   *1975*

Foreign Trade Regimes and Economic Development:
EGYPT

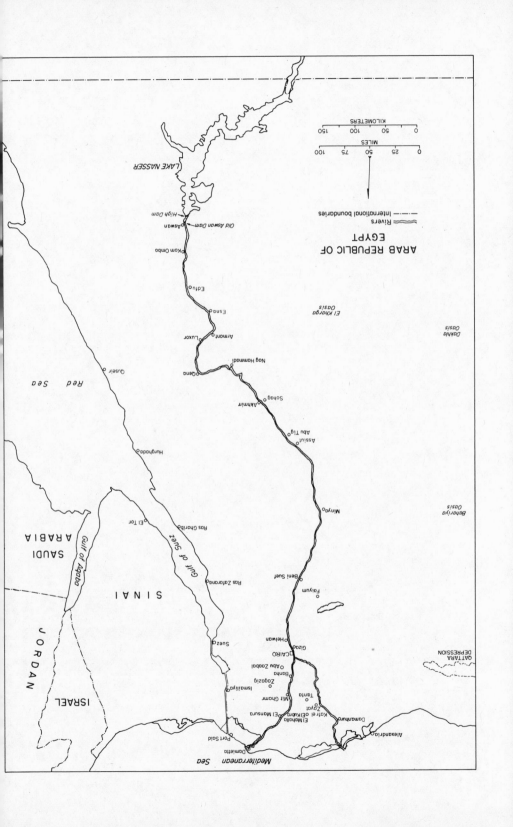

ARAB REPUBLIC OF
EGYPT

Rivers
International boundaries

EGYPT

by **Bent Hansen**

UNIVERSITY OF CALIFORNIA, BERKELEY

Karim Nashashibi

INTERNATIONAL MONETARY FUND

DISTRIBUTED BY Columbia University Press
New York and London

Nᴀᴛɪᴏɴᴀʟ Bᴜʀᴇᴀᴜ ᴏғ Eᴄᴏɴᴏᴍɪᴄ Rᴇsᴇᴀʀᴄʜ

*A Special Conference Series on Foreign Trade Regimes
and Economic Development*

Library of Congress Card Number: 74–82375
ISBN for the series: 0–87014–500–2
ISBN for this volume: 0–87014–504–5

Printed in the United States of America
DESIGNED BY JEFFREY M. BARRIE

390332

Relation of the Directors of the National Bureau to
Publication of the Country Studies in the Series on
Foreign Trade Regimes and Economic Development

The individual country studies have not passed through the National Bureau's normal procedures for review and approval of research reports by the Board of Directors. In view of the way in which these studies were planned and reviewed at successive working parties of authors and Co-Directors, the National Bureau's Executive Committee has approved their publication in a manner analogous to conference proceedings, which are exempted from the rules governing submission of manuscripts to, and critical review by, the Board of Directors. *It should therefore be understood that the views expressed herein are those of the authors only and do not necessarily reflect those of the National Bureau or its Board of Directors.*

The synthesis volumes in the series, prepared by the Co-Directors of the project, are subject to the normal procedures for review and approval by the Directors of the National Bureau.

Contents

Tables and Charts

Tables

Charts

Co-Directors' Foreword

This volume is one of a series resulting from the research project on Exchange Control, Liberalization, and Economic Development sponsored by the National Bureau of Economic Research, the name of the project having been subsequently broadened to Foreign Trade Regimes and Economic Development. Underlying the project was the belief by all participants that the phenomena of exchange control and liberalization in less developed countries require careful and detailed analysis within a sound theoretical framework, and that the effects of individual policies and restrictions cannot be analyzed without consideration of both the nature of their administration and the economic environment within which they are adopted as determined by the domestic economic policy and structure of the particular country.

The research has thus had three aspects: (1) development of an analytical framework for handling exchange control and liberalization; (2) within that framework, research on individual countries, undertaken independently by senior scholars; and (3) analysis of the results of these independent efforts with a view to identifying those empirical generalizations that appear to emerge from the experience of the countries studied.

The analytical framework developed in the first stage was extensively commented upon by those responsible for the research on individual countries, and was then revised to the satisfaction of all participants. That framework, serving as the common basis upon which the country studies were undertaken, is further reflected in the syntheses reporting on the third aspect of the research.

The analytical framework pinpointed these three principal areas of research which all participants undertook to analyze for their own countries.

Subject to a common focus on these three areas, each participant enjoyed maximum latitude to develop the analysis of his country's experience in the way he deemed appropriate. Comparison of the country volumes will indicate that this freedom was indeed utilized, and we believe that it has paid handsome dividends. The three areas singled out for in-depth analysis in the country studies are:

1. *The anatomy of exchange control:* The economic efficiency and distributional implications of alternative methods of exchange control in each country were to be examined and analyzed. Every method of exchange control differs analytically in its effects from every other. In each country study care has been taken to bring out the implications of the particular methods of control used. We consider it to be one of the major results of the project that these effects have been brought out systematically and clearly in analysis of the individual countries' experience.

2. *The liberalization episode:* Another major area for research was to be a detailed analysis of attempts to liberalize the payments regime. In the analytical framework, devaluation and liberalization were carefully distinguished, and concepts for quantifying the extent of devaluation and of liberalization were developed. It was hoped that careful analysis of individual devaluation and liberalization attempts, both successful and unsuccessful, would permit identification of the political and economic ingredients of an effective effort in that direction.

3. *Growth relationships:* Finally, the relationship of the exchange control regime to growth via static-efficiency and other factors was to be investigated. In this regard, the possible effects on savings, investment allocation, research and development, and entrepreneurship were to be highlighted.

In addition to identifying the three principal areas to be investigated, the analytical framework provided a common set of concepts to be used in the studies and distinguished various phases regarded as useful in tracing the experience of the individual countries and in assuring comparability of the analyses. The concepts are defined and the phases delineated in Appendix A.

The country studies undertaken within this project and their authors are as follows:

Brazil	Albert Fishlow, University of California, Berkeley
Chile	Jere R. Behrman, University of Pennsylvania
Colombia	Carlos F. Díaz-Alejandro, Yale University
Egypt	Bent Hansen, University of California, Berkeley, and Karim Nashashibi, International Monetary Fund
Ghana	J. Clark Leith, University of Western Ontario

India   Jagdish N. Bhagwati, Massachusetts Institute of Technology, and T. N. Srinivasan, Indian Statistical Institute

Israel   Michael Michaely, The Hebrew University of Jerusalem

Philippines   Robert E. Baldwin, University of Wisconsin

South Korea   Charles R. Frank, Jr., Princeton University and The Brookings Institution; Kwang Suk Kim, Korea Development Institute, Republic of Korea; and Larry E. Westphal, Northwestern University

Turkey   Anne O. Krueger, University of Minnesota

The principal results of the different country studies are brought together in our overall syntheses. Each of the country studies, however, has been made self-contained, so that readers interested in only certain of these studies will not be handicapped.

In undertaking this project and bringing it to successful completion, the authors of the individual country studies have contributed substantially to the progress of the whole endeavor, over and above their individual research. Each has commented upon the research findings of other participants, and has made numerous suggestions which have improved the overall design and execution of the project. The country authors who have collaborated with us constitute an exceptionally able group of development economists, and we wish to thank all of them for their cooperation and participation in the project.

We must also thank the National Bureau of Economic Research for its sponsorship of the project and its assistance with many of the arrangements necessary in an undertaking of this magnitude. Hal B. Lary, Vice President-Research, has most energetically and efficiently provided both intellectual and administrative input into the project over a three-year period. We would also like to express our gratitude to the Agency for International Development for having financed the National Bureau in undertaking this project. Michael Roemer and Constantine Michalopoulos particularly deserve our sincere thanks.

JAGDISH N. BHAGWATI
Massachusetts Institute of Technology

ANNE O. KRUEGER
University of Minnesota

Acknowledgments

Gathering statistics and other basic information has been one of the major difficulties in our work on this book, which, in several instances, has been severely limited by the lack of data. Egypt may have better statistics than many other less developed countries, but what does exist is not always easily accessible, and administrative practices are, more often than not, difficult to uncover and describe systematically. In this and other respects we are much indebted to Abdel Moneim El Kaissouni, General Manager of the Egyptian International Bank for Foreign Trade and Development; Nazih A. Deif, Executive Director of the International Monetary Fund; Mahmoud Sidky Mourad, formerly Deputy Minister of the Economy and Foreign Trade; Levon Kisheshian, correspondent to *El Ahram;* Said Sonbol, editor, *Akhbar El Yom;* and Mohammed El Sayed Oweida, librarian at the Institute of National Planning, Cairo. Without their great helpfulness substantial parts of the monograph could not have been written.

Much useful information was also obtained on visits to the FAO office in Cairo, the GATT organization in Geneva, and the foreign exchange control authorities in Cairo. Wyn F. Owen, of the University of Colorado, Boulder, read Part Two and gave us valuable comments on agricultural problems.

On the more technical level, we acknowledge statistical, econometric, and computational assistance from Khairy Tourk and Rabab Kreidieh Ward. Thomas Rothenberg, University of California, Berkeley, advised us on econometric problems. We are also grateful to Hedy D. Jellinek for editing the manuscript, and to H. Irving Forman for drawing the charts.

The study of response functions in Appendix A was made possible through a grant from the Institute of International Studies at the University of California, Berkeley. The University supplied free computer time.

Last but not least, we must express our gratitude for the continuous flow of comments and advice received during the last two years from the co-directors of the project, Jagdish Bhagwati and Anne Krueger, and from Hal Lary of the National Bureau of Economic Research, who read draft after draft and often caused us to reconsider results, reorganize material, and clarify obscure points. To have had continuous access to their expert opinion has made participation in this project an unusually rewarding experience for the authors.

This study was undertaken as part of the National Bureau of Economic Research project on exchange control, liberalization, and economic development, under a research contract with the Agency for International Development. Research for the study was carried out at the University of California at Berkeley and at the United Nations in New York prior to the appointment of one of the authors to the staff of the International Monetary Fund. The views expressed in this book are entirely the authors' own.

Finally, we want to call the reader's attention to the authors' NBER Working Paper No. 48, entitled "Protection and Competitiveness in Egyptian Agriculture and Industry," which presents details of the calculations of ERPs and DRCs for both agriculture (Chapter 7) and industry (Chapters 8 and 9), together with the statistical material used in estimates of acreage response functions and elasticities (Chapter 6 and Appendix A) and crop area predictions (Chapter 7), as well as some international comparisons of the competitiveness of Egyptian industries. This Working Paper is available from the National Bureau on request.

BENT HANSEN
KARIM NASHASHIBI

Foreign Trade Regimes and Economic Development: EGYPT

Principal Dates and Historical Events in Egypt

1805   Accession of Mohammed Ali.

1830   Introduction of long staple cotton (Jumel).

1834   Start of Delta Barrage construction at the bifurcation of the Nile near Cairo.

1838   Free Trade Treaty between Great Britain and the Ottoman Empire.

1863–65   Cotton boom (related to the Civil War in the United States).

1869   Inauguration of Suez Canal.

1882   British occupation; appointment of Lord Cromer as British agent and Consul General.

1890   Delta Barrage is brought into effective use.

1902   Inauguration of Aswan Dam.

1907   Resignation of Cromer and appointment of Sir Eldon Gorst.

1914   Egypt is declared a British protectorate.

1920   Establishment of Bank Misr.

1922   Accession to independence (in principle).

1930   Imposition of a new customs tariff.

1947   Egypt leaves the sterling area.

1948   Palestinian War.

1949   Devaluation of Egyptian pound following sterling.

1950   First general election; formation of a nationalistic government.

1951   Korean cotton boom.

1952   July: Coup d'etat by the Free Officers.
September: Creation of a Permanent Council for the Development of National Production.
Land reform limiting property to 200 feddans.

1954   February: Gamal Abd el Nasser takes over.
        July: Agreement on withdrawal of British troops from Canal Zone.
1955   February: Israeli attack on Gaza.
        September: Arms deal with Chechoslovakia.
1956   July: Withdrawal of United States and United Kingdom from Aswan High Dam finance and end of IBRD participation in the project.
        Nationalization of Suez Canal.
        October: Suez War.
1957   January: Creation of Economic Organization for Public Investment; launching of industrial plan.
        Egyptianization laws for financial and trading institutions.
1958   February: Union with Syria; formation of the United Arab Republic.
        Russian commitment to finance Aswan High Dam.
1960   Nationalization of Bank Misr and the National Bank of Egypt.
1960–61 to
    1964–65   First Five-Year Plan.
1961   July: Nationalization of most industrial firms and foreign trade.
        Reduction of land holdings to 100 feddans per individual.
        September: Withdrawal of Syria from Union.
1962   May: Devaluation of the Egyptian Pound.
        September: Egyptian troops intervene in Yemen following military coup.
1963   April: Nationalization of cotton export firms, ginning mills, and some industrial firms.
        October: Formation of the Arab Socialist Union and proclamation of the Charter.
1964–65   Stabilization Policy.
1965   Abrogation of U.S. credits (PL 480).
1967   June War.
1970   July: Inauguration of Aswan High Dam.
        September: Death of Nasser.

Introduction

The political revolution that overthrew the monarchy in 1952 was of little immediate consequence for the Egyptian economy. Land reforms resulted in some redistribution of land and wealth, but the economy continued to be based on private enterprise. As before, quantitative regulations remained directed mainly toward foreign trade and payments, and were largely of the type introduced by many other less developed countries as temporary emergency measures, to be abolished whenever circumstances permitted. It is always difficult to identify precisely what the policy objectives are in such transitional periods, but at least until the Suez War of 1956 there was nothing to indicate that the economy would not continue on a private enterprise basis.

By the end of the fifties government attitudes had shifted in favor of public participation in and direct regulation of the economy, and in 1961 sweeping nationalization measures brought most big business and virtually all foreign trade into the hands of the state. The ideals of private enterprise and free trade were now replaced by those of Arab socialism. In practice, that meant a mixed economy with a large public sector (which included all foreign trade) and with the remaining private economic activities subject to various kinds of direct controls. Prices were regulated for purposes of income distribution and stabilization, and resource allocation in important fields became a matter of administrative decision.

This metamorphosis is described in some detail in Chapter 1. It has the important consequence for our study that the exchange regimes after 1961 have to be appraised as an integral part of the general control system, while their impact on the pre-1961 period has to be analyzed on the basis of the regimes in conjunction with the accompanying aggregative economic policies. The shift in emphasis is related also to a change in the role of prices. In a private enterprise economy the impact of a foreign exchange regime can be gauged through the price distortion it causes, assuming that private producers adjust to the distorted prices. Under extensive price control, domestic market prices will no longer exclusively reflect the exchange regime, and with a large public sector where investment decisions are made by the government, as well as direct intervention in production decisions in both public and private sectors, the allocation of resources will not reflect domestic market prices, either. A system that deliberately intervenes in resource allocation through direct commands may conceivably attain efficiency in production and investment—or create even more inefficiency than would follow from the given exchange regimes under a market system.

Problems of this nature compelled us to supplement the investigation of exchange regimes and trade controls with a rather detailed study of government decisions regarding industrial and agricultural investment and production to gauge directly the degree of efficiency or inefficiency in these areas. As a consequence, we have found it appropriate to divide the monograph into three parts. Part One describes the exchange regimes from World War II until the end of the sixties and examines their effects at an aggregate level; Part Two analyzes cropping patterns in agriculture during the sixties; and Part Three studies the investment and production developments in ten manufacturing industries during the fifties and sixties.

From World War II until 1961 Egypt was the happy owner of very substantial—though largely blocked—foreign exchange reserves in London. During this period Egypt's foreign exchange policies basically consisted in responding to the ups and downs of world economic conditions as they manifested themselves in the international markets for long staple cotton. Their aim was to stabilize both the Egyptian balance of payments and the domestic economy under the constraint set by the speed at which the British government would agree to release Egyptian sterling reserves and convert them into U.S. dollars. The phases of Egyptian exchange policies from the second half of the forties to the beginning of the sixties thus tended to coincide with the phases of the world economy.[1] During an international upswing, cotton prices and export earnings generally increased, generating an upswing with tendencies toward price increases in the domestic Egyptian economy. To stabilize the economy the obvious policy was to relax whatever exchange controls might have existed and to appreciate the domestic currency in an effort to dampen export earnings, expand imports, and keep down domestic prices. Vice versa, during a downswing in world business conditions, cotton prices and export earnings declined and deflationary tendencies were transmitted to the domestic economy. Stabilization now required tightened exchange controls and some measure of currency depreciation. Note that the aim of stabilizing domestic prices and production went nicely hand in hand with that of stabilizing free foreign exchange reserves.

It is along the lines of this paradigm that Chapters 2 and 3 attempt to describe and analyze the Egyptian exchange regimes from World War II to 1961. During this long period the country was vacillating between what the co-directors term Phases I, II, and V;[2] the problem is to trace possible sub-phases to understand these vacillations. To be fully understood, the Egyptian exchange regimes have to be viewed as integral parts of general aggregative stabilization policies, not merely as palliatives adopted to save a troublesome exchange reserve situation or protect domestic industries. Their success was rather limited; generally, they could be characterized as "too little and too late."

In 1962 the foreign exchange reserves were exhausted and Egypt entered a period of permanent, severe foreign exchange crisis—as yet unresolved. A devaluation with unification of exchange rates was undertaken in 1962 (as discussed in Chapter 4). In a sense, it could be said that here we have Phase III, to use the co-directors' terminology: after fifteen years of fumbling with foreign exchange regimes, the government finally decided to devalue overtly.

De facto, however, the devaluation was imposed upon the country by the International Monetary Fund as a condition for obtaining short-term credits in a critical situation, possibly in the hope that it might be an overture to liberalization in the conventional sense of the word. The Egyptian government had not wanted to devalue—it saw no reason for it, and had no intention of liberalizing trade and foreign exchange in any sense of the word. For by that time, the fundamental institutional changes in Egyptian society alluded to above were a *fait accompli,* rendering it difficult and, indeed, inappropriate to pursue the analysis in terms of deviations from and approaches to free trade.

With the introduction of Arab socialism, foreign trade and financial transactions became government prerogatives that were not going to be abolished even if the economy, internally and externally, had been in a state of equilibrium. Indeed, what were emergency controls before 1961 now became the normal institutions of the country, and how the economy would work was going to depend, *inter alia,* upon the rules for their operation. Refusing to see anything but palliatives in such a system would be an absurdity, almost like insisting that the communist system in the Soviet Union is really only an expedient that would be superfluous if that country just pursued appropriate demand management policies and introduced a realistic exchange rate! With controls established as permanent institutions in a system dominated by the public sector and by government ownership and decisions, the basis for their evaluation should be above all how well they serve that particular system, with its particular constraints on private economic activity and its particular economic and social aims (as best as these can be identified).

It is along these lines that Chapter 5—and Parts Two and Three in their entirety—attempt to appraise exchange regimes and domestic controls after 1961. Chapter 5 describes the situation after the nationalizations of that year and the devaluation of 1962, focusing on the formal machinery of exchange allocation. The motives for the actual allocations, apart from certain very general principles, are hidden behind a wall of administrative secrecy which we have not been able to penetrate (yet another reason why we have been compelled to study directly the allocation of resources in Parts Two and Three).

Chapters 6 and 7 study cropping patterns in agriculture during the sixties. An econometric technique was developed to measure the deviation of actual crop acreages from optimal acreages, the portion of the deviation that can be ascribed to price distortions, and the impact of direct government controls. Generally, we find that, rather than neutralizing them, the direct controls have added to the deviations from optimal cropping patterns that the price distortions alone would have created. Thus, on balance, far from improving the situation in regard to efficiency in production, the direct acreage controls only served to make it worse.

Chapters 8 to 10, comprising Part Three, analyze ten important manufacturing industries from the point of view of efficiency and international competitiveness. Because the government—before 1961 with the participation of private industry—attempted to broaden the industrial structure, it did not concentrate investments in the most efficient, traditional industries. Hence, a tendency to a relative decline in measured competitiveness is apparent over the period. It may be partly explained by the emergence of infant industries, but some long-term misallocation of investments clearly did take place. There is no evidence that this went beyond the misallocation that would have occurred in any case as a consequence of genuinely private investment decisions made by private firms on the basis of price distortions created by the government to provide adequate profits in inefficient industries. Before 1961, low efficiency was, in fact, always accommodated by the necessary price distortions. After 1961, inefficiency was reflected in low profits or losses, financed by government subsidies, rather than in greater price distortion. Thus, it can be argued that after 1961 there was less misallocation in respect to manufactured consumer goods in the sense that price distortion of consumption patterns was reduced. Moreover, there was no automatic "resource pull" to inefficient industries. These positive features may have been more than offset, however, by shortages in consumer goods caused by trade controls and by undue concentration of decisions at the ministerial level, severely disrupting the incentive system at the plant level, misallocating labor, crippling its discipline, and generally creating a rather erratic pattern of trade and inventories. Albeit some labor misallocation may have been adopted for the sake of income redistribution, the latter can certainly not serve as an excuse for the nepotism in hiring practices and personnel management prevailing over the whole period and aggravated after 1961. There is, on the other hand, little evidence of production disruptions as a direct consequence of the exchange regimes, although this circumstance is probably related to discrimination in favor of the big, modern manufacturing industries, as discussed in Part Three.

It should be emphasized that our paradigms at best capture only the most essential characteristics of Egyptian foreign exchange regimes. Actual developments were more complex than that. Moreover, the aims of successive governments were never clearly formulated, and more often than not policy moves were badly prepared, poorly executed, and occasionally inconsistent. In explaining our paradigms, we warned against considering the exchange regimes as mere palliatives. To some extent, of course, they were just that. Thus, both the Organization of Free Officers and, later, Nasser himself were obsessed by the idea of the stability of the Egyptian pound—that is, of its official par rate—as a symbol of the soundness of the economy and perhaps even of the nation. (In all fairness, let it not be forgotten that this was conventional wisdom at that time, codified in the IMF.) When, during the fifties, exchange regimes followed each other in rapid succession, they doubtless also served to conceal the true nature of the policy pursued. And the resistance to the 1962 devaluation, not to mention the blunt refusal to devalue further in 1966, may have been more a question of paying homage to the national (and international) symbol than the logical consequence of sponsoring an economic system where prices serve to regulate income distribution rather than resource allocation and where, for that reason, devaluation has a different role to play— if it has a role to play at all—than within a conventional, private enterprise-oriented liberalization program.

While we are fully aware of this aspect of Egyptian foreign exchange policies, making it the focus of our analysis would be misleading. It would tend to hide the real problem that the government was seeking to solve: the administration of a mixed economy, dominated by the public sector, with nationalized foreign trade. How to make such a system function efficiently is a problem that socialist regimes in general and the Egyptian government in particular have yet to solve.

NOTES

1. For a listing of specific phases in tracing the evolution of exchange control regimes, delineated by the co-directors of the present series, Jagdish Bhagwati and Anne Krueger, as an overall guide, see Appendix B, pp. 348–349.

2. See Appendix B, p. 349.

Part One

Foreign Exchange Regimes in Egypt, 1946-1969

Chapter 1

Foreign Trade in the Egyptian Economy

This study highlights foreign trade and exchange controls in Egypt and their impact on economic development during the two decades between World War II and the June 1967 War. The full picture, of course, emerges only in the context of the country's overall economic policy, against the background of its general economic conditions. At the same time, a detailed survey of the Egyptian economy and its development is clearly beyond the scope of a specialized study like ours; moreover, several general surveys are easily accessible to the reader.[1] For these reasons we limit ourselves here to a brief sketch of some major historical, economic, and political features important to foreign trade and exchange policies.

NINETY YEARS OF FREE TRADE, 1840–1930

During the first decades of the nineteenth century, the viceroy Mohammed Ali made an abortive attempt to develop Egypt into an autarchic industrial economy.[2] His policies collapsed around 1840, when agreements between the European powers and the Sublime Porte—of which Egypt, in principle, was a dependency—gave foreigners full freedom of trade and navigation in the country and led to the abolition of government monopolies in trade and production.[3] Until 1930, Egypt continued under a regime of almost perfectly free trade.[4] The conventions signed by the Porte limited import duties to 5 percent ad valorem, later increased to 8 percent, with a few exceptions varying over time. At the end of the twenties the tariff for kerosene was 4 percent, for con-

3

struction timber, 10 percent, and for gasoline and lubricants, 15 percent. Except for special, higher rates for alcohol and tobacco, the uniform 8 percent ad valorem rate was applied to all other imports.[5] A general export duty was first levied at 12 percent ad valorem, but soon lowered to 1 percent. Direct controls were virtually nonexistent, with one important exception from 1916 on: a ban on imports of foreign cotton, which we shall discuss in detail later.

During close to a century of free trade the Egyptian cotton economy was developed to a high level of perfection, but practically no industrialization took place. The very substantial inflow of foreign capital and financial, commercial, and technical expertise were absorbed in agriculture, trade, finance, and infrastructure. With the wisdom of hindsight, it stands to reason that earlier industrialization might have proved beneficial,[6] and the British have been strongly criticized for their free trade, nonindustrialization policy. In all fairness it should be admitted, however, that generally few obstacles were raised against industrialization,[7] and that the development that actually did take place was in the fields where the country obviously had a natural advantage. Also, the British can hardly be blamed for failing to predict the Great Depression.

PROTECTIONISM AND THE BEGINNING OF INDUSTRIALIZATION, 1930–1950

In 1930 Egypt gained tariff autonomy and immediately used her freedom to reform the tariff system in a protectionist direction.[8] Raw materials and fuel were now taxed at lower rates than before; semimanufactured goods, at about the old level, at 6 to 8 percent; and manufactured goods, at 15 to 30 percent. In most cases the duties were specific. During the 1930s they were increased very substantially for manufactured goods such as textiles and footwear. A general import tax of 1 percent ad valorem was introduced in 1932 and subsequently increased. The sugar industry was particularly favored through a variable tariff that kept domestic prices at a high level independently of fluctuations in the world market price of raw sugar. In addition to the tariff reform, the government started supporting industries through subsidies, cheap loans, and other measures.

Behind the tariff wall the few existing industries expanded and a number of new ones were established during the 1930s. (For details, see Part Three.) The low profitability of agricultural investments also helped to shift domestic capital to manufacturing, and industrialization might have been initiated even without the protectionist measures. With the relative fall in agricultural prices, particularly for cotton, Egypt's natural advantages shifted somewhat in favor of manufacturing industry.[9] It has been held that the protectionist measures helped greatly to establish domestic monopolies,[10] and this aspect of protectionism may well have been equally important in the promotion of new industries.

A further impetus to industrialization came with the outbreak of World War II. When Italy entered the war, Egypt was largely cut off from foreign supplies. The combined domestic civilian and Allied military demand led to the emergence of new industries, partly in repair and metal manufacturing, partly in areas based on hitherto ignored domestic raw materials.

The protectionist policies of the 1930s were continued after the war when, for example, the production of nitrogenous fertilizers was taken up and the textile industry expanded vigorously. The general ad valorem duty was raised to 7 percent beginning with 1946, but was lowered again to 3 percent in 1950. Duties on capital goods were lowered.

During the war an elaborate system of direct controls had been set up by both Allied and national authorities for distributing food and scarce raw materials and for regulating prices. This control system was never fully dismantled after the war as commodity and foreign exchange shortages continued to make themselves felt. During a brief spell of liberalization at the time of the Korean boom it was substantially limited, but during the ensuing recession direct controls once again gained in importance and subsequently became the main instruments of Egyptian economic policy.

THE ECONOMIC POLICIES OF THE NASSER REGIME

Using the plural form for the word policy in the title to this section is intentional. The economic policy of the Nasser regime changed radically during its first decade in response to external pressures and internal ideological developments in a way that has never been satisfactorily explored.[11]

The Organization of Free Officers that took power in 1952 was a heterogeneous group of mainly young people with political views ranging from the extreme left to the extreme right. It had no precisely formulated, detailed economic program apart from the land reforms that were implemented almost instantaneously. The latter had the character of political and social rather than economic reforms, and were undertaken for reasons of social justice with a view to redistributing wealth and income. Social justice was probably the single economic idea that the members of the Organization of Free Officers had in common and that clearly distinguished its policy from that of the old regime. With all the imperfections of Egyptian economic policies, it remained a leading principle of the government's political philosophy until recently.

In its general economic policy the new regime did little more than continue that of the old regime until the nationalization of the Suez Canal. The

Free Officers took power after the end of the Korean boom and the collapse of the cotton markets, and fiscal and monetary as well as foreign exchange policies were cautiously tight during the first year or two. In fact, the new regime did not really take over general government until 1954, and in the interim it was the old style politicians who ran economic policy. El Kaisouni, who represented modern economic thinking in the Nasser regime, was appointed Minister of the Treasury in 1954; later he became, in addition, Minister of the Economy and Minister of Planning. Controls over foreign exchange were tightened in 1953, but did not go beyond those found in both European and underdeveloped countries at that time. Defense expenditures had been substantially expanded by the old regime after the establishment of the Jewish state in Palestine, but were not increased further (as a percentage of GNP) by the new regime until the Yemen war in 1962. The old regime had embarked upon a public investment program that, by any standard, was quite impressive. Little was done immediately to expand this program further. The new regime relied basically upon private initiative in investment and production, and sought to promote private investment by protectionism, tax incentives, and other conventional measures. Private enterprise was slow to respond, however. Quite apart from the general recession in the Egyptian economy from 1952 to 1954, both the land reforms and the new regime's rather erratic sequestrations of private property served to create an atmosphere of uncertainty that was not conducive to private investment activities and tended to divert such activities to inconspicuous fields.

In the area of foreign trade and exchange, the major change—before the events surrounding the Suez War in 1956 upset Egyptian trade completely—had already taken place back in 1947, when the old regime decided to leave the Sterling Area and shift trade away from Britain. Bilateral trade was initiated by the old regime but expanded rapidly during the first years of the new regime, particularly with communist countries. In the beginning the expansion of trade with these countries had few ideological overtones: it was merely another opportunity to expand the markets for Egyptian cotton and textiles and thus expand trade in general. Nevertheless, it was trade with the communist countries that, among other things, initiated the radical changes in economic policy that were soon to follow.

This is not the place to discuss the diplomatic and not-so-diplomatic events that led up to and followed the Egyptian-Czechoslovak arms deal of 1955, the peculiar behavior of the United States in relation to the scheduled Aswan High Dam loan from the World Bank, the nationalization of the Suez Canal, the British-French-Israeli aggression and the Suez War, the accompanying foreign exchange and trade blockade by the United States, Britain, and France, and the subsequent shift of Egyptian trade from West to East.[12] This chain of events is of great interest in the present context, however, not only because it changed Egyptian economic policy so fundamentally but also because it poses some challenging problems for the conventional pure theory of optimal trade. When a decision to make purchases (of weapons, in this instance) in one half of the world creates trade and aid obstacles (and even prompts war) from the other half, analysis ceteris paribus with respect to conditions of trade becomes rather uninteresting in itself. Ceteris paribus analysis has, of course, still a role to play. The economic gain or loss from a particular trade or exchange policy measure can be set against the gain or loss from any retaliatory move; and ex post facto, the net gain or loss can be calculated (assuming, of course, that the utility of all measures, including the purchase of weapons, can be expressed in economic terms and is known).[13] But for designing *future* policies such analyses are of little operational value. For here everything depends upon whether retaliation will take place and in what form. An Egyptian decision to purchase more weapons from the Soviet Union may be punished by the U.S. Congress through a ban on Egyptian cotton exports to the United States; this would lead to a shift of Egyptian exports away from the United States to other countries, implying an extra cost for the weapons deal. But the punishment might also take the form of stepped-up military deliveries to Yemen royalists or to Israel, which, in turn, would increase the shadow price of weapons in Egypt and act as an incentive for a further expansion of weapons imports and commodity exports.

This kind of mechanism has played a major role in the development of Egyptian foreign trade policies and patterns since 1956. In the nature of the case, the pure theory of foreign trade has little advice to give about optimal trade strategies under such circumstances.

At the outbreak of the Suez War, Egypt immediately confiscated all property belonging to British and French subjects and nationalized all British and French companies (concentrated mainly in banking, finance, and trade). These steps were in a sense a natural and predictable consequence of the war. What was less predictable is that the events were also followed by a change in the attitude of the regime to *domestic* private business.

The war seems to have convinced the government that, if Egypt was to be able to defend herself, economic development was imperative. The new regime had, it is true, favored development in general terms all along and plans for the Aswan High Dam were a cornerstone of Nasser's developmental thinking. But it was not until after the Suez War that the new regime seriously embarked upon a development policy. Industrial and agricultural investment plans were drawn up in 1957 with emphasis on public investment. The (private) Federation of Industry was not even consulted on the plans and, when disagreement arose about the direction of private investment, nationalization of the big Misr Bank followed in 1960. A comprehensive five-year plan for the first half of the 1960s assumed that virtually all investment should be public. In July 1961 a series of decrees suddenly nationalized all large-scale industry, finance, and trade.[14] Further nationalization decrees, together with an extension of the land reforms, followed in 1963, and a national charter declared Arab socialism to be the basis of the economic system and the economic policy of the country. It should be added that sequestrations (based on presidential decrees) continued erratically (from an economic point of view, at least) to bring private property under public administration.[15]

All these changes added up to the establishment of a new economic system in Egypt. It is not clear, however, what the logic of this new system was. Behind the sweeping changes there was no carefully elaborated, coherent economic and social philosophy. The ideologists of the regime largely limited themselves to ex post comments on whatever decisions had actually been made, and such comment seldom went beyond simplistic rhetoric. Nasser's own speeches—long though they were—were not very illuminating, either. It is not always clear whether changes in the system were ends in themselves, undertaken to satisfy certain ideological requirements, or whether they were used as means, necessary to fulfill the basic aims of the regime: social justice, with its implications for distribution of wealth, income, and opportunity (including employment), economic growth, and (at least from the time of the Yemen war) what can be called military grandeur.[16] Nor should expediency, as well as the erratic responses of a highly impulsive and often badly informed ruler to short-term problems,[17] be ruled out as explanations.[18]

THE NEW ECONOMIC SYSTEM

The following pages outline the major characteristics of the present economic system as it was created at the beginning of the sixties and briefly indicate some major implications for the targets of the regime and for the foreign trade and exchange problems analyzed in detail later in our study.

The present system derives its socialist character mainly from the fact that all big business is in the hands of the government, which has taken over existing businesses and founded new ones. Since little, if any, compensation has been paid for existing enterprises taken over by the government, the change in ownership of big business has been accompanied by the disappearance of the upper tail of the wealth and income distribution. The land reform has worked in the same direction, although it has not directly expanded government ownership of the means of production; with the exception of the royal family, compensation should have been paid to the old owners according to the law, but as a matter of fact nobody has ever received compensation.[19]

There is no legal limit to the size of private enterprises, and such enterprises can be established in principle in almost any field. However, the government would presumably not let any private business grow big without nationalizing it sooner or later, and, of course, this presumption exerts a strong brake on private initiative. It would probably be difficult, if not impossible, to find private enterprises today with more than one hundred employees; the vast majority have a few employees at most. Strangely enough, in urban real estate it is still possible to find big private capitalists. While the regime is not hostile in principle to small-scale private business, it has explicitly favored the idea of cooperative organization as the desirable form of private small-scale enterprise. However, apart from a network of government retail stores named "cooperatives," little has been achieved in the direction of cooperative operations outside agriculture.

Government versus private economic activity by sector is divided as follows: modern manufacturing, mining, electricity and other public utilities, construction, transport and communication, finance, and wholesale trade (including almost all foreign trade) are, by and large, government-owned, while most retail trade, handicrafts and repair, housing, professional services of all kinds, and agriculture are privately owned and operated. Furthermore, the government imposes some control even upon agricultural production through its control over the irrigation system and the compulsory participation of all cultivators in the government-sponsored agricultural cooperatives. About half of the gross domestic product is produced by the public sector.

Government controls may also be classified by expenditure categories. *Private consumption* is largely free in the sense that only a few necessities are rationed, and even those may usually be purchased without controls at higher prices. However, the consumer is, of course, limited in his choice by the available supplies, which, to a large extent, depend directly upon government decisions in production and trade. Consumer credits were given generously until around 1964–65 for purchases of domestically produced consumer durables, but have been difficult to obtain since then. *Public consumption* is determined through traditional budgetary procedures, with large-scale weapons purchases negotiated directly by the president. Investments are public up to 90 percent. Decisions about *public investments* are taken by the ministries within limits set by the government. When a ministry has decided upon an investment within its allocation it will generally give a green light to financing and importation of investment goods. Some large public investments, partly financed from abroad, are decided upon directly by the government in negotiations with foreign donors or lenders. No general criteria for public investments seem to have been laid down. *Private investment* activities are very limited and in most cases conditioned by building or import licenses. Private fixed investment consists mainly in residential building. *Exports and imports,* finally, are almost exclusively a public activity.

The government exercises wide control over the distribution of capital goods, raw materials, and semimanufactures as well as over prices and wages. Historically, most of these controls have had nothing to do with the public ownership of larger enterprises. Both import licensing and price controls (including agricultural support price schemes and the like) grew up during the forties and the fifties, and enterprises have remained subject to such controls even after nationalization. In this regard the present Egyptian economic system resembles the Western European control economies of the late forties more than the current communist economies (including Yugoslavia's). Now the controls seem to have become part and parcel of Arab socialism, but they were originally introduced in Egypt for much the same reasons as earlier in Western Europe: if everything had been left to market forces, shortages of foreign exchange and commodities would have led to strong shifts in relative prices and income distribution, incompatible with prevailing views on social justice. There is a difference, however—whereas Western Europe rapidly overcame the shortages and was able to abolish commodity and price controls as well as foreign exchange controls in the first half of the fifties, Egypt has become more and more deeply entangled in her own web of controls. A decisive factor here is certainly that the administrative feasibility of solutions to problems of social justice through taxes and transfers is much more limited in Egypt than in Western Europe, regardless of the fact that the Nasser regime's commitment to social justice targets may have been no less sincere than that of most Northwestern European governments.

It has already been emphasized that both public and private enterprises are, in principle, constrained by administrative controls. This circumstance does not mean, of course, that public and private enterprises are, in fact, treated equally by the controlling authorities, or that they respond to changing conditions in the same way. Price controls are most effective with respect to public enterprises, which, on the other hand, are clearly favored in the distribution of scarce capital goods, spare parts, and raw materials. Apart from public utilities, public enterprises are in most cases organized as joint-stock companies, with the government as the sole or major shareholder. Decisions on current management, in theory at least, are left to the board of directors and the general manager. Thus, public enterprises in both production and trade could, if so ordered, behave like profit-maximizing private enterprises (given the constraints of administrative price and commodity controls). However, no general directives seem to have been issued for their management; as a matter of fact, there is considerable direct interference with production decisions from the ministries under whose jurisdiction the enterprises operate. There is also some participation in management by the workers, but its main impact seems to have been to create difficulties in enforcing discipline on the shop floor. It is thus exceedingly difficult to generalize about the behavior and responses of public enterprises. One thing is abundantly clear—they do not behave just like profit-maximizing private enterprises.

From this description of the system it is evident that—disregarding black markets—there is relatively little direct, automatic price response to changes in demand and supply conditions. Some agricultural goods enjoy free price formation, and the same is true of most products and services in the area of handicrafts, repair shops, professionals, and so forth. But all major commodity prices are fixed by the government, which also sets wholesale and retail profit margins. Even factor prices are widely controlled. Rentals (but not prices) of agricultural land and urban buildings, as well as interest on loans from all financial institutions, are fixed at low levels. Wages in public enterprises are paid according to a scale set by the government. Statutory minimum wages for both urban and rural workers exist but are enforced only for larger enterprises and public works, and not at all in agriculture. Trade unions are government-controlled and have little impact on wages.

Moreover, with some 40 percent of domestic expenditures for final use, as well as imports and exports, administratively controlled by the government, and about half of the production of goods and services for final use taking place in the public sector—together with some direct government interference in private production—it follows that automatic responses of quantities in demand and supply are, by and large, limited to private consumption and small-scale production (partly including agriculture, to be sure). Thus, market forces have been largely replaced by administrative decisions, although all this does not amount to a centralized command economy of the communist type but resembles, rather, (as already mentioned) the controlled economies of Western Europe during the years immediately following World War II.

Insofar as the 1960s are concerned, it is therefore obvious that we cannot apply uncritically the standard competitive foreign trade models to Egypt and assume that balance of payments measures will have the standard effects upon the balance of payments and the domestic economy. The same is partly true for the second half of the 1950s. With foreign trade and payments entirely in the hands of the government, there is no such thing as an automatic balance of payments response. Effects on the domestic economy through price responses will make themselves felt mainly to the degree that the government deliberately chooses to change domestic prices; indeed, to a large extent, both domestic prices and quantities supplied must simply be considered as policy instruments. In such an economy a devaluation, to take an important example, will only work to the extent that the government takes complementary measures in regard to prices and quantities—measures which could be taken without a formal devaluation.

NATIONAL PRODUCTION AND EXPENDITURES, 1947 TO 1969–70[20]

To highlight the structure of the Egyptian economy and its development since World War II, Tables 1–1 and 1–2 show gross domestic product—

TABLE 1–1

Gross Domestic Product: Growth Rate and Sectoral Origin, 1947 to 1968–69

	1947	1952	1956–57	1963–64	1966–67	1968–69
GDP, at 1959–60 market prices (mill. £E)	764	983	1,074	1,606	1,765	1,813
GDP, annual growth rate (percent compounded)	5.2	2.0	5.9	3.2	1.4	
Share in GDP (percent)						
Agriculture	38	33	30	27	28	29
Industry, mining, electricity	13	13	16	24	22	23
Construction	3	3	3	5	4	5
Transport and communication	6	7	6	9	10	5
Trade and finance	19	19	16	9	9	9
Housing	7	7	6	5	4	4
Other services, including government and public utilities	14	17	22	21	23	25
Total	100	100	100	100	100	100

NOTE: The GDP figures were spliced together from three different estimates. The official data for the sixties had to be corrected for some obvious mistakes in the construction (1963–64) and housing (1968–69) sectors. As far as sector distribution is concerned, 1947 should be fully comparable to 1952, and 1963–64, to 1968–69. 1956–57 is roughly comparable to 1947 and 1952, but only to some extent to 1963–64 and later years. The sharp decline in the share of trade and finance between 1956–57 and 1963–64 and the corresponding increase in the share of industry, mining, and electricity are largely definitional.

SOURCES: 1947, 1952, and 1956–57: B. Hansen and G. A. Marzouk, *Development and Economic Policy in the U.A.R. (Egypt)*, Amsterdam, 1965, Statistical Appendix.

1963–64: B. Hansen, "Planning and Economic Growth in the U.A.R., 1960–65," in P. V. Vatikiotis, ed., *Egypt since the Revolution*, London, 1968.

1966–67 and 1968–69: Central Agency for General Mobilization and Statistics (CAGMS) and Ministry of Planning, Cairo.

TABLE 1-2

Gross National Product and Gross Domestic Product: Distribution by Expenditure Category

(percent)

	1947	1952	1956–57	1963–64	1966–67	1969–70
Gross investments	12.0	11.5	13.4	19.2	15.5	13.0
Public consumption	7.5	12.8	15.6	21.3	19.7	25.4
Private consumption	83.7	79.8	73.8	66.1	65.8	65.8
Exports	n.a.	21.4	19.8	19.0	17.3	13.3
Imports	n.a.	−25.5	−22.6	−26.0	−18.2	−16.5
Foreign balance						
(exports—imports)	−3.3	−4.1	−2.8	−7.0	−0.9	−3.2
Adjustment	—	—	—	0.4	−0.1	−1.0
GDP at current market prices	100.0	100.0	100.0	100.0	100.0	100.0
Net factor income from abroad	n.a.	−1.2	0.1	−0.3	−0.9	−1.3
GNP at current market prices	n.a.	98.8	100.2	99.7	99.1	98.7

SOURCES: 1947, 1952, 1956–57: B. Hansen and G. A. Marzouk, *Development and Economic Policy in the U.A.R. (Egypt)*, Statistical Appendix; and *Economic Bulletin*, National Bank of Egypt, 1970. 1963–64 and thereafter: Central Agency for General Mobilization and Statistics (CAGMS) and Ministry of Planning, Cairo. The shares are calculated on the basis of current price estimates. The table may underestimate both the increase in the real share of public consumption and the fall in that of private consumption. Individual years are not fully comparable. Gross investment does not include stock changes, except for 1966–67 and 1969–70. In the latter year stock investments exceeded 2 per cent of GDP. Private consumption is estimated as a residual. Public consumption does not include military equipment received as grants, and probably includes payments but not deliveries of other foreign military equipment.

GDP—by origin and expenditure categories in years that demarcate the beginning or end of periods particularly interesting from an economic policy point of view.

The 1947–1952 period was one of rapid postwar recovery at a growth rate of about 5 percent per annum. It ended with the Korean boom and is the only period marked by attempts to liberalize foreign trade and payments. Since then the tendency has been, instead, toward more direct control over the foreign sector.

During the period from 1952 to 1955 there was a relative slack in the economy, with only a growth of about 2 percent. These were the years when the new regime was still quite passive with regard to development and overly conservative in the area of fiscal and monetary policy, considering the very substantial gold and foreign exchange reserves.

After the Suez War of 1956 the government's development efforts increasingly dominated the economy, and both fiscal and monetary policies became inflationary. This period lasted until about 1964, when foreign exchange difficulties forced the government to cut back investments and generally pursue a less expansionary fiscal and monetary policy. The fiscal year 1963–64 marked the end of unhampered development efforts. The average growth rate for this period was almost 6 percent.

The following three years were characterized by severe foreign exchange shortages, relatively tight fiscal and monetary policies, and, it should be added, poor crops. The growth rate slowed down to an average of little more than 3 percent. With the June 1967 War, GDP fell, and, despite a subsequent recovery, the growth rate averaged only about 1½ percent during the three years ended June 1969.

Population may have been growing by somewhat less than 2 percent annually at the end of the forties. By 1960 the rate had increased to about 2.4 percent and by 1970 to 2.5 percent. The period 1947–1952 may thus have experienced an annual increase of per capita income of about 3 percent. From 1952 to 1955–56 per capita income probably fell slightly. During the development years, from 1956–57 to 1963–64, there was an annual increase of 3–3½ percent. Thereafter, per capita income first stagnated and then fell somewhat. From 1968–69 to 1971–72 it may have been increasing again by some 3–3¼ percent, but is now nearly stagnant.

The composition of national expenditure closely reflects the policies behind the development of the growth rate. During the nearly ten years between 1947 and 1956–57 the share of gross (fixed) investment remained low at a level of 12 to 13 percent. The share of public consumption increased by about 8 percentage points (partly for defense) over the period, while that of private consumption seems to have dropped sharply—by about 10 percentage points. There was a minor decrease in the balance of payments deficit.

From 1956–57 to 1963–64 the share of fixed investments increased by 6 percentage points to about 19 percent. The share of public consumption increased by another 6 percentage points to 21 percent. These increases were offset (in real terms) by a continued steep decline in the share of private consumption of almost 8 percentage points and an increase in the foreign deficit of 4 percentage points.

The cutbacks in demand initiated in 1964 to curb inflation and improve the balance of payments did not affect the share of private consumption very much. The share of public consumption fell moderately, and that of investments, substantially. The June 1967 War further intensified the fall in the share of investments, while public consumption took a new strong jump to almost 25 percent of GDP and the foreign deficit temporarily increased. Private consumption kept its share almost unchanged despite the war.

Egypt thus ended the sixties devoting almost as low a share of GDP to investments as it had in 1947. But public consumption had more than tripled (to almost 25 percent), while that of private consumption had shrunk by one fourth (to about 65 percent). A largely unchanged payments deficit persisted.

Table 1–2 also brings out a decline in foreign trade relative to GDP. From 1952 to 1969–70 total exports of goods and services fell from 21.4 to 14.3 percent of GDP. Part of this fall is related to the closure of the Suez Canal. Canal revenues amounted to about 4 percent of GDP in 1966–67. Total payments for imports of goods and services (including payments for military equipment but excluding interest and dividend payments) remained at the very high level of about one quarter of GDP until 1963–64, after which the ratio was cut back to about 18 percent. (The balance of payments will be discussed in somewhat more detail in the following section.)

FOREIGN TRADE AND BALANCE OF PAYMENTS, 1947–1969

The Egyptian balance of payments has been persistently in the red since World War II (see Table 1–3). The cumulated current deficit from 1950 through 1967 amounted to £E993 million. It should be noted that deficits existed already before 1950, and that the cumulative figure does not include possible credits for military equipment outstanding at the end of 1967.

The deficits were financed mainly by first drawing on the large foreign exchange reserves accumulated during World War II to a total of £E364 million and then by loans to an amount of £E595 million (net). The reserves (net) of gold and foreign exchange were brought down to a minimum at the beginning of the 1960s (see Table 3–7), when the foreign debt began to build up rapidly. During the first half of the 1960s U.S. funds (U.S. PL

TABLE 1-3
Egypt's Balance of Payments, 1950–1967
(mill. £E)

	1950	1951	1952	1953	1954	1955	1956	1957	1958
Exports[a]	190.2	204.5	148.8	137.8	144.2	139.1	132.5	167.0	163.1
Imports[a]	−222.6	−243.4	−212.9	−166.7	−155.9	−193.9	−196.0	−218.6	−215.5
Balance of trade[a]	−32.4	−38.9	−64.1	−28.9	−11.7	−54.8	−63.5	−51.6	−52.4
Shipping, net[b]	−0.6	0.3	0.0	0.4	−0.2	−0.8	−0.3	−1.9	−2.1
Suez Canal dues	26.2	26.4	26.6	29.1	30.6	31.8	29.3	24.3	43.0
British army expenditures	13.0	14.7	5.8	9.0	5.6	4.8	—	—	—
Interest and dividends, net	−11.2	−12.5	−12.1	−11.1	−13.1	−9.8	−5.1	1.9	2.8
Government expenditure	−5.1	−6.3	−5.7	−6.6	−9.4	−11.0	−12.9	−16.9	−21.7
Other, net	−3.9	1.1	−3.8	0.2	1.8	5.8	19.5	13.0	10.3
Balance on invisibles	18.4	23.7	10.7	21.0	15.3	20.8	30.5	20.4	32.3
Balance on current account	−14.0	−15.2	−53.4	−7.9	3.6	−34.0	−33.0	−31.2	−20.1
Loans, net[c]	−3.6	−4.6	−2.0	−0.4	−0.3	2.2	2.0	−0.1	1.5
Transfers[d]	—	—	—	—	—	—	—	—	—
Deterioration of:									
Foreign exchange and gold reserve	7.4	17.9	57.8	4.1	−6.9	32.3	33.3	33.1	15.7
IMF position	−3.0	—	—	—	—	—	5.2	5.2	—
Nonresident accounts	8.0	1.9	−1.8	4.5	3.8	−0.9	−7.0	−8.1	6.6
Errors and omissions	5.6	—	−0.6	−0.3	−0.2	0.4	−0.5	1.1	−3.7

TABLE 1-3 (concluded)

	1959	1960	1961	1962	1963	1964	1965	1966	1967
Exports[a]	167.3	203.7	164.9	145.2	228.8	227.6	246.8	259.5	258.7
Imports[a]	−237.6	−258.1	−241.4	−294.2	−402.6	−399.4	−413.3	−410.9	−413.2
Balance of trade[a]	−70.3	−54.4	−76.5	−149.0	−173.8	−171.8	−166.5	−151.4	−154.5
Shipping, net[b]	1.0	0.4	0.2	3.6	0.7	0.0	2.7	−1.2	−1.8
Suez Canal dues	44.4	50.1	51.2	53.7	71.1	78.4	86.2	95.3	47.0
British army expenditures	—	—	—	—	—	—	—	—	—
Interest and dividends, net	4.1	2.1	1.3	−2.2	−4.8	−7.8	−7.1	−4.4	−9.0
Government expenditure	−27.9	−25.3	−30.9	−28.4	−28.3	−36.8	−35.5	−32.3	−29.0
Other, net	12.7	3.5	1.4	4.7	12.2	14.9	10.2	18.4	21.8
Balance on invisibles	34.3	30.8	23.2	31.4	50.9	48.7	56.5	75.8	29.0
Balance on current account	−36.0	−23.6	−53.3	−117.6	−122.9	−123.1	−110.0	−75.6	−125.5
Loans, net[c]	11.4	11.1	33.9	80.7	93.7	111.1	80.9	64.2	50.5
Transfers[d]	—	—	—	—	—	—	—	5.0	58.2
Deterioration of:									
Foreign exchange and gold reserve	16.8	27.4	23.4	16.8	1.9	9.1	41.4	28.6	3.8
IMF position	−0.9	6.2	−0.9	20.0	6.4	1.9	−3.7	−7.3	1.4
Nonresident accounts	6.9	−14.2	2.8	4.1	20.0	−2.3	−13.6	−7.4	16.3
Errors and omissions	1.8	−6.9	−5.9	−4.0	0.9	3.3	5.0	−7.5	−4.7

NOTE: Receipts are (+) and payments, (−).

SOURCE: *Economic Bulletin*, National Bank of Egypt, 1970.

a. Including transit trade.

b. Including insurance other than for exports and imports.

c. Includes civilian, but probably not military, credits, U.S. PL 480 counterpart funds as from 1959, IBRD loans, and compensations for nationalizations, the Aswan High Dam lake in Sudan, et cetera. Amortizations on loans are deducted.

d. Includes compensation from Arab countries for loss of Suez Canal revenues. It might be more logical to include this in the current account item.

480 counterpart funds equal to £E131 million at the end of 1966) played an important role, but otherwise the loans have come mainly from communist countries. It was the abrogation of PL 480 in 1965 in combination with the exhaustion of foreign exchange reserves that brought the country's development efforts to a virtual halt already before the outbreak of war in June 1967.

The balance on commodity trade had shown substantial payments deficits during the 1950s, fluctuating between £E12 and £E70 million, and increased to a range of £E150 to £E170 million in the 1960s. Disregarding the Korean boom years of 1950–51, export performance has been rather poor throughout the postwar period. Even when measured from the recession years 1953 and 1954, and adjusting for a depreciation of the Egyptian pound by almost 25 percent in 1962, the value of exports rose by less than 50 percent up to 1967, or by 3 percent annually. The average rate of increase in the U.S. dollar value of world trade during the same period was, of course, much higher. Calculated in the same way, imports rose by almost 100 percent, or about 5½ percent annually, which is a modest increase, too, if compared to world trade.

Another way of presenting the trends in foreign trade is to measure exports and imports as percentages of GNP. This is done in Chart 1–1. From 1953, when the share of exports was about the same as before World War II—15 to 16 percent of GNP—we see a clear downward trend, perhaps flattening at the end, to a level of 12 percent in 1969. Imports first show a downward trend from 22 to 23 percent of GNP in 1951–52 to about 17 percent in 1961. This is followed by a strong upturn, with imports remaining at a very high level until 1968. In the years that followed imports were cut so drastically that in 1969 a trade surplus emerged for the first time since World War II.

During the 1940s the trade deficit ran at a level of 1 percent of GNP, about the same as before the war. After the Korean boom it increased to a level of some 4 to 5 percent of GNP, where it remained until the beginning of the 1960s, when it increased further to some 6 to 10 percent of GNP until 1966.

A substantial part of the widening in the trade gap was covered by an increase in the Egyptian revenues from the Suez Canal. Considering the effects of the nationalization of the Canal, Egypt's[21] net foreign revenue from the Canal increased from about £E10 million in 1953 to £E95 million in 1966, or by about £E85 million. The trade payments deficit rose during the same period by about £E130 million. Increasing government expenditure abroad (mainly for military equipment),[22] however, added another £E25 million to the deficit's growth.

Thus, in the last year before the war of June 1967, the deficit on merchandise trade was £E151 million. Of this £E95 million was covered by

CHART 1–1

Exports and Imports as Percentages of GNP, 1938–39 to 1969–70

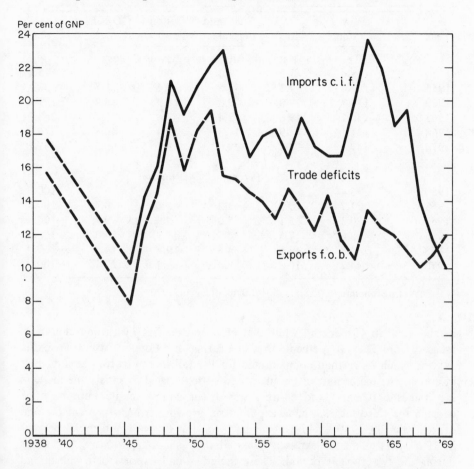

Per cent of GNP

Imports c. i. f.

Trade deficits

Exports f.o.b.

Suez Canal revenue, while other invisibles (net) contributed another £E13 milion, which together would have meant a current deficit of £E43 million. Government expenditure, however, increased the deficit to £E76 million, of which £E64 million was covered by longer-term loans (net) and the remainder by further drains on the reserves.

The composition of both exports and imports has changed substantially over time. Before World War II Egypt was largely a one-product exporter, raw cotton constituting about 9/10 of total exports, while imports consisted mainly of manufactured consumer goods, fuel, and some raw materials. On the export side (Table 1–4), the picture was still much the same in 1950, raw cotton accounting for 85 percent of total exports. During the next two decades

TABLE 1–4

Exports by Commodity Group, 1950–1968

Year	Raw Cotton	Rice	Fruits and Vegetables	Cotton Textiles	Other Exports	Total
			Value in Millions of Egyptian Pounds			
1950	149.8	7.6	2.3	4.0	11.7	175.4
1955	107.4	7.3	4.5	7.4	11.7	138.3
1960	134.7	9.8	9.5	18.9	18.7	191.6
1965	146.2	19.8	12.4	47.0	37.6	263.1
1968	121.1	44.9	11.5	52.4	40.4	270.3
1970	147.8	34.2	29.0	53.7	66.5	331.2
			Percentage Distribution			
1950	85.4	4.3	1.3	2.3	6.7	100.0
1955	77.7	5.3	3.2	5.4	8.4	100.0
1960	70.3	5.1	5.0	9.9	9.7	100.0
1965	55.6	7.5	4.7	17.9	14.3	100.0
1968	44.8	16.6	4.3	19.4	14.9	100.0
1970	44.7	10.3	8.8	16.2	20.1	100.0

SOURCE: *Economic Bulletin,* National Bank of Egypt, 1970.

its share fell to 45 percent, while that of cotton textiles (yarn and cloth) increased from 2 to 16 percent. In value terms the increase in cotton textile exports much more than compensated for the fall in raw cotton exports but, of course, the major part of the processed cotton served to satisfy the increasing domestic demand and entirely wiped out cotton textile imports. Rice became the third largest single export item, growing from 4 percent of total export value in 1950 to 17 percent in 1968, but falling again to 10 percent in 1970. Miscellaneous exports increased their share from 7 to 20 percent during the twenty-year period. These include small exports of a substantial number of manufactured goods (oil and fuel, cement, and footwear, in particular). Counting cotton textiles as two goods (yarn and cloth), as well as fruits and vegetables, Egypt thus developed from a one-commodity exporter in 1950 to a six-commodity exporter in the second half of the sixties.

On the import side (Table 1–5), the share of capital goods imports increased sharply from 1950 to 1955, subsequently remained almost constant at a level of 24 percent until 1968, and increased once more to 31 percent in 1970. The growth in the share of capital goods imports during 1950–1955 was largely compensated for by a decline in food imports, which, however, showed a strong and steady relative uptrend thereafter, reaching 32 percent in 1968. This increase was, in turn, compensated for by an almost equal fall

TABLE 1–5

Imports by Commodity Group, 1950–1968

Year	Food	Other Consumer Goods	Raw Materials	Capital Goods	Total
		Value in Millions of Egyptian Pounds			
1950	50.2	48.4	88.1	31.8	218.5
1955	25.0	37.4	78.8	45.2	186.4
1960	47.9	32.6	88.7	55.8	225.1
1965	110.2	45.3	155.0	95.4	405.9
1968	91.9	28.9	99.3	70.5	290.6
1970	72.6	32.4	129.5	107.5	342.0
		Percentage Distribution			
1950	23.0	22.2	40.3	14.6	100.0
1955	13.4	20.1	42.3	24.3	100.0
1960	21.3	14.5	39.4	24.8	100.0
1965	27.1	11.2	38.2	23.5	100.0
1968	31.6	9.9	34.2	24.3	100.0
1970	21.2	9.5	37.8	31.4	100.0

NOTE: Economic "aid" is not included. ("Aid" here probably means grants; thus, PL 480 aid, a loan, is included.) Military equipment is not included.

SOURCE: *Economic Bulletin,* National Bank of Egypt, 1970.

in the shares of other consumer goods and raw materials. This represents, to some extent, import substitution (cotton textiles, footwear, and fuel, for example), but for the rest became possible only through domestic commodity shortages (manufactured goods consumed by the middle and upper income brackets, materials used in handicrafts, and so forth). More recently the share of food imports shrank again, to 21 percent in 1970, as a result of the increase in agricultural production.[23]

Finally, Table 1–6 shows the development of trade with the communist countries ("Eastern Europe"). In 1950 such trade was insignificant, but in 1955—the year of the Czechoslovakian arms deal—exports increased substantially, with imports unchanged. This export surplus remained characteristic of the trade with communist countries throughout the following period. It has obviously served to cover payments for military equipment not included in the import figures: note that the surplus is of the same order of magnitude as the item "government expenditure" in the balance of payments (Table 1–3). By 1965 imports from these countries were about one quarter of total imports, while exports to them were about half of the total. In 1970, after the 1967 War, imports from the East Bloc reached one third of total imports,

TABLE 1–6

Egypt's Trade with Eastern Europe

Year	Imports Mill. £E	% of Total	Exports Mill. £E	% of Total	Trade Balance (mill. £E) Eastern Europe	Total
1950	13.9	6.4	18.8	10.7	+4.9	−41.4
1955	13.1	7.0	30.1	20.6	+17.0	−41.2
1960	55.8	24.0	83.0	41.9	+27.2	−34.7
1965	92.0	22.7	129.1	49.5	+37.1	−142.6
1968	116.9	40.4	132.1	48.9	+15.2	−19.3
1970	114.8	33.5	201.3	60.7	+86.5	−10.9

SOURCE: *Economic Bulletin*, National Bank of Egypt, 1970. For coverage, see Note to Table 1–5.

while exports to that area increased to above 60 percent of the total, with a trade surplus of no less than £E86.5 million, obviously related to greatly increased payments for military equipment.

NOTES

1. For earlier developments, the basic reference is A. Crouchley, *The Economic Development of Egypt*, London, 1935. See also the articles in C. Issawi, *The Economic History of the Middle East, 1800–1914*, Chicago, 1966, Part VI; Z. Y. Hershlag, *Introduction to the Modern Economic History of the Middle East*, Leiden, 1964; and E. R. J. Owen, *Cotton and the Egyptian Economy, 1820–1914*, Oxford, 1969. For post-World War II developments, see C. Issawi, *Egypt at Mid-Century*, London, 1954, and *Egypt in Revolution*, London, 1963; B. Hansen and G. A. Marzouk, *Development and Economic Policy in the U.A.R. (Egypt)*, Amsterdam, 1965; D. C. Mead, *Growth and Structural Change in the Egyptian Economy*, Homewood, Ill., 1967; B. Hansen, "Economic Development in Egypt," in C. A. Cooper and S. S. Alexander, *Economic Development and Population in the Middle East*, New York, 1972.

2. H. A. B. Rivlin, *The Agricultural Policy of Muhammad 'Ali in Egypt*, Cambridge, Mass., 1961; C. Issawi, op. cit., 1966, pp. 390–402; and Z. Y. Hershlag, op. cit., 1964; Moustafa Fahmy, *La Révolution de l'industrie en Egypte et ses conséquences sociales au 19e siècle, 1800–1850*, Leiden, 1954.

3. Hershlag, op. cit., 1964, Part 4; and A. A. Mustafa, "The Breakdown of the Monopoly System in Egypt after 1840," in P. M. Holt, ed., *Political and Social Change in Modern Egypt*, London, 1968.

4. A. A. I. El-Gritly, *The Structure of Modern Industry in Egypt*, Cairo, 1948, Chapter 10; V. J. Puryear, *International Economics and Diplomacy in the Near East*, Stanford, 1935, pp. 117–125; "History of the Customs Regime in Egypt," *Annual Statement of Foreign Trade, 1933*, Cairo, 1935, pp. 5–13.

5. *Annuaire Statistique,* 1925–1926, pp. 383–384, Cairo, 1927.

6. A. El-Gritly, op. cit., 1948, and C. Issawi, op. cit., 1966, pp. 359–374.

7. This statement may need qualifications; see Chapter 8, p. 207.

8. A. El-Gritly, op. cit., 1948, Chapter 10.

9. Ibid., p. 376.

10. Ibid., Chapter 8.

11. P. O'Brien, in *The Revolution in Egypt's Economic System,* London, 1966, has so far given the best description of the economic policy changes from 1952 to 1962. A. Nutting's *Nasser,* London, 1972, contains interesting additional information about the process of change.

12. A. Nutting, op. cit., Chapters 5 to 10, gives a detailed account of the politics behind these developments.

13. Weapons are difficult to include in economic analysis not only because of the secretiveness with which they are surrounded and because no world market exists with market prices for heavy weapons, but also because they are part of public consumption and thus give rise to the problems in modern welfare theory related to the existence of public goods.

14. Nutting, in "The Socialist State," op. cit., Chapter 15, gives a very different account of these events, in particular the relations to the Misr concern. However, he got the chronology of events wrong. His main point—that Nasser should have suspected the Misr group of a conspiracy to destroy the union with Syria and that the nationalizations were a punishment for this conspiracy—makes little sense. The breach with Syria occurred only in September 1961, while the big nationalization sweep took place in July 1961 and the Misr concern was placed under control as early as February 1960, when Bank Misr was nationalized. Nutting seems to believe that the Misr concern was nationalized after the breach (see pp. 295–300). It is quite another thing that a wave of sequestrations did, in fact, follow after September 1961.

15. A reversal of the sequestrations was promised by President Sadat, but it is not clear how much property has actually been returned to its old owners.

16. Maxime Rodinson, in *Israel and the Arabs,* New York, 1968, suggests that *grandeur* was, in fact, Nasser's main concern from the very beginning, and that his economic development policies have to be seen as a means to this end. But most observers agree that his concern with social justice and improvement of the standard of living of the broad masses was genuine and always pervaded his thinking (see, for instance, Anwar Abdel Malek, *Egypt: Military Society,* New York, 1968; and, particularly, Anthony Nutting in his 1972 book cited in footnote 11).

17. Thus, it has been maintained that the nationalizations in 1963 were largely undertaken to create retirement positions for officers dissatisfied with the Yemen War.

18. For a more general discussion of the motivations for the changes in the system, see the somewhat diverging views in O'Brien (see footnote 11), and Hansen (see footnote 1), pp. 72–78. But these are views of economists and may not be very relevant for the political issues. Nutting, who probably knew Nasser personally better than anybody else, gives the impression that the whole thing for Nasser was a power game. To "protect the revolution," powerful private capitalists could not be allowed to exist, and this was something that apparently Nasser should have felt right from the beginning. The nationalizations thus became the instrument for the ultimate consolidation of both the revolution and Nasser's personal power. (See Nutting, op. cit., Chapters 3 and 15.)

19. This is a fine point that has escaped most authors who write about the consequences of the Egyptian land reforms.

20. Throughout this volume the notation 1963–64 refers to fiscal year July 1 to

June 30, unless otherwise indicated. As of 1960, Egyptian statistics are increasingly presented on a fiscal year basis. This is, unfortunately, an inconvenience that we can do nothing about. The reader should note that in some connections the agricultural year (November–October) or the cotton year (September–August) is used.

21. The major part of the Canal dues before nationalization accrued to the foreign-owned Canal Company.

22. Military equipment has been obtained from the communist countries as grants, against cash payment, and with loans. The total and its distribution among these three classes are not known. Only payments (at delivery or deferred) appear in the balance of payments, and they are classified as current payments, lumped together with expenditure for representation abroad, students' scholarships, support of revolutions, and other government payments.

23. For the first time since World War II, in 1970 Egypt was again a net food exporter by £E26 million.

Chapter 2

Foreign Exchange Regimes, 1946-1961: Oscillations between Phases I, II, and V

The years between the end of World War II and the nationalizations of 1961 form a convenient period for the start of our survey. During its entirety Egypt continued to rely mainly upon private enterprise and, until the last year or two, applied only policy measures that were consistent with it and that had been used in Europe until the trade liberalization of the mid-fifties. The period started with the country leaving the sterling area and saw the introduction and termination of a number of exchange control arrangements, as well as a strong expansion of bilateral trade.[1] After the Suez War of 1956, trade with communist countries rose sharply and a substantial effective depreciation of the currency took place, leading up to the official devaluation of 1962.

The beginning of the period under review was characterized by the postwar recovery, and until 1947 a number of wartime restrictions disappeared. Thus, it may be said that the immediate postwar years somewhat resembled the co-directors' Phase V (see p. 349), although strongly influenced by the special postwar conditions.

Despite a huge exchange reserve, the improving cotton price, and a continued economic upswing, from 1947 onward Egypt ran into serious exchange problems, closely related to the difficulties of the British economy and the pound sterling. A number of foreign exchange measures were taken, and during the years 1947 to 1950 the country clearly found itself in Phase I on the road to balance of payments and exchange controls. (See pp. 26–32 below.)

During the Korean boom, 1950–1952, the country experienced a brief spell of import liberalization—not unlike Phase V—but also an integrated portion of anti-inflationary policies. (See the discussion on pp. 32–39 below.)

With the breakdown of the Korean boom, exchange controls were tightened again, and, since various arrangements introduced during the years 1947–1950 (Phase I) were never abrogated, it makes sense to identify the period from 1953 to 1961 as Phase II. Although the nature of the controls varied quite substantially during these years, they generally tended to become ever tighter.

The changed institutional framework in the wake of the nationalization of foreign trade in 1961 makes it difficult to identify further developments in terms of the phases set up by the co-directors.

THE POSTWAR RECOVERY

Egypt came out of World War II—during which, although theoretically neutral, the country served as the main Middle East base for the Allied forces—without much direct destruction. The productive machinery was worn out, however, and agriculture suffered from soil exhaustion due to insufficient fertilizing during the war years. Stocks of imported raw materials and consumer goods, including food, were emptied. On the other hand, the country had accumulated substantial stocks of cotton and a very large foreign exchange reserve, held in pounds sterling in London. This reserve amounted to more than two-thirds of Egypt's national income, or about four years' imports at the 1945 level.

Under these circumstances, there could be only one course to follow: to use exchange reserves for replacement and modernization in industry and communications, replenishment of exhausted commodity stocks, and recovery of soil fertility. The policy was successful in terms of production, which increased rapidly in industry and agriculture. Large trade deficits did appear (although improvements in the terms of trade favored the country greatly), but foreign exchange reserves declined slowly as British military spending continued, Suez Canal toll revenues increased, and exchange controls contained the pressure on the balance of payments. The major developments are shown in Tables 2–1 and 2–2, as well as in Table 1–3.

THE DOLLAR SHORTAGE, TRIANGULAR
TRANSACTIONS, AND THE EXPORT POUND:
PHASE I

The exchange control regime in Egypt originated at the outbreak of World War II. At that time Britain imposed exchange controls on her foreign trans-

TABLE 2-1

Production, Income, and Foreign Trade, 1945–1949

Year	Gross National Product, at Constant 1954 Prices (mill. £E) (1)	Growth Rate (%) (2)	Gross National Income, at Constant 1954 Prices (incl. terms of trade gains) (mill. £E) (3)	Growth Rate (%) (4)	Agricultural Production (major field crops) (5)	Industrial Production (6)	Barter Terms of Trade (1945=100) (7)	Imports (% GNP) (8)	Exports (% GNP) (9)	Trade Deficit (mill. £E) (10)	Foreign Exchange Reserve (end of year, mill. £E) (11)
1945	711	—	673	—	100	100	100	10.2	7.8	n.a.	379
1946	744	6.4	704	4.6	97	101	121	14.2	12.3	35.8	n.a.
1947	776	4.3	731	3.8	102	110	122	16.1	14.5	37.6	353[a]
1948	877	13.0	908	24.2	121	124	180	21.2	18.9	29.9	323
1949	927	5.7	937	3.2	119	139	159	19.1	15.8	18.0	321

SOURCES: Cols. (1) and (2): B. Hansen and G. Marzouk, *Development and Economic Policy in the U.A.R. (Egypt)*, Amsterdam, 1965, p. 319.

Cols. (3) and (4): Ibid., p. 319.

Col. (5): M. El Imam, "A Production Function for Egyptian Agriculture," *Memo No. 259*, Institute of National Planning, Cairo, December 31, 1962, Table VIII, p. 43.

Col. (6): Hansen and Marzouk, op. cit., pp. 115–118.

Cols. (7)–(11): Ibid., pp. 186–187, 174, 176, and 190.

a. October 4, 1947.

TABLE 2–2
Trade with Sterling Area and Nonsterling
Countries, 1946–1950
(mill. £E)

Year	Merchandise Exports		Merchandise Imports		Balance on Current Account	
	Sterling Area	Non-sterling	Sterling Area	Non-sterling	Sterling Area	Non-sterling
1946	24.4	27.5	39.0	49.6	+8.4	−27.8
1947	31.4	35.8	37.1	63.3	+12.2	−43.9
1948	67.0	65.6	68.9	93.6	+29.5	−41.7
1949	64.7	74.0	57.8	100.5	+33.2	−38.9
1950	73.0	111.9	84.7	132.0	+8.1	−22.5

SOURCE: *Economic Bulletin,* National Bank of Egypt, various issues.

actions, a move which was followed by similar measures in Egypt and other countries belonging to the sterling area. While trade and capital movements within the sterling area were unrestricted, transactions in currencies other than sterling were tightly controlled. Egypt, as a member, deposited all of her foreign exchange earnings in the London pool, where they were credited to her in sterling, while, in turn, Britain would annually release foreign currencies to Egypt according to a quota system instituted for her trading partners. Even then, the composition and origin of Egyptian imports were controlled from the Allied Center for the Supply of the Middle East.

It was only in December 1944 that Egypt regained her freedom to import and the administration of exchange control was shifted from London to the Foreign Exchange Control Committee at Cairo, an Egyptian government authority. In practice, however, Egypt was limited by the inconvertibility of her sterling balances, the restrictions (through the quotas mentioned above) imposed on her access to hard currencies, and the commodity shortages in the sterling area.

The sterling balances stemmed mainly from the expenditures by the Allied forces in Egypt and the inability of the Allies to meet Egypt's import requirements. The reserves, on a steady uptrend during the war, reached their peak immediately afterwards at £E425 million. The Egyptian government found it both natural and desirable that in this situation it should be able to utilize its sterling balances to finance a dollar trade deficit for a number of years. Hence, an Egyptian delegation was sent to London in June 1947 to negotiate along these lines on the disposal of the sterling balances. The agreement that emerged, however, was to fall significantly short of Egyptian plans and hopes. The British position on all such sterling balances accumulated during the war years was that (1) a part of the balances would be released and made freely convertible immediately; (2) another part would be gradually released over a period of years; and (3) the remainder would be "readjusted" or "scaled down."[2] It meant, simply, that her colonies and dependencies were expected to pay part of the costs of World War II. In Egypt's case, the part released as "No. 1 sterling account" was £ 8 million, with an additional £ 12 million put on standby to meet any deficit; the remainder was blocked as "No. 2 sterling account."

Faced with these terms, Egypt decided to leave the sterling area, although the British threats of "scaling down" the balances never materialized. An additional consideration in this decision was that Britain was still unable at that time to deliver the raw materials and capital equipment that Egypt badly needed. Wheat, in particular, which Egypt needed to import on a large scale, was not available for export in the sterling area. Thus, sterling as such was not very useful. Egypt's imports form nonsterling countries exceeded those from the sterling area, resulting in a substantial current hard currency deficit. At the same time, on top of her accumulated sterling balances, her current sterling account was also in surplus (mostly because of continued British military expenditures in Egypt and increasing Suez Canal revenues).

It should be recalled that Britain was committed to the United States (as a condition for loans obtained in 1946) to introduce full convertibility of the pound sterling. Egypt thus had good reason to expect that whatever was released from her blocked balances would be fully convertible into hard currency. As of July 15, 1947, the British actually did introduce full convertibility, and the Egyptian exchange position then looked fairly satisfactory. This situation did not last long, however, and the problem of her deficit vis-à-vis non-sterling area countries was again accentuated when Britain, on August 20, 1947, reneged on its commitment to full convertibility.[3] Egypt found herself placed outside the sterling area, with all her reserves in sterling and partly blocked, and with no right to convertibility of released balances and of current sterling earnings. The subsequent transfer of £ 21 million from No. 2 to No. 1 account under a 1948 agreement had no effect in alleviating the shortage of nonsterling currencies, nor any relevance to her sterling trade, where Egypt was running a surplus in any case. At the same time, Egypt's efforts to increase her exports to dollar countries were frustrated as the United States imposed import restrictions on cotton.[4]

This situation resulted in two Egyptian policy moves: (1) relaxation and subsequent removal in March 1948 of trade regulations against sterling area countries and any other country accepting sterling; and (2) adoption of auxiliary trade methods to alleviate the dollar shortage.

Triangular Trade.

One such auxiliary method was to engage in triangular trade relations with other sterling area countries which, instead of selling their dollar earnings to the London pool, would manage to buy dollar goods and resell them against sterling at prices higher than those corresponding to the official parity. Through these arrangements Egypt was able to convert part of her transferable sterling into dollar goods, although at a premium. The premium was in the range of 20 to 25 percent, as quotations for most third countries' transferable sterling accounts were in the range of U.S. $2.95–3.10 per Egyptian pound, compared with a par rate of U.S. $4.027 per Egyptian pound.

Conversely, Egyptian cotton bought with sterling was offered against hard currencies "at a considerable discount," thus making direct purchases from Egypt by hard currency countries unprofitable. Hence the government resorted to direct cotton sales against hard currencies from its surplus stocks (accumulated during the war) at low prices. It also reserved certain export goods, such as rice and cottonseed cake, for hard currency purchasers.[5] These transactions clearly represented a partial depreciation of the Egyptian pound vis-à-vis the U.S. dollar and other hard currencies.

Barter Trade and Bilateral Agreements.

Other auxiliary trade methods adopted at the same time were barter and bilateral agreements with countries facing similar problems. The first such barter agreement was concluded with the Soviet Union in 1948, shortly followed by a bilateral agreement with France. Bilateral trade was increasingly resorted to throughout the 1950s in coping with balance of payments difficulties (see p. 43 below).

Licensing.

A licensing system for exports to and imports from countries outside the sterling area was also introduced in 1948. Export products were divided into four schedules which differed as to means of payment and restrictions on the volume exported. For instance, shoes and hides could only be exported against hard currency, while yarn and textiles could only be exported after domestic demand was fulfilled. Most imports were licensed as to country of origin; licenses were given freely to imports from countries with which Egypt had bilateral agreements, while tight restrictions were imposed on imports from the dollar area. With imports thus restricted, the government moved to limit excess profits through price control, specifying maximum profit margins according to the type of goods involved (for example, woolens, 30 percent, agricultural machinery, 22 percent, tea and coffee, 18 percent).[6] There is no evidence that significant shortages developed in these commodities. By and large, it seems that quantities sufficient to clear the market at the controlled prices were imported; this, of course, indicates that prices and profit margins must have been set at generous levels.

The Export Pound.

In March 1949 a new agreement was reached with Britain, converting £E5 million into dollars and shifting £E12 million from the No. 2 to the No. 1 (released sterling) account. As the Egyptian No. 1 sterling balances at that time stood at £E7.4 million, the new releases were of little immediate consequence. Indeed, the problem continued to be Britain's inability to deliver commodities at competitive prices. Moreover, a critical restrictive amendment was attached to the agreement: Britain insisted that the right to use sterling be restricted to direct current transactions on goods originating in the country to which the payment was made.[7] By thus barring triangular transactions, it deprived Egypt of an important access to hard currency goods. In response, Egypt created a transferable Egyptian pound on "export account" to finance trade with soft currency countries.

As a background to a discussion of the export pound arrangement, a few words are in order on the international devaluations that took place in September 1949. Britain devalued against the U.S. dollar by over 30 percent, and Egypt, which sent roughly half of her exports to sterling area countries, followed suit immediately. Since Egypt's trade with the United States was very small at that time, the average depreciation involved was very small as well. The result was some rise in cotton prices in Egypt and a reorientation of cotton exports toward hard currency countries, while expectations of price increases in Britain as a consequence of the sterling devaluation induced a temporary increase of imports from the sterling area. Egyptian sterling balances fell steadily as exports to the United Kingdom were reduced. The development of a deficit in sterling and the subsequent reduction of free Egyptian sterling balances prompted the government from 1952 on to follow a path of increasing general intervention in foreign trade (see pp. 41–45).

We mentioned that Egypt created so-called "export accounts" so that Egyptian pounds could be used in trade with soft currency countries in lieu of the abolished triangular transactions in pounds sterling. Under this arrangement Egyptian importers of specified hard currency goods from specified soft currency countries could make their Egyptian pound payment to nonresidents' "export accounts." Egyptian pounds from these accounts were freely transferable to other nonresidents and could be used to pay for Egyptian exports to a long list of soft currency countries. The "export pounds," being freely transferable, were traded and quoted at a discount in third-country exchange markets. In this way Egypt could acquire hard currency goods indirectly through third countries, while exports from Egypt to such countries were promoted.

The whole arrangement amounted, of course, to a partial, floating exchange rate for Egyptian pounds and involved a depreciation of the currency. While the official rate set in September 1949 was U.S. $2.87 per Egyptian pound, the price in Tangiers of Egyptian pounds on export account ranged between U.S. $2.24 and $2.48 during 1951, with a tendency to increase over the next several years (Table 2–3, col. 2). Thus, the depreciation of the export pound averaged about 17 percent in 1950, but only about 9 percent from 1953 to 1955. The rates depended mostly on the quantities of wheat Egypt was buying abroad with export pounds.

The depreciation was partial since it affected only a small part of total trade: at its peak in 1953 the export pound covered only 14 percent of exports and 12 percent of imports. Therefore, the average depreciation accomplished by this means was small, ranging from 1.17 to 0.18 percent over the period 1950–1955 (Table 2–4). Since export pounds were also bought to pay for exports to dollar areas—resulting in reduced dollar receipts—the government found it appropriate to replace the export pound gradually by an import entitlement system, and to expand bilateral trade.

THE KOREAN BOOM AND IMPORT LIBERALIZATION IN EGYPT: PHASE V

The Korean War, responsible for a strong increase in cotton prices (by about 130 percent from 1949 to 1951, calculated on annual averages) and, hence, an improvement in the barter terms of trade (by about 75 percent, as shown in Table 2–5), helped to create a kind of "stag-flation" in the Egyptian economy. The boom was accompanied by some domestic price increases (see Table 2–6); the cost of living rose by about 7 percent annually from 1949 to 1951.

Production was rather stagnant during this period. Agricultural output fell by 8 percent, while industrial production rose by only 4 percent. Real GNP increased by less than 5 percent from 1949 to 1951 (Table 2–7). But the strong improvement of the terms of trade brought a rise in real national income (GNI) of 8 percent in 1950 and another 7 percent in 1951. Although the accompanying uptrend in demand certainly influenced domestic prices, it found a partial outlet in increased imports, which, despite a rise of about 50 percent in export value, caused both the balance of trade and the balance of current payments to deteriorate during the boom.

TABLE 2-3

Exchange Rates for the Egyptian Pound

Year	Par Rate (U.S. $/£E) (1)	Export Pound Quotations Tangiers (U.S. $/£E) (2)	Import Entitlement Premiums Quotations from Alexandria (buying, percent, end of year)			Quotations Abroad (buying rates for £E on "B accounts," end of year)		
			£ (3)	DM (4)	U.S. $ (5)	Amsterdam (florin/£E) (6)	Zurich (Sw. fr./£E) (7)	Brussels (Belg. fr./£E) (8)
1950	2.87	2.24–2.48	—	—	—	n.a.	n.a.	—
1951	2.87	2.34–2.63	—	—	—	n.a.	n.a.	—
1952	2.87	2.31–2.72	5	n.a.	11	9.6	12.10	—
1953	2.87	2.57–2.62	5⅚	11⅛	8	10.07	11.65	128.82
1954	2.87	2.55–2.75	7⅛	8³⁄₁₆	10	10.06	11.18	135.37
1955	2.87	2.50–2.73	10³⁄₃₂	12³⁄₃₂	14	10.30[a]	11.90[a]	129.25[a]
1956	2.87	—	—	—	—	9.25[a]	10.50[a]	126.00[a]
1957	2.87	—	—	—	—	8.60[a]	9.50[a]	109.25[a]
1958	2.87	—	—	—	—	9.00	9.80	109.00
1959	2.87	—	—	—	—	8.70	9.90	110.50
1960	2.87	—	—	—	—	—	11.50	—
1961	2.87	—	—	—	—	—	10.40	—
Cross rates at official U.S. $ par rates, 1950–1961						10.40	12.40	142.05

SOURCES: *Economic Bulletin*, National Bank of Egypt, various issues; IMF, *International Financial Statistics*, various issues.
a. November figures.

TABLE 2–4

Depreciation through the Export Pound

(percent)

Year	Export Pound, Depreciation in Relation to Par Rate (1)	Proportion of Total Trade Effectuated via Export Account Exports (2)	Imports (3)	Average Depreciation for Total Trade through Export Pound Exports (4)	Imports (5)
1950	17	5	2	0.85	0.34
1951	13	10	9	1.30	1.17
1952	12	7	5	0.84	0.60
1953	9	14	12	1.26	1.08
1954	7	6	5	0.42	0.35
1955	9	3	1	0.27	0.09

SOURCES: Col. (1): Averages of Table 2–3, col. (2).

Cols. (2) and (3): Calculated on basis of figures for payments on export account from *Economic Bulletin,* National Bank of Egypt, 1953 and 1959, and for total export and import from Hansen and Marzouk, op. cit., pp. 186–187.

TABLE 2–5

**Cotton Prices, Terms of Trade,
and Foreign Trade, 1949–1953**

Year	Cotton Price for Crop of Previous Year, £E/Kantar (1)	Barter Terms of Trade (1938–39 = 100) (2)	% of GNP Exports (3)	Imports (4)	Value (mill. £E) Balance of Trade (5)	Balance on Current Account (6)
1949	11.05	137	15.8	19.1	−18	−4
1950	14.93	176	18.2	20.8	−32	−14
1951	25.14	243	19.4	22.1	−39	−15
1952	18.24	155	15.5	23.0	−64	−53
1953	12.28	118	15.3	19.2	−29	−8

SOURCES: Col. (1): *Annuaire Statistique,* Cairo, 1960–1961. The prices are averages for cotton season (Sept. 1–Aug. 31) for all varieties.

Col. (2): Hansen and Marzouk, op. cit., p. 176.

Cols. (3)–(6): Ibid., p. 174 and Table 1. III.

TABLE 2–6

Prices and Wages

Year	Wholesale Prices (1953 = 100) (1)	Cost of Living (1953 = 100) (2)	Industrial Wages: Weekly Earnings (£E) (3)
1949	88	94	1.46
1950	97	99	1.69
1951	108	108	1.94
1952	105	107	1.90
1953	100	100	2.03

SOURCE: D. Mead, *Growth and Structural Change in the Egyptian Economy*, Homewood, Ill., 1967, Tables VI–F–1 and II–B–7.

TABLE 2–7

National Income and Production, 1949–1953

Year	Real GNP, at 1954 Prices (mill. £E) (1)	Growth Rate of Real GNP (%) (2)	Real Gross National Income[a] at 1954 Prices (mill. £E) (3)	Growth Rate of Real GNI (%) (4)	Agricultural Production (1949 = 100) (5)	Industrial Production (1949 = 100) (6)
1949	927	5.7	937	3.2	100	100
1950	945	1.9	1,013	8.1	95	105
1951	971	2.8	1,084	7.0	92	104
1952	992	2.2	1,001	−7.7	102	107
1953	981	−1.1	956	−4.5	94	108

SOURCES: Cols. (1) to (4): Hansen and Marzouk, op. cit., p. 319.
Col. (5): See Table 2–1, col. (1).
Col. (6): See Table 2–1, col. (2).
a. Includes terms of trade gains.

A more detailed analysis of events is, unfortunately, handicapped by the existence of two different series of government budget figures: the official series (see Table 2–8, A) and a revised series compiled by the Institute of National Planning, Cairo (Table 2–8, B). The latter is based on United Nations definitions and classification and is known to be a thorough and compe-

TABLE 2–8
Egypt's Budget
(mill. £E)

A. Government Budget: Official Presentation

Budget Year July 1 to June 30	Surplus (1)	Expenditure		Revenue	
		Total (2)	"Economic Administration" (3)	Total (4)	Customs Duties (5)
1948–49	−15	158	34	143	53
1949–50	−15	164	36	159	62
1950–51	2	190	38	185	75
1951–52	−39	233	n.a.	194	77
1952–53	−10	208	n.a.	198	74

B. Government Ordinary Budget: Special Study

Budget Year July 1 to June 30	Surplus (1)	Expenditure		Revenue			
		Total (2)	"Economic Services" (3)	Total (4)	Duties on		
					Imports (5)	Exports (6)	Total (7)
1948–49	−2	145	34	143	46	10	56
1949–50	−28	187	75	159	50	11	61
1950–51	46	204	72	250	80	24	104
1951–52	−25	219	54	194	60	14	74
1952–53	−4	202	43	198	57	14	71

SOURCES: A: *Annuaire Statistique,* 1949–1950, 1950–1951, Cairo, 1953; 1951–1952, 1952–1953, and 1953–1954, Cairo, 1956.

B: Mead, op. cit., Tables VI–E–3 and VI–E–4. These figures are based on an unpublished study by Rasheed Khalid of the IMF at the Institute of National Planning, Cairo. Khalid's reclassification and presentation follows the principles laid down in *A Manual for the Economic and Functional Classification of Government Transactions,* United Nations, 1958.

tent piece of work. It also makes more sense than the official budget series insofar as it shows strong uptrends in government spending for 1949–50, when the government embarked upon a development program, and in customs revenues for 1950–51, when foreign trade reached its peak—two phenomena neither one of which shows up in the official series. On the other hand, it is difficult to reconcile the revised series' large surplus figure for 1950–51 with data on changes in the banking system's net claims on the gov-

ernment (see Table 3–5). Considering the known government loan transactions outside the banking system, in particular the large Palestinian War
Loan of £E30 million in 1948–49, the official surplus figures tally reasonably
well with the changes in the banking system's net claims on the government.
The revised surplus figures do too, except for 1950–51. We suspect that—
being based on U.N. definitions—the revised revenue figures reflect tax liabilities rather than actual tax collections; it stands to reason that large tax arrears
were built up during the boom years (a very normal phenomenon in Egypt)
which, after the collapse of the boom in 1952 and the land reforms and other
events that followed, were never paid. These considerations have led us to use
the revised figures for all years except 1950–51, for which we have preferred
to use the official revenue figures. But we call the reader's attention to the fact
that the analysis of 1950–51 depends critically upon which budget revenue
figures are used; since both sets of figures may be correct (in terms of their
own definition) our problem is, in effect, whether budget analysis should be
based on actual tax receipts or on tax liabilities. Our choice is to work on a
cash basis.

Inflationary tendencies were already beginning to build up in the economy before the outbreak of the Korean War in June 1950. The development
program implied an increase of government expenditure in 1949–50 by about
£E40 million, corresponding to 4 percent of the national income, and a
budget deficit of close to £E30 million (Table 2–8, B). At first, the main
impact of the expansionary forces was on imports rather than on prices and
domestic production. Imports started to increase as a result of a reduction in
tariff rates accompanying the removal of trade regulations with the sterling
area (see below), the increasing export capacity of the member countries of
the area, and some shift from grain crops to cotton in Egypt.

From the second half of 1950, exports took the lead in the expansionary
process. The major driving force was certainly the rising world demand for
raw materials of strategic importance. Both export and import values soared,
exports through price increases, imports mainly through volume increases.
The expansion of the value of imports in 1950 was stronger than the value
of exports, which by itself suggests that domestic forces added to the export
boom. The money supply began to increase—by 4.2 percent in 1950 and 6.5
percent in 1951, as compared with a slight fall in 1949 (see Table 3–5).
Even so, money supply was hardly a decisive factor in the process.[8] More
importantly, government expenditures expanded further during 1950–51 and
1951–52. On the other hand, production tended to stagnate during 1950
and 1951, partly because crops were small (due to low floods and plant dis-
ease), but also because industrial expansion slowed down. Government revenue in 1950–51 (even according to the official figures) rose so much that the
deficits of the earlier years were replaced by a small surplus, serving to dampen

domestic demand somewhat. The revenue increase was, however, mainly an automatic response to the expansionary forces emanating from both exports and government expenditure; in 1951–52 the growth in expenditure actually exceeded that in revenue, and a substantial deficit developed once again.

The peculiar stagnation in industrial production was, of course, partly related to the bad crops, but increased liberalization and stronger competition from imported goods most probably played a role as well. Deliberate liberalization measures were taken during these years, partly to stimulate growth, partly to induce imports as an anti-inflationary measure. Licenses were issued more generously. In early 1950 the ad valorem duty was reduced from 7 to 3 percent; duties on machinery for new industrial undertakings were reduced from the 6–10 percent range to 4 percent; and wheat, barley, beans, and lentils were exempted from all duties. Later in 1951 tariffs on a number of foodstuffs were abolished altogether, and the ad valorem duty on imports of machinery and certain foodstuffs was reduced to 1 percent.[9] Revenue duties on tobacco and alcoholic beverages were, on the other hand, increased sharply, together with duties on automobiles.

The combination of an inflationary boom and stagnation in industry thus seems to be explained by two circumstances. *First,* when a country experiences a strong improvement in its terms of trade through a rise in export prices, national income and expenditure are bound to expand more strongly than national product in real terms. The difference consists, of course, in the terms of trade gain. Business indicators related to expenditures are therefore also bound to show stronger expansion than indicators related to production. And there is nothing to prevent real expenditure from increasing even with falling production. *Second,* high cotton prices and the expenditure boom did not lead to a production boom but, rather, the opposite because, on the one hand, full capacity in cotton acreage was already reached before the Korean boom and, on the other, economic policy as expressed in trade liberalization served to divert domestic demand toward imported goods. But, of course, as we have pointed out, there were also exogenous factors that affected manufacturing adversely through the poor agricultural crops.

The international cotton market collapsed at the end of 1951, and, after a vain attempt by the Egyptian government to keep international prices for extra long staple cotton at a high level (among other things, by taking over all futures contracts at the Alexandria Bourse and buying in the spot market for stockpiling), Egyptian cotton prices fell drastically during 1952.[10] Export revenues shrank, and the trade deficit soared to a peak of £E65 million that year. The rapid drop in the exchange reserves generated a fall in money supply (Table 3–5), and for 1952–53 the government cut expenditure by about 10 percent. The general situation thus shifted very rapidly from an expenditure boom to a recession.

With the end of prosperity, Egypt's liberalization policy vanished, too. It had helped to stabilize prices, but had probably also contributed to the stagnation in domestic production. It was too short-lived to have had any importance for long-term growth. (For a discussion of this policy in a more general setting, see Chapter 3, p. 75.)

POST-KOREAN RECESSION, LICENSING, AND THE IMPORT ENTITLEMENT SYSTEM: THE BEGINNING OF PHASE II

In its first years, the economic policy of the revolutionary government, except for the land reforms, was generally conservative. Both monetary and fiscal policy were, on balance, deflationary, and production expanded only slowly until around 1955. Between 1952 and 1955, the budget deficit averaged only about £E3 million and the money supply remained nearly constant. From virtual stagnation in 1952–53 the growth rate of GNP rose to about 3½ percent in 1955–56. A major reason for the stagnation was the lack of appreciable growth in agricultural production (slightly above 1 percent annually on the average from 1952–53 to 1956–57). This slow growth was partly a result of the depressed prices[11] and partly a result of the government's area restriction policies, which from 1953 on aimed at shifting agricultural production from cotton to wheat (see Chapter 6 and Appendix A). Cotton export taxes (temporarily abrogated in 1952) remained high for some time despite the depressed international prices. At the same time, industrial growth was also slow until 1955 (see Table 2–9).

Until 1952 Egypt had a small deficit in its balance of trade with the sterling area. However, this was more than offset by a surplus generated on the invisible accounts (stemming mostly from Britain's military expenditures in Egypt). This surplus, as well as the gradual release of old sterling balances, had financed a large deficit vis-à-vis dollar and soft currency countries, initially through triangular transactions and later through the export pound.

In 1952, following the collapse of cotton prices, sales to the United Kingdom (Egypt's largest customer) fell to about a fifth of their average in the years since the end of the war.[12] This would not deserve special mention if it had been a temporary phenomenon related to the post-Korean recession in the developed countries, but, in fact, it marked the beginning of the downward trend of cotton exports to Western countries. Long-run factors included the decline of the Lancashire textile industry, the gradual substitution of synthetic fibers for cotton, and technological innovations that permitted the use of medium and coarse counts of cotton in the production of fine cloth. Demand shifted away from extra long staple—the Egyptian speciality—to long

TABLE 2-9
Production and Foreign Trade, 1953–1956

Fiscal Year	GNI at 1953–54 Prices (mill. £E) (1)	Growth Rate (%) (2)	Agricultural Production (1952–53 = 100) (3)	Industrial Production (1952–53 = 100) (4)	Exports as % of GNP (5)	Imports as % of GNP (6)	Balance on Current Account (mill. £E) (7)
1952–53	947	0.6	100	100	15.4	21.1	−30.5
1953–54	963	1.7	101	103	14.9	17.9	−5.7
1954–55	999	3.7	104	110	14.2	17.3	−18.8
1955–56	1,032	3.3	103	118	13.5	18.1	−33.5
1956–57	1,045	1.3	106	126	13.8	17.4	−32.1

NOTE: In cols. (3) to (7) the budget year figures are averages of calendar year figures.

SOURCES: Cols. (1) and (2): Hansen and Marzouk, op. cit., p. 320.

Col. (3): See Table 2–1, col. (5).

Col. (4): See Table 2–1, col. (6).

Cols. (5) and (6): Hansen and Marzouk, op. cit., p. 174.

Col. (7): Table 1–3.

TABLE 2–10
Trade with Sterling Area and Nonsterling Countries, 1951–1957
(mill. £E)

Year	Merchandise Exports		Merchandise Imports		Balance on Current Account	
	Sterling Area	Nonsterling	Sterling Area	Nonsterling	Sterling Area	Nonsterling
1951	74.5	127.4	77.2	164.7	27.3	−42.5
1952	27.7	117.9	52.8	157.7	−3.6	−49.8
1953	35.2	100.1	31.4	133.8	27.7	−35.6
1954	36.3	103.5	36.5	114.2	17.2	−13.6
1955	24.3	108.8	40.7	149.5	−4.7	−38.7
1956	19.9	110.0	42.9	149.4	−5.7	−38.7
1957	8.8	157.2	18.1	199.4	−5.7	−25.5

SOURCES: *Annuaire Statistique* and *Economic Bulletin,* various issues.

and medium staple, which favored Sudanese and American varieties. At the same time, Sudan emerged as a major producer of long staple cotton and substantially eroded the Egyptian share of the Western market.

Not surprisingly, therefore, Egypt experienced a deficit in her current transactions with the sterling area and other countries in 1952 (see Table 2–10). By the end of the year her free sterling reserves were down to a negligible amount (£E6.3 million). The total free reserves including gold (£E 98 million) were still roughly equivalent to five months' imports.[13] The external deficit on current account was reduced considerably in 1953, and in 1954 there was even a slight surplus, actually a sign of domestic slackness rather than of soundness in the economy. In 1955 and 1956 the deficit became significant once more as a result of a strong expansion in imports (Table 2–10) of credit-financed capital goods.

In view of the unfavorable balance of payments picture in 1952, the government felt that it had to take strong corrective measures, but it was certainly too deflationary in its general policy. Exchange regulations and controls now became so comprehensive that developments can be identified with the co-directors' Phase II, which lasted until the nationalization of 1961.

General Import Licensing.

The first step taken by the government to improve the foreign exchange position was to extend import licensing in 1952 to all countries and to limit imports from the sterling area to necessities. Further, a 10 percent surcharge was imposed on all remittances abroad, and customs duties on tobacco and luxuries were raised. On the other hand, licenses for imports from countries with which Egypt had bilateral agreements were issued without limit. In general, imports in hard currency were confined to essentials, while semi-essential imports, such as textiles, were restricted to the export pound or to barter agreements.

The Import Entitlement System.

The second step was to introduce a comprehensive import entitlement system in 1953. Under this arrangement exporters who shipped goods to the dollar or sterling areas received an import entitlement for 75 percent of the value of exports (66 percent for goods shipped to West Germany) and for 100 percent in the case of exports of cotton yarn and textiles. The entitlement was transferable. Exporters could now sell cotton at a discount, recouping any losses by the premium they obtained through selling their import entitlement to importers. Import entitlements commanded a premium ranging over the next several years from 8 to 14 percent for dollars, 5 to 10 percent for sterling, and 8 to 12 percent for German marks (Table 2–3, columns 3–5). They could be used to import the commodities on the list for the export account (essentials and semi-essentials); but they were less restrictive in that they permitted importation from the sterling and dollar areas. Moreover, in order to encourage foreign investment and as an exception to the import entitlement regulations, all products could be imported from dollar and sterling areas provided that the proceeds of the sales were invested in Egypt. The value of such imports could not exceed 65 percent of the total foreign capital to be invested in Egypt; the remainder had to be invested in dollars or sterling at par.[14]

The import entitlement system was far more comprehensive than the export accounts, and it spread the partial devaluation to a larger segment of trade. At their peak, export accounts financed only 12 percent of imports, while the import entitlement system covered 40 percent of imports in the first year of its operation.[15] The supplementation of the export pound by the import entitlement system thus represented a further depreciation of the Egyptian currency. Nevertheless, the depreciation as reflected in the import entitlement quotations throughout 1953 and 1954 remained small; by the end of 1954, the premiums were 7.13 percent for sterling and 10 percent for the U.S. dollar (Table 2–3).

Through the relative rise in import prices in terms of domestic currency and the discount on exports, the import entitlement system, together with tighter import control on nonessentials, probably contributed to the marked improvement in the balance of payments and the resulting small current account surplus in 1954. However, it applied to only three currencies, which created severe imbalances with other currencies. Imports from France, to which entitlements did not apply, were relatively cheap, while exports to France were relatively expensive. This contributed to a severe Egyptian deficit vis-à-vis France which the government tried to reduce by ad hoc measures (for example, granting cotton a discount of 6.5 percent when exported to France).[16]

BILATERAL TRADE

With the shortage of transferable sterling as well as hard currencies, bilateral agreements appeared increasingly attractive to Egypt and its trading partners in Western and Eastern Europe. Italy, Belgium, West Germany, and the Netherlands concluded payments and trade agreements with Egypt in the years 1952 and 1953. The proliferation of these agreements was such that, by the end of 1953, no less than 55 percent of Egypt's foreign turnover was governed by bilateral agreements, as shown in Table 2–11.

Most of the payments agreements were based on Egyptian pounds (stipulated in those concluded with Eastern European countries) or on various combinations of the two partners' currencies (stipulated in the agreements concluded with Western European countries).[17] The exchange rates of the two currencies were fixed vis-à-vis the U.S. dollar, and the agreements guaranteed adjustment of the outstanding net balance in the event of a change in the exchange rate. They specified the manner in which any outstanding balance might be settled (usually in goods) and fixed a debt ceiling. The agreements allowed for triangular settlements, as Egyptian exchange control "often

TABLE 2–11
**Egypt's Balance of Payments with Bilateral
Agreement Countries**
(mill. £E)

Year	Merchandise Trade Account		Other Transactions		Total Deficit	Turnover as % of Total Foreign Transactions
	Receipts	Payments	Receipts	Payments		
1951	42.3	51.0	10.9	26.1	−23.8	21
1952	70.0	73.5	16.0	31.3	−18.8	39
1953	90.8	92.1	27.1	33.3	−7.5	55

NOTE: The United Kingdom is excluded. Transactions in any one year cover only those countries with which there were agreements during that year.
SOURCE: *Economic Bulletin,* National Bank of Egypt, 1954, p. 166.

approves on an administrative basis the export of cotton to an agreement country with payment being received from the account of another agreement country."[18]

Transferability of outstanding balances enhances the efficiency of bilateral trade. Nonetheless, bilateral agreements usually imply an effective depreciation of one of the two currencies involved vis-à-vis hard currencies. For, with the addition of bilateral trade, the volume of competitive commodities traded (i.e., with a c.i.f. price equal to or lower than the world market price at the official exchange rate) is likely to exceed that which would have been contracted under pure multilateralism. Moreover, its composition is also likely to include goods for which c.i.f. import prices exceed world market prices at the official par rate. This expansion in trade volume can only be achieved by paying relatively more for imports or receiving less for exports (in terms of world market prices, not domestic prices), which amounts to some degree of currency depreciation.[19] Such implicit depreciation was brought out explicitly through the special arrangement with Switzerland commonly referred to as the "B-account." In 1950, when the agreement with Switzerland was renewed, it was decided that certain transactions should be carried in Swiss francs and others (specified in the form of a list of goods) in Egyptian pounds—the B-account. Instead of having a fixed exchange rate between the Egyptian pound and the Swiss franc, the exchange rate of the Egyptian pound in Switzerland was left to be decided by market conditions. The same arrangement was later incorporated into the agreements with Belgium and the Netherlands. The quotations for the Egyptian pound in the three markets are shown in Table 2–3. At the end of 1953 these rates reflected a depreciation of the Egyptian pound of 3 percent vis-à-vis the dollar in Amsterdam, 6 percent in Zurich, and 10 percent in Brussels.

THE ABOLITION OF THE EXPORT POUND AND IMPORT ENTITLEMENTS, 1955

The multiplicity of rates existing for identical commodities gave rise to lucrative arbitrage transactions. In 1955 Britain insisted, as part of the agreement on further sterling No. 2 releases, that the entitlement on sterling be dropped and the Egyptian pound be treated at par with sterling. The agreement was implemented in September 1955; entitlements on all other currencies were terminated as well. Earlier in the year export accounts had also been abolished, having lost all practical importance. Thus Egypt resorted again to a uniform exchange rate. But instead of devaluing its currency, which would have consolidated and generalized the previous partial depreciations, she chose to maintain the par value of the currency with the imposition of an import surcharge of 7 percent and a premium on cotton exports. The 7 percent surcharge applied to all imports except industrial equipment needed for investments and raw materials, which implied the exemption of roughly 50 percent of imports from the surcharge. The premium on cotton exports took the form of a reduction in the export tax (for example, from 300 to 160 piasters per kantar on Karnak) which corresponded to an 8 percent reduction in price. But other exports (in particular, cotton textiles, agricultural products, and leather goods) no longer benefited from any kind of premiums.

However, this was not sufficient to permit relaxation of exchange control measures; in fact, in view of the reappearance of a large balance of payments deficit in 1955, import controls were tightened. A new import policy was announced in March 1956 whereby licenses were issued on a half-yearly basis, with the aggregate value of licenses issued for each half-year period corresponding to 50 percent of the preceding year's export earnings. This was the first systematic attempt to establish a foreign exchange budget with import quotas determined in relation to exports. Old importers (somewhat inconsistently) were granted licenses up to 50 percent of their average imports during the last two years, while new importers were considered on the basis of the price of their imports and the type of currency involved.[20] The degree of restriction differed according to the priority given to various commodities (automobile and other consumer durables imports were prohibited altogether), and the 7 percent import surcharge had to be paid at the time of the issuance of the license. Later in the year an attempt was made to link import authorization to export performance by granting import licenses to any firm which succeeded in expanding its exports. A firm could import its own inputs up to 50 percent of the value of exports.

In the fall of 1956 the British-French-Israeli attack on the Suez Canal upset all these arrangements and we shall never know how they would have worked.

ECONOMIC RECOVERY AFTER 1956 AND THE SHIFT TOWARD EAST BLOC TRADE

The conservative caution of the government in regard to monetary and fiscal policy continued until 1959. Money supply, which had increased substantially during the Suez War, was only slightly higher at the end of 1958 than at the end of 1956, and government net borrowing from the banking system was modest until 1960–61 (see Table 3–5). Significant external current account deficits of about £E20 to 30 million were experienced each year from 1957 to 1960, partly caused by bank-financed capital goods imports for development purposes and weapons purchases. The remainder of the blocked sterling reserves was finally released, however, and some aid was obtained from both West and East. At the end of 1959, with all sterling reserves released, Egypt still had a gross exchange reserve corresponding to seven months' imports *plus* government payments abroad (including payments for military equipment) and a net reserve corresponding to about 3 months' imports *plus* government payments abroad.

The events surrounding the Suez War of 1956 severely disrupted the flow of trade and shifted its geographic distribution toward Eastern Europe and the Soviet Union (see Table 1–6). In the immediate aftermath of the Suez War, Egypt again concluded a number of barter agreements with Western countries in which highly inflated import prices reflected substantial discounts on sales of Egyptian cotton. At the same time, large purchases of cotton by the USSR and Czechoslovakia were re-exported to the West at discounts reaching 28 percent.[21] As a result, Western markets refrained from buying Egyptian cotton directly even when equivalent discounts were granted. Subsequently, the communist countries were to readjust their cotton policies to allow for much larger consumption of Egyptian cotton.

Nevertheless, Egyptian imports continued to reflect heavy reliance on Western sources. The deficit on current transactions was mainly with Western countries, and the need for an expansion of exports to the West was strongly felt. The payments situation in 1954 and 1957 is shown in Table 2–12.

THE FOREIGN EXCHANGE BUDGET

At the beginning of 1957 Egypt adopted a number of measures intended to encourage exports to the West and to restrict further the imports of non-essentials. A foreign exchange budget was set up, and a quarterly quota was established for imports on the basis of past export performance. The exchange budget first determined the import requirements of the Ministry of Supply (wheat, tea and coffee, et cetera), and then allocated a monthly quota for the importation of pharmaceuticals. Thereafter, it allocated to raw materials imports by industrial producers a *global* quota equal to one-fourth of the quantity imported in the previous year.[22] Finally, it allowed for seasonal imports, which were deducted from subsequent quotas.

EXPORT PREMIUM SYSTEMS AND IMPORT DUTIES, 1957–1961

As part of the policy outlined above, the government also announced a system of export premiums, which varied by currency and destination and

TABLE 2–12

**Distribution of Current Payments and Receipts
by Country Group, 1954 and 1957**

	1954		1957	
	(mill. £E)	(%)	(mill. £E)	(%)
Current receipts from:				
Eastern Europe	21.6	10	85.2	37
West	169.3	76	95.7	40
Other countries	31.3	14	56.3	23
Total	222.2	100	237.2	100
Current payments to:				
Eastern Europe	18.3	8	84.4	31
West	174.4	80	119.2	44
Other countries	25.9	12	64.8	25
Total	218.6	100	268.4	100
Balance on current account:				
Eastern Europe	3.3	—	0.8	—
West	−5.1	—	−23.5	—
Other countries	5.4	—	−8.5	—
Total	3.6	—	−31.2	—

NOTE: "Eastern Europe" includes Austria, Bulgaria, Czechoslovakia, East Germany, Greece, Hungary, Poland, Rumania, Turkey, the USSR, and Yugoslavia. "West" includes American monetary area, sterling area, and European countries not included in Eastern Europe.
SOURCE: D. Mead, op. cit., Table V–A–10.

were adjusted periodically in response to cotton prices and the general trends in the current balance of payments. From February to May 1957, the premium was applied only to cotton; it amounted to 10 percent on exports against Indian rupees and Italian liras, 15 percent on exports to Germany in DMs, 15 percent on exports against dollars to countries other than the United States and Canada, and 20 percent on exports against dollars to the United States and Canada. In May 1957, the premiums were extended to exports of onions (20 percent) against convertible currencies, and those on cotton were raised across the board by 5 percentage points.

An import fee of 10 percent was imposed in February 1957 on all imports against convertible currencies. The 7 percent surcharge that had been intro-

duced in 1955 was extended to all nonessentials and later increased to 9 percent. In June the fees on government purchases with the currencies mentioned
above were doubled to 20 percent.

The premium system was the third example of partial, de facto depreciation introduced in the postwar period. It was accompanied by a rise in wholesale prices (8 percent between August 1956 and August 1957), which was
concentrated on import goods such as tea, coffee, fuel, and paper. Imports
of textiles and consumer durables (automobiles, for example) fell during
1957, as did imports of intermediate products (paper, wood, jute bags).[23]
For the first time in the postwar period "a general scarcity of imported goods
and raw materials" was reported.[24] Part of this phenomenon was certainly
due to the disruption of trade caused by the Suez War, but it also marked
the beginning of a recurrent pattern of commodity shortages in the Egyptian
economy. It should be mentioned that the period 1955–1957 saw the launching of several large industrial plants (such as the iron and steel plant at
Helwan, and fertilizer and tire plants), entailing heavy imports of capital
equipment. At this time most Western European countries returned to convertibility, thereby increasing the number of currencies sold at a premium
and reducing the opportunities for bilateral agreements, which Egypt now
relied upon heavily.

In 1958, the premium on exports was extended to all commodities except rice and oil products through the reintroduction of nonresident "export
accounts," which were freely transferable to other nonresidents. However,
while in the old system (1950–1956) the premiums had been left to the
market, in the new system the premiums were fixed by the central bank.
The premium developed as follows:

	(percent)
March 1 to March 10, 1958	30.0
March 10 to June 6, 1958	26.5
June 7 to September 1, 1958	25.0
September 2, 1958 to April 20, 1959	17.6

Starting with April 1959, the premium on cotton was changed frequently,
sometimes from week to week. It was adjusted according to the international
supply and demand situation in an attempt to assure the competitiveness of
cotton abroad at relatively stable producer prices. When the cotton season
of 1958–59 was near its end and unusually large supplies were still available, the premium averaged around 53 percent (between May and July of
1959). The new season (1959–60) started with premiums around 23 percent; they were frequently adjusted downward as supplies became gradually
smaller toward the spring of 1960. At that time the premium averaged 6

percent and the carryover was about half that of the previous season. When the availability of two crops overlapped, a higher premium was quoted for the old crop than for the new one. It should be added that during the cotton seasons 1958–59 and 1959–60 the cotton export taxes were lowered and subsequently abolished for almost all varieties and grades; by itself the lowering of export taxes implied a depreciation.[25] Thus, the policy shifted from taxing to subsidizing cotton cultivation for a few years until 1962.

By the middle of 1959, exports of cotton received a premium fluctuating around 25 percent, onions and textiles, a premium of 29 percent, and other exports with the exception of rice and oil products, a premium of 17.5 percent. On the import side, fluctuating premiums prevailed through 1958 at rates between 30 and 17 percent, with a higher premium applied to government purchases. At the same time all imports were paying the 9 percent surcharge. Note that trade with Eastern European countries was subject to no premiums, either on imports or on exports: export prices higher than world market prices were offset by higher import prices.[26]

In September 1959 the "export account" system was abolished and replaced by a system in which premiums on the Egyptian pound were applied to receipts and payments in convertible currencies. All current transactions were grouped into categories, as follows:[27]

1. Imports of goods and invisibles were to pay a premium of 27.5 percent, except for certain capital goods and raw materials.

2. Exports of manufactured products, except textiles and cement, were to receive a premium of 17.5 percent.

3. Exports of cotton, textiles, and onions were to receive a variable premium which would be adjusted periodically according to international market prices (each week in the case of cotton). It averaged between 25 and 30 percent in December 1959.

4. Exports of rice and cement, which were sold at the official exchange rate, occasionally carried an export tax.

As the balance of payments situation improved again, the premium on most exports was reduced, first to 20 percent in January 1960 and then to 10 percent in July. At the same time, the "statistical" ad valorem tax of 1 percent on all imports was raised to 5 percent. Moreover, the 9 percent import surcharge was extended to imports from countries with which Egypt had bilateral agreements. Half the premium was, however, refunded in the case of imports of foodstuffs, raw materials, and industrial equipment; such imports exceeded two-thirds of total imports. Thus, by adding the import surcharge of 9 percent, the premium (½ of 10 percent), and the statistical tax (5 percent), we reach an effective premium (not including tariffs) of 19 percent on imports of food, raw materials, and industrial equipment, as compared with an effective premium of 10 percent on all exports.

THE NATIONALIZATION OF FOREIGN TRADE, 1961

In July 1961 the government nationalized a large number of companies. A virtual government monopoly was established for imports: the right to import was restricted to state-owned import companies, with some state-owned industrial companies authorized to import directly the commodities and equipment needed for their own use.

With respect to exports, the government acquired majority participation in all export trade companies that dealt principally in cotton. The cotton futures market was abolished and the Alexandria bourse was closed. The Egyptian Cotton Commission (ECC) was given a monopoly in internal trade and became the sole supplier to the export companies.[28] Instead of the earlier policy of giving exchange premiums to private exporters, who could then sell cotton at a discount, the ECC now simply fixed export prices periodically in line with world prices. These fell below domestic buying prices, as on previous occasions. On the other hand, the ECC sold cotton to domestic mills at prices 11 percent higher than its own purchase prices from agriculture.[29] This price differential, which was reflected in a rise in textile prices, helped check domestic consumption and increased exportable supplies; it reversed the earlier policy of sales to domestic mills at prices below world market prices (at a margin equal to the export taxes abolished during the years 1958–1960). With respect to cotton textile exports, the price differential was made up by a premium until 1962 and by a subsidy later. While cotton export prices were constantly adjusted in response to the supply and demand situation abroad, domestic buying and selling prices were adjusted occasionally only in response to cost movements or to adjust the profitability of alternative crops.

Trade in rice was also monopolized by the government, but a number of small private export companies dealing in fruits and vegetables remained in business.

FOREIGN EXCHANGE CRISIS AND DEVALUATION, 1962

During 1961 and 1962 the balance of payments suffered several setbacks. In 1961 the cotton crop experienced a major failure; production was down by 40 percent despite a record sown acreage. This crop failure was reflected in the export figures for both 1961 and 1962. Moreover, a decrease in the rice crop, together with a rise in domestic rice consumption, in 1962 cut exports of that commodity to almost half of the level they had reached in previous years. Imports of food, particularly of cereals, increased drastically in 1961 and even more so in 1962; but this increase was financed by PL 480 counterpart funds and thus did not strain exchange reserves. Egypt was, however, committed to certain extraordinary capital expenditures, such as compensations to the old Suez Canal stockholders, to the Sudanese Government on account of the Aswan High Dam construction, and to the United Kingdom for "Egyptianized" property.

All these circumstances pointed toward an acute foreign exchange crisis in 1962. The unification of the premiums on imports and exports to 20 percent at the end of 1961 and the reintroduction of a simple multiple-exchange system with three rates[30] later finally led to devaluation in May 1962.

NOTES

1. These systems are explained later in this chapter.

2. *National Bank of Egypt, 1898–1948,* National Bank of Egypt, 1950, p. 97; *Economic Bulletin,* National Bank of Egypt, Vol. 1, 1948, pp. 50–51.

3. For a description of the abortive British convertibility attempt of 1947, see L. B. Yeager, *International Monetary Relations,* New York, 1966, pp. 378–380.

4. *Economic Bulletin,* N.B.E., 1948, p. 187.

5. Ibid., Vol. 1, p. 187; Vol. 2, p. 114.

6. Ibid., Vol. 2, p. 220.

7. Ibid., Vol. 2, p. 13.

8. Whereas the increase in real GDP was 1.9 and 2.8 percent in 1950 and 1951, respectively, the increase in real GNI (including terms of trade gains) was 8.1 and 7.0 percent. We are here up against an old issue in monetary policy: should money supply be proportional to commodity (and services) output or to total factor input? To put it another way: should output prices or factor prices be kept constant? The issue arises clearly in case of productivity changes. In underdeveloped countries the two most important instances of productivity change in the short term are crop fluctuations and terms of trade changes. The issue was discussed years ago by K. Wicksell and D. Davidsson, who agreed that factor prices rather than commodity prices should be stabilized in the short term. Contemporary attitudes in developed countries are, rather, that, if anything, it is commodity prices that should be kept constant. However, there seem to be good reasons for the standpoint of Davidsson and Wicksell in the context of crop and terms of trade fluctuations in underdeveloped countries.

9. *Economic Bulletin,* N.B.E., 1950, p. 186, and 1951, p. 132.

10. Critics of the old regime maintain that the policy basically aimed at bailing out bullish speculators, among them people closely related to the establishment.

11. Once the cotton acreage has reached its technical maximum, a further cotton price increase has no effect on production. But a sufficiently strong price decline may, of course, bring cotton production down below this maximum.

12. The United Kingdom's shift of cotton purchases to the Sudan was also partly politically motivated, as it coincided with Egyptian attempts to assure British withdrawal

from the Suez Canal area. See "An Unwanted Customer?," *Economic Bulletin*, N.B.E., 1952, p. 170.

13. *Economic Bulletin*, N.B.E., 1953, pp. 31–32.

14. *Economic Bulletin*, N.B.E., 1954, p. 181.

15. *Economic Bulletin*, N.B.E., 1953, p. 198.

16. The discount was to be financed by a premium of 6.5 percent on imports of tea from Ceylon. See *Economic Bulletin*, N.B.E., 1956, p. 36.

17. In the agreement with the Netherlands, payments for goods were to be effected in Egyptian pounds, and for invisibles, in florins. In the agreement with Belgium one third of the value of Egyptian imports was to be settled in Belgian francs and the rest in Egyptian pounds, while Egyptian exports were to be settled in either currency at the option of Belgium.

18. *Economic Bulletin*, N.B.E., 1954, pp. 163–164.

19. For a theoretical treatment, see Karim Nashashibi, "Bilateral Trade as a Development Instrument under Global Trade Restrictions," NBER Working Paper 54, 1974. As an example, suppose that bilateral trade between Egypt and Belgium results in an outstanding balance in favor of Belgium. If this balance is to be settled in goods, which is the aim of bilateral trade, either Egypt has to offer additional exports at lower prices, or the balance of Egyptian pounds could be auctioned off on the Brussels currency market. In either case this would imply a partial depreciation of the Egyptian pound, which would vary according to the importer's relative demand for Egyptian goods (either for local consumption or for reexport).

20. *Economic Bulletin*, N.B.E., Vol. 9, p. 46.

21. M. S. Mourad and F. Moursy, *The Foreign Exchange Budget and the Exterior Financing of Development*, Cairo, 1967, p. 246 (in Arabic).

22. *Economic Bulletin*, N.B.E., 1957, Vol. 10, p. 31.

23. Ibid., p. 43 and pp. 162–163.

24. Ibid., p. 282.

25. B. Hansen and A. Marzouk, *Development and Economic Policy in the U.A.R. (Egypt)*, Amsterdam, 1965, pp. 198–204.

26. *Economic Bulletin*, N.B.E., Vol. 14, 1961, p. 384.

27. *Yearbook of Exchange Controls*, International Monetary Fund, 1960, pp. 318–319.

28. The Commission was established in 1942 to handle government stock purchases during World War II. Continuing its activities after the war, it was the instrument of the government's price support policy vis-à-vis the cultivators and exerted an influence on export prices through its stock policies.

29. In 1960 the difference between cotton prices at delivery to ginning mill and at arrival at Alexandria was slightly less than 10 percent. Since the buying price of the ECC relates to ginned cotton, it would seem that the 11 percent price differential more than covered the trade and transport margin of the old middlemen and implied a certain taxation of domestic consumption.

30. The three rates were: (1) the official rate ($£E1 = US\$2.87$), applying to Suez Canal tolls, and rice, oil products, onions, and groundnuts; (2) a depreciated rate—by 10 percent—on imports such as raw materials, foodstuffs, and capital equipment; and (3) a depreciated rate—by 20 percent—on all other imports and exports.

Chapter 3

The Effective Exchange Rate, 1948-1961: An Appraisal

At this point it may be useful to interrupt the narrative and attempt to appraise the foreign exchange regimes that were applied during the years from 1948 to 1961. It is difficult to get a clear idea of what it all amounted to from brief summaries of the regimes and their general economic setting. Since they all implied changes (partially or totally) in the effective exchange rate, it would seem natural to summarize them in terms of an average effective depreciation. The question is only how such an average should be defined and what it could tell us about the exchange regulations as a whole.

THE CONCEPTS OF AVERAGE DEPRECIATION AND PRICE DISTORTION

Consider a small country, in a competitive environment, in equilibrium, without foreign exchange regulations but with unified, pegged exchange rates. Assume now that a general 10 percent tax is imposed on all foreign trade for financing domestic government expenditure, which is equivalent to a 10 percent depreciation for all imports and a 10 percent appreciation for all exports. A simple average of the effective exchange rates for exports and imports would show that there has been no change in the exchange rate. In what sense, if any, is this regime equivalent to an unchanged exchange rate?

Looking at the impact on the economy, we find, of course, a tendency for both exports and imports to decrease, releasing factors of production from export industries to industries competing with imports. Under certain condi-

53

tions of demand and supply elasticities and factor price flexibility, export value and import value in terms of foreign currency will shrink by the same amount, so that current foreign payments will remain in balance and the factors released from export industries will be absorbed completely by industries competing with imports. Macroequilibrium is thus preserved, and the regime is equivalent to unchanged exchange rates. It will also be seen that the effects on the domestic price level will tend to cancel each other out; prices of exportables will fall and those of importables rise. In regard to resource allocation and productive efficiency, on the other hand, the regime is clearly not equivalent to unchanged, uniform exchange rates.

These considerations suggest that, if we calculate a simple average of the partial exchange rate changes, we may use this "average depreciation" as an expression of the aggregate effect on the balance of payments surplus and, perhaps, on domestic prices. But we cannot use such an average as an indicator of allocative effects. For the latter it is, rather, the distribution of the changes in effective exchange rates around the mean that matters. If we have only one effective rate for exports and one for imports, a simple indicator of the allocative effects would be the absolute value of the difference between the two, perhaps normalized by the average effective rate. In the example discussed here the average depreciation would become $\frac{1}{2}$ $[10 +(-10)] = 0$, while the distortion index would become $|[10 - (-10)]| = 20$, or, normalized, 0.2. At 20 percent simultaneous appreciation and depreciation, the average depreciation would again become $\frac{1}{2}$ $[20 +(-20)] = 0$ and the distortion index $|[20 - (-20)]| = 40$. While thus the aggregate effects on the balance of payments surplus would be the same in these two cases, the allocative effects would be accentuated—which, of course, is in line with standard theory.

Needless to say, quite a number of conditions have to be fulfilled for things to work out that neatly, and it is not difficult to imagine some weighted means as well as dispersion measures that might be more satisfactory, were the necessary information about demand and supply elasticities available.[1] This is not the case, however, and we shall therefore proceed in the manner described in the previous paragraph and take a simple average of the (average) effective depreciation for exports and imports, respectively, with the absolute difference as a distortion indicator. We do not need to emphasize that these are the crudest possible measures of the combined effects of the exchange regulations. Nonetheless, we hope that they may at least indicate orders of magnitudes and directions of effects.

The results of our calculations are set out in Tables 3–1 to 3–3. Since a depreciation, from the Egyptian point of view, means an increase in the dollar rate, we have indicated depreciation by a positive and appreciation by a negative sign.

THE STATISTICAL PICTURE

Table 3–1, column 1 shows, first, the average export tax calculated as export tax revenue over the value of total exports of commodities. The average rate of export taxation—levied mainly on cotton but occasionally also on rice and other exportables—rose from almost nothing in 1947 to a level of 9 to 11 percent during the years 1950 to 1954. In the following years the export taxes were gradually reduced and, by 1961, they had virtually disappeared.[2]

The calculated rates are probably on the high side. First, they are based on official customs statistics on exports, which for various reasons have always tended to show lower values than statistics on payments. Second, adjustment should be made for the fact that the export tax on cotton lint served as a subsidy for exports of cotton textiles (yarn and fabrics) by enabling the cotton textile industry to acquire its basic raw material at a price correspondingly lower than the world market price. Exports of cotton textiles developed from virtually nothing before 1948 to about 10 percent of total export value in 1961. But even in 1959, the last year in which the export taxes were of any importance, the volume of cotton lint exported in the form of textiles was little more than 6 percent of the volume of raw cotton lint exported. The adjustment of the average export tax rates needed for this reason is thus negligible. Other forms of export subsidies have been granted, in particular to cotton textiles; they have always been small relative to export tax revenues, but information about them is insufficient for the purpose of quantification.

Columns 2 to 5 of Table 3–1 quantify the depreciation involved in exports by triangular transactions (1948–1949), the export pound (1950–1955), import entitlements (1953–1955), and export premiums (1957–1961). The short-lived export performance scheme of 1956 is not included. The depreciation rates are calculated in all cases in relation to total export value.[3] Special calculations of the rate of net depreciation for two major cotton varieties for the cotton years 1956–57 through 1960–61 are shown in the note to Table 3–1. They corroborate the overall results for these years.

The net depreciation for exports is set out in column 6 (recalling that an export tax implies an appreciation). It so happens, mainly as the result of the high export taxes, that, after a slight depreciation in 1948, the Egyptian pound was de facto appreciated for exports at varying degrees from 1949 to 1956. During the years 1951–1953, this appreciation amounted to about 8 to 9 percent. From 1957 to 1959, depreciation (as compared with 1947) was the dominant trend, reaching a maximum of 16 percent in 1959. Thereafter the rate of depreciation fell to about 10 percent in 1960, but rose to 20 percent at the end of the year.

TABLE 3–1

Average Net Effective Depreciation (+) or Appreciation (−) Compared with 1947: Exports

(all figures expressed as percent of total export value)

| Year | Export Tax Collections (change from percent for 1947) (1) | Depreciation through | | | | Total (2)+(3)+(4) +(5)−(1) (6) |
		Triangular Transactions (2)	Export Pounds (3)	Import Entitlements (4)	Premiums (5)	
1947	0	—	—	—	—	—
1948	3	7	—	—	—	0
1949	7	5	—	—	—	4
1950	10	—	1	—	—	−2
1951	9	—	1	—	—	−9
1952	9	—	1	2	—	−8
1953	11	—	+0	3	—	−7
1954	10	—	+0	4	—	−7
1955	7	—	—	—	—	−3
1956	6	—	—	—	—	−6
1957	4	—	—	—	10	6
1958	5	—	—	—	18	13
1959	4	—	—	—	20	16
1960	1	—	—	—	14	13
1961	+0	—	—	—	10	10
1962		—	—	—	—	
Pre-devaluation	+0	—	—	—	20	20
Post-devaluation	+0	—	—	—	24[a]	24

TABLE 3–1 (concluded)

NOTE: The following calculations for two major varieties offer an interesting corroberation for the overall results.

Cotton, Net Depreciation: Premium minus Export Tax
(percent of official par rate)

Cotton Year (Sept. 1–Aug. 31)	Karnak	Ashmouni
1956–57	−6.3	−2.1
1957–58	−0.9	6.2
1958–59	15.4	20.1
1959–60	19.2	13.8
1960–61	19.0	11.9

SOURCE: Hansen and Marzouk, *Development and Economic Policy*, 1965, p. 204.

SOURCES: Col. (1): *Annuaire Statistique*, several issues; and D. Mead, *Growth and Structural Change*, 1967, Table VI–E–3.

Cols. (2)–(5): Our estimates.

Cols. (3) and (4): Tables 2–3 and 2–4.

a. Official par rate change.

Table 3–2 gives corresponding figures for commodity imports. Two series are calculated for the changes from 1947 in the tariff rates—with and without tobacco duties.[4] The tobacco duties are formally customs duties, but are partly levied upon the production (sales) of tobacco products; cultivation of tobacco is forbidden in Egypt, and the import duties on raw tobacco are pure revenue duties. To the extent that they are levied on manufacture (sales) of tobacco products, they should not be included here, since we do not include any other production or excise taxes. However, lack of data does not permit a breakdown of the tobacco duty revenues between those collected on imports and those collected on production and sales. The development over time of these two series is, unfortunately, quite different. Tobacco duty revenues increased over the period, while other tariff revenues generally fell. Thus, including tobacco duties raised the level of duties (implying depreciation) until 1954, when a maximum of 11 percent was reached. This depreciation disappeared almost completely by 1958, after which a certain uptrend started once again, mainly through an increase in the so-called statistical tax. Excluding tobacco duties, however, we find an appreciation of about 3 percent during 1951–1953. It disappeared in 1955 but reappeared in 1956, reaching a maximum of 7 percent in 1958; thence it dropped and was down to about 2 percent by the time of the devaluation in 1962.

The decline in the level of import duties after 1957 seems surprising against the background of the exchange regimes described in Chapter 2 (pp. 44–46). However, although tariff and import tax rates were increased sharply in 1957 and 1959, exemptions were widespread; in addition, the composition of imports shifted strongly toward low-tariff commodities (food, capital goods, and raw materials and other inputs), while high-tariff commodities (in particular, nonfood consumer goods) fell both in relative and absolute value (see Table 1–5). Here we are up against a difficult problem of weighting import duties. For problems of allocation, of course, they should somehow be weighted by domestic production (value added). From a macro point of view, with interest centered upon the balance of payments deficit, it is much less obvious what the correct weighting is; weights based on trade as it would be without the regimes might be appropriate. It should also be emphasized that part of the shift in the composition of imports was brought about by the direct play of import controls, and we are not attempting to include these in our calculations of the average effective exchange rate. There is, unfortunately, nothing we can do about the problem beyond calling the reader's attention to it.

Taking into account the effective depreciation related to triangular trade, export pounds, import entitlements, and premiums (columns 3 to 6), we have two series for the net depreciation for imports in Table 3–2 (columns 7 and 8). According to the series that includes tobacco duties, the depreciation for imports progressed fairly steadily (with interruptions in 1952 and 1956) from

1948 to 1959, when a maximum of 23 percent was reached. The depreciation diminished substantially in 1960 and 1961, but then increased again to a predevaluation height of 26 percent. According to the other series (excluding tobacco duties), the effective exchange rate for imports vacillated between minor depreciation and appreciation until 1957, after which there were two years of relatively strong depreciation in the order of 13 to 14 percent. During 1960 and 1961 most of this depreciation disappeared, but shortly before the devaluation of 1962 a depreciation of 18 percent was reached.

In Table 3–3, column 3 we have calculated the average depreciation for the balance on current account. It is the simple average of the average depreciations for exports and invisibles shown in column 1 and for imports in column 2. The average depreciation for exports and invisibles was obtained from the figures for average depreciation for commodity exports in Table 3–1, column 6, reduced by the ratio of commodity exports to total exports plus the net of invisibles (to account for the fact that payments related to the three dominating items among the invisibles—British army expenditure, Suez Canal dues and government expenditure abroad—were effected at par throughout the period). The average depreciation for imports was taken directly from Table 3–2, column 8.

In interpreting the table it should be noted that the average depreciation set out in column 3 is calculated with 1947 as the base year. The average depreciation or appreciation from year to year is shown in column 4 as the change in the average depreciation from 1947. A decrease in the average depreciation implies, of course, an appreciation over the previous year (designated by a minus, as explained above).

In column 5, finally, we have calculated our index of distortion as the absolute value of the difference between columns 1 and 2, divided by 100.

Before average depreciation, the index of distortion, and their development are traced through the period, a brief discussion of some foreign exchange measures and regimes not included in the calculations is in order.

First, we have not taken into account the depreciation of 1949 against the dollar. Here Egypt followed the sterling pound, and thus her exchange rates remained unchanged except against the U.S. dollar and the few currencies that followed the dollar. Her direct trade with the dollar countries was still very small in 1949 and, using trade at that time as weights, the average depreciation on this occasion amounted to only 1 to 2 percent. The simplest way to take this into account would be to lower the figures in Table 3–3 (columns 1 to 3) by 1 or 2 percentage points for the years 1947, 1948, and 1949, but it would not really change the picture.

Second, and much more important, is the fact that we have not included the effects of import licensing, which began in 1948 and continued throughout the period. In principle, the effect of licensing could be translated, commodity

TABLE 3–2

Average Net Effective Depreciation (+) or Appreciation (−) Compared with 1947: Imports

(all figures expressed as percent of total import value)

Year	Customs Duty Collections (change from percent for 1947)		Depreciation through				Total	
	Incl. Tobacco Duties (1)	Excl. Tobacco Duties (2)	Triangular Trade (3)	Export Pounds (4)	Import Entitlements (5)	Premiums (6)	Incl. Tobacco Duties $(3)+(4)+(5)+(6)+(1)$ (7)	Excl. Tobacco Duties $(3)+(4)+(5)+(6)+(2)$ (8)
1947	0	0	—	—	—	—	0	0
1948	0	0	7	—	—	—	7	7
1949	0	0	5	—	—	—	5	5
1950	5	0	—	+0	—	—	5	0
1951	3	−3	—	1	—	—	4	−2
1952	−1	−3	—	1	—	—	0	−2
1954	5	−3	—	1	2	—	7	0
1953	11	−3	—	+0	3	—	14	2
	10	0	—	+0	4	—	14	4

	(1)	(2)	(3)	(4)	(5)	(6)		
1956	8	−2	—	—	—	—	8	−2
1957	7	−4	—	—	—	10	17	6
1958	1	−7	—	—	—	20	21	13
1959	3	−6	—	—	—	20	23	14
1960	5	−5	—	—	—	10	15	5
1961	6	−2	—	—	—	10	16	8
1962								
Pre-devaluation	6	−2	—	—	—	20	26	18
Post-devaluation	—	−2	—	—	—	24[a]	30	22

SOURCES: Cols. (1) and (2): *Annuaire Statistique*, several issues; and D. Mead, *Growth and Structural Change*, 1967, Table VI-E-3.
Cols. (3)–(6): Our estimates.
a. Official par rate change.

TABLE 3–3

Average Depreciation and Index of Distortion, 1947–1962

| Year | Average Depreciation from 1947 (percent) | | Balance on Current Account | | |
	Exports and Invisibles (1)	Imports (2)	Average Depreciation from 1947 (percent) ½[(1)+(2)] (3)	Year-to-Year Change in Average Depreciation (percent) (4)	Index of Distortion (2)−(1) 100 (5)
1947	0	0	0	—	0.00
1948	4	7	5½	5½	0.03
1949	−2	5	1½	−4	0.07
1950	−8	0	−4	−5½	0.08
1951	−7	−2	−4½	−½	0.05
1952	−7	−2	−4½	0	0.05
1953	−6	0	−3	1½	0.06
1954	−6	2	−2	1	0.08
1955	−2	4	1	3	0.06
1956	−5	−2	−3½	−4½	0.03
1957	5	6	5½	9	0.01
1958	11	13	12	6½	0.02
1959	13	14	13½	1½	0.01
1960	11	5	13	−½	0.06
1961	9	8	8½	−4½	0.01
1962					
Pre-devaluation	16	18	17	8½	0.02
Post-devaluation	24	22	23	6	0.02

SOURCES: Col. (1): Table 3–1, col. (6), adjusted for net invisibles to which par rate applies. Col (2): Tables 3–2, col. (8).

by commodity, into an equivalent depreciation. From a practical point of view such calculations are not feasible, however. The necessary information about black market prices for durable consumer goods and other inessentials is not available; these goods were most effectively hit by licensing. In general, we can only say that licensing meant some further depreciation and distortion from 1953 on, accentuated after 1956.

Third, there is the trend to bilateral trade during the first half of the fifties, continued after the Suez War with a shift toward trade with communist countries. We argued in Chapter 2 (p. 44) that bilateral trade tends to imply a depreciation for the country which runs a deficit on bilateral account. The free-market quotations of Egyptian pounds on bilateral "B-accounts" with Belgium, the Netherlands, and Switzerland (see Chapter 2, p. 44) reveal the depreciation in relation to these three countries. Taking simple averages of the quotations in Brussels, Amsterdam, and Zurich (averaging end-of-year figures) we arrive at the depreciation of the Egyptian pound shown in Table 3–4.

TABLE 3–4

**Depreciation of the Egyptian Pound
on "B-Accounts"**

(percent)

1953	5.1
1954	6.5
1955	5.7
1956	9.7
1957	20.8
1958	25.6
1959	24.4
1960	16.2
1961	13.5

SOURCE: Table 2–3.

The rate of depreciation varied widely among these three countries, and one should probably not generalize from their experience as to other countries, particularly not communist countries. There is no doubt, however, that there must have been some depreciation caused by bilateral trade in general, since Egypt has tended to be in the red on bilateral accounts everywhere. All we can say is that bilateral trade points to some further depreciation from about 1950 on, accentuated for a time after the Suez War.

Finally, it is worth noting that the free gold price in the Cairo bazaars at Musky also shows a significant depreciation of the Egyptian pound when compared with the free gold price on the world market. Chart 3–1 shows the gold parity of the Egyptian pound, the free gold price at Brussels (expressed

CHART 3–1

Gold Prices

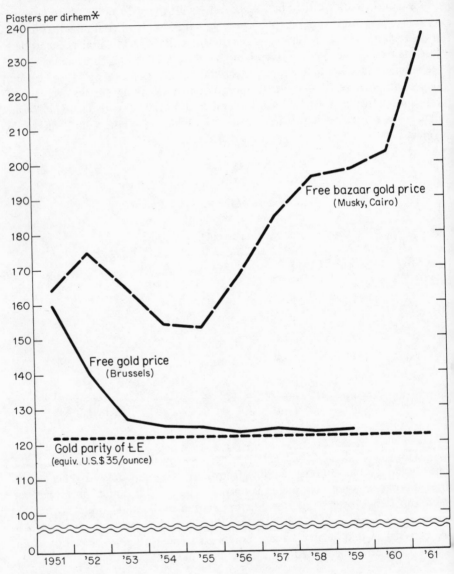

in Egyptian currency at par), and the free Musky bazaar price. Private gold importation was subject to control beginning with 1951 and was soon thereafter stopped completely. Since gold has served to a large extent as a means of smuggling capital out of the country, the free gold price has tended to follow the black market price of foreign currency (dollars). Accordingly, the National Bank regularly reported the bazaar gold price in its quarterly *Bulletin* —until its nationalization. From 1953 to 1956 the bazaar price was about 25 percent higher than the free world market price, after having been at the same level in 1951 and 1952 when import was still possible; from 1957 on the premium in the bazaar increased steadily and reached about 100 percent in 1961. Once again the picture is one of increased depreciation after the Suez War, although, of course, trade in the bazaar gold market is too limited to permit generalizations about the general depreciation of the Egyptian pound.

WORLD BUSINESS CONDITIONS AND AVERAGE DEPRECIATION IN EGYPT

Egypt has traditionally been an open economy in which foreign trade plays a relatively large role. (See Chart 1–1.) For that reason the country tends to be strongly influenced by international business conditions. With cotton still accounting for about four fifths of her total export value after World War II and almost one-quarter of her total agricultural output value, the price of raw cotton has necessarily been a major link between the international and the domestic economy.

In Chart 3–2, covering the period 1949 to 1962, we have, therefore, first included the international price for a leading Egyptian cotton variety at that time (Karnak, Fully Good, Liverpool, spot price in U.S. cents per kilogram). A glance at this series shows immediately that, in the short term, Egyptian cotton prices have fluctuated heavily and depend directly upon the business cycles in Western Europe and the United States. Indeed, this series could almost be used as a business cycle indicator for the United States. It clearly reflects all American booms and recessions, upswings and downswings, with only minor deviations in regard to timing. The basic difference is that the general upward trend in production and prices in the Western World here is replaced by a downward trend, reflecting increasing competition from synthetics and changed technology in the cotton textiles industry in favor of short and medium staple cotton at the expense of long staple varieties. The cyclical fluctuations and the downward trend in cotton prices are fundamental facts behind Egyptian exchange policies during this period.

In considering these as exogenous forces imposed upon the Egyptian economy from the outside, we have taken sides on the issue whether Egyptian

CHART 3–2

Cotton Prices and Average Depreciation

———— Karnak, fully good, spot price, Liverpool, USc/kg
– – – – Karnak, good, spot price, Minet El Bassal, USc/kg, at official par rate
············1.0 + 5 times average rate of effective depreciation

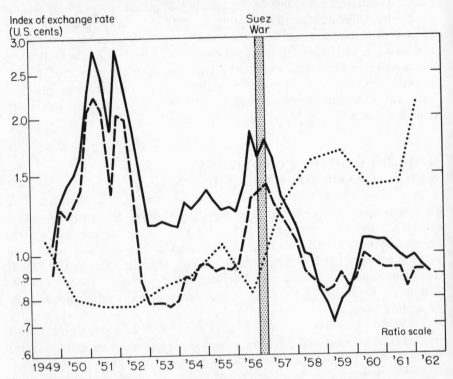

policies themselves have determined the development of cotton prices in international markets: without denying that, to some extent, Egyptian policies may have influenced world market prices for long staple cotton, we feel that they have at most modified cyclical swings and the longer-run trend (see below, p. 83). All along Egyptian policies have been responding to and following—never leading—the changes in international cotton prices; and Egypt no longer dominates the international market as it did before World War II.

In addition to the international cotton price, Chart 3–2 presents a series showing domestic cotton prices (converted to U.S. cents per kilogram at par) to illustrate how far the Egyptian exchange regimes and export taxes have modified the relationship between the international price fluctuations and the domestic cotton prices—and, hence, the domestic economy. These two are the most comparable series we could unearth. Both are spot prices for the variety Karnak; however, the Liverpool quotations are for a slightly better grade (Fully Good) than the Minet El Bassal (Alexandria) quotations (Good). Moreover the former are c.i.f. Liverpool, whereas the latter are prices at delivery from warehouse, unbaled, Alexandria. Together these two differences should account for a margin of 5 to 10 percent in the foreign over the domestic series. It should also be noted that Karnak is the variety that has carried the highest export taxes and has exhibited the strongest short-term price fluctuations as well as the strongest downward trend among all Egyptian varieties. Before March 1951, we had to use the variety Ashmouni for both price series in Chart 3–2. The British prices here were not free market prices, and represent averages for all grades of Ashmouni; hence, comparability is low between 1949, 1950, and the following years, and between foreign and domestic prices for 1949 and 1950.

The period started and ended with domestic prices (converted at the official par rate) at the same level as international prices. The picture is consistent with the fact that the cotton export taxes, although introduced already in 1948, did no become important until 1950 and were largely abolished at the end of the fifties, as explained earlier. In the interim—between 1950 and 1957—domestic prices ran at a much lower level than the corresponding international prices.

Finally, Chart 3–2 also includes our series from Table 3–3 for average depreciation, drawn to an exaggerated scale. It shows that average depreciation has tended to be both countercyclical and counter-to-trend in relation to the international cotton prices—until the fall of 1961, when other considerations gained the upper hand.

The price of cotton completely dominated the terms of trade,[5] the balance of payments, and the economy as a whole over the period in question. High cotton prices tended to create a balance of payments surplus and produce a booming domestic economy; low cotton prices, on the other hand, tended to bring a balance of payments deficit and push the economy into a recession, ceteris paribus, and a long-term downward trend in cotton prices would depress the economy and keep the balance of payments in the red permanently. It cannot be emphasized strongly enough that during most of the period we are now discussing, 1949–1961, it was the balance of payments that disturbed the domestic economy rather than the other way around.

THE OVERVALUATION
OF THE EGYPTIAN POUND

A full understanding of the balance of payments problem during the forties and the fifties also requires a comparison with the prewar situation. It has been maintained that the Egyptian pound became overvalued already during World War II, and that this is the basic explanation of the persistent deficits after the war. According to this interpretation, the successive depreciations during the second half of the fifties, culminating in the devaluation of 1962, were the delayed response to this overvaluation, taken by the government when the exchange reserves finally began to be exhausted.

There is much to be said in favor of this interpretation, and it does not in any way contradict our observation that the average depreciation tended to be countercyclical until 1961 and that the tendency to depreciation was precipitated by the downward trend in cotton prices after the Korean boom. It is not possible, however, to produce unequivocal evidence that the Egyptian pound was already overvalued by the end of World War II. The terms of trade seem to have improved substantially from 1938–1939 to 1949,[6] and the net of the exogenous invisibles (British army expenditure, Canal dues, and dividends) probably increased. Prices and costs, on the other hand, appear to have risen much more in Egypt than in the major developed countries. In 1949 both prices and industrial money wages were about three times higher in Egypt than before the war; in the United States and Britain prices had risen by only about 50 percent. The situation in 1953 and 1954, when the country was in a recession, with its current payments and receipts in balance (Table 1–3), certainly points toward overvaluation.

We accept the view that the currency was, in fact, overvalued already in the forties in the sense that, at a normal level of domestic economic activity, the balance of current payments would tend to be in the red. With the term "overvalued" thus defined, it may be perfectly rational for the government to keep the currency overvalued. For, if the country has too large an exchange reserve and wants to bring it down, it must run deficits for some time, and this means that it must have an overvalued currency until the reserves have reached their desired level.

DOMESTIC POLICIES AND BALANCE OF PAYMENTS DEFICITS

Although the pre-1961 balance of payments deficits can be seen as a hangover, partly at least, from the inflation of World War II, the period we are now discussing was not generally characterized by domestic inflation. Table 3–5 gives the data necessary for appraising the degree of inflation and the underlying fiscal and monetary policies.

Retail prices were quite stable for the period 1949–1961 as a whole; on the average they rose by less than 2 percent per year. Wholesale prices increased slightly more, about 3 percent per year. After an uptrend related to the Korean boom, retail prices again fell back in 1952 and 1953. Apart from an increase by 6 percent around the time of the Suez War, retail prices then remained constant, practically speaking, until 1962. The relatively modest increase in prices was not primarily the outcome of price control. There was not much to control (apart from some prices of scarce import goods), because most of the period was characterized by deflationary tendencies. From 1949 through 1960, money supply increased year by year at a slower pace than real national income (including terms of trade gains). The only exceptions are the year 1956, when money supply increased by 12 percent, and the recession period 1952–1953, when money supply *fell* less than real national income. From the standpoint of a simplistic quantity theory of money, it would actually be hard to understand how—with retail prices increasing by about 10 percent from 1955 to 1960 and money supply, by about 20 percent —there could be, during the same period, an increase of real GNI by almost 30 percent. The obvious explanation would be that velocity must have increased, but when this kind of ad hoc explanation has to be added, money supply really ceases to tell us anything. All that we can safely say is, therefore, that money supply developments do not indicate the prevalence of inflationary tendencies until the beginning of the sixties.

From Table 3–5 it also appears, however, that a very substantial expansion of bank credit did, in fact, take place during most of the period. Is this not an indication that inflationary, or at least expansionary, domestic forces must have been at work? During the years of the Korean boom, government borrowing was on the order of 3 to 5 percent of GNI; it was used partly for covering ordinary budget deficits, partly for financing operations in the cotton market. Beginning with 1954, substantial credits were extended to either government or the private sector or both. The government borrowed heavily in 1955 and 1956, partly in connection with the Suez War, and from 1960 on government borrowing from the banking system dominated the picture completely. For the years 1954 and 1957–1959, however, the credit expansion took place largely in the private sector (either directly or through the specialized banks).

At the time of the Korean boom and the Suez War, the expansion of government borrowing from the banking system worked as one would usually expect: domestic expansion (inflation) was induced and money supply increased, with a positive effect on prices and a negative effect on the foreign exchange reserves through an increased balance of payments deficit. But in the years when the credit expansion occurred in the private sector, as well as in 1955 and 1960, two years when the government borrowed heavily, the money supply was not affected—the whole impact seems to have been directly upon the foreign exchange reserves. The obvious explanation of this phenomenon is that credit expansion in these years stemmed largely from purchases

TABLE 3-5
Prices and Money Supply, 1949–1962

Calendar Year	Retail Prices		Money Supply, M_2[a]			Counterpart of Change in Money Supply (mill. £E)			
	(1953=100) (1)	Increase (%) (2)	End of Year (mill. £E) (3)	Increase (mill. £E) (4)	Increase (%) (5)	Net Foreign Assets[b] (6)	Net Claims on Government[c] (7)	Claims on Private Sector (8)	Claims on Specialized Banks (9)
1949	93	1	402.7	-0.6	-0.1	-9.7	-18.4	23.9	3.6
1950	101	5	418.9	16.2	4.2	2.6	-6.9	12.1	8.4
1951	110	9	446.3	27.4	6.5	-7.4	37.5	2.9	-5.6
1952	107	-3	428.8	-17.5	-3.9	-72.5	61.3	-11.9	5.6
1953	100	-6	420.1	-8.7	-2.0	-9.4	-1.4	7.2	-5.0
1954	101	1	425.3	5.2	1.2	-13.3	-11.6	35.1	-5.1
1955	102	1	433.2	7.9	1.9	-33.8	33.0	5.5	3.2
1956	104	2	482.9	49.7	11.5	-42.2	70.0	15.1	6.8
1957	110	6	485.0	2.1	0.4	-57.3	16.5	14.5	28.4
1958	110	0	489.7	4.7	1.0	-18.4	-12.9	27.6	8.4
1959	111	1	513.4	23.7	4.8	-48.9	9.8	34.0	28.8
1960	112	1	525.5	12.1	2.4	-44.9	46.8	4.4	5.8
1961	113	1	584.7	59.2	11.3	-20.8	66.9	6.5	6.8
1962	113	0	629.2	44.5	7.6	-75.6	82.1	28.8	9.0

SOURCES: Col. (1): D. Mead, *Growth and Structural Change*, 1967, Table VI–F–1.
Cols. (3)–(9): Ibid., Table VI–A–1.

a. Including P.O. savings bank deposits.
b. Including bilateral balances, IMF position, and U.S. counterpart funds.
c. Including capital and profits, and other items. These items were very constant and their inclusion in net claim on government does not significantly change the picture. As of 1956, most private banks did, in fact, belong to the government and in 1960 the last two private banks were brought under government ownership.

directly from abroad of capital goods and, in the case of the government, of weapons. It is precisely from 1955 on that weapons purchases for defense and capital goods purchases for development strongly increased their share of total imports.

Domestic credit expansion thus played an important role in the exhaustion of the exchange reserve during the period under consideration. But for most of this time it occurred through deliberate credit financing of purchases directly from abroad, not through domestic inflationary mechanisms.

It is a common practice in the analysis of exchange rates to adjust nominal exchange rates (official or estimated effective) for domestic and foreign price developments along the lines of purchasing power parity theory. Egyptian price increases for the period 1949–1961 were low by international standards. In America, retail prices increased slightly more than in Egypt from 1949 to 1960, and wholesale prices, slightly less, while in most European countries price increases were substantially higher than in Egypt.

Such comparisons are of dubious value, however, unless the difference in price developments is very striking (as was the case, for instance, during World War II). First, it is not obvious what domestic and foreign price indexes should be used in this kind of exercise, retail prices, wholesale prices, or implicit GNP deflators; which countries should be included; how they should be weighted together; and so on and so forth. Second, available price indexes for Egypt are not very good (their weighting is inadequate for almost any purpose), and some prices were controlled even during the years under review. Instead of deflating the effective exchange rate by some inadequate price index, therefore, we prefer to present some figures to show the development of competitiveness in manufacturing industry. As an expression of competitiveness we shall use unit labor costs in Egypt and in highly industrialized countries.

From 1952 to 1960, money wages (weekly earnings) in industry (establishments with more than ten employees) increased by 2.9 percent annually, while the corresponding increase of output per hour was 4.0 percent. Adding all fringe benefits, hourly wages increased by 4.7 percent. For the years before 1952 information is very shaky; existing data point to an annual rate of increase in wages from 1947 to 1960 of 4.4 percent (5.5 percent when all fringe benefits are included), whereas labor productivity for this period increased by 4.7 percent annually.[7] Thus, for the period as a whole it would seem that wage increases in industry almost remained within the range of the increase in productivity.

It would also seem that wage cost movements in Egyptian industry compared favorably with those of the highly industrialized countries in Europe and America. Measured in the respective country's domestic currency, wage costs per unit of output (excluding fringe benefits) increased annually during the period 1955 to 1961 by ¾ percent in the United States, by 3½ percent in the United Kingdom, and by an average of 3 percent in the European Common Market countries. The corresponding figure for Egypt is −¾ percent.[8]

Comparisons of prices and wage costs in Egypt and abroad thus indicate that there was no fall in the relative "intrinsic value" of the Egyptian pound from 1947 to 1960. If anything, there may even have been a slight improvement, and it is not a circumstance that helps to explain the persistent balance of payments deficits during these years.

Summarizing, we can state that the persistent external deficits of the postwar years until 1960 seem to have been the combined outcome of (1) a certain overvaluation of the currency created by the inflation of World War II; (2) credit expansion, in some years for financing domestic government expenditure but in most years for financing direct purchases abroad of capital goods and weapons; and, finally, (3) the downward trend in cotton prices.

FOREIGN EXCHANGE POLICY TARGETS

In appraising an exchange rate policy one should ascertain whether the policy was well designed from the point of view of the Egyptian government's targets. (Albeit a popular method, an appraisal of a government's policy measures from the viewpoint of somebody else's targets does not make sense.) The exchange rate policy should, of course, be coordinated with all other measures to fulfill all the government's policy targets.

The broad targets of the Nasser regime were already discussed in Chapter 1. In the present context it should be emphasized that price stability was always a major concern of the government. All governments favor price stability, of course, but it would appear that the successive Egyptian governments attached exceptional importance to this objective. It may have been partly an inheritance from the British colonial administrators,[9] and thus simply represented prudence and conservatism; but after 1952 it was also closely related to the government's strong emphasis on equity in income distribution. Income stability in real terms for the peasants and the lower urban income brackets makes general price stability a natural concern, both in regard to agricultural inputs and outputs and in response to the cost of living. With cotton the major cash crop for agriculture and food the major expenditure item for urban low income groups, the government naturally concentrated on stabilizing cotton and food prices—that is, agricultural prices.

The balance of payments and the availability of foreign exchange were naturally another subject of concern. A glance at the level and development of the free gross reserves (Table 3–6) conveys the impression that Egypt could not possibly have had much to worry about in this regard. At the end

TABLE 3–6
Foreign Exchange Reserves, All Banks
(book values, mill. £E)

End of Year	Gold (1)	Pounds Sterling No. 1 (free) (2)	Pounds Sterling No. 2 (blocked) (3)	Pounds Sterling Total (4)	U.S. Dollars (5)	Other Currencies (6)	Total Exchange Reserve Gross Total (7)	Total Exchange Reserve Gross Free (8)	Total Exchange Reserve Net (9)	Free Gross Reserves as % of Yearly Import Payments (10)
1945	n.a.	n.a.	n.a.	n.a.	n.a.	n.a.	n.a.	n.a.	379	n.a.
1946	n.a.	n.a.	n.a.	n.a.	n.a.	n.a.	n.a.	n.a.	n.a.	n.a.
1947	n.a.	n.a.	n.a.	n.a.	n.a.	n.a.	n.a.	n.a.	n.a.	n.a.
1948	13	71	264	335	6	10	364	100	323	62
1949	19	63	247	309	21	8	357	111	321	70
1950	34	52	224	277	26	18	355	140	312	63
1951	61	24	196	220	37	12	330	134	292	55
1952	61	6	174	180	20	11	272	98	232	47
1953	61	19	164	183	12	10	266	102	224	62
1954	61	35	146	181	13	15	270	124	227	82
1955	61	21	125	146	21	10	237	113	195	59
1956	66	7	100	107	21	17	210	111	159	58
1957	66	27	61	87	16	19	188	128	101	58
1958	61	45	42	87	4	10	162	120	85	56
1959	61	63	—	63	7	19	150	150	62	64
1960	60	n.a.	—	n.a.	n.a.	n.a.	157	157	43	62
1961	61	n.a.	—	n.a.	n.a.	n.a.	136	136	16	57
1962	61	n.a.	—	n.a.	n.a.	n.a.	n.a.	-7	n.a.	n.a.

SOURCES: *Economic Bulletin*, National Bank of Egypt, various issues; *Economic Review*, Central Bank of Egypt. various issues. For details, see Hansen and Marzouk, op. cit, p. 190.

of the most troubled year, 1952, free gross reserves were about 47 percent of the same year's import payments, and in most years they corresponded to about 7 months' imports. It may be argued, of course, that until 1953–1954 the problem was one of dollar shortage and that free sterling reserves were not automatically convertible into dollars. It might also be argued that seasonal fluctuations of exports are relatively large in Egypt (at least, as compared with developed countries), and that the bad experience in 1947 with the breakdown of sterling convertibility, the uncertainty of future releases of No. 2 sterling, and the conflicts with Western powers gave Egypt some good reasons for keeping relatively large reserves. Even so, it is hard to understand the Egyptian exchange reserve policy. During the critical years of the dollar shortage, 1948–1951, when Egypt struggled with triangular trade arrangements and first introduced the export pound, the central bank increased its gold stocks from about £E19 million to £E61 million[10] corresponding to two to three months' imports in those years. It would seem that, without the gold accumulation policy, the dollar problem for Egypt would have been a minor one. The increase in the gold reserve could have covered about two years of non-sterling deficit at the end of the forties. The official motivation for the gold policy was the need to keep gold as a note cover; but there may also have been an element of speculation in the free dollar price of gold—in fact, the IMF at that time encouraged member countries to sell "legal" gold in the free market. Be that as it may, once acquired, the gold reserve was considered sacrosanct. It was not touched until the mid-sixties, when the government was forced to pledge part of it as collateral for trade credits from European banks. In our appraisal of the exchange rate policies we thus have to acknowledge that we are dealing with a country with an unusually strong international liquidity preference. When things went wrong in 1961–62, it was out of miscalculation and the coincidence of unhappy circumstances rather than disregard for the reserve position.

The government's attitude to the exchange reserve seems to have been that, whereas the total reserve (including the blocked sterling balances) was considered to be unreasonably large and in need of reduction, the free reserves over and above the untouchable gold stock were considered to be too small. Given this attitude, it made sense to keep the currency overvalued and let the total exchange reserve fall to the desired level and, at the same time, to be concerned with the balance of payments to prevent reserves from falling faster than the blocked reserves were released and from being used for low priority purposes. At the end of the process a devaluation would then logically follow.

Summarizing, it is probably correct to say that during the whole period until 1962, both domestic price stabilization and balance of payments considerations were reflected in the policy of effective depreciation—but that the foreign exchange position was so comfortable until 1961 that price stabilization could be given top priority, with the balance of payments only a secondary problem. From the summer or fall of 1961, the priorities were reversed. This interpretation is consistent with the development of the effective depreciation. From 1949 to 1960–61, the average effective depreciation, according to Table 3–3, was about 7 percent. The dominating cyclical fluctuations in average effective depreciation were superimposed upon a slow trend of effective depreciation. From the fall of 1961 to the formal devaluation in May 1962, a further 9 percent effective depreciation took place and the formal devaluation added another 6 percent.

It is true that the formal devaluation of May 1962 only added marginally to the effective depreciation already in existence at the time of the formal devaluation. But in appraising the effective exchange rate policy in relation to the underlying targets, it is preferable to consider the effective depreciation that took place from the fall of 1961 together with the formal devaluation of May 1962 as one single policy move designed to save the balance of payments. Looking at things in this way, the 1962 devaluation amounted effectively to about 15 percent in one year against an earlier creeping effective depreciation of about 7 percent over twelve years. When we turn to the 1962 devaluation in Chapter 4, we shall appraise it with this approach.

COUNTERCYCLICAL EXCHANGE RATE POLICY

In examining the rationale of countercyclical exchange rate policies, we start out from some simple assumptions and subsequently bring the discussion in line with the conditions actually confronting the Egyptian government during the 1940s and 1950s.

In the simplest possible case, the world business cycle may be assumed to develop through uniform expansions and contractions, with all prices uniformly rising during the upswing and falling during the downswing. A small country in competitive circumstances would experience no fluctuations in its terms of trade (relative prices), and the whole problem would be either (1) to protect the domestic economy from the uniform price fluctuations that would be inevitable under a pegged exchange rate policy combined with full employment, or (2) to protect it from the balance of payments deficits and surpluses and from the domestic booms and recessions in production that would follow if the country did not let its domestic price level adjust to that of the world market. Uniform countercyclical changes in exchange rates in inverse proportion to world market prices would then be the ideal policy. Domestic prices would remain constant, foreign payments would remain balanced, and domestic production would be unaffected. Similarly, changes in the world price level could always be completely neutralized through appropriate changes in exchange rates. Indeed, this discretionary exchange rate policy would be tantamount to letting the exchange rates float.

Against the background of this simplified model there could be no doubt about the rationality of a policy like Egypt's appreciations and depreciations, although their timing may have been imperfect and the magnitude of the average appreciations and depreciations, inadequate.

It should also be emphasized that we are here talking about the *average* effective exchange rate changes implied by the exchange regimes. Even if this average rate were to move in a way that looks rational from a macroeconomic stabilization point of view, it does not follow, of course, that the exchange regimes and their manipulations would in any sense be the best possible policy. With uniform rates, and free trade, the average rate could be moved in the same way without the allocative drawbacks of the various exchange regimes. All we are saying is that—granted the existence and use of quantitative regulations—countercyclical tightening and relaxation of the regulations would appear rational from a stabilization point of view.

However, international price fluctuations were *not* uniform during the period considered here. Egypt's terms of trade exhibited clear and strong cyclical movements, as could be expected from a country whose exports largely depend upon one primary commodity and whose imports are quite diversified. The terms of trade fluctuated in the short term up and down with cotton prices; this was particularly true during the time of the Korean boom. Their long-term trend over the period has probably more or less followed that of cotton prices, too.[10] We have to think, rather, in terms of a model with export (cotton) prices increasing faster than import prices during an upswing and increasing less fast (or decreasing faster) during a recession. The change in relative prices and the resulting terms-of-trade gain or loss must be taken into account in our analysis.

Appreciation (depreciation) equal to the average change in export and import prices is here a possible policy that would permit domestic prices to remain unchanged on the average. But in the short term it might not prevent domestic imbalances from arising. An upswing in the world business cycle, for example, with increasing export prices would produce a tendency to overheating in the export sectors and to recession in the sectors competing with imports, because the appreciation is simultaneously too small to prevent export prices in domestic currency from increasing yet big enough to cause import prices in domestic currency to fall. It is difficult to say generally whether the balance of payments would improve or deteriorate in the short run. In case there were a net improvement, that would also create a general tendency toward expansion (inflation) in the country. The appreciation could, of course, be made stronger to secure balance of payments equilibrium, but then the domestic price level might decline and the domestic imbalance be reinforced insofar as the industries competing with imports would suffer a further setback.

For purposes of domestic macrostabilization, a multiple exchange rate policy with stronger appreciation for exports than for imports would seem more appropriate. If the appreciation for exports and imports were made proportional to the respective export and import price increases, domestic prices would be left unchanged, production and the allocation of resources would be unaffected, and the whole terms of trade gain would be skimmed off by the government and invested in larger foreign exchange reserves. During a world recession with a fall in the terms of trade, the opposite policy could be pursued, with more depreciation for exports than for imports; the terms-of-trade loss would be carried by the government sector and financed through a diminution of the exchange reserves.

From a macrostabilization point of view, this multiple exchange rate policy looks perfectly rational; it implies complete domestic stabilization and full employment of resources. But, in contrast to the case of uniform price movements, we are now up against problems of allocational efficiency. For, if export prices are relatively high during upswings and booms and low during recessions, allocative efficiency would "normally" require that the volume of trade, of exports as well as imports, should tend to be high during booms and low during recessions.[11] The cyclical multiple exchange rate policy suggested here to secure domestic stabilization in the face of cyclical fluctuation in foreign prices and terms of trade would prevent the cyclical adjustment of production and trade that efficiency requires.

If the possibility of stockpiling is included—and in cotton this is, of course, a very real one—our analysis changes again. In the extreme case where prices in the future are perfectly foreseen, the foreign markets are perfectly competitive, and carrying costs are negligible, the optimal policy would be simply to produce cotton constantly to the margin determined by the cyclical top prices, stockpile whenever prices are lower, and sell out when prices are at the top. Foreign exchange reserves would then have to fluctuate correspondingly. The conditions for the success of such a policy are not likely to be fulfilled, and under more realistic assumptions the problem of stockpiling as an optimal policy is much more complicated. Our discussion of the countercyclical exchange policy assumes only that sale prices are fully foreseen at the time of sowing, but nothing more than that. In real life, prices are never perfectly foreseen, but the policy discussed here seems to be the one that requires the least foresight; in this sense it is likely to be the optimal policy. But it has to be admitted that even the foresight required for this policy may exceed what can be expected from the authorities. Without going deeper into the important matter of uncertainty regarding future prices, we assume here that a priori it rules out stockpiling as the best policy. Looking at the actual stock policy of the Egyptian government (see below), this assumption certainly seems to be justified.

Note that the importance of this allocational problem depends, of course, upon the possibilities and costs of short-term reallocation of resources. Generally, one might be inclined to think that such reallocation possibilities are small, and that it might be preferable in the short term to let factors continue producing inefficient lines rather than leaving them unemployed. However, land and labor in agriculture may be reallocated easily among field crops. When reallocation takes place not only within the same industry but even within the same enterprises (farms), the short-term costs from reallocation must be negligible. If so, the short-term allocational losses may take on serious proportions.

For Egypt, therefore, the concrete problem relates to the extent to which the cotton acreage and export volume should respond procyclically to international cotton prices. We are here up against an old issue in Egyptian economic policy on which opinions have been divided. It concerns the alleged technical upper limit of about 2 million feddan to cotton cultivation.[13] One argument has held that, even at relatively low prices, cotton cultivation is always so profitable that it should be close to the technical upper limit. If this were correct, there would be no cyclical allocation problem,[14] and excessive cotton prices could simply be taxed away. The relatively low elasticities of acreage with respect to prices that we have found for cotton in Egypt (Table 6–3) support this view. Against this argument it has been contended that, although cotton is and always has been a very profitable crop and land is a relatively homogeneous factor of production in the Nile Valley and the Delta, there are, nonetheless, marginal cotton lands. Hence cotton acreage should indeed respond significantly to changes in relative cotton prices, and at very low prices even a large decrease in acreage might be justified on grounds of efficiency. The consensus has been, however, that the technical upper limit could not and should not be surpassed even at very high relative prices for cotton. Thus, the conclusion seems to be that at low prices export taxes would have allocative effects, but only income distributional effects once prices are so high that the upper limit to the acreage is reached. The latter case is clearly relevant to the Korean boom, when the acreage actually reached the upper limit (see Chart 3–3).

In the Egyptian setting we therefore have to distinguish between two cases:

First, relative cotton prices may be so high that, even at an international cyclical trough, cotton should be cultivated to the upper limit. In that case, the general exchange rate should be made to fluctuate with the average import price, and a cotton export tax or subsidy (depending upon the phase of the world business cycle) should be levied to absorb the relative change in international cotton prices. No allocational problems would arise, but the government would have to have a policy for the distribution of the terms-of-trade

CHART 3–3

Cotton: Output, Exports, Price, Stocks, 1946–1962

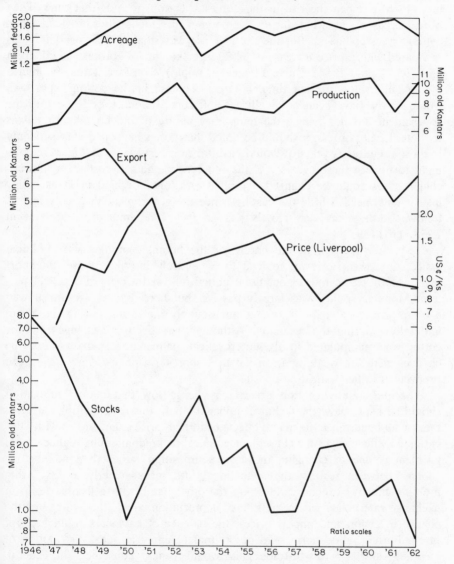

gains and losses that would be absorbed through the cotton export taxes or subsidies. Stabilization of real national income over time would require that export tax revenues during booms be sterilized and invested in a corresponding increase in foreign exchange reserves. During recessions the subsidies should then be deficit-financed and the exchange reserves correspondingly diminished.

The policy outlined in the last paragraph would apply to the years of the Korean boom (see Chapter 2, p. 32). Cotton export taxes were introduced in 1948 to dampen the rise in the domestic cotton price at that time. They were increased somewhat during the boom and temporarily abrogated when cotton prices collapsed. But the tax increase was small (£E3 per kantar as compared with a price increase of £E21 per kantar for Karnak, Good, from mid-1950 to mid-1951, to take a typical example). Considering the dominance of big landowners at that time, a larger increase in the cotton export tax would hardly have been politically feasible, but it would also seem that the government did not realize the temporary nature of the boom until it was too late. In all fairness, it should be noted that things happened very suddenly in those tumultuous years. It would have taken a very clever and alert government to foresee these events. On the other hand, both export taxes and exchange rates could be changed overnight and, once decided upon as policy instruments, needed little forecasting, since the government then only had to follow cotton prices very closely—as, in fact, it attempted to do later in 1958 and 1959.

Misinterpretation of the nature of the boom, combined with political expediency, was, however, to lead to an entirely insufficient use of export taxes. At the same time, inept fiscal policy followed a clear procyclical pattern. Monetary policy was largely passive, but here, too, the result showed a clear procyclical pattern, with money supply increasing during the boom and falling during the recession. Although the effective exchange rate for cotton was manipulated in a countercyclical manner during these years, the changes were too weak, and, on balance, short-term policies may have been procyclical rather than the opposite.

Second, relative cotton prices may be so low that cotton cultivation should be kept below the technical upper limit. In this case multiple effective rates would neutralize the macro effects of foreign price changes, but with allocational inefficiency as the consequence. Since the predominating reallocational problem is one of changing the crop composition rather than moving resources between sectors, the allocational loss speaks clearly against using multiple effective exchange rates. On the other hand, with a flexible uniform exchange rate policy where the rate of depreciation equals the average of the change in export and import prices, the balance of payments could be kept in equilibrium, allocation would be optimal (granted an ideal distribution of income), and a terms-of-trade gain would benefit consumers in general. Farmers would experience an increase in cotton prices and a proportionate fall in all other output prices, and their money income would tend to be unchanged.[15] But with all other agricultural prices lowered, the cost of living would be lower and, since there would be no pressure on money wages, all real wages and profits would increase. This policy would imply that, though private money income would be constant, private real income would fluctuate cyclically with the terms of trade.[16] If that is not considered suitable, the government could theoretically keep private real income constant over the cycle by levying countercyclical food taxes (subsidies) and letting the terms-of-trade gains and losses be absorbed in fluctuating exchange reserves.

Our discussion thus leads up to the conclusion that domestic stabilization over the cycle without misallocation would require countercyclical, uniform exchange rate changes in inverse proportion to some kind of average of export and import prices, combined with export taxes when the upper limit for cotton cultivation is reached and with food taxes (subsidies) in all other situations, both changing procyclically. The timing and magnitude of such measures would be a problem even for the best of governments, but in principle we do not believe them to be beyond the administrative capabilities of the Egyptian government. Indeed, it worked deliberately with instruments of this kind in the late 1950s.

AN APPRAISAL OF THE EFFECTIVE
EXCHANGE RATE POLICY

We are now in a position to assess analytically the effective exchange rate policy from 1948 to the devaluation of 1962. To this end, let us recall that the statistical picture drawn earlier in this chapter revealed a policy that, on balance, was countercyclical and counter-to-trend in relation to cotton prices and the terms of trade.

A first problem is whether this really was the result of a deliberately designed policy. For, in light of our discussion, so far, such a policy looks quite sophisticated, indeed, and the reader might wonder whether Egyptian foreign exchange policies were really all that sophisticated—if for no other reason, simply because governments usually are pretty unsophisticated in this regard and certainly were so at that time, when pegged rates had just been made the cornerstone of the international monetary system. Moreover, our description of the policy is based on overall averages of a bewildering array of exchange measures, and it would be natural to ask whether the authorities themselves really were able to see the wood for all the trees. Are our "policy cycles" perhaps nothing but the sum of a large number of erratic policy moves?

We do not think so. Were the whole thing nothing more than that, it is inexplicable why the Egyptian policy cycles should have been synchronized with the world business cycles—themselves perhaps nothing but the sum of another set of erratic events. (We shall show, however, that in at least one instance—1955–56—the countercyclical nature of the policy was, indeed, fortuitous.) It should also be recalled that what is considered in many quarters an advanced and rational exchange policy today, i.e., floating rates, was at that time frowned upon as little more than a frivolous, primitive reaction to problems that should have been solved without (effective) exchange rate changes.

Granted now that the statistical picture we have drawn above (see p. 55) of the exchange policy is more than just a technical artifact, the question remains how well adapted it was to actual circumstances. From our discussion of countercyclical exchange rate policy it follows that an answer to this question requires careful consideration of the cotton situation. In Chart 3–3, therefore, we have brought together data for acreage, production, stocks, exports, and international prices of Egyptian cotton from 1946 to 1962. To prevent the chart from being too crowded we have abstained from showing domestic prices, too. However, the international price series in Chart 3–3 is identical with that in Chart 3–2 (except that the present one is on an annual basis), so that Chart 3–3 is directly comparable to Chart 3–2 (with due regard to the difference in scale).

Egypt came out of World War II with large stocks of cotton, roughly corresponding to one year's normal crop. Acreage restrictions (see Appendix A) had kept production at a low level during the war; yet production exceeded domestic consumption, and the government accumulated large stocks until 1946. After the reopening of trade with Europe and America and the rise in international cotton prices, acreage restrictions were relaxed; in 1947, they were abolished. Production increased rapidly, but demand was so brisk that stocks were drawn down rapidly at increasing prices. By the outbreak of the Korean War, they were practically exhausted. Despite record acreages, low yields in 1950 and 1951 led to a decline in production and, with stocks exhausted and domestic consumption rising, the export volume fell strongly— during a period of very high cotton prices. Private speculation and, later, the government's attempt to prevent the international price from falling (in 1952) led to a substantial increase of stocks (which reached their maximum level in 1953), but a good crop in 1952 made it nonetheless possible for exports to increase in 1952 and 1953. From 1953 on the government imposed restrictions on the cotton area which, although relaxed slightly in 1954, remained in force until 1960 (with increasing evasion). Export taxes were continued (see below). Production and stock developments together led to a fall in exports from 1953 to 1956, when prices reached a new peak. Thereafter, with prices in a downturn again, exports rose quickly.

The net result of acreage restrictions, stock policies, and domestic consumption, together with strong erratic fluctuations of yields, turned out to be a movement in the volume of cotton exported that was almost perfectly countercyclical to international prices—high in years of low prices and low in years of high prices. Thus, the cotton export policy for these years looks like a complete failure, with results that were just the opposite of what an optimal exchange policy should bring about.

But here we face the problem of the elasticity of foreign demand for Egyptian cotton. In principle, these developments could, after all, be interpreted the other way around: Perhaps it was world market prices that responded to Egyptian exports along a downward sloping demand curve? In that case it would not be obvious that the Egyptian policies were a failure. To appraise this position we would first have to estimate optimal acreages and exports at shifting demand curves; the actual development could conceivably also be the optimal one.

We do not believe, however, that such an interpretation is realistic. Most probably the demand for Egyptian cotton was highly elastic. Before World War I Egypt held a dominating position as supplier of extra long staple cotton, difficult to replace with substitutes. Estimates of demand functions based on data for the pre-World War I and interwar periods point to a total price elasticity on the order of -1 to -2[17], with the long-term elasticity somewhat lower. Since then competition from new long staple producers (Sudan and Peru, among others), from medium staple cotton, and from synthetics has not only shifted the international demand curve for Egyptian cotton downwards but probably also increased the elasticity of demand significantly. We do not know of any attempt to estimate the demand elasticity for Egyptian cotton for the years after World War II, but the consensus is that Egypt has lost her old near-monopoly position for long staple cotton, and that the prices she now faces in the international markets are by and large only slightly influenced by Egyptian supply policies. Even if the Liverpool price of Egyptian cotton should show some reaction to the Egyptian supply policy, this would not justify the cotton policy, although it would imply that its countercyclical nature was somewhat exaggerated.

If that is so, we can only conclude that, to the extent that cotton exports between 1948 and 1956 were the outcome of deliberate government cotton policies, these were indeed a failure. However, the government should not be blamed for having sold the wartime stocks before the onset of the Korean boom, which it could not possibly have foreseen; also, it must be acknowledged that erratic yield fluctuations contributed much to the outcome. Nonetheless, this circumstance clearly deprives the average depreciation policy of much of its rationale. To the extent that it should have worked on the volume of exports, it was influenced by uncontrollable events and superseded by other policies that went awry. It was only on imports and the remaining exports other than cotton that it may have worked. The stabilizing effect on domestic prices is obvious, however.

Since the upper limit for the cotton area was reached in 1950 and prices continued increasing, it would have been perfectly rational in 1950 and 1951 to levy high export taxes for domestic stabilization purposes. Cotton prices by far exceeded the level necessary to bring the acreage to its maximum. It would seem (see Appendix A) that a producer price of £E15 per metric kantar would have been sufficient to keep the acreage at its maximum. Export taxes, therefore, could probably have been higher by at least £E10 per metric kantar in 1950 and by £E3 in 1951. When, on the other hand, international prices fell in 1952 and reached such low levels in 1953 that the optimal cotton acreage must have been below the upper limit, the export taxes should have been abolished altogether, according to our previous reasoning. The export taxes were, in fact, cut in 1953 (after a temporary suspension in 1952) to about half their size during the peak of the boom. The sharp price drop, however, meant that the rate of taxation remained about the same. In addition, acreage restrictions were imposed and the cotton acreage was most certainly below the optimum. The taxes continued at this level until 1955, when they slowly began to be phased out. If export taxes had been completely abolished as far back as 1952, and no cotton area restrictions had been adopted, the recession of 1953–1954 would have been mitigated, probably without detrimental effects on the balance of payments. The fall of the domestic price level in 1952 and 1953 would, of course, have been less pronounced, but since wages had risen more than prices during the Korean boom, there was no strong social motivation for a reversal of the price increase. The excessively low level of the cotton export taxes in 1950 and 1951, together with their continuation after 1952 and the introduction of the cotton area restrictions, added up to be the greatest mistake in the trade and exchange policies from 1948 to 1962.

In the statistical section of this chapter we saw that from 1948 through 1951 there was an average appreciation of 12 percent for commodity exports and of 9 percent for imports (Tables 3–1 and 3–2), with the possible deduction of 1 or 2 percent related to the devaluation against the dollar in 1949. Both on the export and the import side, about 6 percent of the appreciation was due to the disappearance of triangular trade with the introduction of the export pound. There is little to object to in this part of the policy. With the improvement of Egypt's dollar situation, the motivation for triangular trade became weaker, and, although the introduction of the export pound arrangements in 1950 shows continued government concern about the country's dollar earnings, general allocational arguments certainly speak for letting the appreciation as far as possible take the form of canceling the multiple exchange rate arrangements. On the export side, the rest of the appreciation was related to export taxes. From our discussion it follows that they should have been increased even more, and that the appreciation from the export side should have been correspondingly stronger. On the import side, the rest of the appreciation was related to lower customs duties. The appreciation policy for this period thus consisted in a move toward more unified exchange rates, with a reduction of customs duties and raising of export duties that had no allocational effects in the given situation. Up to this point, the whole package seems well designed, with the important qualification that the export taxes could have been much higher.

As mentioned in Chapter 2, however, the boom was accompanied by recessionary tendencies in industrial production, with increased competition from abroad as a possible contributing cause. If that is so, the appreciation on the import side may have been too strong. Purely from a stabilization point of view, a larger increase in export taxes with a smaller decrease in import duties might then have been preferable.

From 1952 through 1955 the average effective depreciation was about the same for exports and imports—5 to 6 percent. About half was related to the import entitlement system introduced in 1953. The remainder was due to a drop in the average rate of export taxation (partly a consequence of the rise in cotton prices) and an increase in the import duties. Abolition of the export taxes together with a general depreciation would certainly have been preferable. The timing was not very appropriate, either; the depreciation should have reached its peak already in 1953.

The average appreciation from 1955 to 1956 was largely caused by the cancellation of the import entitlement system, which, in turn, was the result of British pressures; the need for an appreciation came afterwards (and completely unexpectedly, of course), with the speculative increase in cotton prices after the nationalization of the Suez Canal. It is at this point that the countercyclical nature of the policy was entirely fortuitous. To some extent, moreover, the appreciation was counteracted by a tightening of import licensing, which we have not been able to consider in our calculations of the average effective exchange rate.

After the Suez War, various premium systems dominated the picture completely, although the depreciation was enhanced by the abolition of the export taxes. The average rate of import duties fell, but this was largely related to the change in the composition of imports that took place with the rise in food imports and the decline in imports of other consumer goods. The premium system was closely geared to the international development of cotton prices with the effective exchange rate deliberately used as a means of domestic price stabilization for this period, but a unified exchange rate with a high degree of flexibility could probably have produced about the same result. It is another thing, of course, that overtly flexible exchange rates probably would have met stiff opposition from the international monetary authorities at that time.

The premium system implied a more definitive depreciation of the Egyptian pound than earlier measures. Nonetheless, the balance of payments deficit was large and persistent, and exchange reserves were rapidly falling. The release of blocked Sterling No. 2 balances, however, served to keep the free reserves at a high level until 1961, and the government probably did not feel the need for further depreciation until the cotton crop's failure and the consequent fall in exports in 1961 suddenly created an acute payments crisis. Even without the failure of the cotton crop payments problems would have arisen sooner or later had the policies of 1957–1960 continued. It is very doubtful, however, whether the government would have devalued in 1962 without the payments crisis, which made it dependent upon credits from the International Monetary Fund.

ALLOCATIONAL EFFECTS OF EXCHANGE POLICIES

At the beginning of this chapter we suggested a crude indicator of the distortions created by the exchange regimes. Calculated in Table 3–3 (column 5), it shows increased distortion from 1947 to 1950 and then remains at a high level until 1955. After 1956, the distortion appears much smaller, except for a single year, 1960.

From the foregoing discussion of the effective exchange rate policy, however, it follows that for this purpose we should disregard the export taxes, at least for 1950 and 1951 and perhaps also for 1952. Once that is done, the index of distortion falls to a low level for these three years. It seems, then, that after some distortion in 1948 and 1949, misallocation almost disappeared during the years 1950–1952 (the years of liberalization), reappeared between 1953 and 1955, and tended to disappear again beginning with 1957, partly because the export taxes were lowered and abolished, partly because the premium systems implied relatively uniform exchange rates.

There are several reasons, however, why our index may not correctly describe the degree of distortion. First, the index is formed as the (absolute) difference between the averages of depreciation for exports and imports, respectively, so that some distortions may have been averaged out on both the export and the import side. Although we could probably improve the index by taking the (absolute) difference between the highest depreciation and the lowest appreciation for the individual regimes (Tables 3–1 and 3–2), we could easily exaggerate the distortion in this way (although the method actually applied tends to do the opposite), since the various regimes more often than not applied to the same commodities. (Cotton, for example, was, in 1953, simultaneously subject to export taxes, the export pound, and the entitlement system.)

Second, import licensing is not included in our calculations of the average rate of depreciation. We have seen that licensing was tightened in 1953 and again in 1957. It stands to reason that licensing by itself has created distortions. The licensing system was largely used for cutting down imports of nonfood consumer goods, partly to promote import substitution (footwear and apparel, for instance), and partly to save foreign exchange regardless of the consequences of the shortages created (in luxury goods and automobiles, in particular). In the first case there may be inefficiency in production, in the second case, inefficiency in consumption. We shall make an attempt to consider the inefficiency in production in agriculture and some major industries in Parts Two and Three of this volume. The possible inefficiencies in consumption are a much more tricky issue, closely related to the problem of equity in income distribution. Import licensing was clearly used as a means of cutting down the standard of living of the upper income brackets. If no other means of making income distribution more equitable were at hand, import licensing would not necessarily involve a loss from inefficiency in consumption. We see no possibilities of quantifying this aspect of licensing.

It seems clear, however, that we should allow for increased distortion both in 1953 and 1957. To some extent, import licensing has even served to keep down our distortion index. We noted above (p. 58) that the average rate of import duties was falling after 1956 despite increases in individual tariff rates; the explanation was that licensing served to change the composition of imports so as to increase the share of low-tariff goods in total imports. Without this effect of import licensing, our index of distortion would not show a diminution in distortion after 1956.

Most probably, therefore, distortions increased throughout the whole period, apart from a temporary interruption during the years of liberalization during the Korean boom.

NOTES

1. In defining "average depreciation" we might, for instance, proceed along the lines of the Bickerdike-Robinson partial analysis (see Joan Robinson, "The Foreign Exchanges," in *Essays in the Theory of Employment,* London 1937). We would then write $q_x p_x\$ - q_m p_m\$ = B\$$ in easily understood notation and assume that the volume of exports depends on domestic price of exportables, $p_x = p_x\$ r_x$, and volume of imports on domestic price of importables, $p_m = p_m\$ r_m$, where r_x and r_m are the exchange rates for exports and imports, respectively. Differentiating, we find then directly $e_x{}^s X\$ (dr_x/r_x) + e_m{}^d M\$ (dr_m/r_m) = dB\$$, where $e_x{}^s$ and $e_m{}^d$ are domestic export supply and import demand elasticities, respectively, defined with positive sign, and $X\$$ and $M\$$ are dollar values of exports and imports, respectively. Assuming the initial values of r_x and r_m to be equal to r, we find the uniform exchange rate change, dr, that is equivalent to dr_x and dr_m in the sense that it brings about the same $dB\$$, as $dr/r = [e_x{}^s X\$ (dr_x/r) + e_m{}^d M\$ (dr_m/r)]/ (e_x{}^s X\$ + e_m{}^d M\$)$.

With the balance of payments in equilibrium, the expression is reduced to (dividing r out) $dr = (e_x{}^s dr_x + e_m{}^d dr_m) / (e_x{}^s + e_m{}^d)$, and, furthermore, if the two elasticities are equal in size, $dr = 1/2 (dr_x + dr_m)$, which is, indeed, the expression we shall use. This derivation serves to bring out both the rationale and the weaknesses of our definition of "average depreciation." The formula for dr can be extended to any number of multiple rates in export and import.

2. They reappeared later in the sixties as the margin between the Cotton Commission's buying prices and selling prices for exports.

3. This method of calculation, of course, amounts to weighting each regime according to the share of exports to which it applies (in line with the formulas developed in footnote 1).

4. Import values are based on customs statistics and tend to be underreported.

5. Figures for the terms of trade do exist for 1938–39 and 1945 through 1959 (see, for instance, B. Hansen and G. A. Marzouk, *Development and Economic Policy in the U.A.R. (Egypt)*, Amsterdam, 1965, p. 176). They were calculated by the National Bank of Egypt, but suffer, unfortunately, from very incomplete coverage and particularly from being based on export and import values expressed in domestic currency. They are, thus, distorted by the premium system for later years. Until 1957 this series followed the international cotton prices series in Chart 3–2 very closely and we have omitted it from the chart. For the years 1957 to 1959 it points to an improvement in the terms of trade despite the weak international cotton prices. This improvement is probably an optical illusion created by the premium system; we believe that the terms of trade, measured in foreign currency values, tended to deteriorate further after 1957.

6. By 37 percent, according to the sources discussed in footnote 5 above.

7. Hansen and Marzouk, op. cit., p. 143.

8. Ibid., p. 158.

9. It is probably not without significance that the National Bank of Egypt (the central bank) continued as a private bank with a strong governor until 1960, when it was nationalized and divided into the Central Bank of Egypt, taking over the central banking functions of the old National Bank, and the new, purely commercial National Bank of Egypt. There is little doubt that the old bank served as a spokesman for cautious, not to say deflationary, policies and for old-fashioned British ideals of commercial banking (self-liquidating loans, prime trade bills, and all that).

10. These figures do not include any increase in the book value of the gold reserves in 1949 after the British depreciation.

11. See footnote 5, on the terms of trade statistics.

12. Exceptions can be constructed but they seem to assume that import goods are inferior.

13. The problem of this technical upper limit to cotton cultivation will be discussed in some detail in Chapter 6.

14. The argument carries over to rice, another export crop. Before the Aswan High Dam was built, rice cultivation was also considered to be subject to an upper limit imposed by the available water supply at the time of rice planting. And the argument applies, of course, to any export commodity with capacity limits.

15. If the composition of foreign trade and agricultural production differs this statement is not quite accurate, of course.

16. See Chapter 2, footnote 10.

17. B. Hansen (assisted by G. Duguay), "The Demand for American and Egyptian Cotton, 1889–1913 and 1920–1938," University of California at Berkeley, 1975. The unusual result—lower long-term than short-term elasticity—is perfectly possible when dealing with *total* elasticities and disregarding speculation over the long term.

See also C. Bresciani-Turroni, "Rélations entre la récolte et le prix du coton Egyptien," *L'Egypte Contemporaine*, Vol. 19, 1930; and S. Soliman Nour El Din, "A Statistical Analysis of Some Aspects of Cotton Production and Marketing with Special Reference to U.S.A. and Egypt," Ph.D. dissertation, London University, 1958, pp. 146–147.

Chapter 4

The Devaluation of 1962

The devaluation of 1962 appeared as a small ripple on the surface of the Egyptian economy, hardly noticed by the general public. It was overshadowed by more spectacular and publicized measures—the five-year plan of 1960, which included projects like the Aswan High Dam, the nationalizations in July 1961, the proclamation of Arab socialism as the official policy of Egypt, and the extension of land reforms in 1961. Nevertheless, the devaluation was an important reminder of a basic weakness in Egyptian economic policy which was to make development grind to a complete halt only a few years later. Therefore it deserves to be looked at in some detail.

THE FOREIGN EXCHANGE CRISIS OF 1962

At the end of 1961 foreign exchange reserves were still comfortably large. Gross reserves were £E136 million and corresponded to half a year's imports plus government payments abroad. Half of the reserve, however, was the sacrosanct gold stock; net reserves had decreased to a mere £E16 million (Table 3–6). Moreover, in view of the cotton crop failure in 1961, a difficult year was known to lie ahead, and during 1962 the drain on the reserves was heavy. Apart from gold, almost no foreign exchange reserve was left at the end of 1962.

Several factors combined to create the foreign exchange crisis described in Chapter 2 (p. 50). Not even the very substantial increase in foreign aid (PL 480 and Soviet aid) that took place during these years could fill the

89

resulting balance of payments gap. The coincidence of the payments crisis with the nationalizations of 1961 was, however, a fortuitous circumstance. The government asked for credits from the IMF, and in May 1962 a stabilization program was officially adopted. Credits to an amount of £E20 million were extended by the IMF. Domestic interest rates were increased and some belt-tightening was announced. The exchange rate was to be unified and increased from 35.2 to 43.5 piasters per U.S. dollar for all transactions except Suez Canal tolls and students' scholarships abroad. At the same time, the government refused to change the official par rate, which was still unchanged at the 1949 level in the early seventies.

There is little doubt that the government, despite its commitments to the IMF, had no intention whatever to cut down domestic demand; at any rate, domestic demand continued to expand vigorously. The government refused to scale down its investment program; Arab socialism was taken to mean, in addition to the nationalization of big business, increasing wages (according to the interpretations of its ideologist, Ali Sabri), and on top of it all, there were the rapidly increasing defense expenditures related to the Yemen War. The figures in Tables 4–1, 1–3, and 3–5 illustrate the main developments during the years around 1962.

During 1962–63, the fiscal year following the devaluation, the balance of payments continued deteriorating, and during 1963–64 and 1964–65, the deficit on current account remained at a high level, around £E120 million. The driving force in the expansion of domestic demand was clearly public consumption (civil until 1962–63, military thereafter), but gross investments (entirely dominated by government investment projects) were also expanding until 1964–65. Private consumption as a proportion of GDP fell from 1957–58 to 1960–61, but then stayed until 1962–63 at a higher level than in 1960–61. The commodity shortages that began to appear in 1957, characteristic of suppressed inflation, became more and more general. In 1964 people in the big cities were queueing at times for elementary necessities such as rice, fat, and meat. Black markets, too, began to be important for many ordinary commodities. Effective measures to curb domestic demand were not taken until 1964–65; the expansion of investments was stopped, and private consumption started falling in relative as well as absolute terms. Money supply in the private sector shrank slightly in the first year after the devaluation, but, with the strong expansion in the public sector through nationalizations, this tells us little about total demand. Prices, by and large government-controlled, were kept stable through 1963. This constancy, while partly due to index inadequacies,[1] mainly reflects price control. Beginning with 1964, prices were increased at an average rate of around 10 percent per year as part of the government's demand-management policies.

The devaluation of 1962, followed by strongly expansionary domestic demand policies over the next two years, was doomed to be an empty gesture.

TABLE 4–1

**Growth Rate of Gross Domestic Product
and National Expenditure, 1957–58 to 1963–64**

Fiscal Year (July–June)	GDP Growth Rate at Constant Prices (1)	Expenditure as Percentage of GDP			
		Gross Investment (2)	Public Consumption (3)	Private Consumption (4)	Total Expenditure[a] (5)
1957–58	5.9	13.8	14.4	75.6	103.8
1958–59	5.1	14.4	13.8	73.1	101.3
1959–60	6.8	12.4	14.0	73.3	99.7
1960–61	5.5	15.5	16.9	68.8	101.2
1961–62 Devaluation	3.0[b]	16.6	17.3	71.7	105.6
1962–63	8.0[b]	17.8	18.9	69.5	106.2
1963–64	6.4	19.8	22.0	65.5	107.3

NOTE: Figures for 1957–58 and 1959–60 are not always comparable to later years, but incomparability is relatively insignificant and can be disregarded for the present purpose.

SOURCES: Col. (1): 1957–58 to 1959–60, B. Hansen and G. Marzouk, *Development and Economic Policy in the U.A.R. (Egypt)*, 1965, p. 320; 1959–60 to 1963–64, B. Hansen in Vatikiotis, *Egypt since the Revolution*, p. 31. The figures for 1963–64 differ slightly from those on Table 1–2; they were obtained from a different source.

Cols. (2)–(5): 1957–58 and 1958–59, Hansen and Marzouk, op. cit., p. 322; 1959–60 to 1963–64, B. Hansen, "Economic Development of Egypt," in Charles A. Cooper and Sidney S. Alexander, *Economic Development and Population Growth in the Middle East*, Elsevier, New York, 1972, p. 59. The figures for 1963–64 differ slightly from those in Table 1–2, having been obtained from different sources.

a. The excess of total expenditure over 100 percent equals the foreign trade deficit.

b. The cotton crop failure in 1961 was followed by extraordinary bumper crops in 1962.

To a large extent it codified earlier de facto devaluation undertaken via the exchange premium system introduced in 1957,[2] but the unification of the exchange rates was a decisively new feature which by itself removed some of the protection enjoyed earlier by some industries highly dependent upon imported raw materials.

THE POSITION OF AGRICULTURE

That the devaluation of 1962 was partly a formal shift from premiums on foreign exchange to higher official rates is only one reason for its small impact on agriculture. More important was the fact that, despite the devaluation, the government did not change the prices on its purchases from agriculture, and little happened to output prices ex farm from 1961 to 1963 and 1964, the years studied here. (The system of government intervention with agricultural prices is described in Chapter 6.)

On the input side developments were rather uneven. Fertilizer prices were, on balance, lowered somewhat, with a substantial price cut for nitrates and a price increase for superphosphate, both under government control. The price cut for nitrates was related to the expansion of domestic capacity, with production on a larger scale in more modern plants, while the increase for superphosphate was apparently in line with the devaluation. Prices for fuel were kept unchanged, and prices for other produced inputs tended to increase.

The result was that domestic value added (DVA^{dom})—defined as outputs *minus* traded inputs, evaluated at actual ex-farm prices—on average remained almost unchanged at £E41 per cropped feddan for fourteen field crops from 1961 to 1963 (see Table 4–2).[3] An increase by about 16 percent from 1963 to 1964 (ten field crops) was mainly due to exceptionally high yields in 1964. For 1965 there was probably a substantial decline, but we do not have the data. DVA^{dom} includes some nontraded inputs, together with wages, rental of land, and returns to capital and management. Despite an increase in rural wages by about 13 percent from 1961 to 1963 and 44 percent from 1961 to 1964, with maximum land rentals, fixed by the government, unchanged, nominal returns to capital and management (on average £E13) almost remained the same from 1961 to 1963, but real returns, deflated by the wage index,[4] declined somewhat, from £E13.03 in 1961 to £E11.50 in 1963. In 1964 nominal returns increased sharply but real returns remained unchanged. From data on agricultural output prices, input prices, sales proceeds, and costs for 1961, 1963, and 1964, it would be impossible to infer that a devaluation had taken place in 1962.

To analyze the balance of payments deficit, its underlying causes, and possible remedies, we must gauge the competitive position of agriculture in 1961, the year before the devaluation. After all, agriculture was directly responsible for over three quarters of total 1961 exports of commodities and competed with food imports, which amounted to more than 20 percent of total 1961 imports.

Table 4–2 gives the average domestic resource costs, DRC, in piasters per U.S. dollar, for fourteen field crops in 1961 and 1963 and for ten field crops in 1963 and 1964. Domestic resources are defined here as labor, land, capital, and management, and nontraded inputs minus nontraded outputs. Two sets of DRCs were calculated, one excluding and the other including domestic transport costs and trade margins between farm and port.

The remarkable result is that the average DRC for agriculture in 1961 was only slightly lower or higher than the official exchange rate—32.7 or 36.4

TABLE 4–2

Domestic Value Added (DVA), Effective Rate of Protection (ERP), and Domestic Resource Cost (DRC) in Agriculture, 1961, 1963, and 1964

	Fourteen Field Crops		Ten Field Crops	
	1961	1963	1963	1964
DVA per feddan crop area, weighted average (£E) at actual ex farm prices, DVA^{dom}	41.339	41.033	41.097	47.652
at imputed, international prices, DVA^{int}	41.500	54.731	54.873	63.013
ERP, weighted average (%)	−0.4	−25.1	−25.2	−24.4
DRC, weighted average (piasters per U.S. dollar) excl. domestic trade and transport margins	32.9	32.2	32.5	32.7
incl. domestic trade and transport margins	36.4	36.6	36.7	36.9
Official exchange rate (piasters per U.S. dollar)	35.2	43.5	43.5	43.5
Surplus to capital and management per feddan crop area, weighted average (£E) at actual ex farm prices, wages, and official rents	13.028	12.993	12.839	16.029
deflated by rural wage index	—	11.498	11.362	11.131

NOTE: The four crops not included in 1964 are sesame, peanuts, lentils, and chickpeas. These are secondary crops with a combined acreage of about 3 percent of the total acreage for the fourteen crops included in 1961 and 1963. The fourteen crops with their individual ERPs and DRCs are listed in Table 6–4. Since there is no international price for cane, the calculations for sugar include the domestic sugar industry and thus really pertain to refined sugar and cane as an integrated industry. Hence, the field crops include what is usually called the sugar industry. This method of procedure, of course, affects the DVA, ERP, and DRC estimates. Surplus to capital and management in the last two rows, however, only includes surplus in cane cultivation.

SOURCE: Authors' calculations. See Hansen and Nashashibi, "Protection and Competitiveness in Egyptian Agriculture and Industry," NBER Working Paper No. 48, New York, 1975.

piasters (depending on how trade and transport margins are treated) against 35.2 piasters per U.S. dollar. And in 1963 the DRC was almost unchanged, at 32.3 or 36.6 piasters alongside the rise in the official rate to 43.5 piasters per U.S. dollar. Thus, there should have been nothing in the agricultural cost situation in 1961 to require devaluation. Indeed, judging from agriculture's "shadow rate" of 32.9–36.4 piasters in 1961, the official rate of 35.2 looks much like an equilbrium rate. In 1964 the shadow rate still seems to have been at the level of the official rate of 35.2, but then yields were abnormally good that year.

We do not think that our estimates of the average DRC for agriculture contain anything (such as incomplete coverage, mainly regarding animal products, or misleading prices) that can explain away this result. (The estimates will be discussed in detail in Chapter 7.) Egyptian agriculture as a whole was a highly competitive industry which, despite some misallocations (Chapter 7), could have withstood the introduction of free trade in 1961 without any change in the official exchange rate; and after the devaluation, it would have been a splendid business in 1963 and 1964 under conditions of free trade.

We want to point out, however, that the choice of exchange rate is of limited importance for agriculture as a whole in a less developed country, where at least two major primary factors—land and labor, together responsible for more than 80 percent of value added—have prices that tend to adjust passively to output prices and marginal productivity values, so that agriculture tends to become "normally" profitable whatever the sales prices are. Carried to its logical conclusion this consideration implies that no exchange rate problem ever exists as far as primitive agriculture is concerned.

Table 4–2 also shows that the average effective rate of protection, ERP, was slightly negative, at −0.4, in 1961 and developed into a much more substantially negative number, −25.1, by 1963. In 1964 it was about the same as in 1963. The reason is partly the 1962 devaluation, combined with relatively constant domestic prices for traded outputs and inputs; but there were also very sizable world price increases for three important commodities—cotton, rice, and sugar—and, in 1964, very high yields. Despite the strong increase in negative protection, actual returns to capital and management remained a good deal above normal: £E13 per cropped feddan against a normal of perhaps about £E7 in 1961 and £E16 against about £E10 in 1964. Even with trade and transport margins included in the domestic farm price, returns to capital and management probably remained above normal, but tended to fall in real terms.

THE EFFECTS ON MANUFACTURING

After 1962 profits in manufacturing experienced a terrible squeeze between increasing raw materials costs (related to both the devaluation and the government's cotton price policies) and increasing wage costs, on the one hand, and the government's reluctance to increase controlled domestic prices, on the other. Table 4–3 reproduces the available facts.

Unfortunately, detailed information about manufacturing is only available at current prices. A comparison of gross domestic product in total manufacturing industry at constant 1959–60 prices and an index of labor input (hours) in establishments with over ten employees (row 1) points to largely unchanged labor (hourly) productivity (row 2) from 1960 to 1964–65. Assuming productivity per hour to have been approximately constant, indexes of output values and input values per hour tend to be price indexes for outputs and inputs. On this assumption, Table 4–3 (rows 3 to 7) shows the developments from 1960 to 1965–66 of output price, raw materials and fuel prices, gross value added, gross profits, and wage costs, all per unit of output and input. The table also gives the shares of raw materials and fuel costs, gross profits, and wages in output value, and the shares of gross profits and wages in gross value added. Until 1962 manufacturing industry was generally fairly profitable—at the actually ruling domestic prices and wages and given the protection it enjoyed. Productivity per hour seems to have increased by some 4 percent per year from 1952 to 1960,[5] and 1961 does not show much of a departure from this trend. The share of profits in gross value added increased from 60 percent in 1952 to 68 percent in 1960, and inched up further during the next two years to reach a peak of 71 percent in 1962. The share of gross profits in output value reached a high of 26 percent in 1962, with the corresponding share of net profits at 22 percent. At a capital-to-gross output ratio of 3, this would result in a net profit of 7 to 8 percent on capital, which is a bit low, considering the costs of capital in the country, but compares well with many other less developed countries.

From 1962 to 1963–64, however, profitability declined radically. The share of gross profits in value added fell from 71 to 40 percent (measured on the basis of output value, from 26 to 9 percent). In terms of net profit on capital this development implies a fall from 7 or 8 to only 1 or 2 percent. Not until 1965–66 did profits begin to recover.

The decline in profits from 1962 to 1963–64 was the result of increases of 35 percent in raw materials and fuel prices (costs per hour) and of 42 percent in gross wage costs (per hour), accompanied by an only modest increase of 12 percent in output prices (output value per hour).

From 1957 to 1962 the prices of raw materials and fuel (costs per hour)

TABLE 4–3
Outputs, Inputs, and Profits in Manufacturing Industry, 1960 to 1965–66

	1960	1961	1962	1963–64	1964–65	1965–66
Labor input (hours) (1960 = 100)	100	106	124	130	140[a]	149[a]
Labor productivity (output per hour) (1960 = 100)	100	103	96	105	102	n.a.
Output value (per hour) (1960 = 100)	100	105	108	121	125	140
Raw materials and fuel	100	101	100	135	140	154
Gross value added	100	114	129	89	92	109
Gross profits	100	117	133	53	52	72
Wages	100	107	119	169	178	187
Share of output value (percent)						
Raw materials and fuel	69	66	63	77	77	76
Gross profits	21	24	26	9	9	11
Wages	10	10	11	14	14	13
Share of gross value added (percent)						
Gross profits	68	70	71	40	38	45
Wages	32	30	29	60	62	55
Social security contribution	2–3	3–5	3–5	10	12	15

NOTE: Data cover establishments with over ten workers. Wages seem to include social security contributions for all years, while profits probably include workers' share in profits after 1962. The percentage of social security contributions in total wages, actually paid, was 17 percent in 1963–64, 19 percent in 1964–65, and 28 percent in 1965–66. For years before 1963–64 no figures have been published, but they may have been around 5–10 percent in 1960 and 10–17 percent in 1961 and 1962. The employer contribution was fixed by law at 10.1 percent as of 1959 and at 17 percent as of 1961, but before the nationalizations there was probably substantial evasion.

The following consideration corroborates the data given above. From special wage censuses the hourly earnings per week are known (see ILO, *Yearbook*). Adjusted for hours per week, the earnings per hour are as shown in col. 1 of the table below. Adjusting these figures for social security contributions with 5 percent for 1960, 10 percent for 1961, 17 percent for 1962 and 1963–64, 19 percent for 1964–65, and 28 percent for 1965–66, we obtain the figures in column 2. Apart from 1963–64 and 64–65, this series corresponds closely to the wage costs series in Table 4–3, row 7.

Hourly Earnings in Manufacturing

	Not Adjusted (1960=100) (1)	Adjusted for Social Security Contributions (1960=100) (2)
1960	100	100
1961	101	103
1962	112	118
1963–64	124	140
1964–65	133	155
1965–66	152	184

SOURCES: ILO, *Yearbook*: hours per week; *Economic Bulletin*, No. 2, 1970: Number of employees, value of output, wages and raw materials; Bent Hansen, "Planning and Economic Growth in the U.A.R. (Egypt), 1960–65," in P. J. Vatikiotis, ed., *Egypt since the Revolution*, London, 1968: GDP at fixed 1959–60 prices, by industry.
a. For 1965–66 there is a peculiar increase in hours per week which, considering legislation and development of production, simply does not make sense. We have assumed unchanged hours per week from 1964–65 to 1965–66.

remained virtually unchanged, but from 1956 to 1957 they went up 19 percent. It would seem, therefore, that the premium system, described in Chapter 2, had its major impact on raw materials and fuel costs already in 1957. Profits at that time were not allowed to suffer; at a 14 percent increase in output value per hour (implying a 10 percent increase in output price per unit at a productivity increase of 4 percent), profits remained unchanged, practically speaking, from 1956 to 1957. From 1960 to 1962 there was a certain rise in output price (value per hour), exclusively reflecting increases in both gross wages and profits (particularly the latter) per unit.

Clearly, of the 35 percent increase (per man-hour) in raw materials and fuel costs from 1962 to 1963–64, only a minor part can be explained by the devaluation of 1962. If the total devaluation for imports from 1956 to 1962 was about 22 percent (see Table 3–3), and a 2 percent appreciation was accomplished by 1956, that makes about 25 percent from 1947 to 1962. Thus, if users of imported raw materials were not refunded *all* premiums, etcetera, it stands to reason that the devaluation may have meant a maximum rise in imported raw materials prices of about 20 percent, if all raw materials were imported. A large part of the 35 percent increase in raw materials and fuel costs must therefore be ascribed to higher prices for domestic raw materials and fuel. It would seem that the change in the government's cotton price policy (see Chapter 3, pp. 55 and 85)—from subsidizing (through export taxation) to taxing (through export premium) domestic cotton consumption—can explain much of the discrepancy.

The uptrend in wage costs was partly the outcome of the government's employment policy and partly the result of government-decreed increases in wage rates and social security contributions. The normal workweek in large enterprises was cut from 48 to 42 hours around 1962, and there was a drive for expanding employment in 1962 and 1963, which probably led to overstaffing. Since the reduction in hours was to leave weekly wages unaffected, it implied a rise in hourly wages by some 15 percent in the enterprises involved. At the same time, the statutory minimum wage for industry was increased, paid holidays, sick leave, and other fringe benefits were introduced, and a new system of wage grading brought a further increase in average wage rates. Social security contributions, to be paid by employers, were increased substantially. (They are included in wage costs in Table 4–3 and deducted from profits.) Since they were largely paid to social security funds and little was distributed as benefits, part of the wage rise and profit fall was only nominal (see note to Table 4–3) in the sense that both profits and social security contributions accrued to the public sector. But, even so, the increase in wages and the decline in profits were very substantial.

For a privately run industry these developments would, presumably, have led to a decline in both current production and investments. For a nationalized industry, however, such consequences do not follow automatically. As it happened, the main impact was on domestic savings. Public savings (including both nationalized business profits and social security fund accumulations) fell sharply; private savings must have increased, but it is impossible to trace their movements.

The information contained in Table 4–3 does not help in evaluating the competitiveness of manufacturing industry before and after the devaluation in terms of domestic resource costs, DRCs, or in any other absolute sense. But it certainly suggests a deterioration in the competitive position of industry during the year of devaluation. The detailed industry studies reported in Part Three, generally corroborate this impression, although individual industries exhibit widely divergent developments in regard to competitiveness. In Table 4–4 we have brought together the fragmentary information available about DRCs in selected manufacturing industries before and after the devaluation. (For details, see Part Three.) Note that Table 4–4 includes only a minor part of total manufacturing; for example, certain new high-cost industries are not included.

Three industries—phosphates, nitrates, and tires and tubes—show unchanged or even declining DRCs during the years straddling the devaluation. Note, however, that all three of them were characterized at that time by the introduction of important technological innovations sufficient to wipe out the adverse effects of cost inflation and unification of the exchange rate (the latter being particularly important for the tires and tubes industry, with its high import content). Although the cement industry experienced a slight rise in its DRC, it remained highly competitive even at the old official exchange rate. There were no major technological improvements in this industry, but capacity utilization increased substantially while wage increases were, for some reason, relatively modest.

The cement, phosphates, nitrates, and tires and tubes industries are exceptions, however; they contribute only a minor part of total value added in manufacturing industry. In the big old industries—sugar and cotton textiles—which are probably more representative of manufacturing as a whole, the picture is drab, corresponding to the impression given by Table 4–3. The sugar industry was particularly hard hit by wage increases, since wages in rural areas, where the sugar factories are situated, increased much faster than urban industrial wages during the period under consideration. It should be added that the sharp upturn in rural wages was not by government design, but reflected, rather, a strong demand for rural manpower for public works as well as military conscription. The textile industry also suffered badly from cost inflation, and there was little innovation in this industry to offset the effects of rising wages. In fact, during a period when most developed countries and some less developed countries reorganized and modernized their textile

TABLE 4–4

**Domestic Resource Costs (DRCs) in Selected Manufacturing Industries
before and after the Devaluation of 1962**

(piasters per U.S. dollar)

Industry	Before 1962	After 1962
Cement	28	31
Fertilizers		
Phosphates	36	33
Nitrates	61	52
Sugar	34	54
Tires and tubes	59	59
Cotton textiles		
on actual domestic raw materials base	56	80
on hypothetical foreign raw materials base	38	54
Weighted average		
with cotton textiles		
on actual domestic raw materials base	46	58
with cotton textiles		
on hypothetical foreign raw materials base	37	50
Official exchange rate	35.2	43.5
"Realistic" exchange rate suggested by IMF, 1966	—	61

NOTE: "Before" and "after" 1962 refers to the following years: cement, 1960 versus 1965–66; phosphates, 1957 versus 1964–65; nitrates, 1957 versus 1964–65; sugar, 1960 versus 1970 (based on long-term prices); tires, 1960 versus 1962–63; and textiles, 1960 versus 1970.

The averages were weighted by DVA at international prices for the years in question.

SOURCE: Authors' calculations; see Hansen and Nashashibi, NBER Working Paper No. 48, 1975, and Chapter 10 of this volume, Table 10–2. The rate of return on capital is assumed to be 10 percent.

industries, Egypt's first five-year plan seems to have positively neglected textiles—hence the strong increase in the DRC. The level of competitiveness of the textile industry depends, however, entirely upon the source of its primary raw material, cotton. Since 1916 the industry has been compelled to use domestic cotton as input, and imports of foreign cotton have been banned, which means producing fairly coarse yarns from relatively expensive medium staple cotton in lieu of cheap short staple cotton. With the actual domestic cotton input, the DRC was 56 piasters in 1960; with foreign cotton as input it would have been only 38 piasters. In the second half of the sixties the corresponding figures were 80 and 54 piasters, respectively.

As a consequence of showing two DRCs for textiles we also present two weighted averages of DRCs for the industries included in Table 4–4. On either basis, the increase in the average DRC exceeds the devaluation of 1962 so that, to break even at international prices, manufacturing industry was even more in need of protection or, alternatively, of devaluation after 1962 than before. It should be emphasized that our unrepresentative sample of industries probably gives too much weight to the "good" industries. Moreover, it should be recalled that in equilibrium it is not the average but the marginal industry that rules the roost. The equilibrium exchange rate must permit the least efficient industry that has to survive for the sake of full utilization of resources or maximization of production to do so. It is difficult to say which industries should actually survive in the long run, but let us assume that the industries included in Table 4–4 should, in fact, continue to exist. The implication would obviously be that before the devaluation of 1962, a "realistic" exchange rate would have been about 60 piasters per U.S. dollar, as compared with the official rate of 35.2. From the mid-sixties on, a "realistic" rate might even have exceeded 80 piasters, against an official rate of 43.5. And that was at a time when the IMF's suggestion of a rate of 61 put Nasser into paroxysms and made his cabinet resign.

Had the government been bold enough to shift the raw materials basis of the textile industry to cheap foreign cotton, the picture would have looked much better. Before 1962 a rate of about 60 piasters would still have been needed, not for the sake of textiles but to permit the nitrogenous fertilizer and tire industries to break even at international prices; and after 1962 the same rate would have sufficed to make all industries break even. Thus, with a sharper devaluation in 1962, combined with a shift in the raw materials basis of the textile industry, the government probably could have, in one stroke, put manufacturing industry on a permanently competitive footing despite the actual cost inflation and other factors detrimental to industrial efficiency.

GENERAL APPRAISAL OF THE DEVALUATION OF 1962

The devaluation of 1962 is an example of exceptionally badly designed and badly coordinated economic policies. Politically, this was the outcome of partly unrelated independent forces: the government's firm determination to carry through simultaneously both its investment programs and its military policies; the ideologists' determination to demonstrate to the workers the benefits of Arab socialism; and the IMF's equally firm determination to impose upon the country a stabilization program the execution of which the IMF could control only in its outward manifestations of a devaluation with unification of the exchange rates.

This is clearly a situation in which it makes sense to discuss costs and demand aspects separately, since higher wage costs were imposed upon the enterprises by decree and were not the result of endogenous forces in the economy. It is true that rural wages were pulled up strongly in 1963 and 1964 because of increasing public expenditure; but this happened largely after the devaluation of 1962 and could have been avoided had the devaluation been accompanied by adequate demand management.

Thus, the first question is whether a devaluation would have been required beyond the average level corresponding to the premiums introduced during the years 1957 to 1961, assuming that the cost inflation had been avoided and that export industries and those industries competing with imports should break even under free trade.

We answered this question to some extent in the preceding two sections. The general agricultural cost position in 1961 did not require further devaluation (see Table 4–2). From the more detailed analysis in Chapter 7 (see Table 7–1) it will be noted that the traditional export crops were heavily taxed but highly competitive at the official exchange rate of 35.2 piasters, while some important import-competing crops, particularly autumn corn, wheat, and beans, enjoyed substantial protection. But this is not really a problem. For if agriculture had been exposed to free trade at the official exchange rate at that time, one out of two possibilities would have materialized: Had substitution between crops been substantial, a shift in crop composition toward the more profitable export crops or other import-competing crops would have taken place, and that could only have improved the balance of payments situation. Had, on the other hand, rigidities in crop rotation made substitution between crops negligible, cultivation of wheat and beans would have largely continued, although income from these crops would have been low (Table 7–7). These crops are to some extent subsistence crops (particularly for those tenants who would experience losses in money terms). There is no reason to believe that land would be taken out of cultivation or left fallow during the winter season because of low profitability for these crops. And as for corn, a rapid shift was taking place from autumn corn to the more profitable summer corn at that time. In any case, the cost position of agriculture is of limited consequence because rural wages and land rentals (without controls) are highly flexible and tend to adjust to a competitive situation.

We have also seen that in manufacturing, even before the cost inflation had made itself felt, important industries were in need of a sizable devaluation if they were to break even at international prices. Even if the nitrogenous fertilizer industry and the tire industry were considered infant industries, and one assumed that the government had indeed been prepared to take the bold step of shifting the raw materials base of the textile industry, a devaluation on the order of the one that actually did take place in 1962 appears to have been a minimum necessity. The conclusion is inescapable that, to make a sufficient number of export industries, together with the import-competing industries, competitive before the advent of the cost inflation, a substantial devaluation would have been required, perhaps to the level of 50 piasters per

U.S. dollar. This is in line with our earlier contention (see Chapter 3, p. 68) that the Egyptian pound was overvalued since the inflation of World War II.

If a devaluation of that order of magnitude was needed to make the marginal industries break even before the cost inflation, it goes without saying that the actual devaluation of 1962 was entirely insufficient after the cost inflation. Our calculations in the preceding section pointed to an exchange rate of about 80 piasters as a realistic rate from the cost point of view (disregarding the possibilities of a shift in the raw materials base of the textile industry). At such rates, agriculture would have been extremely profitable, but an adjustment of agricultural output and input prices would have mainly served to bring rural wages and land rentals (if rent controls had been abolished) into line with the higher price level; real wages in both agriculture and industry would have returned by and large to their starting point in 1961. If the government, in the event of a further devaluation, had continued its policy of keeping agricultural output and input prices (ex farm) unchanged, a sizable shift would have taken place in the terms of trade between agricultural and industrial products in favor of the latter. Such a policy would have been in line with the exploitation of agriculture which was preached by some development economists, was practiced by the Soviet Union for long periods of time— and actually took place in Egypt to some extent during the years to follow. Quite apart from the question of the wisdom of this kind of policy, from both development and equity points of view, it is doubtful whether it would have proved at all feasible in the longer run. Wages in agriculture might sooner or later have been pulled up to the level of industrial wages, and, with a policy of keeping agriculture profitable, it would have been necessary to adjust the level of agricultural prices upward in line with the devaluation.

The cost situation, however, was only one aspect of the exchange rate problem. Macroeconomic effects via demand should, of course, be considered, too. It might be argued that in the complete absence at that time of rational demand management policies—defined as policies that keep total domestic demand within the limit set by domestic production *plus* whatever loans could and should be obtained from abroad—the question of the demand effects of the devaluation remains a rather academic issue. We shall discuss it, nevertheless, as part of the more general question, What is the place, if any, of exchange rate policies in a country where government controls and decisions predominate in production, investments, prices, and trade?

DEVALUATION IN A CONTROLLED ECONOMY

A completely controlled economy should, in principle, have no need for an exchange rate policy. An exchange rate must exist, of course, to translate foreign prices into domestic ones and vice versa. Production (and consumption) commands could, however, be used (in principle) for achieving efficiency in the economy. And if a command economy were not thought feasible or desirable, controlled prices could (in principle) be manipulated so as to provide the necessary incentives or disincentives to production and consumption in the spirit of market socialism. The present Egyptian economic system, however, is a mixed one in all respects. Its command over prices is far from complete and effective. Politically, the government has never been sufficiently strong to lower industry wages and is probably not strong enough to let wages, rents, and profits fall significantly in agriculture, either, although factor prices in agriculture are certainly flexible downward. For political reasons, therefore, factor prices can be regulated downward only under very exceptional circumstances (such as the outbreak of the 1967 war, when salaries of civil servants were slashed ruthlessly). This means that, if reduction of domestic resource costs is felt to be necessary in relation to the price of foreign exchange, the latter will have to be adjusted upward. The political arithmetic of publicly administered prices is like that.

As already mentioned, the Egyptian government did not feel any need for devaluing in 1962. Whatever discrepancies did exist between foreign prices (at the old exchange rate adjusted for premia) and domestic prices were filled in by subsidies and taxes on exports and imports (including public enterprise and organization profit or loss margins). At completely unchanged domestic prices, these taxes and subsidies would have needed adjustment in line with a devaluation, but that would have been purely a bookkeeping matter within the public sector. Any increase that the Central Bank might have charged import organizations (public enterprises) on their purchases of foreign exchange would have been paid back as a subsidy to the importer, while, correspondingly, exporters would have had their higher earnings in Egyptian pounds automatically taxed away. In this way a devaluation as such need have had no effects whatever on domestic demand and could have appeared a completely empty gesture.

In the 1962 devaluation, however, the government did take the opportunity to let the higher foreign exchange rate be passed on to some domestic prices.[6] To the extent that import prices for consumer goods were passed on to consumers (which was actually the case for the few nonessentials that were still imported) and that higher prices for imported raw materials were passed on to domestic users (consumers or producers) via higher domestic prices for outputs from Egyptian manufacturing industry, government revenue would increase and a corresponding curb on domestic demand would be imposed. None of the higher export earnings in Egyptian pounds were passed on to agriculture, and for manufactured products and oil, increased profits would accrue to the public sector. For capital goods the devaluation probably did not mean any decline in demand. For all practical purposes, all investment requiring imports of capital goods was public investment, which, once decided upon, always got the financing needed to cover costs; and there is nothing to indicate that the government was led to diminish the rate of investment because imported capital goods became more expensive in terms of Egyptian pounds.

It is not possible to assess the extent to which anti-inflationary demand restraint was actually accomplished through the devaluation and the subsequent rise in some prices. The simultaneous increase in industrial wages and squeeze on profits in manufacturing industry make it conceptually impossible to gauge how much of the approximately 15 percent price increase for manufactured output from 1961 to 1963–64 was due to higher prices of imported raw materials. But it is probably fair to say that the possible anti-inflationary impact must have been insignificant. The effects of the devaluation were, by and large, delayed till 1964 and 1965, when the government, faced with a severe foreign payments and credit crisis, finally began to take steps to rectify the domestic demand situation. The domestic price increases which were then decided upon, however, could just as well have been made without the devaluation—through diminished subsidies, increased taxes, higher sales prices from public enterprises, and higher purchasing prices for agricultural products. It would therefore seem that in a system like that of Egypt, the role of devaluation was mainly to reduce the tax increase that would otherwise have been necessary. It may have had a certain beneficial effect through simplifying the administration of such taxes, but from the more general point of view of resource allocation and productive efficiency it was of no consequence, since domestic prices and imports remained controlled by the government as before and income distribution effects continued to be its major consideration.

The inevitable conclusion is that, if a country is not prepared to let the price mechanism play a dominating role in the economy in general, foreign exchange rate policies cannot possibly have any important role to play, either; efforts from the outside—for example, from the IMF, the World Bank, or a consortium—to impose exchange rate adjustments upon the country make little sense without forcing the country to make more use of the price mechanism and market forces. Whether a change in this direction is good or bad for the country against the background of the authorities' ability to handle their controls, the possible imperfections of the market forces, and the whole setup of the policy makers' economic and social targets is a complex matter on which the following chapters will have more to say.

NOTES

1. Certain noncontrolled prices, not appearing in the indexes, did increase, and for some commodities black market prices were important.

2. In fairness to the IMF staff, it is understood that it had suggested at the time a higher devaluation to a rate of $2 per Egyptian pound. The effective depreciation in May 1962 would have thus been 26 percent instead of the 6 percent actually attained.

3. For the sake of comparability, it has been assumed in the estimation that cotton yield for 1961 was the same as in 1960. Otherwise, the cotton failure of 1961 would have lowered the average for 1961 substantially.

4. Farm labor is the major alternative source of income for small peasants.

5. B. Hansen and G. A. Marzouk, *Development and Economic Policy in the U.A.R. (Egypt)*, Amsterdam, 1965, p. 143. Unfortunately, the quality of data concerning manufacturing industry deteriorates rapidly as we go backward in time (partly due to more and more incomplete coverage).

6. In discussing the devaluation we include not only the effects of the formal devaluation but also that of the strong increase in the premium that took place shortly before the formal devaluation. See the discussion of foreign exchange policy targets in Chapter 3.

Chapter 5

The Administration of Foreign Trade and Foreign Exchange since 1961

Practically speaking, all exports and imports were taken over by government organizations or public enterprises in 1961. Since that time, the volume of exports and imports, prices, and all foreign payments have been the outcome of interaction between the Egyptian administration and the "world market." For a significant part of Egyptian trade and payments, the "world market" means the actions of the authorities of other countries, Communist countries in particular. The administration has, of course, been forced to operate within the constraints of the domestic supply situation, and domestic supply, particularly in agriculture, is to some extent still determined by market forces. Domestic demand, on the other hand, influences foreign trade and payments only to the extent deliberately permitted by the administration.

These circumstances make it difficult to describe the operation of the system. When everything is left to administrative discretion, only detailed studies made on the inside can disclose exactly which mechanisms or criteria are crucial for the decisions made. Unfortunately, we have not been in a position to study how the system functions from the inside, and with a single exception,[1] nothing has been published about it. Moreover, it is conceptually impossible to single out the impact of the nationalizations as separate from the effects of import, foreign exchange, and other controls. To a considerable extent foreign exchange allocation has been undertaken by the same ministries and organizations that administer the nationalized industries.

It is also clear that actual developments in foreign trade and payments should not be interpreted as simply revealing the preferences of the Egyptian authorities, for they did not always correctly foresee the consequences of

107

their decisions and may have based them on inadequate information. Miscalculation has certainly not been absent. And since much of Egypt's foreign trade has been on a bilateral basis, what has actually taken place may reflect the relative bargaining position of the countries involved rather than preferences. Complicating this issue is the fact that, intimately related to the problem of weapons deliveries, the Egyptian position vis-à-vis the Communist countries has become increasingly weak. To what extent these countries have taken advantage of the situation economically is hard to say. For political reasons they may even have been inclined to subsidize (rather than exploit) Egypt. It seems clear, however, that had weapons and loans been available to a larger extent from the West, Egypt's East Bloc trade would have been much more limited.[2]

ECONOMIC STAGNATION AND FOREIGN PAYMENTS COLLAPSE: 1964–1967

Table 5–1 shows some indicators of developments from 1963–64 to 1970–71. The GDP growth rate, which had been 6.4 percent in 1963–64, declined to 4.9 percent in 1964–65, to 4.4 percent in 1965–66, and finally dropped to 0.3 percent in 1966–67. While the outbreak of war in June 1967 may have lowered the growth rate for that last year somewhat, it can explain the complete stagnation of GDP only to a minor degree. With the war, the growth rate became negative; the closure of the Suez Canal (which normally produced some 4 percent of GDP), the occupation of Sinai, the evacuation and destruction of Suez, Ismaileya, and some minor towns, together with the destruction of some major industries, including oil refineries and fertilizer plants, brought about a fall in GDP by 3.1 percent.[3] In 1968–69 a recovery by about 6 percent took place, but it did little more than compensate for the fall in 1967–68. For the three years from 1966–67 to 1968–69, the GDP growth rate averaged only about 1 percent; per capita income must have fallen by about 6 percent during this period.[4]

It is usually assumed that it was the mounting foreign exchange crisis during 1965 and 1966 that brought development (in terms of GDP growth) to a complete stop around 1966–67—before the 1967 war. The foreign exchange crisis (which had been looming since 1961) became acute in 1965, when the United States abrogated PL480 sales of wheat, and Egypt suddenly had to purchase large quantities of wheat in convertible currency at a time when the exchange reserves were exhausted. The exchange crisis reached such proportions in 1965 and 1966 that Egypt was unable to fulfill contractual debt service obligations, got involved in short-term financing through European (particularly Italian) commercial banks at interest rates that even

TABLE 5-1

Economic Indicators, 1963–64 to 1970–71

Year (July 1–June 30)	Growth Rate (percent)		Production (1963–64 = 100)			Expenditure on GDP (% of GDP at current market prices)				Foreign Trade Deficit (−) or Surplus (+) (mill. £E)	Deficit on Current Account (−) (mill. £E)
	GDP (1)	GDP, Excluding "Other Services" (2)	FAO Index, Total Agricultural Production (3)	Agriculture (4)	Industry and Mining (5)	Gross Investment (6)	Public Consumption (7)	Private Consumption (8)	Foreign Balance (9)	(10)	(11)
				Value Added at Constant Prices							
1963–64	6.4	6.6	100	100	100	19.7	21.3	66.0	−7.0	−176.8	−126.0
1964–65	4.9	3.5	103	105	104	17.2	19.8	66.1	−2.5	−135.5	−119.5
1965–66	4.4	3.5	104	107	107	18.6	20.5	65.9	−5.1	−204.8	−96.2
1966–67	0.3	−0.5	103	104	108	15.5	19.7	65.8	−1.0	−115.2	−103.9
1967–68	−3.1	−5.5	107	108	102	13.5	22.7	69.6	−5.3	−99.3	−117.4
1968–69	5.9	6.1	117	109	114	11.8	23.9	67.8	−2.4	32.8	−118.7
1969–70	6.9	6.8	120	116	121	14.0	24.1	65.3	−4.1	5.9	−160.4
1970–71	4.8	3.6	118	115	134	14.2	25.8	66.9	−5.2	−61.2	−211.4

NOTE: Imports do not include delivery of military equipment, but the balance of payments on current account does include payments for such equipment. Public consumption probably includes payments for military equipment from abroad, and not deliveries.

SOURCES: Cols. (1), (2), (4), (5): Official estimates of Central Agency for General Mobilization and Statistics; estimates for 1959–60 to 1964–65 at constant 1959–60 prices; those from 1964–65 on, at constant 1964–65 prices. Both estimates are corrected for obvious flaws. Concerning the 1959–60 to 1964–65 estimate, see Bent Hansen in Vatikiotis, op. cit. In the estimate at 1964–65 prices, housing jumps up by more than 50 percent from 1966–67 to 1967–68. Since housing does not behave like that, particularly not at a time when houses are destroyed and about half a million people driven from their homes, we have assumed that housing in 1967–68 and 1968–69 increased by the normal 1–2 percent. "Other Services" consists mainly in government.

Col. (3): FAO, *Monthly Bulletin*, 1972 and 1974, No. 1, for averages of agricultural years. Overlapping of years makes year-to-year comparisons between cols. (3) and (4) difficult.

Cols. (6) to (9): CAGMS.

Cols. (10) and (11): *International Financial Statistics*, IMF, U.S. dollar values converted at the official rate of £E0.435 per U.S. dollar.

TABLE 5-2
Money Supply, 1962–1968

Year End of	Price Indexes (1962=100) Wholesale Prices			Money Supply, M_2ᵃ			Counterpart of Change in Money Supply (mill. £E)				Net Foreign Assets minus Clearing Accounts (11)
	Cost of Living (1)	Food-stuffs (2)	Industr. Mat. and Prod. (3)	Total (mill. £E) (4)	Increase (mill. £E) (5)	Increase (%) (6)	Net Foreign Assets, etc.ᵇ (7)	Net Claims on Governmentᶜ (8)	Claims on Private Sector (9)	Claims on Specialized Banks (10)	
1962	100	100	100	629.2							−0.1
1963	102	100	102	748.1	118.9	18.9	−32.5	120.5	26.0	4.7	7.6
1964	114	110	105	864.0	115.9	15.5	−25.7	114.7	12.0	14.9	−6.3
1965	127	124	110	923.7	59.7	6.9	−17.3	69.7	8.5	−0.8	−22.8
1966	133	141	111	938.5	14.8	1.6	−65.4	101.5	−4.9	−16.4	−77.8
1967	132	153	113	983.8	45.3	4.8	−26.1	64.5	−8.9	15.8	−101.9
1968	—	147	116	1,015.8	32.0	3.3	−13.7	4.9	44.4	−3.6	−103.1

SOURCES: Cols. (1) to (3): *Economic Bulletin*, various issues; cols. (4) to (11): *International Financial Statistics*, IMF, various issues.

a. Includes time and savings deposits with banks and Post Office Savings Bank deposits; does not include government and semigovernment deposits.

b. Net foreign assets (including gold) *minus* clearing and other accounts in £E, U.S. counterpart funds, and IMF accounts.

c. Including capital, reserves, et cetera (since all banks are government-owned).

TABLE 5–3
Imports, 1963–1968
(mill. £E)

	1963	1964	1965	1966	1967	1968
Foodstuffs	113.6	119.8	110.2	126.1	137.7	91.9
Other consumer goods	42.2	33.8	45.3	47.0	32.3	28.9
Raw materials	133.9	153.2	168.1	175.8	106.3	100.5
Capital goods	98.5	107.6	92.3	117.0	67.9	68.3
Total	398.4	414.4	405.8	465.4	344.3	289.6

SOURCE: *Economic Bulletin*, National Bank of Egypt, 1970.

the Khedive Ismail would have found immodest, and had to ask for moratoria from both West and East.

The payments crisis was a financial matter, of course, but it could have been expected to lead to a reduction of imports. This was not the case, however. From 1964 to 1966, total commodity imports remained at a very high level in relation to GDP (see Chart 1–1), increasing by 12 percent over the two years, which should have been sufficient for sustaining the growth rate at a level of 6 percent. Not only is it surprising, therefore, that the authorities were able to increase imports in the face of the desperate payments situation, but also that production suffered from the payments crisis when imports were actually on the rise.

Before discussing this matter in some detail, we want to emphasize that other factors did, in fact, serve to dampen the GNP growth rate from 1964 to 1967.

Both agriculture and industry stagnated, but in both cases exogenous forces were at work none of which can be traced back to the foreign exchange crisis. Agriculture experienced very good crop years from 1962 to 1964, and this helped to create the rather high growth rates of GDP in that two-year period. From 1964 to 1966, however, the yield of cotton fell by about 20 percent. There was a little "green revolution" in corn, with yield increasing by about one third. Nevertheless, corn being a much less valuable crop than cotton, agricultural output and value added stagnated, albeit at a relatively high level, from 1964 to 1967. In industry, oil production (extraction as well as refining) fell because certain wells began to run dry, a circumstance that also tended to create stagnation in the total exports of manufactured products other than textiles during these years (Table 5–4). The same happened with manganese. In addition, the slowdown in agricultural output alone would have tended to create stagnation in industries processing agricultural products, such as cotton ginning and pressing, flour milling, canning, and sugar refining.[5]

TABLE 5–4

Exports, 1963–1968

(mill. £E)

	1963	1964	1965	1966	1967	1968
Cotton						
Raw	121.0	166.6	146.2	143.4	121.6	121.1
Yarns and fabrics	32.9	31.8	47.0	47.9	47.6	52.4
Rice	19.5	30.4	19.8	21.2	29.8	44.9
Other agric. products	15.2	14.6	14.5	15.3	16.2	13.7
Crude oil and oil						
products	20.0	20.9	16.8	15.3	9.1	7.5
Cement	1.2	1.0	2.0	2.3	1.9	5.1
Other	5.6	5.8	5.5	5.1	5.5	6.5
Total	226.8	234.4	263.2	263.1	246.1	270.3

SOURCE: *Economic Bulletin*, National Bank of Egypt, 1970.

However, these factors can, at best, only partially explain the stagnation of industrial production.

The foreign exchange crisis could have worked directly on industrial production through a decline in imports of raw materials, parts, and machinery, and through greater maldistribution of the production requirements actually imported. However, the total value of imports of both capital goods (including transport equipment) and raw materials continued to rise through 1966, as shown in Table 5–3. Raw materials imports rose by about 15 percent and capital goods and transport equipment, by about 9 percent, (in value terms) from 1964 to 1966, while industrial value added at constant prices rose by only 3 percent from 1964–65 to 1966–67. Relevant import price indices are not available, but international raw materials and capital goods prices did not rise markedly during these four years. A unit price index for total Egyptian imports rose by 3.3 percent from 1963 to 1965,[6] while the IMF's import price index for less developed areas rose by 3 percent from 1963 to 1967.[7] It seems clear that imports of both raw materials and capital goods increased much more than industrial production in real terms.

Moreover, data are available which point in the direction of higher stocks of industrial raw materials and parts during this period. Table 5–5 presents value figures for inventories in state-owned industrial enterprises. Nothing is known about the inventory valuation principles applied, but finished products are presumably at current prices, and raw materials and spare parts, at ingoing prices. It is not clear how goods in process—if at all included—have been classified. Two comparisons with inventory values have been made, one

TABLE 5-5
Inventories in State-Owned Industrial Enterprises

	1964–65		1965–66		1966–67	
	(mill. £E)	Percent of Total Output Value	(mill. £E)	Percent of Total Output Value	(mill. £E)	Percent of Total Output Value
	(1)	(2)	(3)	(4)	(5)	(6)
Finished products	56.2	6.6	77.9	7.6	100.3	9.4
Raw materials	84.1	9.8	112.9	11.0	107.2	10.0
Spare parts	29.8	3.5	34.5	3.4	39.6	3.7
Total inventories	170.1	19.8	225.3	22.0	247.1	23.1
Index Numbers						
Total inventories, value	100	—	132.4	—	145.3	—
Industry and mining, value added at constant prices	100	—	102.5	—	103.2	—
Wholesale prices, industrial materials and products	100	—	103.1	—	107.1	—

SOURCES: Value of inventories: Cols. (1), (3), (5), *Follow-up and Appraisal Reports for the First Five-Year Plan*, Ministry of Planning, Cairo, for the years indicated in the tables. Cols. (2), (4), (6), our calculation—Cols. (1), (3), and (5) divided by total output value in industrial enterprises with ten workers and more; 1964–65 and 1965–66, from *Economic Bulletin*, N.B.E., 1970; 1966–67, obtained by applying percent increase of "Value of Industrial Production" (undefined) for averages of 1965–1966 and 1966–1967 in *Yearbook, 1969*, Federation of Industries, Cairo, p. 10, to the 1965–66 figure for output value in industrial enterprises with ten workers and more.
Industry and mining, value added: *Economic Bulletin*, N.B.E., 1971, No. 4.
Wholesale prices: *Economic Bulletin*, N.B.E., 1970, end of calendar year figures.

with total output value in enterprises employing ten workers and more (which must include practically all state-owned enterprises but also some private ones) and the other with total value added at constant prices in industry and mining (which includes all private industrial enterprises and handicrafts).

Compared with total output value, there was a clear relative increase in total inventory value from 1964–65 to 1966–67, whereas during the first five-year-plan period, 1960–61 to 1964–65, there had been no change in relative inventory value.[8] Almost the whole (relative) increase was in finished products, although relative value of inventories of both raw materials and spare parts showed a slight increase, too.

In physical terms, inputs of raw materials and consumption of spare parts can be expected to change roughly in proportion to physical output and value added at constant prices (unless there is strong pressure on capacity, in which case at least consumption of parts might increase more than proportionately); and inventories need not increase fully in proportion to current inputs. Value added at constant prices in the industry and mining sector increased by 3 percent from 1964–65 to 1966–67. Wholesale prices for industrial materials and products increased by 7 percent. Assuming that this price index can be used for deflating the values of both raw materials and spare parts, and identifying increase of real value added with increase in physical output, one finds a sharp rise in real inventories relative to real output, not only of finished products but also of raw materials and parts. There is admittedly more than one snag in this argument. Presumably, production increased more in state-owned enterprises than in small private enterprises: raw materials allocations discriminated clearly in favor of state-owned enterprises. And the assumptions about prices may be misleading. Nevertheless, it would take a very strong discrepancy in the relative increase of production in public and private enterprises, or a shift in relative input and output prices, to upset the conclusion that relative inventories of raw materials and parts increased somewhat during the years in which the growth rate of production slowed down. Certainly, it is beyond a reasonable doubt that relative inventories of finished products increased substantially during these years.

Data for individual industries also point to the accumulation of excessive inventories of spare parts. The cement industry, for example, which experienced an increase in production from 2.0 million tons in 1960 to 2.3 million tons in 1965–66, at the same time showed an increase in consumption of spare parts from £E5.12 million to £E6.15 million (this nominal increase may have implied a certain fall in real terms), while inventories of spare parts rose from £E2.10 million to £E4.99 million.

Thus, looking at the *totals* of imports and inventories of raw materials and parts, there is nothing there to help us understand the stagnation of industrial production during the period of the foreign exchange crisis. Totals, however, tell us nothing about distribution between enterprises. There may be plenty of inventories—of the wrong things. Indeed, the simultaneous occurrence of inventory surpluses and commodity shortages is a well-known phenomenon in the centralized economic systems of the Communist countries. Would it not be natural for something similar to take place in Egypt, and perhaps even more so in Egypt than in a Communist country? Also, enterprises may have been stockpiling in anticipation of shortages.

Be that as it may, nothing is easier than giving examples of shortages leading to unintentional production curbs during these years. In 1965–66 superphosphate production declined because of insufficient supplies of pyrites and sulphur (both imported). Production of rubber tires declined from July to December 1966 because of the shortage of imported raw materials.[9] During these years, the newspapers—which are often quite outspokenly critical of the lower levels of government—contained reports of extraordinary accumulations of import goods in the customs warehouses in Alexandria. Moreover, the durable consumer goods industries were severely affected by deliberate curbs on imported components; automobile assembling is the outstanding example. Thus, there is little doubt that behind the apparently satisfactory import and inventory totals there were, indeed, commodity and sectoral shortages that exerted an adverse effect on production.

A striking feature of Table 5–5 is the sharp absolute and relative increase in inventories of finished industrial products. In a market economy this would normally be interpreted as a sign of slack demand. In a controlled economy it might just mean that a lot of unsaleable rubbish is piling up. But although domestic purchasers certainly preferred imported goods (apart from cotton textiles, where Egyptian quality is superior), there is no indication that they would have chosen to abstain from all buying when only domestic products could be obtained. We have, then, the last possible explanation of the industrial stagnation: measures to curb private demand and investment were taken as of 1964–65. Since the situation was one of repressed inflation, however, it is difficult to find clear indicators of total demand ex ante.

Let us first consider money supply as a demand indicator (Table 5–2). The expansion in money supply, including quasi money (in the terminology of the IMF), slowed down rapidly during 1965 and 1966. After spurts of 19 percent in 1963 and 15 percent in 1964, the increase was only 7 percent during 1965 and less than 2 percent during 1966. The corresponding figures for increases in GDP at current market prices were 12, 18, 9, and 4 percent. Thus, while some excess liquidity may have accumulated during 1963 (and earlier), during the following three years liquidity in the private sector showed a relatively declining tendency. These developments in the money supply do not exclude the possibility that some deflationary pressure may have emanated via the private sector during 1965 and 1966.

The course of money wages points in the same direction. While annual wages increased from 1963–64 to 1964–65 by 17 percent in agriculture, by 9 percent in industry, and by 5 percent in services, the corresponding increases during the following year were only 4, 3, and 0 percent. Real wages in agriculture rose slightly during these two years, but those in industry and services fell. Developments in private profits are not known.

The composition of national expenditure, measured as a percentage of GDP at current market prices (Table 5–1, columns 6 to 9), permits some further conclusions. The characteristic feature of national expenditure from 1963–64 to 1966–67 is that gross investment (including stock changes) shrank from 19.7 to 15.5 percent of GDP, while the foreign deficit fell from 7.0 to 1.0 percent of GDP. Of the improvement by 6.0 percentage points in the foreign deficit, 4.2 percentage points was financed (in real terms) by a decline in gross investment; fixed gross investment even fell as much as 5 percentage points. Gross investment thus occupies a central place in explaining events. The remainder of the improvement in the foreign deficit is related almost exclusively to the share of public consumption, while private consumption by and large kept its share.

Before analyzing the demand situation, we sound a word of caution concerning the improvement in the foreign deficit noted above. A glance at col. 11 of Table 5–1 shows that the deficit in foreign *payments* improved less during the same period. Apart from the deficiencies of the statistics, this apparent contradiction is most probably explained by the fact that the computation of the foreign deficit for the national expenditure estimates is based on commodity and services *deliveries* in foreign trade (with the exception of weapons), whereas the foreign payments deficit is a deficit on *payments*. The difference would then be the well-known phenomenon of leads-and-lags in foreign payments, and it is crucial for understanding the payments situation. From around 1963 to 1966, payments abroad were postponed as the foreign exchange situation became increasingly strained; when, therefore, purchases and deliveries of imports were cut down after 1966, payments continued to run at a high level for some time because deferred payments fell due and could not be postponed. The alleviation of the payments situation was thus a prolonged process and did not occur instantaneously with the reduction of imports.

The diminution in the share of gross investments partly reflects the government's deliberate policy of reducing investment expenditure; the Mohieddin cabinet felt that expenditure on investment could safely be reduced without detrimental effects on real investment in the sense of capacity creation.[10] The reduction of investment expenditure goes far in explaining why a domestic slack should appear with little or no immediate improvement in the balance of payments in terms of capital goods deliveries, and why the effects on imports tended to lag behind the domestic measures of demand management.

In the year 1964–65, the decision of the government was not to embark upon any new investment projects, only to finish projects already started. Since at the start of an investment project (particularly in industry and electricity) expenditures are usually concentrated on construction, shifting to machinery and equipment only later, and since construction is an activity using domestic materials—whereas machinery and equipment are largely imported into Egypt—it follows that a decision to cut investments by refraining from starting new projects leads to a drop in construction activity and, hence, in the production of building materials, while capital goods imports continue and may even rise for some time. This time pattern is well-known in developed countries and is clearly discernible in Egypt for these years. In real terms construction activity (measured by value added) fell by 5 percent from 1964–65 to 1966–67, while capital goods imports increased by 8 percent during the same period.[11] To some extent the development was fortuitous, since the Aswan High Dam project happened to pass from the construction phase to the installation of generators and transmission lines around 1965. In terms of money value, fixed investment remained constant from 1964–65 to 1966–67; in real terms it probably fell, but in terms of finished capacity it may quite well have increased in line with the government's intentions. Not until 1967 did capital goods imports fall, but then the fall was very dramatic (to less than two thirds), and now real investment fell to a very low level.[12] For the years we are interested in—1964 to 1966—the investment policies thus created a domestic slack without alleviating the strain on the balance of payments.

The available data on public and private consumption are less helpful. Public consumption data (and the foreign deficit) may include payments for military equipment acquired from abroad, but certainly not deliveries (otherwise something much more dramatic would have taken place from 1966–67 to 1967–68, when the Soviet Union replaced a very substantial part of the army's equipment); this fact distorts the size of all shares, and most of all that of public consumption. Moreover, the only available expenditure data (Table 5–1) are at current market prices, which are particularly deceptive for a comparison between public and private consumption shares for this period. About two-thirds of public consumption consists of government wages and salaries, which were kept unchanged (in principle, at least) from 1964 to 1967, while prices for consumer goods increased much more than other prices, by about 30 percent from the end of 1963 to the end of 1966 (Table 5–2, columns 1–3). The almost unchanged share of private consumption at current market prices thus hides a substantial decline in real terms. The share of public consumption in real terms, on the other hand, must have declined far less, and probably even increased somewhat from 1963–64 to 1966–67. How this shift in the composition of real demand affected private production and the balance of payments is difficult to say a priori, but it stands to reason that it must have tended to reduce demand for domestically manufactured products and perhaps strained the balance of payments. For public consumption consists of direct labor services to a much larger extent than does private consumption; and the Egyptian government, involved in the Yemen War at that time, probably had a relatively high propensity to import (even disregarding heavy military equipment, included here only insofar as payments are concerned): the army procurements of food, an important import item, and of other imported goods probably increased rapidly.

It is more difficult to gauge the shifts in income distribution in the private sector and their effects on demand for domestically produced manufactures and import goods or exportables. It is beyond a reasonable doubt that private sector income distribution shifted strongly in favor of labor during the 1961–1963 period, when nationalizations, Arab socialism, and other policies of the Nasser regime dominated the scene (see Chapter 4). But from 1964 on the picture is less clear. The rise in the cost of living was largely the result of public enterprise pricing, and to that extent did not serve to increase private profits. Some increases in producer prices in agriculture did take place, however, and black market profits probably became more widespread. It seems possible, therefore, that from 1964 to 1967 there was, indeed, a shift back in favor of private profits. There is some evidence that terms of trade between agriculture and manufacturing shifted in favor of agriculture from 1964 to 1967, with the peasantry tending to consume more food, textiles, and fuel, and little else. How shifts in income distribution within the private sector generally affect the demand for domestic products and the balance of payments ex ante is not obvious. The effects may go either way.[13]

Possibly all of these factors must be brought into the picture to explain fully the stagnation of industrial production. Industries processing agricultural products tended to stagnate because agricultural crops were mediocre. Durable consumer goods industries declined because supplies of imported components were deliberately cut down. Private sector liquidity stopped increasing, generally dampening private demand. Building materials industries suffered from the change in public investment policy and a decline in residential building. The shifts in the composition of demand may, at least temporarily, have affected the balance of payments adversely. On top of all this, the growing complexity of controls and the increase of red tape generally created imbalances and obstacles to production, inter alia through increased maldistribution of available imports. However, to quantify the individual impact of all of these factors does not seem feasible.

A final problem to be considered is the coordination of domestic demand management measures with foreign trade and exchange policies. Through

1963–64, a high degree of coordination was possible insofar as the two key ministries—the Treasury and the Ministry of the Economy (in charge of foreign trade and banking, including the central bank)—together with the Ministry of Planning (a body without any real importance), were gathered under the same minister. Thereafter, these three ministries were headed by three different ministers, and coordination of policy may have suffered from this change. Coordination between ministries has always been a weak point in Egyptian government, and it became worse during these years when the president lost contact with domestic realities and his interest was almost exclusively directed toward foreign affairs.[14] It must not be excluded from our consideration, either, that, at the same time as the Treasury embarked upon an honest attempt to mop up purchasing power, the foreign trade authorities continued to consider it their main task to secure higher commodity imports regardless of the foreign exchange position. Pressures from other ministries and the natural tendency under a control system for enterprises and authorities to ask for more than is really needed may have contributed to keeping the issuance of licenses at too high a level.

The deficit in the balance of current payments during these years was largely with Western Europe and the United States and therefore a deficit in convertible currency. Payments vis-à-vis Communist countries were almost balanced (Table 5–6). Trade with the latter yielded a surplus averaging almost £E20 million during the years 1961 to 1966, but this surplus was by and large used for covering payments for deliveries of military equipment from, and debt service to, the Communist countries. Between one-half and two-thirds of total imports continued to be purchased from Western Europe and the United States (the Communist countries being unable to supply wheat, to take one important item), and during the years 1963 to 1966 the trade deficit with these countries was on the order of £E150 to £E200 million. About half of this deficit was covered by revenues from the Suez Canal. The remainder had to be covered by credits and, apart from some long-term development loans and PL480 counterpart funds (until 1965), this meant short-term commercial credits.

Contacts with the IMF led the latter to present in 1966 a "background stabilization plan" which, among other steps, involved a rise in the foreign exchange rate by about 40 percent, as well as certain price and tax increases and a lowering of subsidies on consumer goods. The Mohieddin cabinet seems to have agreed to the stabilization plan; some further price and tax increases were actually implemented to reduce private consumption and investments were further curtailed. But the president considered the devaluation proposal as an intolerable interference in Egypt's economic affairs, and it led to the resignation of the cabinet. At this time there seems to have been a clash between president and cabinet about policy in general, and the Yemen War in

TABLE 5-6
Distribution of Foreign Trade by Area, 1961–1968

Year	Exports			Imports			Trade Balance (mill. £E)		
	Total (mill. £E) (1)	Eastern Europe (%) (2)	Western Europe and America (%) (3)	Total (mill. £E) (4)	Eastern Europe (%) (5)	Western Europe and America (%) (6)	Total (7)	Eastern Europe (8)	Western Europe and America (9)
1961	168.9	40.5	30.9	243.8	23.6	50.9	−74.9	10.9	−79.9
1962	158.3	38.7	35.4	301.0	24.2	56.7	−142.7	−11.5	−114.7
1963	226.8	44.3	31.5	398.4	18.7	64.0	−171.6	25.7	−183.2
1964	234.4	45.1	30.1	414.4	19.1	62.9	−180.0	26.7	−190.0
1965	263.2	48.7	25.2	405.8	22.7	55.2	−142.6	37.1	−157.8
1966	263.1	51.7	19.9	465.4	25.7	55.1	−202.3	16.4	−204.1
1967	246.1	50.3	23.5	344.3	43.5	37.1	−9.2	−26.0	−70.0
1968	270.3	49.5	20.8	289.6	40.4	42.4	−19.3	15.4	−66.6

NOTE: Based on customs statistics. Except for 1963 and 1964, "aid" (see Note, Table 1–5) is not included. No military equipment is included in the import figures.
SOURCE: *Economic Bulletin*, N.B.E., 1970.

particular. Mohieddin seems to have insisted upon a termination of the Yemen War as the only way of improving the economy.[15]

DEVELOPMENTS AFTER THE 1967 WAR

The outbreak of war with Israel in 1967 changed the picture in several respects. The immediate consequence was a sharp increase in imports (excluding military equipment) from the Communist countries, with exports to them remaining almost unchanged. But after 1968 the tendency was reversed, to a fall in commercial imports from and a strong increase in exports to these countries, obviously to cover payments for military equipment. The deficit vis-à-vis Western Europe and the United States in 1968 was cut down to £E66 million, which was more than covered by the transfers received from other Arab countries as compensation for the loss of revenues from the Suez Canal. The reduction of the deficit with Western Europe and the United States was accomplished exclusively through a substantial reduction of imports from these countries. Thus, in 1968–69 Egypt, for the first time since World War II, found herself with a trade surplus.[16]

Beginning with that year, however, GDP started recovering. The growth rate was 5.9 percent in 1968–69, 6.9 percent in 1969–70, and 4.8 in 1970–71. Agricultural production played an important part in the recovery, and it would seem that the returns from the Aswan High Dam began to materialize at that time. From 1967 to 1969, the FAO index of total agricultural production rose by 12 percent. The uptrend continued over the following two years at a slower rate, with an increase of little more than 4 percent, but, the overall increase for the five-year period from 1966 to 1971 did reach about 25 percent, or some 5 percent per year. By comparative standards this is quite a substantial rate of growth for agriculture. It should also be recalled that the normal growth rate of Egyptian agriculture had been about 2½ percent; the additional 2½ percent per year, therefore, was almost certainly the result of the High Dam. Since the dam had originally been expected to increase total agricultural output by some 20 percent, this means that almost two-thirds of the expected increase (12½ percentage points out of 20) had materialized by 1971. Fertilizer shortages related to the destruction of some industries and the decline of imports may have inhibited faster agricultural growth in these years, notably because the High Dam itself meant a strong increase in fertilizer requirements.

More important from our point of view is the fact that industrial production recovered, too, despite the destruction of important industrial plants. After a decline in 1967–68 of 5 or 6 percent in industrial value added, an increase of 12 percent in 1968–69 brought industrial production 5 percent above the pre-1967 War level. Since this recovery took place in the face of capital goods and raw materials imports in 1967 and 1968 running at only two-thirds of the average for 1965 and 1966, it is hard to believe that supplies of imported capital goods and raw materials could have been the decisive factor in limiting industrial growth during the years immediately *before* the war.

THE ADMINISTRATIVE SYSTEM [17]

Initially, the nationalizations of 1961 changed little in the formal setup of exchange and trade controls. Exchange control continued to be supervised by a Supreme Committee for Foreign Exchange, set up by the Minister of the Economy. Laws, decrees, and instructions issued by the latter were implemented by a Director of Exchange Operations. Technical problems were left to the Central Exchange Control attached to the Central Bank of Egypt.

Commodity exports were controlled by a special Export Board. In principle, they continued to be free of licensing, and, as mentioned earlier, some exports of fruits and vegetables actually remained in private hands. However, most foreign sales were now handled by public enterprises, and exports of cotton could take place only through the intermediary of the Egyptian Cotton Commission.

All imports required licenses by the Import Control Office. Imports were largely effected through state organizations, which initially had to apply for licenses to import. Government departments could import directly, but state import organizations as well as industrial firms had to submit applications to the appropriate ministry, which scrutinized each application in relation to the foreign exchange budget (see below) and forwarded it to the Import Control Office. The imports of industrial firms were limited to their own requirements of raw materials, parts, and equipment. Thus, there was no scope left for imports by private traders, and as of August 1963, the right of private industrial firms to import directly was also abolished.

Import licenses were issued within the framework of the foreign exchange budget, drawn up by a Supreme Committee with members from the Central Exchange Control, the Cotton Commission, and representatives from the ministries of Industry and Planning. Initially, the Supreme Committee was only expected to evaluate the foreign exchange budget estimates prepared by the other exchange control authorities, but after 1962 it was directly in charge of the allocation of foreign exchange. The intent was to keep imports within the limits of export performance and the availability of foreign loans, and to coordinate the allocation of foreign exchange with the expenditures under the overall government budget, which included the gross expenditure and revenue of all state-owned enterprises from 1962 on.

The allocation process developed roughly as follows: In January the Foreign Exchange Office of the Ministry of the Economy sent questionnaires to the various state organizations and firms, requesting details about their production requirements for imported raw materials and capital equipment for the next fiscal year. On the basis of these questionnaires a foreign exchange budget was drawn up after extensive bargaining between the various authorities and organizations. The allocations were made according to the type of goods to be imported, the type of currency required for payment, and the method of settlement. Allocation of foreign exchange to an importer was accompanied by an import license, and the import transaction was initially carried out by the licensee. However, import licenses became superfluous, since private traders and private industrial firms (beginning with 1963) were not allowed to import. Licensing was therefore abolished as of October 1964.

In October 1964 the economy was divided (administratively) into a number of major sectors. Each was allotted a total amount of foreign exchange by the budget of the Supreme Committee, but it was left to the authorities (ministries) at the top of each sector to determine the detailed allocation within it. These authorities also determined whether imports should be made directly by themselves or left to the (state-owned) import organizations. A special bank was attached to each sector to take care of the technical matters pertaining to import payments. These changes implied a certain degree of decentralization of the allocation system, with the aim of placing the responsibility for investment, production, and import decisions with the same authority.

Within the framework of the annual budget, the foreign exchange allocations to the main sectors were first made on a weekly basis by a special Interministerial Committee. The total amount allocated each week equaled the actual exchange earnings of the previous week *minus* foreign debt obligations and other payments for invisibles falling due in the following week.

A system as myopic as that could hardly be expected to work in a satisfactory way. For instance, it would seem to link sectoral allocation of foreign exchange to the seasonalities of exports and debt servicing, but how this, in turn, affected allocations within the sectors is not known to us. The system was changed in the following year—1965—to one of less frequent periodic allocations, but operated on the basis of the same kind of simple arithmetic as that of the weekly system. A step in the direction of increased centralization was taken later, when it was decided that a central financing committee should meet periodically to decide upon import transactions recommended by the sectors for the period under consideration and within the given, periodic foreign exchange allocation. The intention was obviously to permit appraisal of the relative need for foreign exchange among the various sectors. It should be added that the annual foreign exchange budget continued to set fixed annual quotas for each particular sector, but what precise relation the foreign exchange budget had to the periodic allocations of foreign exchange and import approvals is not clear.

In regard to import priorities little was changed after the nationalizations of 1961. The Ministry of Defense had top priority along with the Ministry of Supply (in charge of basic foods). Next in line came raw materials, machinery, and parts. How allocations were made within the main sectors during the period of decentralization in 1964 and 1965 is not known, though the priorities were probably largely the same. It is clear, however, that actual allocation was greatly influenced by bargaining among parties of unequal bargaining power, and that all kinds of imponderabilia, from ministers' whims and personal favoritism to baksheesh, played their role.

It should also be emphasized that construction of new plants financed through special arrangements with foreign sources and, of course, purchases of weapons fell outside the foreign exchange allocation system just described.

No information is available on the import requests of the various sectors and the extent to which they were satisfied, but we have compiled a partial list of quotas actually allocated by the Foreign Exchange Budget to the ministries and government authorities in the fiscal year 1963–64 (Table 5–7). The

TABLE 5–7

Foreign Exchange Quotas Allocated to Various Ministries and Organizations in the Fiscal Year 1963–64

(mill. £E)

	Total	Convertible Currency	Inconvertible Currency
Ministry of Industry (raw materials, industrial equipment, spare parts)	105	76	29
Ministry of Agriculture (seeds, pesticides, agric. equipment, livestock)	14	12	2
Ministry of Supply (wheat, tea, coffee, fertilizer, sugar, etc.)	105	27	78
Ministry of Housing (steel and electrical equipment, drainage and sewage requirements)	7	3	4
Transportation	4	3	1
Pharmaceutical Organization	14	13	1
Petroleum Authority	28	22	6
Agricultural Organization (fertilizer and seeds)	4	3	1
Total	281	159	122

SOURCE: M. S. Mourad and F. Moursy, *The Foreign Exchange Budget and the Exterior Financing of Development*, Cairo, 1967, pp. 206–208.

total amounts to £E281 million (67 percent of all imports), which exceeds exports for that year (£E238 million) by roughly the service surplus (£E45 million). However, to these import allocations one should add capital goods imported in implementation of the investment program for new plants, as well as imports of consumer goods (such as woolen textiles, furniture wood, appliances, and automobiles) allocated directly to government agencies. Moreover, to the £E135 million deficit on current account in 1963–64, foreign payments obligations on capital account amounting to £E54.6 million should be added. Against this, foreign loans of £E148.1 million were available (including £E75.5 million under PL480), leaving an overall deficit of £E41.5 million. This deficit, maintained at that level until 1966, had then to be covered ad hoc by short-term credits and postponement of foreign debt service obligations. The Supreme Committee, thus, does not seem to have had the authority to balance its budget, and lack of power in negotiating with ministries and organizations may have confronted it with an impossible task.

APPRAISAL OF THE SYSTEM'S PERFORMANCE

Any attempt to appraise the performance of the administration of foreign trade and exchange after 1961 runs into two basic problems. Information about the actual working of the administrative machinery is scarce and may not really be sufficient to evaluate what was going on. In any case, a standard of comparison has to be chosen, and it is not obvious what this standard should be. Before proceeding, therefore, we have to make up our minds in this regard.

The information we have been able to collect about the administrative machinery summed up above does not amount to much more than a crude outline of the organizational setup. We could have added some more details of the same type, giving lists of state-owned trade agencies and organizations, et cetera, but this would hardly contribute to answering the basic question of how the machinery worked and how well or badly it performed. Indeed, such detail might help prejudice the analysis; for there is probably a tendency to assume that the larger a bureaucratic machinery is, given the problems to be solved, the worse it works. But that does not necessarily follow. Bureaucratic machinery may have an optimal size and may thus be too small, too. Moreover, with any system there is a concomitant bureaucracy. Even the "market forces" have their office employees and the less-than-perfect markets have many of them. It is only in abstract theory that perfect market forces as such do not use up resources and do not depend for their performances on the capabilities of these resources.[18] Once it has been decided, therefore, to replace private enterpreneurship with state ownership and not to depend on market forces, the bureaucracy of the market forces has to be replaced by another allocative machinery, another bureaucracy. The mere fact that the new bureaucracy is larger than the old one does not prove that the new system is less efficient.

Connoisseurs of Egyptian bureaucracy may, at this point, smile and ask whether these are not fairly superfluous rites in the name of academic objectivity. After all, would anybody acquainted with Egyptian bureaucracy be in doubt about the answer? The authors, who have long personal experience with Egyptian bureaucracy, do not suffer from illusions in this regard[19] but feel, nevertheless, that some caution is warranted. First, there is a clear tendency in the economics profession, particularly in the United States, to take it for granted that any market system, however imperfect, is better than any other system. Second, private enterprise and market forces in Egypt were never perfect; they performed only reasonably well under the umbrella of a government that was always at their disposal and ready to bail out losers, be it through protective measures, support in the cotton futures market, or otherwise. In the case of Egypt (as anywhere else, of course) the choice is between (highly) imperfect systems, and we do not think that it is obvious a priori which one is preferable.

These considerations lead us directly to the basis of comparison. The reader will already have understood that we do not think that a system should be condemned just because it demonstrably fails to imply a perfect theoretical Pareto optimum or convergence toward such an optimum. No existing system is known to succeed in that unfailingly. The only basis of comparison that makes sense is the hypothetical performance of a realistic alternative system that could conceivably operate in Egypt. We know of at least one such system —that which preceded the one introduced in 1961. To choose that system as a basis of comparison has the great advantage that we do not need to hypothesize about its possible performance: we know what it was. Hence, we shall simply compare performance during the two five-year periods 1956–1961 and 1962–1967, and see which period made the better showing. The objection might be raised that the transition to the present system already began in the first of these two periods: important nationalizations took place in connection with the Suez War (nationalization of the canal itself, with a number of British- and French-owned companies, particularly in the field of finance); the purely domestic Misr Bank, the center of the Misr concern, was nationalized in 1960; and, in general, government activities in investments were increasing during the entire period. Hence it might be more interesting to go further back in time when private entrepreneurship was still unchallenged. Disregarding the immediate postwar years when the economy was still dominated by war controls, their dismantling, and the recovery of the economy, this would lead us to take as our point of reference the period from around 1948–49 to 1955. However, we shall refrain from this choice, mainly because this period is dominated by the Korean boom and post-Korean recession and therefore can hardly be termed characteristic of the private enterprise system.

The Balance of Payments Deficit.

We emphasize first that the extraordinary increase in the balance of payments deficit after 1961, with the subsequent payments collapse, should not be taken as proof, or even as an indicator, of the inferiority of the present system. It was the logical, direct result of the ambitious targets for economic policy formulated by the government during the years 1960 to 1962, as we already noted in our discussion of the 1962 devaluation. The five-year plan of 1960–61 to 1964–65, Arab socialism, and the involvement in the Yemen war implied targets for gross investments, private consumption and public consumption far beyond the expansion of GNP. It is not clear whether this was understood by those who set these targets. Indeed, it is by no means clear whether target setting during these years was performed with any consideration of the problem of consistency. The men who pushed the first five-year plan and its investment targets (El Boghdady and El Kaisouni, among others) were not the same individuals as those who pushed for Arab socialism, with its consumption effects (Ali Sabri and his entourage). Also, the rise in defense expenditure may have been an unexpected consequence of the Yemen war (which was the president's personal responsibility and was initially expected to be brief and painless), much as the increase in U.S. defense expenditure in 1966 came unexpectedly as a consequence of the escalation of the Vietnam war. Furthermore, the president, upon whom the ultimate decisions about these matters rested both formally and de facto, may not have been correctly informed about the implications of these ambitious targets. Given the targets, however, the "system" had no choice but to increase the payments deficit and do its best to finance it.

The dangers of this policy were comprehended at the lower levels of government at an early stage, and the Treasury as well as the Central Bank tried to get messages through to the president in this connection. Whether these did not reach him, he did not take notice of them, or whether he thought that he would be able to continue playing off the United States and the Soviet Union against each other[20] and thus obtain financing beyond what the Treasury and the Central Bank thought realistic or justified is not known. As long as the two powers agreed to play the game, the payments problems were overcome. But when first the Soviet Union, in 1964 (when Khrushchev refused to postpone High Dam loan payments), and one year afterwards the United States (abrogating PL480 sales) backed out, the potential inconsistency immediately became an established fact and targets had to be sacrificed.

While thus the balance of payments policy turned out to be entirely unrealistic and the export performance, against this background, entirely inadequate for financing the import requirements of the economy at a satisfactory rate of growth, these are failures for which the top decision makers rather than the administrative system as such should be blamed.

Given the public sector's expenditure targets and the government's wage, tax-subsidy, and exchange rate policies, any system would run into balance of payments difficulties. Whether it would have been possible under another and better allocation system to realize the general expenditure targets at lower balance of payments deficits, either by maintaining production increases at lower import levels or, at given levels of imports, by increasing production and exports is another matter. This is largely a matter of production efficiency, the problem we are turning to now.

Resource Allocation.

Productivity data certainly point to inefficiency in production. While productivity per man-hour in industrial enterprises with ten employees and more increased by 4 percent per year from 1952 to 1960,[21] and faster in the second than in the first half of this period, there does not seem to have been any increase at all in industrial labor productivity after 1961.[22] To some extent the decline in labor productivity may reflect overemployment created first by the government's employment drive of 1961 (yet another ambitious policy target related to Arab socialism), when public enterprises were forced to employ workers beyond their needs, and after 1965 by the slack in demand which, as in any other system, tends to create labor redundancies. However, the increasing complexities of the bureaucratic system, deterioration of management, commodity shortages, and disciplinary difficulties—all directly or indirectly related to the change in the system—probably did much to keep down labor productivity. And if these circumstances had harmful effects on labor productivity, it stands to reason that they also had harmful effects on the productivity of other inputs, including imports.

There is the further question whether the *composition* of domestic production became more or less suboptimal during the 1960s—the allocation problem of neoclassical theory.[23] Did explicit and implicit price distortions increase or decrease? This matter will be discussed in some detail in the following chapters on agriculture and industry. A clear answer is difficult to give, however, because we are confronted not only with direct price distortions and trade controls—which certainly did increase—but also with government interference with domestic production patterns. Our tentative conclusion on the basis of the following chapters is that resource allocation in both agriculture and manufacturing industry deteriorated during the 1960s.

The problem is closely related to that of the *level* of foreign trade, or, given the deficits, the level of exports or imports. In Chapter 1 (Chart 1–1) we presented exports and imports as percentages of GDP at current market prices. The important feature in the present context is the clear downward trend of exports in relation to GDP from the time of the Korean boom until around 1963; from that year on the level is approximately constant.

Before World War II, exports seem to have been about 15 or 16 percent of GDP. Immediately after the war the percentage was low, but it recovered quickly. After the high export prices of the Korean boom years had subsided, the export level in 1952 was about the same as before World War II. From then on the share was shrinking until 1963 (the very low levels of 1961 and 1962 should be disregarded here, since they were the result of the cotton crop failure in 1961). The gradual (cyclical and structural) depreciation during the 1950s (Chapter 3) was clearly insufficient to stop, let alone reverse, the downtrend in the share of exports. In that respect the system after 1961 actually performed better—at least it stopped the downward trend. But by then exports had reached a very low level, and it was partly the rise in cotton and rice prices on the international markets that halted the decline. A volume index for exports shows an increase of 40 percent from 1956 to 1960 and of only 25 percent from 1960 to 1966. The corresponding unit value index fell by 6 percent between 1956 and 1960 and rose by 10 percent between 1960 and 1966.[24]

Assuming the level of exports in 1952–53 (the same as before World War II) to have been about optimal under free trade, given the deficits, the falling level of exports during the 1950s could have only been optimal if the concurrent downward trend in imports had been optimal. The fact that import licensing gained in importance during this period and commodity shortages began to appear is probably sufficient corroboration of the hypothesis that imports were running at an increasingly suboptimal level. In addition, some ill-advised import substitution took place in manufacturing (the steel works in Helwan being the most important example), but the removal of export taxes in agriculture and the increasing evasion of area controls (Chapter 6) worked in the opposite direction. All things considered, our judgment is that the optimal level of imports in 1961 as a percentage of GDP, given the deficit, may have been about the same as, or even higher than, in 1952–53. It follows that exports were running at too low a level in 1961 (even disregarding the cotton crop failure).

The roughly unchanged level of exports after 1962–63 was accompanied by an increase in the balance of payments deficit and a sharp rise in imports. If now, starting from an optimal situation with balanced foreign payments, the government decided to run a balance of payments deficit, imports should have increased and exports decreased (unless there were inferior goods), at least measured as a percentage of GNP. Since exports were not lowered when imports soared from 1962 onwards, the export level, ceteris paribus, must have become less suboptimal. The development of exports by commodity groups points in the same direction; (see Table 5–4). The government's export efforts during the 1960s were concentrated on rice and cotton textiles. The expansion of rice production and exports was certainly a move in the direction of better resource allocation (Chapter 7), and so was probably the expansion of textile production (Chapter 8). The fall in the export of other manufactured goods was mainly the consequence of the exhaustion of oil wells. However, despite these efforts, it seems pretty clear that the level of exports was too low during the whole period of the 1960s, even granted the size of the deficits. If that is true, there must also have been some loss of efficiency, and with better resource allocation the targets could have been fulfilled at a higher level of trade with a smaller deficit.

In conclusion, the economic system is not export-oriented; exports are simply viewed as necessary to pay for imports. Neither have exports been designated as a specific target supported by a planning machinery, nor have they been actively promoted abroad. Indeed, they have often served as a buffer to domestic supply fluctuations. The adaptation of domestic products to foreign specifications, particularly with regards to packaging and grading, has been virtually nonexistent, and only recently have some efforts been made in this direction.[25] This deficiency may be odd for an economy long based on exports of cotton, but even here there are strong indications that export promotion has not been pursued thoroughly and has often succumbed to considerations of self-sufficiency, diversification, and equitable income distribution.

Problems of Foreign Exchange Administration.

The changes made in the foreign exchange allocation system in 1962, 1964, 1965, and 1966 reflect all the difficulties such allocation systems face.

Although, to work rationally, a system must be comprehensive and cover all sources of demand and supply, Egypt's foreign exchange allocations to defense and new plants and other projects remained outside the system even after 1962, while orders from the top could always supersede existing allocations.

Foreign exchange budgets, indispensable for administrative exchange allocation, have been in existence since 1957. The budgets seem to have systematically overestimated foreign exchange availabilities in relation to requirements. One reason may have been the lack of comprehensiveness, but inadequate forecasting methods may also have been at fault. The survey method, apparently the major forecasting device, does not work well when the surveyed enterprises, organizations, and authorities know that their answers will have direct consequences for themselves: the requirements will tend to be overstated. Although the budget may try to adjust for such a bias, doing so correctly requires long experience with the survey method in this particular field. The tendency for imports of raw materials and parts, and inventories of such inputs, to increase more than production (for which we have given some evidence) could be a consequence of this kind of bias in the surveys. It is more difficult to know how replies to questions about future foreign exchange earnings would be biased. Exaggerated statements could be expected from enterprises and organizations if the import allocating authorities were known to discriminate in favor of foreign exchange earners—which, in fact, they probably were. Management may also have a personal career interest in drawing up a rosy picture of the future. With upward biases in both requirements and expected earnings, it is easy to imagine a situation where excessive import licenses are issued and unexpected foreign exchange shortages arise.

Under such circumstances it is tempting to supplement the annual foreign exchange budget with a primitive "cash flow" system by which any dollar is allocated at the moment it is earned but never before. The weekly allocation system adopted in October 1964 came close to a completely synchronized earnings-allocation system. Such a system is foolproof in the sense that it does not allocate more than has been earned, but only if it is comprehensive—which this system was not. In addition, it rules out all possibility for optimal allocation over time, at least if it is applied at all stages of allocation. And it does not, of course, solve the problem of allocation between users. If, for instance, the weekly allocations simply applied the proportions of the annual allocations in the budget, by the end of the year all users would have received the same x percent of their annual allocations; this is not necessarily a rational way of adjusting the annual budget. The change to a system with less frequent "cash flow" allocations in 1965 was obviously a compromise between annual budgeting and mechanical synchronization.

It appears that improvement in Egypt's exchange allocation administration partly hinges upon the development of better forecasting methods for demand and supply of foreign exchange. The short-term forecasting methods used in highly developed countries could presumably be adapted for this purpose. But it should be emphasized that, even under free trade, exports and imports tend to be difficult to forecast and that, even with the best possible forecasting methods, a substantial foreign exchange reserve may be indispensable as a shock absorber. Certainly, forecasting trade with Communist countries gives rise to special problems that, we think, nobody has tackled so far.

Centralization versus decentralization was another problem encountered in Egypt during these years. The decentralization move in 1964, when the economy was divided into sectors that were allotted lump sums of exchange to be allocated within an individual sector by the sector's own authority, was clearly undertaken to enable each sector to coordinate its decisions in regard to production and allocation of both domestic and imported inputs. But this system left open the problem of coordination among the various sectors, which probably explains the switch back to centralization in 1966 whereby the individual sector's detailed allocation of its overall quota had to go back to the central organ for approval. The government may have hoped to combine the advantages of centralization and decentralization in this way; the paper work must certainly have increased.

One of the basic shortcomings since 1961 in the Egyptian system is that it has never succeeded in formulating clear, simple, operational allocation criteria to replace those of private profit maximization, be it in long-term investment planning or in short-term commodity allocation. Hence the vacillation between centralization and decentralization. It would probably help greatly if the government could formulate such criteria—and stick to them; they might come close to private profit maximization, and, if so, the whole problem of relying upon price mechanisms to a larger extent than at present would naturally have to be reconsidered.

Our discussion in this section is not very conclusive. It does, however, indicate that—even apart from the basic targets—the administrative systems after 1961 were less efficient than the earlier system in the areas of production and imports. In exports the performance may have been better, although it was far from satisfactory. The possibilities of substantial improvements in the present administrative system are evident. Given such improvements, it is not clear to us which system would prove superior in the long run, particularly if weapons purchases continue to necessitate substantial trade with Communist countries.

NOTES

1. M. F. Mourad and F. Moursy, *The Foreign Exchange Budget and the Exterior Financing of Development,* Cairo, 1967.
2. This view pervades Nutting's discussions of Nasser's foreign policy. See A. Nutting, *Nasser,* London, 1972.
3. Excluding the sector "Other services," which mainly consists of government (including defense), the growth rate was -0.5 percent in 1966–67 and -5.5 percent in 1967-68.
4. Excluding "Other services," the fall in per capita income averaged about 3 percent per year, or 9 percent for the three years 1966–67 to 1968–69.
5. But this was not true of the cotton textiles industry. After a bad cotton crop the government has always preferred to let exports of raw cotton suffer rather than the textiles industry. The crop failure in 1961 is the clearest example of this policy.
6. *Statistical Indicators for the U.A.R., 1952–1965,* Central Agency for General Mobilization and Statistics, Cairo, 23 July 1966, p. 97.

7. IMF, *International Financial Statistics,* 1968.

8. *Follow-up and Appraisal Report for the First Five-Year Plan,* Ministry of Planning, Cairo, 1967, pp. 119–143.

9. Federation of Industries, *Yearbook,* Cairo, 1967, p. 209.

10. According to the Minister of the Treasury, Nazih A. Deif, in conversation with one of the authors in 1965.

11. The increase of 8 percent in capital goods imports is in value terms, but even allowing for some price increase it seems likely that capital goods imports rose in real terms.

12. Capacity creation may not have fallen—the completion of the Aswan High Dam during 1969–70 added enormously to capacity in electricity.

13. D. L. Chinn, "Effects of Income Redistribution on Economic Growth Constraints: Evidence from the Republic of Korea," *Economic Bulletin for Asia and the Far East,* Vol. 13, No. 1, United Nations, ECAFE, June 1972, pp. 61–76.

14. Nutting, op. cit., Chapter 15.

15. Nutting, op. cit., p. 381.

16. In terms of customs statistics. The surplus is actually smaller because a small part of the accumulated imports at ports of entry were released under the "temporary admission" procedure, whereby imported goods can be withdrawn from customs without payment of duties (and entry into the custom statistics) to relieve port congestion. Duties would be collected (and imports recorded) at a later date. On a payment basis, however, there is a substantial deficit (£E77 million), in a steady uptrend in subsequent years, reflecting increasing payments for armament deliveries after the 1967 war.

17. This section depends heavily upon the annual reports of the IMF on exchange regulations, and Mourad and Moursy, op. cit.

18. So-called information theory is, however, beginning to reform abstract theory at this point.

19. See, for instance, B. Hansen, "Economic Development in Egypt," in C. A. Cooper and S. S. Alexander, eds., *Economic Development and Population Growth in the Middle East,* New York, 1972.

20. Nutting, op. cit., pp. 374–76, seems to imply that the abrogation of U.S. aid was largely the result of Nasser's actions rather than a deliberately designed policy on the part of the Johnson administration. But this is irrelevant for our problem, since the policies we are discussing were launched during the time of the Kennedy administration.

21. B. Hansen and G. Marzouk, *Development and Economic Policy in the U.A.R. (Egypt),* Amsterdam, 1965, p. 143.

22. See Chapter 4, Table 4–3; and George Abed, "Industrialization, Employment Growth, and Economic Development (with Special Reference to the Case of Egypt)," Ph.D. dissertation, University of California at Berkeley, 1972.

23. In the preceding paragraphs we suggested that the actual production point might be below the production frontier. Here we are concerned with the question whether the best point on the frontier has been chosen.

24. L. E. Preston, in association with K. Nashashibi, *Trade Patterns in the Middle East,* New York, 1970, Appendix (by K. Nashashibi), p. 78.

25. Exports of citrus fruits have increased from negligbile amounts to over 100,000 tons solely as a result of standardization and packaging.

Part Two

Protection, Controls, and Competitiveness in Egyptian Agriculture

Chapter 6

Basic Characteristics of Egyptian Agriculture

In Part Two we study the effects within agriculture of government intervention in prices, production, and foreign trade. We have emphasized that in an economy like that of contemporary Egypt it makes little sense to select the controls at the border (tariffs and other trade taxes, import and export licensing, foreign exchange restrictions, and so forth) for special study without considering the concurrent controls in the interior. The latter have usually been designed with some regard to the former and vice versa, and each may be intended to reinforce or neutralize particular effects from the other set of controls.

Agriculture in Egypt is characterized by a number of special features that critically influence the impact of government controls. Although descriptions of Egyptian agriculture can be found in a number of publications,[1] this chapter provides a brief summary, for the benefit of the general reader, of those of its characteristics relevant to the problems under review. We also present some new estimates of supply (area response) elasticities and a general description of quantitative regulations directed specifically at agriculture.

OUTPUTS, INPUTS, AND VALUE ADDED

Table 6–1 shows the production account of agriculture for 1965. It is a gross account; seeds and fodder are agricultural outputs the value of which is included in field crops, and natural manure and eggs for hatcheries appear as both output and input. On the other hand, the expenditure by public authori-

137

TABLE 6–1

Production Account, 1965

(mill. £E)

Receipts			Payments		
Field crops					
(incl. fodder)	383.9		Seeds	20.7	
Vegetables	45.5		Chemical fertilizers	40.6	
Fruits, etc.	22.6		Natural fertilizers	36.2	
			Insecticides	4.6	
Total plant			Fodder	53.5	
production		452.0	Eggs for hatcheries	1.6	
			Fuel	11.0	
Dairy products	42.3		Maintenance and		
Meat, etc.	41.7		depreciation	3.9	
Poultry	24.1				
Natural fertilizers	36.2		Total intermediary inputs		172.1
Fish and game	13.7				
Total animal					
production		158.0	Net value added		437.8
Total output		610.0	Total inputs (incl. profits)		610.0

SOURCE: "Estimates of National Income from the Agricultural Sector, 1965," Central Agency for General Mobilization and Statistics (CAGMS), 1964 (in M. Clawson, H. H. Landsberg, and L. T. Alexander, *The Agricultural Potential of the Middle East*, Elsevier, New York, 1971, p. 280).

ties for operating the irrigation and drainage system is not included among the costs. Current government expenditure for indirect services to agriculture and irrigation was estimated at £E4.4 and 4.6 million, respectively, or a total of £E9 million in 1959–60.[2] These "hidden" production costs amount to about 7 percent of the value of produced intermediary inputs (including feed and seed), or 2½ percent of value added at that time. They are difficult to distribute by crop.

Table 6–2 presents detailed information for 1965 on area, production, value ex farm, exports, and imports of major field crops (covering more than 90 percent of the total crop area). They are divided into summer, winter, and autumn crops, and crops that are either perennial or can be grown at any time of the year. This table also gives some impression of the substitution possibilities.

Substitution between outputs often implies substitution between inputs, since input requirements differ substantially between crops (at given prices).

Sugar cane and cotton are heavy fertilizer consumers, whereas beans, lentils, and clover need relatively little fertilization. Cotton needs nitrates, beans and clover need phosphates. Crops have also very different requirements for other inputs: water, draught-power, labor, etcetera. Substitution between inputs for a given crop is also possible, of course. It should be added that, although soil quality and climatic conditions are unusually homogeneous in the Nile Valley and the Delta, there are nevertheless significant differences between regions with regard to soil characteristics, temperature, and water supply, and a change in the acreage for a particular crop may by itself imply changes in the input coefficients.

THE IRRIGATION SYSTEM

Apart from a narrow strip of poor land along the Mediterranean Sea where barley, figs and a few other crops can be grown on rain-fed land, Egyptian agriculture is based entirely on irrigation with water from the Nile. The modern irrigation system in the Nile Valley and the Delta is dependent upon the control of the river itself.[3] With the new Aswan High Dam (completed in 1971), the Nile's control has been brought to the absolute maximum as far as Egypt is concerned.

Before the Aswan High Dam began modifying the water flow in 1965, evening out the difference between water levels during the flood season and the rest of the year, about one-sixth of the total cultivated area was still under basin irrigation (the ancient method), with only one crop per year (mainly in Upper Egypt). Now that the High Dam is completed, basin irrigation should virtually disappear, and much more water is available during the first half of the year. In 1963 the total cropped area (not including certain vegetables) was 10.4 million feddan[4] on a cultivated area of 6.1 million feddan,[5] with the number of crops per year thus averaging 1.7; on areas with perennial irrigation two crops per year are typical.

Before the modern irrigation system was initiated a century ago, basin irrigation predominated and Nile silt was the only fertilizer (aside from natural manure). The silt was fertile, giving very high yields for most crops. With basin irrigation, the silt is deposited on the soil; with perennial irrigation, it tends to settle in the canals. The introduction and expansion of perennial irrigation and continuous cropping and the predominance of cotton, in particular, made the application of chemical fertilizers a necessity.

The consumption of chemical fertilizers increased rapidly, and at the beginning of the sixties Egypt had one of the highest nitrate fertilizer inputs (measured by nutritional content per acre) among LDC's. With the completion of the High Dam, almost all the silt is being deposited as sediment in the new

TABLE 6-2
Major Field Crops, 1965

Crop	Acreage (000 feddan)	Quantity (000 MT)	Value ex farm[a] (000 £E)	Exports (000 MT)	Imports (000 MT)
Summer					
Cotton, lint[b]	1,900	508	149,542[c]	330	—
Cotton, seeds	1,900	961	6,267	—	—
Rice	842	1,783[d]	39,453	330	—
Corn	931	1,599	46,242	—	137
Millet	441	739	20,588	—	134[e]
Onions, incl. green	144	319	4,595	—	—
Peanuts	55	51	4,537	—	—
Sesame	52	22	2,294	—	—
Autumn					
Corn	520	542	16,472	—	—
Rice	6	6	116	—	—
Millet	59	67	1,804	—	—
Winter					
Wheat	1,144	1,272	57,297	1	1,230[f]
Barley	125	130	4,426	1	4
Beans	433	432	20,732 ⎫		
Lentils	89	61	5,150 ⎬	76[g]	6[g]
Chick-peas	12	9	835 ⎭		
Helba (fenugreek)	52	37	2,380	—	—

Lupin	16	13	806	—	—
Onions, incl. green	50	373	4,348	170	—
All year					
Sugar cane	129	4,736	3,400	16[h]	44[h]
Berseem (clover)[i]	2,493	n.a.	60,767	—	—

SOURCES: *El iqtisad el zirai* [*Agricultural Economics*], Ministry of Agriculture, Cairo, July 1968; and *Trade Yearbook*, FAO, Rome, 1965.

a. Including value of straw and stalks.
b. Including lintners.
c. Calculated as value of unginned cotton minus value of seeds at official price.
d. Paddy.
e. Cereals not elsewhere specified.
f. Not including flour.
g. All pulses.
h. Refined and raw sugar, at raw basis.
i. Including seeds.

lake to the south of the dam and has almost completely disappeared from the irrigation water; preservation of fertility has thus required a further increase in the use of chemical fertilizers. In accordance with plans, fertilizer input did, in fact, increase substantially from 1960–61 to 1965–66 (nitrates, by 77 percent, phosphates, by 82 percent), but fell somewhat thereafter, due partly to the war in 1967 and partly to the foreign exchange shortages starting around 1965–66. Fertilizer input must have been suboptimal since 1966, and this circumstance may have influenced crop yields negatively.

The basic problem in Egyptian irrigation has always been the provision of an adequate water supply for the profitable summer crops, particularly cotton, rice, and summer corn. The flood time lasts from the end of July to October–November, and there is, practically speaking, always sufficient water for autumn and winter crops (sown in August and November–December, respectively). The supply during the first half of the year depends partly upon the previous year's flood level and partly upon storage possibilities.

Before the closure of the river by the High Dam in 1965, rice cultivation fluctuated sharply with the level of water supply in May and June. At a low level of supply, the rice acreage would be low, and acreages of other crops, especially corn, would be expanded instead. Rice may also be cultivated as an autumn (flood) crop (sown in August), but the yield of autumn rice is poor. Corn may be cultivated as a summer crop, when it yields much more than in autumn. However, summer corn, too, is dependent upon an abundant water supply. Hence, a low flood one year and a low water supply during the following spring implied a decrease in the acreage of high-yielding summer rice and an expansion of low-yielding autumn corn, with land fallow from May to August. In modern times the effects on the rice and corn crops constituted the most important implication of variations in the water supply. Since the erection of the High Dam, thanks to its large storage capacity, the water flow can be kept almost constant. A substantial expansion of the rice area and a substantial shift from low-yielding autumn corn to high-yielding summer corn have been the most conspicuous agricultural gains from the High Dam.[6]

The irrigation system is largely controlled by the government, and its technical characteristics seem to make a relatively centralized form of regulation essential. In fact, the irrigation system—with respect to both investment outlays and current operation—has always been a government responsibility, with the implication that the government cannot be neutral in regard to conditions of cultivation.

Water is distributed free, and irrigation costs are partly paid from the public budget. Advocates of market forces have recommended that irrigation water be priced, but so far nobody has been able to design a system that would work from a technical and administrative point of view. The introduction by the British of the uniform land tax, based on rental value, at the beginning of this century was partly motivated as a payment for water. At present, however, the land tax, based on assessments of 1949 and perforated by numerous exemptions, has little relation to water supply.

CROP ROTATION

With land under continuous crop cultivation, crop rotation takes on paramount importance. Egyptian peasants are well aware of this, and for ordinary field crops they have traditionally applied rotation systems, with cotton grown once every two or three years. Cotton tends to exhaust the soil as to nitrates, and is therefore grown after berseem (Egyptian clover, the major animal feed), which builds up the nitrate content of the soil; but even then, it is widely believed, in the longer run cotton could probably not be grown every year. Opinions have been strongly divided with respect to the long-run feasibility of the two- and three-year system, but the prevailing (official) attitude favors the three-year rotation.[7] It has been argued by British cotton breeders, however, that with adequate fertilization cotton could, indeed, be cultivated every year without detrimental long-term effects on fertility. The economically optimal rotation must, of course, also depend upon relative output and input prices, and with improved technology, particularly improved fertilizing, a wider range of rotations than those traditionally applied may become available. In practice both two- and three-year rotations are applied by farmers.[8, 9]

Examples of modern rotations follow.

Two-Year System
Rotation

First year: Clover (from last year, one cut)–cotton–wheat.

Second year: Wheat (from last year)–rice (or, at low water supply, fallow, followed by autumn corn, or millet)–clover (to next year), etcetera.

Three-Year System
Rotation

First year and second year: Same as above, except that beans would be planted instead of clover at the end of the second year.

Third year: Beans (from last year)–rice (corn, millet)–clover (to next year), etcetera.

The crop rotation problem has relevance for the present study in two respects. First, substitution between crops is only possible if it is feasible to change the rotation. If the technically feasible rotations are limited in number, the possibilities of substitution among crops are limited as well. Moreover, it takes time to shift from one rotation to another one.

Second, it may be argued that we should, in principle, consider rotations rather than particular crops when discussing protection, profitability, competitiveness, etcetera. For a given rotation, the individual crops are joint products. But if a large number of alternative rotations are feasible, substitution may be almost smooth.

The possibility of continuous cropping and the necessity of crop rotation complicate the appraisal of Egyptian agriculture in regard to optimality because we find both competition and complementarity between crops. Summer (autumn) and winter crops tend to be complementary simply because the summer is too hot for certain crops and the winter too cool for others. Yet summer and winter crops may overlap and thus compete for land (cotton grows from February–March to October–November, wheat from November to April, and corn, from July to December). Other crops are complementary from a fertility point of view (cotton as against clover and pulses). Competitive crops may not be equally competitive with respect to the basic inputs of land, labor, and water. Two crops that compete for land may not compete seriously for labor, not only because input coefficients differ but also because input seasons differ. Cotton and corn are a good example: the growth periods in the Delta are March to October–November for cotton and May to October, or July–August to December, for corn (summer and autumn corn, respectively); the inputs of land do overlap in time, whereas the inputs of labor do not because most labor input takes the form of soil preparation and sowing at the beginning of the growth period and of harvesting at the end. The seasonalities and hence the competition for inputs form an intricate jigsaw puzzle and play an important role in evaluating the relative profitability of crops and rotations. Chart 6–1 gives an impression of the crop seasons in Lower (Delta) and Upper (Nile Valley) Egypt. (The graph dates back to 1914, but it is the best we could find and the seasons have not changed significantly.) It should not be overlooked, however, that the seasons are not absolutely rigid, although they are geared to climate (mainly temperature) and irrigation cycles. Seeding of cotton in the Delta may, for instance, be postponed until April, albeit with detrimental results for yields, yet another substitution possibility to complicate the picture even further.

The rigidity of the crop rotation is difficult to ascertain, and opinions seem to differ widely. If it were true, for example, that cotton cannot be grown more often than every third year for purely technical reasons in the long run, there would be an upper limit of at most one-third of the cultivated area at which the long-run marginal costs of growing cotton become forbidding. At this upper limit cotton export taxes, for instance, would have no direct influence upon resource allocation and would only affect income distribution. The fact is, that the cotton acreage has never exceeded about one-third of the total cultivated area. This could be due to lack of imagination and know-how, insufficient availability of fertilizers, or persuasion and direct interference by

CHART 6–1

Dates of Sowing and Harvesting Important Egyptian Crops

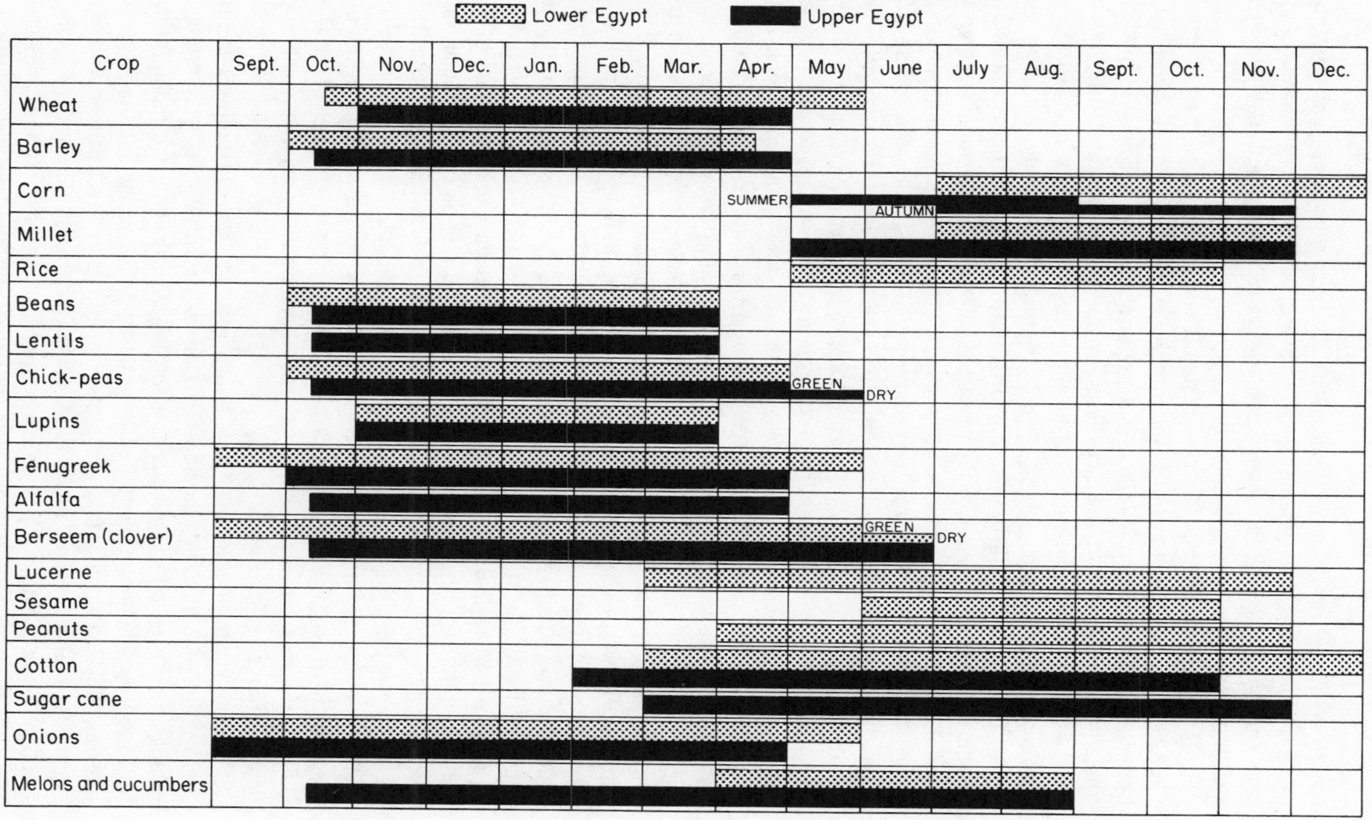

Legend: ▒ Lower Egypt   ■ Upper Egypt

Crop	Sept.	Oct.	Nov.	Dec.	Jan.	Feb.	Mar.	Apr.	May	June	July	Aug.	Sept.	Oct.	Nov.	Dec.
Wheat																
Barley																
Corn								SUMMER		AUTUMN						
Millet																
Rice																
Beans																
Lentils																
Chick-peas									GREEN	DRY						
Lupins																
Fenugreek																
Alfalfa																
Berseem (clover)									GREEN	DRY						
Lucerne																
Sesame																
Peanuts																
Cotton																
Sugar cane																
Onions																
Melons and cucumbers																

the authorities, and does not necessarily mean that a three-year crop rotation is a physical necessity. As mentioned before, however, both three- and two-year rotations have, in fact, prevailed for crops other than sugar cane, fruits, and vegetables.

Rice cultivation requires an abundant water supply, and as noted above, fluctuated strongly with the water supply in May and June prior to 1964. Quite apart from the possibility that greater reliance could have been placed upon pumping water to the rice fields in the northern part of the Delta, one also wonders whether these fluctuations were a technical necessity or partly resulted from the management of the irrigation system. The storage facilities in the Delta give the authorities some flexibility in regulating the water supply to the fields in May and June regardless of the concurrent discharge of the Nile. Until the beginning of the sixties, the short-term management of the system was subordinated to the water requirements of cotton, while rice was treated as a residual crop. Before World War I, when the irrigation system was originally designed, rice was generally a poor crop except in the salty lands of the North, where it was relatively the best crop. But the relative profitability of rice has increased over time (both yield and price have improved in relative terms), and the long-term investment policy for irrigation has led to an uptrend in rice cultivation. The question with respect to earlier performance is, however, whether it was necessary to let rice be the residual on an annual basis. The answer is that rice probably could have been kept more stable at the expense of cotton and corn. When the rice prices on the world market began rising around 1960, a substantial crop expansion took place that was not related to high flood levels but, rather, to the storage facilities in the Delta.

We shall return to these problems in connection with individual crops. At this point we only emphasize that the limitations on crop rotation in Egypt may be less rigid than sometimes assumed, but that, at least until the beginning of the sixties, the authorities may have tended to plan agricultural production within too narrow a technical frame. The latter was, after all, largely outlined by British hydrological and agronomical engineers at a time when the technology of irrigation was less developed than, and the relative profitability of crops different from, today.

Finally, let us note that fruits and vegetables (except onions) are in most cases cultivated in areas outside the standard rotations of field crops. Vegetables tend to be cultivated around the big cities, while fruit plantations can be found everywhere except in the northern part of the Delta. Although the natural conditions for growing vegetables and fruits and the proximity to the European markets might make these crops very profitable under conditions of free trade (in Egypt as well as in Europe), this study did not include them, since price and cost data were missing or entirely inadequate. This is unfortunate also because both crops have shown relatively fast growth during the last twenty years and are more important than some of the crops we did include. The area of vegetable cultivation (not including onions) increased from 252,000 feddan in 1952 to 495,000 feddan in 1961 and 706,000 in 1970, while the area planted with fruit trees increased from 94,000 feddan to 137,000 feddan and 232,000 feddan over the same period.

SUPPLY (ACREAGE) ELASTICITIES FOR FIELD CROPS (1913–1961)

Appendix A reports on an attempt to estimate supply (or acreage) responses with respect to profitability (price), total area, total labor, and total water input for a number of field crops. The estimates were based on data for the years 1913 to 1961, with due regard to area controls. The response functions —of the Nerlove type—were set up primarily to help in the appraisal of the cropping pattern after 1961 (see Chapter 7). As a by-product, the average short- and long-term elasticities set out in Table 6–3 were obtained. It should be emphasized that these are not partial but total elasticities. They were calculated on the (estimated) reduced forms of a complete general equilibrium model for agriculture. Thus, the elasticities take into account all repercussions on other crops and are constrained by actually existing total acreage, labor force, and water supply.

Two features stand out as rather remarkable.

1. Generally, the short-term price elasticities are low—for the basic food crops (corn, millet, wheat, onions, beans, and lentils) even close to zero. There are four possible explanations for the very low short-term elasticities: our elasticities are "total" with individual crop area responses constrained by the total crop area; rigidities in the crop rotation—it takes time to shift from one rotation to another even when alternative rotations are available; rigid operation of the irrigation system; and the fact that some of the basic food crops are essentially subsistence crops.

2. The long-term elasticities for all the big crops—cotton, rice, corn, millet, and wheat—as well as onions and lentils are small, too, and close to the short-term elasticities. Once more the fact that our elasticities are "total" may be the explanation. Rotational rigidities, on the other hand, can hardly explain low long-term elasticities, but the phenomenon adds to our suspicion that the government's operation of the irrigation system has, indeed, always tended to freeze cropping in a rather rigid pattern.

For *cotton* (lint and seed as joint products) the short- and the long-run elasticities are 0.25 and 0.30, respectively, both highly significant. Nerlove[10] and, in particular, Krishna[11] have obtained much higher elasticities for the

TABLE 6–3

Average Elasticities of Crop Acreages

| | | Elasticity with Respect to Price or Yield | | Long-Term Elasticity with Respect to | | |
| | | Short-Term | Long-Term | Total Crop Area | Labor | Water Supply |
Season	Estimate					
Summer–Autumn						
Cotton	I.V.2	0.25[a]	0.30[a]	0.79	0.07	−0.17
Rice	I.V.1	0.41[b]	0.49	0.30	0.61	1.39
Corn	I.V.1	−0.02	−0.02	1.59	−0.26	−0.04
Millet	I.V.1	0.05	0.09[b]	−1.16	0.77	0.32
Winter						
Wheat	I.V.2	0.03	0.04	0.33	0.36	−0.27
Onions	L.S.	0.13	0.25[b]	6.01	−0.60	1.12
Barley	I.V.2	0.25[a]	4.99[a]	−0.49	−2.15	−8.89
Beans	I.V.1	0.17	0.67	0.91	−0.96	0.21
Lentils	I.V.1	0.17	0.30	−0.02	0.29	0.14
Helba	I.V.2	0.33[a]	3.64[a]	7.94	−4.31	0.00
Perennial						
Cane	I.V.2	0.11[a]	0.81[a]	4.17	−1.12	0.29

NOTE: The elasticities presented here were obtained from the estimates chosen for the area predictions in Chapter 7. The price elasticity is equal to the corresponding F-value elasticity times one *minus* the crop's weight in F. The elasticities are based on mean values of acreage and F for the period 1913–1961. The response functions do not assume constant elasticities. L.S. denotes ordinary least squares estimate, I.V.1 and I.V.2 denote instrumental variable estimates, steps 1 and 2, respectively.

SOURCE: Appendix A.

a. t-value > 3: short-term, profitability variable; long-term, lagged area.

b. t-value > 2: short-term, profitability variable; long-term, lagged area.

United States and India, respectively. Using simpler functions, however, other authors have also come out with relatively low elasticity values for the Egyptian cotton area. Thus, for the period 1870–1913, Bresciani-Turroni found an elasticity of 0.4; for the years 1915–1941, Nour El Din obtained an (average) elasticity of 0.2; Stern, using all the years from 1913 to 1937, came up with an elasticity of about 0.4; and, excluding twenty-four years with area restrictions between 1913 and 1959, one of the authors of this volume, unlike the other three who disregarded area restrictions, estimated an elasticity of only 0.09.[12]

Rice is the only major crop with a substantial short-term price elasticity, 0.41; its long-term elasticity is only slightly higher. It may cause surprise that rice should have the highest short-term price elasticity among the crops studied here. It is usually assumed that rice cultivation is largely determined by the available water supply. Water is, indeed, an important determinant of the rice acreage (see Table 6–3); both short- and long-term elasticities of rice acreage with respect to water are high. The short-term price elasticity is based on a coefficient for relative output value per feddan (F) that is significantly different from zero only at the 95 percent level, and therefore it cannot be excluded that the true price elasticity is much lower than 0.41. However, the substantial short-term price elasticity may be due to the circumstance that rice is partly grown in the northern part of the Delta, where salinity is substantial and thus, on the one hand, the standard rotations are less appropriate and, on the other, the extensive margin of cultivation is more flexible than in the rest of the Delta and the Nile Valley. This, however, does not explain why the long-term elasticity should only be slightly higher than the short-term elasticity. The government's management of the irrigation system may be responsible for both features (see below).

Corn, millet, and wheat have negligible price elasticities, both short- and long-term. For corn the elasticities are even negative. For both corn and millet the natural explanation is that these crops are subsistence crops, mainly grown for the farmers' own consumption.[13] But for wheat this explanation is hardly satisfactory. A substantial part of the wheat crop is sold in the market, and before 1900 wheat was an important export crop.

Barley and *helba* (fenugreek) differ from the other crops in having sizable short-term elasticities and high long-term elasticities.[14] For barley the explanation is probably that this crop is mainly grown in the northern part of the Delta and along the coastal strip. It is thus partly grown outside the standard rotations, where the extensive margin of cultivation is flexible. Helba is mainly grown in the valley, but being a very small crop it has no important place in the rotations and may for that reason be easily adjusted to changing profitability.

Sugar cane has a very low short-term, but quite a substantial long-term, elasticity. This feature is easy to explain. Cane remains on the fields for up to three years (and thus yields two or three crops), and it may take three years until it is replaced by another crop. Moreover, the largest part of the cane area is cultivated under contract with the (government-controlled) factories, which fix both prices and acreage. The remainder is produced for the free market and sold to small private molasses factories. In the long term, however, the sugar factories, too, have to pay enough to call forth the supplies they want to buy—hence the relatively high long-term elasticity.

We note, finally, that the explicit inclusion of animal feed (clover) and fruits and vegetables, which may themselves have higher elasticities (at least in the long run) than field crops, might have increased elasticities somewhat for the field crops listed in Table 6–3. Independent observers believe that the rapid increase of both vegetable and fruit acreages during the last two decades is a response to rising relative prices, and that the same is true of the expansion of the clover area during the sixties.

QUANTITATIVE RESTRICTIONS IN AGRICULTURE

Even apart from the inevitable government intervention in the management of the irrigation system and in the problems of externalities related to plant diseases, agricultural policies in Egypt have made much use of quantitative regulation in regard to production, prices, and foreign trade. With foreign trade almost completely nationalized since 1961 and run by government organizations, both prices and quantities supplied are open to direct government intervention. And, although agriculture is almost exclusively based on small, privately owned farms (since 1969, the maximum area is 50 feddan per owner and cultivator), it is now organized in a way that permits centralized control of both prices and cultivated areas, at least for major crops.

Production Restrictions.

Production restrictions were already in use at the end of the last century, when cultivation of tobacco, a big and lucrative crop, was prohibited for purely fiscal reasons (while imports could be taxed effectively, domestic production evaded taxation on a large scale).[15] Area limitations were frequently applied to cotton from World War I onward to enforce the allegedly optimal three-year rotation, to prevent cash-hungry peasants from exhausting the soil (see Appendix A, Table A–1), and also, allegedly, to take advantage of Egypt's monopolistic position in the long staple market. It has been argued, on the other hand, that it was Egypt's supply-limiting policy that was at least partly responsible for the introduction of long staple production in the Sudan, Peru, and some other countries. And when, in the thirties, synthetics appeared as a serious competitor to long staple cotton, there was little basis left for the optimum tariff argument with respect to Egyptian cotton.[16] The increasing input of chemical fertilizers, at the same time, seems to have put an end to the soil exhaustion argument.

Another factor was also to enter the picture. From ancient times to the end of the nineteenth century Egypt had always been a wheat exporter. With the growing population, the country found itself unable to satisfy the domestic demand for wheat at the prevailing low prices without imports; therefore, area restrictions for cotton were in force both during World War II and the 1953–1960 period, coupled with prescriptions for wheat acreage as an import substitution device. (Cotton and wheat cultivation overlap in February, March, and April, and wheat can be grown every year.) The restrictions on the cotton area and the prescriptions for wheat were not much respected by the farmers except, perhaps, during the first year or two: "The *minimum* area fixed by law for wheat throughout 1955–1959 . . . was exactly the *maximum* fixed for cotton, but in actual fact the wheat area—designed to be higher than or at least equal to that of cotton—was 19 percent lower."[17] Chart A–1 in Appendix A shows all years with cotton area restrictions from 1913 to 1961; only some of these indicate a clear impact of the restrictions. The area prescriptions were abrogated in 1960, and the export taxes were by and large formally abolished during 1959 and 1960 (as described in Chapter 2). Beginning with 1962 they were reintroduced de facto through the price policies of the Cotton Commission (see below).

Whereas simple area prescriptions thus may have had only a minor impact on actual cultivation during most of the fifties, other developments, not unrelated to the land reforms of 1952, slowly created possibilities for extensive government control over the production of major crops. In connection with the redistribution of land, the Ministry of Agriculture instituted an ingenious compulsory common crop rotation system for the new farmers on reform estates. The system was originally invented by the British during the interwar period and applied to the Gezira project in the bifurcation of the White and Blue Nile in the Sudan, whence the Egyptians took over the idea. It aims at combining the advantages of private ownership and small farmers' initiative with some large-scale economies in irrigation, soil preparation, financing, and trading, and gives the individual farmers land in different parts of the area under common rotation. The three-year rotation system (as usual, favored by the ministry) would thus imply that farmers be given land in three different places, each one under a different crop. In this way large areas can be grown with the same crop, while the individual small farmer will experience on his three plots of land the same rotation he would apply individually, and always have a food crop for the family, a feed crop for the buffalo, and a cash crop for his expenses. Soil preparation, including ploughing, and irrigation may become more rational, taking advantage of large-scale economies in these processes (even with traditional technology), and mechanization becomes possible, whereas seeding, weeding, fertilizing, and harvesting (so far) are left to the individual owner. Seeds and fertilizers with other chemicals are provided by the cooperative of the particular area concerned, which thus controls plant varieties and fertilizer input, extends credit in case of need,[18] and takes care of marketing of major crops. All decisions are, in principle, taken by the council of the cooperative, formally elected by democratic methods, whose chairman (usually an agronomist) however, is appointed by the ministry. It is believed that de facto it is the chairman, and thus ultimately the ministry, who is the real decision maker, at least in matters of importance for cultivation.[19]

All observers seem to agree that the compulsory rotation system on the land reform estates has been as conducive to productivity in Egypt as it had been in the Sudan. While these estates constitute less than one-sixth of the total cultivated area, the government, inspired by the success of the system, started experimenting in the mid-fifties with cooperation along the same lines outside the reform estates. In the opinion of the government these experiments proved successful,[20] too, and at the end of 1964 the system (still without redistribution or consolidation of ownership of holdings) was virtually extended to the whole country. Each village is now organized into a cooperative where membership is compulsory.

The intention of the government was to use the cooperative system for controlling production of major crops. Detailed rules were laid down for cultivation of cotton and some other crops (beans and barley), prescribing the varieties that should be grown in the individual regions of the country and the amounts of seeds and fertilizers to be used per feddan.

The Ministry of Agriculture estimates the total area allotted to all major crops. In this sense, the country has had an annual plan for crop acreages since 1960. The plans were released by the Ministry of Planning for the (budget) years 1960–61 to 1964–65 and 1966–67. For 1965–66 and all budget years after 1966–67, the acreage plans do not seem to have been released. Until 1963–64, however, these plans were (except for rice) little more than passive forecasts of the farmers' expected behavior. It was not until the agricultural year November 1964–October 1965 that the government possessed the administrative machinery—the cooperative system—to impose its acreage plans upon the farmers.

Apparently the government has used this system mainly for controlling the total cotton acreage and its distribution by staple length.[21] The acreages for most other crops, except rice, wheat, and sugar cane seem to reflect the choice of the farmers, given the adjustments they have to make to fulfill the cotton acreage requirements. Rice, of course, has continued to be influenced by the government's management of the irrigation system, and the cultivation of sugar cane has been tightly controlled. Apart from these crops it is difficult to assess the impact of government control through the cooperative system.[22]

Wholesale Trade and Prices.

Wholesale trade in cotton is carried on by a special Cotton Organization; it handles purchases from agricultural cooperatives, storage, exports, and sales to domestic industry. Wholesale trade in cereals, sugar, and some other food-stuffs is in the hands of the Ministry of Supply, which also takes care of imports of food and its distribution to retail trade. Domestic trade in vegetables, onions, fruits, poultry, and the like is mainly handled by private business, although a network of government retail stores (so-called cooperative stores) has been established. Also, there are free markets where surplus quantities of grain can be sold by the farmers. The supply of manufactured inputs—mainly fertilizers, pesticides, and fuel—is entirely in the hands of government organizations.

Since World War II the government has fixed prices for its purchases from producers or has established support prices for major crops. Until 1964 such prices were fixed mostly to stabilize both farm income and the domestic cost of living, and their level was chosen to strike a desirable balance between rural and urban income; allocational considerations seem to have played a secondary role. It is not clear how these policies, over all, have affected rural-urban income distribution, but until 1964 they certainly helped to stabilize domestic prices and may have had consequences for allocation of resources in agriculture. With control over both price and supply, the possibility cannot be excluded that, for any particular commodity, the country may be off the demand, as well as the supply, curve. During the second half of the sixties, in addition to area prescriptions, compulsory sales (in various proportions) of certain food crops (rice, wheat, onions, ground nuts, beans, and lentils) at low official prices to village cooperatives were introduced, with the possibility of selling surplus output at higher prices in the free market. Actual deliveries, however, tended more and more to fall short of requirements, and the system was changed in 1969.[23]

In recent years production at predetermined prices has been introduced for cane, rice, onions, tomatoes, and other crops. Contracts are concluded before sowing and stipulate delivery of specified quantities, at defined standards and specified prices.[24] This is a particularly important innovation from our point of view because it tends to break the lag between prices and production (see below). This system is not compulsory and its extent is not known to the authors.

It will be understood that the determinants of producer prices for outputs differed considerably from crop to crop during the sixties. At one extreme are crops like cotton (lint as well as seeds), which the authorities purchase in their totality at prices fixed by the government itself. Sugar cane, cultivated under contract with the factories, belongs to this category. At the other extreme we have crops with free price formation; clover (berseem) and other feed crops (not included in our estimates) are by far the most important items in this group. Between these extremes we find most of the other field crops, cereals and pulses, with producer prices influenced by both the government and domestic market forces. When the Ministry of Supply purchases cereals and pulses it is always at prices fixed by the government. For some cereals (rice and wheat) and pulses there was compulsory delivery of certain proportions of the crops at very low prices until 1969. Other deliveries to the government are voluntary, and farmers (usually via the cooperatives) have the option of selling directly to private wholesale or retail dealers. For some crops there are organized markets in Cairo and Alexandria. Price formation in these markets, however, is constrained within rather narrow limits by government prices for purchases from producers, on the one hand, and on the other, by the maximum retail prices for products based on these crops (bread, flour) or for the crops themselves (pulses, for instance). The latter prices are often low and subsidized to the extent retail trade is based on government supply.

Rents.

An unusual feature, finally, is maximum rent for agricultural land, introduced in 1952 and kept unchanged since then. Tenancy is important: in 1960 about half the area was cultivated by tenants. Short-term tenancy was abolished in 1952, and it has become increasingly difficult for owners to evict tenants. Rents predominate, although some share-cropping takes place.[25] The maximum rents, based on land tax assessments made in 1949, should correspond in principle to market rents in that year.[26] Market rents in 1952–53 may also have been below that level due to the collapse of the Korean boom. But since then agricultural output has more than doubled in value, and the maximum rents are entirely out of line with hypothetical market rents.

Wages.

There are also statutory minimum wages for rural labor, but they have never been enforced except in public works. By the mid-sixties, rural wages reached the statutory level, but that was the result of a strong demand for such labor and quite unrelated to the existence of statutory wages.

Shortages and Black Markets.

It might be expected that an economy with both price and quantity controls would have extensive black markets. This has increasingly been the case since the second half of the fifties for certain manufactured products as well as for housing, but only to a minor extent for food and other agricultural products. The government has geared its food import and export policies to the domestic demand-supply situation; imports and exports have tended to be determined as residuals. Rationing at low prices has been applied only to some goods (tea, sugar, vegetable oils, kerosene), with free sales permitted at high prices.

Shortages of food have nevertheless occasionally occurred: rice, fat, and meat are examples. Such shortages have usually arisen in connection with unexpected import difficulties or crash export programs (related, for instance, to repayment of Russian loans), and black markets in food have emerged on such occasions. Black markets are in most cases imperfect, however, and it is in the nature of things that reliable black market price data are hard to obtain. Black market rents for land (and housing) played a minor role in the fifties, but are now the rule rather than the exception. They are often paid for the right to obtain (or cancel) a rental contract in the form of a "bon de sortie," which represents the capitalized value of the difference between the hypothetical market rent and the prescribed maximum rent and is difficult to translate into an annual rental. Moreover, systematic information is not available.

NOTES

1. C. Issawi, *Egypt in Revolution,* London, 1963; B. Hansen and G. Marzouk, *Development and Economic Policy in the U.A.R. (Egypt),* Amsterdam, 1965; D. Mead, *Growth and Structural Change in the Egyptian Economy,* Homewood, Ill., 1967; M. Clawson, H. H. Landsberg, and L. T. Alexander, *The Agricultural Potential of the Middle East,* Elsevier, New York, 1971. On cotton, see, in particular, E. R. J. Owen, *Cotton and the Egyptian Economy, 1820–1914,* Oxford, 1969.

2. *General Frame of the Five-Year Plan for Social and Economic Development,* July 1960–June 1965, Cairo, 1960, p. 141.

3. W. Willcocks and J. I. Craig, *Egyptian Irrigation,* Vols. 1 and 2, 3rd edition, London and New York, 1913 (see also 2nd edition, London and New York, 1899), contains a wealth of detailed technical and economic information about the Nile and the irrigation system. Problems related to the change in the system after the Aswan High Dam are discussed by W. F. Owen, "Land and Water Use in the Egyptian High Dam Era," *Land Economics,* Vol. 15, No. 3, August 1964.

4. One feddan = 1.04 acres = 0.42 ha.

5. Official data show an increase from 1964 to 1969 in the total crop area of 474,000 feddan, with a growth in the cultivated area of 392,000 feddan (*The Development of the Agricultural Sector,* CAGMS, 1971). Accepted at face value, these figures imply that the crop area has increased mainly through land reclamation and only to a minor extent through conversion from basin to perennial irrigation. However, the relatively slow growth of the crop area may be related to the strong uptrend in fruits and vegetables, which are only counted as one crop per year.

6. While the rice area expanded from 695,000 feddan in 1960 to 1,140,000 feddan in 1970, summer corn went up from 128,000 to 1,153,000 feddan and autumn corn went down from 1,698,000 to 351,000 feddan.

7. C. H. Brown, *Egyptian Cotton,* London, 1955, Chapter 1. See also E. R. J. Owen, op. cit., p. 191.

8. Total cultivated area was about 6 million feddan in 1960. At that time about 0.9 million feddan were dependent upon basin irrigation and thus not suitable for cotton. In

addition, 0.1 million feddan were under sugar and 0.1 million under fruit. Rotations with cotton were thus probably applied to less than 5 million feddan. With a 3-year rotation, this would imply a cotton acreage of 1.6 million, with a 2-year rotation, of about 2.4 million. The cotton acreage has frequently reached 1.9–2.0 million feddan, indicating that the two rotation systems have been applied to about the same extent. C. H. Brown, op. cit., Ch. 1, himself an outstanding cotton breeder who worked for many years in Egypt, claims that systematic experiments that could settle the issue as to which rotation is more efficient have never been made (1955). Before World War I, 2-year rotation prevailed; see J. I. Craig, "Notes on Cotton Statistics in Egypt," *L'Egypte Contemporaine*, Vol. 2, No. 6, March 1911.

9. Willcocks, op. cit., 1899, pp. 379–382.

10. Marc Nerlove, "Estimates of the Elasticities of Supply of Selected Agricultural Commodities," *Journal of Farm Economics*, Vol. 38, No. 2, May 1956.

11. Raj Krishna, "Farm Supply Response in India-Pakistan: A Case Study of the Punjab Region," *Economic Journal*, Vol. 73, No. 291, September 1963.

12. See C. Bresciani-Turroni, "Rélations entre la récolte et le prix du coton Egyptien," *L'Egypte Contemporaine*, Vol. 19, 1930; S. Soliman Nour El Din, "A Statistical Analysis of Some Aspects of Cotton Production and Marketing with Special Reference to U.S.A. and Egypt," Ph.D. dissertation, London University, 1958; Robert M. Stern, "The Price Responsiveness of Egyptian Cotton Producers," *Kyklos*, Vol. 12, 1959, and "The Price Responsiveness of Primary Producers," *Review of Economics and Statistics*, Vol. 44, May 1962; B. Hansen "Cotton versus Grain: On the Optimum Allocation of Agricultural Land," *Seminar on Economics and Industrialization of Cotton*, Ministry of Scientific Research, Cairo, 1964.

These results do not necessarily imply, of course, that area restriction tends to increase elasticity. There are many other differences among these studies. However, the government has at times imposed restrictions to keep up prices and may have reacted more strongly than the farmers would have done.

13. As has recently been shown, risk considerations imply that the sign of the response of a subsistence crop's acreage to price changes is uncertain; see V. F. Nowshirvani, "Land Allocation under Uncertainty in Subsistence Agriculture," *Oxford Economic Papers*, Vol. 23, No. 3, November 1971.

14. The high long-term elasticities appeared in the I.V. estimates only. The L.S. estimates resulted in relatively low long-term elasticities for all commodities, although also here barley and helba came out with the highest long-term elasticities, 0.75 and 0.85, respectively. See Appendix A, Table A–2.

15. Willcocks commented in 1899 that this "is a very distinct hardship to the poor in this country, and in estimating the great advantages conferred on the country by the British occupation this fact must always be remembered as counting on the opposite side. The absolute prohibition of so valuable and suitable a crop can never be considered as anything but a makeshift while there are sound financiers in the country." (Willcocks and Craig, op. cit., 1899, pp. 385–386.) Independence in 1936 did not lead to any change in this burden on the poor, nor did the revolution of 1952. Only now is the government contemplating the readoption of tobacco cultivation.

16. Export taxes existed since 1840, but the rates were low (1 percent since 1869) and the taxation thus without serious consequences. In the early 1920s a production tax was levied on cotton, but tax rates were quite low.

17. *Economic Review,* Central Bank of Egypt, Vol. 1, No. 2, p. 217.

18. Farmers are obliged to purchase the minimum amounts of fertilizers stipulated; they can purchase in excess of these amounts at higher prices. See Ezz El Din Hammam

Ahmed and M. G. Abu El Dahab, *Fertilizer Distribution in the Arab Republic of Egypt*, OECD, Paris, 1972, p. 35.

19. D. Warriner, *Agrarian Reform and Community Development in U.A.R.*, Cairo, 1961.

20. No evidence seems to have been published.

21. No systematic account has, to the best of our knowledge, been published about the way in which the government operates through the cooperatives. A detailed verbal description of the modus operandi of the cotton acreage allotments to one of the authors by a high civil servant who was involved for several years in the system at the top level indicates that it is not really a question of a centralized command system. The procedures were described as follows:

At the beginning of each agricultural year, the Ministry of Agriculture, together with export, foreign exchange, and other authorities, decides upon a plan for the areas to be cultivated with various varieties of cotton that year. It subsequently enters into discussions with the directors of agriculture for the individual provinces and reaches agreements with them about a plan for each province. Together these plans may bring about a revision of the original plan. Each provincial director then takes up discussions with the district inspectors of his province, and plans are drawn up for the individual districts. Once more a revision of the total may evolve. Finally, the individual inspector meets with the village cooperatives in his district and reaches agreement with each village about its cotton cultivation. These agreements—which again may imply a revision of the total— are signed by the individual cultivators, who, however, have the right to appeal to a higher authority for a revision of their "contracts"; such appeals are often approved.

The whole procedure can perhaps best be described as a stepwise bargaining process, and it is not clear who has the upper hand in the negotiations at the various levels. It is obviously a long way from the original top-level allotments to the final obligations of the cultivators. Evasion by the cultivators is, finally, a possibility that should not be ruled out, but it is not considered important. Nonfulfilment related to shortages of seeds of prescribed varieties is believed to have been of importance on some occasions.

22. Each farmer has a "farm holding card," issued by the Ministry of Agriculture, which "identifies the location of the farm, its size and the crop rotation pattern prescribed for it—these being the basis for the fertilizer quota." (H. Ahmed and A. El Dahab, op. cit., p. 11.) The fact that each farmer is prescribed a rotation pattern does not imply that all crop acreages are centrally planned.

23. N. Saad, "Structural Changes and Socialist Transformation in Agriculture of the U.A.R., Egypt," *L'Egypte Contemporaine*, Vol. 55, 1968, p. 285, Table 8 gives prices for compulsory and noncompulsory deliveries of wheat, rice, and onions.

24. N. Saad, op. cit., pp. 284–285.

25. *Agricultural Economy*, Ministry of Agriculture, Cairo, 1961, pp. 22–23.

26. As with all other assessments for tax purposes, there may, of course, have been deviations from market values in individual cases and on average.

Chapter 7

The Impact of Protection and Controls on Agriculture

The effect on Egyptian agriculture of the trade, price, and production restrictions reviewed in the preceding chapter must be assessed. In gauging the impact, positive and negative, of protection and controls we have adopted the conventional approach of estimating effective rates of protection (ERPs) and domestic resource costs (DRCs). (The results are reported on pp. 160 ff. below.) This approach, however, does not yield the information about effects on production and resource allocation needed in this context. Therefore, we have worked out a methodology for direct measurement of the effects on land use of all government intervention in agriculture and applied it to the major crops. (See pp. 168 ff. below.) The details of the methodology and statistical estimates are given in Appendix A. On this basis, conclusions are drawn in regard to the economic effects of price distortions and quantitative regulations. Since income-distributional aspects have played a major role in government policies vis-à-vis agriculture, the final section of the chapter discusses the implications of agricultural price policies for income distribution within that sector.

THE PROTECTIVE POSITION, 1961–1968

For fourteen major crops we have calculated both effective rates of protection (ERP) and domestic resource costs per U.S. dollar (DRC) to show the degree of protection, positive or negative (see Table 7–1). The years 1961, 1963, and 1964 were selected partly because these were the only years for which

158

adequate data on both outputs and inputs by crops were available.[1] Moreover, these are the years straddling the devaluation of 1962: we thus obtain a clear picture of what happened to the competitive position of Egyptian agriculture in connection with the devaluation. The year 1962 was excluded although data were available, since for several crops it cannot be determined to what extent they were sold before or after the devaluation.

ERPs and DRCs were estimated on the basis of standard definitions, but a number of problems in regard to data and concepts were encountered.[2] Here we shall only point out that both ERPs and DRCs are calculated for refined sugar instead of cane, which has no applicable international price.[3] Note, also, that DRCs are based on imputed market prices for land and capital.

Looking first at 1961 in Table 7–1, we find wide differences in the ERPs enjoyed by various crops. Some crops—corn, millet, sesame, wheat, beans, chick-peas, and sugar—enjoyed positive protection, while others—cotton, rice, peanuts, barley, lentils, and onions—suffered negative "protection."[4] Typically, it is the export crops that were negatively "protected." The degree of protection is generally exaggerated and the degree of negative protection overstated for 1961, because value added at international prices was calculated at official exchange rates whereas in fact, at various times during the year, exchange premiums applied. In the autumn of 1961, however, there was a period without premiums and our calculations are relevant for that time. For cotton (including cottonseeds) we should add, as appears in Table 7–3, that the negative protection in 1961 was the result of excessive negative protection for cottonseed; lint was actually positively protected in 1961. Since different cotton varieties have different proportions between lint and seed output, the system obviously discriminated in favor of the varieties with relatively high output of lint. After 1962 both lint and seeds were negatively protected, but seeds much more so than lint.

Domestic resource costs, DRCs, show a fairly similar picture for 1961. Cotton, rice, peanuts, lentils, onions, and chick-peas had DRCs below the official exchange rate; the rest had DRCs higher than the official rate. For barley and chick-peas, the positions are reversed; barley appears as negatively protected but has a DRC below the official rate, while chick-peas, with a high positive ERP, nevertheless show a DRC lower than the official rate. But for the other crops there is a clear correspondence between ERP and DRC (see pp. 188 ff. below).

On the average there was a slight negative protection in 1961 (−0.4 percent), and domestic resource costs were at the level of the official exchange rate. We thus reach the interesting conclusion, already mentioned, that there seems to have been no need in agriculture for protection or devaluation in 1961. From the point of view of resource allocation, the average ERP (close to zero) is, of course, deceptive. Behind the innocent-looking average there is

TABLE 7-1

Effective Rates of Protection (ERPs) and Domestic Resource Costs (DRCs) for Major Field Crops, 1961, 1963, and 1964

| | ERP (percent) | | | DRC (piasters per U.S.$) | | | | | |
| | | | | 1961 | | 1963 | | 1964 | |
	1961	1963	1964	Excl. Trade and Transport Margins	Incl. Trade and Transport Margins	Excl. Trade and Transport Margins	Incl. Trade and Transport Margins	Excl. Trade and Transport Margins	Incl. Trade and Transport Margins
Summer crops									
Cotton (lint and seeds)	-7	-21	-22	29	32	32	36	27	32
Rice	-26	-48	-54	24	29	21	26	24	29
Corn	18	1	-14[a]	35	39	40	45	48[a]	53[a]
Millet	0	-2	16	36	40	49	55	68	75
Peanuts	-50	-52	n.a.	18	22	17	21	n.a.	n.a.
Sesame	35	10	n.a.	35	39	39	44	n.a.	n.a.
Autumn crops									
Corn	16	0	-14	48	52	56	62	48	53
Winter crops									
Wheat	16	-13	-10	45	50	44	49	46	51
Barley	-6	-2	-3	34	38	41	46	43	47
Beans	62	51	51	64	69	60	65	54	59
Lentils	-5	4	n.a.	29	33	38	43	n.a.	n.a.
Onions	-31	-47	-56	14	18	11	16	11	16
Chick-peas	45	56	n.a.	27	31	50	55	n.a.	n.a.

Perennial crops

Sugar, incl. refined	46	−69	−47	53	53	22	22	30	30

Weighted average

All 14 crops	−0.4	−25.1	n.a.	32.9	36.4	32.3	36.6	n.a.	n.a.
10 crops	—	−25.2	−24.4	—	—	32.5	36.7	32.7	36.9

Official exchange rate (piasters per U.S.$)

	35.2	43.5	43.5

NOTE: ERP is calculated as domestic value added at domestic prices *minus* domestic value added at international prices (in domestic currency) divided by the latter. DRC is calculated as current market wages *plus* imputed current market rental of land *plus* "normal" market return to capital and management per U.S. dollar of net foreign currency earnings.

SOURCE: B. Hansen and K. Nashashibi, "Protection and Competitiveness in Egyptian Agriculture and Industry," NBER Working Paper 48, New York, 1975, Tables 2 to 10.

a. Average of autumn and summer corn, the latter of rapidly increasing importance.

a wide dispersion of effective rates of protection, presumably with an impact on allocation.

From 1961 to 1963 there was a sharp drop in the effective rate of protection at largely unchanged domestic resource costs, and after the devaluation of 1962, agriculture continued to remain competitive at the old official exchange rate. The fall in the effective rate of protection is mainly the result of the fact that devaluation was not reflected in domestic agricultural prices. Its magnitude is exaggerated for the reason mentioned before—the ERPs of 1961 are at the official exchange rate and disregard the foreign exchange premiums occasionally applied during that year. Partly, however, the decline in the ERPs is due to improved terms of trade; prices for cotton, rice, and sugar improved substantially on international markets. Thus, the strong shift in the ERP position of sugar from 46 percent to −69 percent was largely due to the very high international sugar price in 1963, which was not reflected in domestic sugar prices.

Despite the devaluation and some domestic inflation of factor prices, there was on average little change in the DRCs. This was possible because yields increased substantially from 1961 to 1963 (and 1964),[5] while foreign prices for some outputs increased. In 1964, average DRCs were almost the same as in 1961. We note the very strong decline in the DRC for sugar: with a DRC well above the official exchange rate in 1961, sugar became highly competitive in 1963 due to the international price increase, even at the old exchange rate. The case is interesting because it shows how difficult it can be— on the basis of information for a single year—to judge which commodities should be produced in the longer run. We shall return to the problem in Chapter 8.

In addition to the weighted averages of DRC calculated in Table 7–1 for all crops (fourteen in 1961 and 1963, ten in 1963 and 1964), Table 7–2 shows DRC calculated for a full three-year rotation, including all the big crops, cotton, rice, corn, wheat, and beans, as well as clover. It was not possible, however, to calculate either international value added or domestic resource costs for clover, which is a nontraded commodity (even within the country trade with clover is limited, and an imputed price, based on the value of animal output, would have to be applied). Since, moreover, it is complementary with cotton, it presents great difficulties in estimating "value added." Thus, clover is not really included in the estimate. The DRCs obtained for the rotation as a whole for 1961 and 1963 were slightly above the weighted average calculated for all crops in Table 7–1.

To get an impression of the changes in the protective position of agriculture from 1964 onwards, we calculated a proxy for the ERPs from 1961 to 1968, shown in Table 7–3. On the basis of domestic ex farm prices and international prices converted at the official exchange rate, we have calculated the nominal, de facto rate of protection, that is, the implicit rate of tariff defined

TABLE 7-2

Example of Domestic Resource Costs for Full Three-Year Rotation

(£ E per feddan)

	1961		1963	
	Net Foreign Exchange Earnings[a]	DRCs[b]	Net Foreign Exchange Earnings[a]	DRCs[b]
First year				
Clover (1 cut)	—	—	—	—
Cotton	71	64	90	74
Second year				
Wheat	18	26	30	34
Corn (autumn)	19	28	20	29
Third year				
Beans	13	25	20	29
Rice	14	36	70	41
All years	165	179	230	207
DRC, full rotation[c,d]	38		39	
Official exchange rate[d]	35.2		43.5	

SOURCE: B. Hansen and K. Nashashibi, NBER Working Paper 48, New York, 1975, Tables 2, 3, 5, 6, 8, and 9.

a. Converted to £ E at official exchange rate.

b. Including domestic trade and transport margins.

c. Obtained by dividing net foreign exchange earnings expressed in U.S. dollars into DRCs expressed in Egyptian pounds.

d. In piasters per U.S. dollar.

as the difference between domestic and international prices divided by the international price. A weighted average was calculated as the difference between the total value of all crops at domestic and at international prices divided by the total value at international prices. The nominal rate of protection, thus defined, differs from the ERP in two regards: there is no deduction for traded and nontraded produced inputs; and nontraded outputs (straw and stalks) are not considered. Moreover, the calculation does not include some small crops.

A comparison between the ERPs in Table 7-1 and the nominal rates in Table 7-3 for the years 1961, 1963, and 1964 shows that the difference be-

TABLE 7-3

Nominal de facto Protection (+) or Taxation (−), Nine Major Field Crops, 1961–1969

(percent)

Crop	1961	1962[a]	1963	1964	1965	1966	1967	1968	1969
Cotton									
Lint	6.0*	—	−10.6	−12.7	−1.4	−17.0	−23.6	−28.8	35.2
Seed	−81.5*	—	−83.7	−85.0	−85.7	−85.6	−84.6	−84.1	−83.5
Total	−12.8	—	−23.1	−27.0	−20.5	−30.5	−33.7	−37.2	41.2
Rice	−22.9	—	−46.3	−52.2	−48.4	−36.4	−36.3	−41.9	−37.5
Corn	20.0	—	4.1	−7.0	−8.6	20.0	34.4	13.5	23.3
Millet	9.2	—	3.0	16.0	18.1	30.1	37.7	11.1	8.7
Wheat	39.7	—	−1.8	−12.5	7.7	20.1	35.2	30.7	35.8
Barley	−3.3	—	−0.6	0.0	−18.3	−12.4	4.2	−10.4	−9.2
Beans	78.3	—	45.2	56.5	38.1	28.3	66.0	4.0	−16.4
Onions	−22.0	—	−45.8	−52.3	−41.1	−49.2	−69.9	−65.2	−69.2
Cane	41.0	—	−50.9	−28.7	130.3	162.6	157.0	158.8	50.5
All crops, weighted average	−0.5	—	−22.6	−24.5	−16.6	−12.4	−15.2	−22.5	−25.3
All crops, weighted index of distortion	17.6	—	28.9	28.7	25.2	31.1	38.4	35.3	36.8

SOURCES: Our calculations; see B. Hansen and K. Nashashibi, NBER Working Paper 48, New York, 1975, Tables 2 to 10, 16, and 18.

a. Exchange rate was changed in May 1962.

tween these two measures is small in most cases, wheat (with a high value for straw) being the major exception. The weighted averages are also quite similar. These findings should cause no surprise; after all, in Egyptian agriculture traded produced inputs are small compared with outputs, and rates of protection for such inputs are small, too. It appears that we can use the nominal rates as a reasonably good proxy for ERPs, at least as far as the weighted averages are concerned.

Four facts then stand out as characteristic of agricultural price policies during the 1960s:

1. The increase in the average negative rate of protection—that is, the rate of "taxation" of agricultural production—that took place from 1961 to 1963 in conjunction with the devaluation of 1962 turns out to have been a permanent increase of "taxation."[6] After a certain decline in 1965 and 1966, the weighted average rate of "taxation" increased to 22 percent in 1968, and to one quarter in 1969. Since 1963, agricultural production has thus been heavily taxed as compared with a state of free trade.

2. This rise in taxation was mainly the result of a widening difference between international prices and domestic ex-farm prices for cotton, rice, and onions, in other words, for the export crops. The taxation of cotton increased steadily from 1963 to 1969, when it reached a peak of 41 percent, with cotton valued at international prices; with cotton valued at domestic prices, the tax rate was more than 50 percent. Rice was taxed at about 43 percent during the years 1963 to 1969. Thus, the policy of the fifties to lower and abolish export taxes was reversed, not through formal export taxes but through the government agencies' buying and selling prices. In itself, this price policy must have been detrimental to exports and generally must have affected allocation in agriculture. Increased land taxes would have been a feasible alternative insofar as government revenues are concerned, but the wider distributional problem of keeping the cost of living low and distribution within agriculture equitable would then have remained to be solved (see below). As we shall try to show in the following section, the price policy is not the whole story, however, because direct intervention in production overlaps with the allocative effects of pricing between crops. But the overall effect of discrimination against agriculture remains. Also, there must have been effects on allocation *within* agriculture.

3. The two big domestic food crops, wheat and corn, show a development entirely different from that of the export crops. Wheat and corn are important import substitutes. From a high level in 1961, 39.7 and 20.0 percent, respectively, protection gradually fell until 1964, when it was negative for both wheat and corn. In 1965 it fell further for corn but increased somewhat for wheat. After 1965 the rate of protection rose again, and levels of about one-third were reached in 1967. This development is closely geared to

the rise and fall of PL480 deliveries of grain. We recall that PL480 deliveries, beginning at the end of the 1950s, increased rapidly during the first half of the 1960s and were abrogated in 1965. The development of domestic producer prices was not the outcome of deliberate government pricing. For wheat the government's official purchasing price remained constant during the 1960s; for corn it remained constant until 1965, when it was increased slightly. What probably happened was a drop in the free market prices (the farmers had the right to sell surplus production in the free market) during the PL480 years of abundant supplies, followed by a rise when supplies became scarcer. (For wheat, however, see below, pp. 179 ff.)

PL480 deliveries thus had an impact upon the domestic prices of wheat and corn. For both crops the acreage fell substantially until 1965. While PL480 aid has often been accused of "distorting" agricultural production in the receiving countries in this fashion therefore harming the development of agriculture, this is just not the case for Egypt. Aside from the fact that acreage restrictions, indirectly, appear to have been more dominant in affecting corn production, the fact is that these crops had been highly protected before PL480 deliveries began pouring in. Protection then disappeared with the inflow of PL480 deliveries, and reappeared when PL480 was abrogated. Thus PL480 actually tended to remove (if only temporarily), rather than cause, distortion in agricultural production.[7]

Cane shows a development in the rate of protection similar to that for wheat and corn, albeit for quite different reasons. After the strong international price increase for sugar in 1963, the rate of protection became negative in 1963 and 1964 because domestic producer prices were kept unchanged by the government. When international prices fell to a low level in 1965, it became positive once more and very high. However, toward the end of the 1960s, cane once again moved toward a competitive position.

For the small crops, finally, development has depended on domestic demand and supply conditions, with relatively little domestic government intervention.

4. The degree of *output* price distortion *within* agriculture—as compared with conditions of free trade—increased substantially from 1961 to 1963, with a further substantial rise in 1967. In Table 7–3 (bottom row) we show a dispersion measure of price distortion. It is defined as the sum of all absolute differences (without regard to sign) between crop values at domestic prices and at international prices, expressed as a percentage of the total crop value at international prices. This measure of price distortion has, of course, a close affinity to the primitive aggregate distortion measure we suggested in Chapter 3 (p. 54).

Our price distortion measure rose from 18 percent in 1961 to 29 percent in 1963, and remained at this level until 1966. In 1967 it jumped further to

38 percent. The growth of price distortion within agriculture was mainly the consequence of the government's failure to pass on to the farmers the full increase in the international prices of cotton and rice that took place during the sixties.

We conclude that it was not only general price discrimination *against* agriculture as a sector that increased sharply from 1961 to 1969 (with a temporary reversal in 1964 and 1965)—price distortion *within* agriculture did, too. In both regards, price distortion probably diminished somewhat again in 1970 when the international prices of cotton and rice declined.

It is one thing, however, to calculate ERPs and DRCs on the standard definitions, as well as indices of price distortion; it is quite another to interpret the numbers that emerge from such calculations. On the assumption of increasing costs (realistic in agriculture), it is usually held that (a) the ERP tells us whether at existing prices an industry (commodity) should expand or contract if protection were removed and general equilibrium prevailed, and (b), ceteris paribus, the larger the ERP (numerically), the larger the expansion (contraction) to be expected. But that does not follow.[8]

The DRCs do inform us in principle whether production in particular industries should be expanded or contracted in general equilibrium without protection, because DRCs are supposed to be measured at shadow prices for domestic resources under conditions of nonprotected general equilibrium, and should be compared with the equilibrium shadow exchange rate. Note, however, that even if we limit ourselves to ranking industries, we now have to know the shadow factor prices. The crux of the matter is, of course, that we do not really know these shadow prices. As a matter of fact, what we have used in the calculations leading to the DRCs in Table 7–1 are the (actual or imputed) market prices of labor, land, and capital (and nontradables) in Egypt for 1961, 1963, and 1964, respectively.

Since the questions that the ERPs and DRCs attempt to answer are important, indeed, for appraising current economic policies and production and development potentialities, and since neither measure is satisfactory as to either theoretical soundness or computational accuracy, we try a different approach to these questions in the following section. Finally, the results of these three approaches to an evaluation of Egypt's agricultural policies will be compared.

AN ATTEMPT TO QUANTIFY THE SUBOPTIMALITY OF CROP POLICIES, 1962–1968

During the last decade, the Egyptian government has had, as we know, the power and machinery to interfere systematically with both agricultural prices and cropping patterns. Certainly, domestic prices differed from international prices, and acreages could differ from what cultivators would have chosen them to be at the given domestic prices.

From an efficiency point of view, the basic question is whether actual crop areas differed from the optimal level at the given international prices. After all, the government might just conceivably have interfered with crop areas to obtain an optimal pattern, even though domestic prices were not aligned with international prices. And it might be perfectly rational to allocate resources via direct command and to use prices exclusively for solving targets of income distribution. The problem is only to do it well! Since the Egyptian government has to some extent favored this kind of policy, it should not be assumed a priori that allocations of land by crop must have been suboptimal just because ERPs and DRCs point in that direction at actual government-determined ex-farm prices. Even less can we infer, under these circumstances, the degree of misallocation of resources, the losses from inefficiency, and so forth from the size of ERPs and DRCs. In addition we have the general problem that even at market-clearing prices, the ERPs and DRCs do not accurately indicate the allocational effects of intervention with inputs. The actual outcome of price distortions must be studied together with direct interference as compared with an optimal allocation before concluding whether government direct intervention has led toward or away from the optimum.

To calculate an optimal cropping pattern at given international prices would be a formidable exercise in operations analysis, and the information needed would probably not be available.[9] Hence, we have chosen a simpler, indirect method which, if the underlying assumptions are correct, may permit us to quantify the degree of suboptimality of the actual cropping pattern and calculate the loss from such suboptimality. (For a detailed discussion of methodology and estimates, see Appendix A.)

Methodology.

Assume that we know what the area response functions are for individual crops in the complete absence of direct government intervention with areas. Such response functions would tell us how cultivators actually reacted in the past to changes in prices and other relevant circumstances, such as yields, available area, labor, water supply, and so forth. Let the response functions be of the Nerlove type. We can then predict crop areas for a period with government controls on the assumption of (1) actual domestic prices and actual (short-term) response functions; (2) actual international prices and actual (short-term) response functions; and (3) actual international prices and hypothetical instantaneous long-term adjustment.

A comparison between prediction 1 and actual crop areas will yield an estimate of the extent to which the government's interference has forced cultivators to deviate from the cropping pattern they would have chosen at the given domestic prices without government area interference.

A comparison between prediction 2 and actual crop areas will tell us whether or not government area interference has forced cultivators to adopt a crop pattern similar to what they would have chosen themselves had the domestic prices been equal to international prices. Should this happen to be the case, the government has performed as well as the market forces would have done at the given international prices without area controls.

A comparison between predictions 2 and 1 will show the difference between the result of private market forces at actual domestic prices and at perfectly free trade and thus illustrate the effects of price distortion.

A comparison between prediction 3 and actual crop area will indicate the distance of the actual pattern from the optimal crop pattern—assuming that the cultivators' long-term response is optimal. If the government could instantly accomplish a cropping pattern according to this prediction, area allocation would be optimal and perhaps better than what the cultivators could accomplish under free trade. It should be understood that such perfect planning would require that there be no extra (social) costs involved in instantaneous adjustment, and that the government be capable of making perfect forecasts of both prices and yields for the crops to be sown. We assume that these conditions are fulfilled.

As Appendix A shows in detail, straightforward application of the conventional neoclassical trade model at given resources and Hicks-neutral technical progress, linearization, and the introduction of a special variable, K (to account for past government restrictions on cotton acreage) lead directly to the following (reduced form) area response function of the Nerlove type:

$$A_i = \alpha_{1i} + \alpha_{2i}(F_i)_{-1} + \alpha_{3i}A_{-1} + \alpha_{4i}A_{-2} + \alpha_{5i}L + \alpha_{6i}L_{-1} \qquad (1)$$

$$+ \alpha_{7i}W_\tau + \alpha_{8i}W_{\tau-1} + \alpha_{9i}K + \alpha_{10i}(A_i)_{-1},$$

where the α's are coefficients, A_i denotes area of crop i, A, total crop area, L, total labor input in agriculture, W, total water supply (discharge of Nile at Aswan), and K expresses government restrictions on the cotton acreage. The variable F_i expresses relative profitability of crop i and is defined as the ratio of output value per feddan of crop i to a weighted average of output values per feddan for all crops. F_i is influenced by both relative prices and relative yields.

These response functions were estimated on the basis of data for the years 1913 to 1961. The estimates—with $K = 0$—were then used for predictions 1 and 2 for the years 1962 to 1968. For prediction 3, the "optimal area," we used the stationary form, deleting K,

$$A_i = \frac{\alpha_{1i}}{1 - \alpha_{10i}} + \frac{\alpha_{2i}}{1 - \alpha_{10i}} F_i + \frac{\alpha_{3i} + \alpha_{4i}}{1 - \alpha_{10i}} A \tag{2}$$

$$+ \frac{\alpha_{5i} + \alpha_{6i}}{1 - \alpha_{10i}} L + \frac{\alpha_{7i} + \alpha_{8i}}{1 - \alpha_{10i}} W_\tau.$$

In both equations (1) and (2), the index τ, attached to water, refers to the months May–June for summer and autumn crops and to September of the preceding year for winter and perennial crops.

The results of the predictions are given in Appendix A, Table A–3, and depicted in Charts 7–1 to 7–11. Three estimates were made of all response functions, a least squares estimate (denoted L.S.), and instrumental variables estimates, Step 1 (I.V.1) and Step 2 (I.V.2). Since the L.S. is biased and I.V.2 has theoretical advantages over I.V.1, we have used the I.V.2 estimate wherever possible. However, in some cases this estimate had to be given up for computational reasons, or it led to unstable response functions. In such cases I.V.1 was chosen. In one case I.V.1 led to an unstable response function and the L.S. had to be used. The charts indicate which estimate is used.

The Predictions for 1962–1968.

Our area response functions are estimated on the basis of data for the period 1913–1961. In applying the response functions to the years 1962 to 1968, the conventional procedure would be to compare predictions with actual developments during these years to test the predictive power of our estimated functions. We are prevented from proceeding like this because we know that our functions are not well-specified for these years: government intervention was much more extensive and took on other forms than during the estimation period. Indeed, we want to use the deviation of actual from predicted acreage as a measure of the impact of government intervention. This leaves us in the awkward position of having to accept our estimated response functions as articles of faith for the period 1962–1968, although it is clear that, even if the functions should happen to be correctly specified for 1913–1961, that may not be the case for 1962–1968—quite apart from the problem of the nature and extension of controls (for example, the effects of the radical change in the water supply after 1964 may not be correctly described by the water variable in the response functions).

A simple test of the predictive power of our model could, nonetheless, be made for 1962 because that year was relatively free from direct intervention in acreages: a comparison was made between the errors of prediction 1 and the errors of two "primitive" predictions. Prediction 1 was clearly superior to both kinds of primitive prediction. This test offers us little comfort, however, because ours is the much more ambitious task of forecasting recursively all the years from 1962 to 1968.

Moreover, it is very disturbing for an analysis of the predictions that theoretical confidence limits for our kind of problem have not been established to the best of our knowledge. A related problem is that, while the coefficient of lagged relative output-value, F_i, in all cases (except corn, millet, and wheat, where the coefficient is very close to zero in any case) and the coefficient for the lagged acreage (in most cases) are significantly different from zero, the coefficients for the other determinants—total acreage, labor, and water—more often than not are insignificant in regard to sign. This latter circumstance is not without importance for total acreage and labor, although these did not change much from 1962 to 1968; in relation to water it takes on primary importance because water supply changed so much beginning with 1965, far beyond anything experienced during the period of estimation. All we can do about this problem is to throw in whatever a priori knowledge we have about the influence of water on the individual crops.

We shall keep these problems in mind in interpreting the predictions, and consider for each particular crop whether other systematic factors beside controls may have caused actual developments to deviate from predictions or whether some coefficients determined with great uncertainty are leading us astray. But generally we are disregarding stochastic disturbances and treat our estimated response functions as if they exactly and correctly explained the development of crop acreages in the absence of controls—unless we have positive reasons for not doing so.

COTTON

We know that cotton acreage has been subject to government interference and that 1965 was the year when the government's administrative capability for controlling the cotton acreage was greatly enhanced through the cooperative system.

A glance at Chart 7-1 immediately reveals that something dramatic happened between 1964 and 1965. From 1962 through 1964, actual cotton acreages had been very close to the acreages predicted on the basis of actual ex-farm prices, assuming no controls (prediction 1). In 1965, the actual acreage jumped up by about 20 percent, while prediction 1 shows almost no change for acreage. From 1965 onwards there are declines in both actual and predicted area, with actual area running 200,000 to 300,000 feddan above the forecast until 1968, when the gap shrinks to about 75,000 feddan.

There is little doubt that the upward shift in actual acreage in 1965 can be ascribed to government intervention. The acreage allotments to cotton were 1.8 million feddan for 1961 and 1962, but were lowered to 1.6 million feddan for 1963 and 1964. In 1964, the allotment was only slightly larger than actual

Legend to Charts 7–1 to 7–11

Line 1 represents area prediction 1: farmers' response to actual domestic prices

Line 2 represents area prediction 2: farmers' response to hypothetical domestic prices = current international prices

Line 3 represents area prediction 3: "optimal area," i.e., instantaneous long-term adjustment to current international prices

Vertical line represents standard error of regression (SER)

Circles represent official acreage allotments (plans)

Individual years are agricultural years: previous November 1 to current October 31

Sources: Actual area: NBER Working Paper 48, New York, 1975; predictions 1, 2, and 3: Table A–3; SER: Table A–2; official acreage allotments: Ministry of Planning, Cairo. We have assumed that the Ministry's "year" is the budget year and that the crops are included in the budget year in which they are harvested—the only solution for making the Ministry of Planning data consistent with those of the Ministry of Agriculture.

CHART 7–1
Cotton: Actual versus Predicted Crop Areas

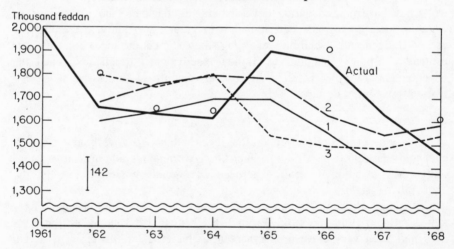

acreage.[10] With little administrative power behind them, the allotments for those years were probably little more than passive predictions. For 1965, however, the allotment was increased to 1.95 million feddan.[11] The upward shift in actual acreage by 0.3 million feddan in 1965 reflects both the increased allotment and the strengthened arm of the government.

The change in water supply in 1965 stemming from the High Dam at Aswan can easily be dismissed as a possible explanation of the upward shift in actual acreage. Taking our response function at face value, the increased water supply that year should have led to a fall in the cotton acreage; both in the short and the long run, water is estimated to have a negative (albeit insignificant at the 5 percent level) impact on cotton acreage (see Appendix A, Table A–2). It might be argued, however, that the response function does not correctively identify the impact of water supply on cotton acreage. While undoubtedly in the short term greater water supply leads to more rice cultivation at the expense of other summer crops, including cotton, in the long term increased summer water supply has historically gone together with an increase in perennial irrigation and in total summer crop acreage—and therefore in cotton cultivation. Our response function includes both total crop acreage and water supply as explanatory variables, and due to the long-term correlation between these two, our estimates may not correctly distribute their roles.[12] At any rate, the positive long-term effect of water supply on the cotton acreage should work through an expansion of perennial irrigation, and we know that conversion in Upper Egypt from basin to perennial irrigation, which should be one of the major benefits of the High Dam, did not take place immediately after the closure of the Dam and had made only partial progress by the end of the sixties.

But the possibility should not be excluded that part of the downward trend in all three predictions from 1965 on is due to mis-specification in this regard. Also, note the low significance of the negative sign of the coefficients for water. Disregarding the change in water supply as of 1964, prediction 3 ("optimal acreage") would show only a slight decline in 1965 and 1964; and 1968 would again be about the same as in 1964. Since relative output value at domestic prices, F_{cotton}, fell sharply in 1965 and 1966, predictions 1 and 2 would show a decline in 1966 and 1967, even apart from water.

Why, then, did the authorities push cotton acreage so strongly in 1965? It is clear that export considerations were responsible, but not nearly as clear how the authorities reached their decision. Having no information about the government's internal deliberations, we have to infer our answers from circumstantial evidence. The strong fall in "optimal acreage," as just pointed out, may not be significant, but there is nothing to indicate that the true optimum should be larger than for 1964; on the contrary, the relative output-value of cotton was lower in 1965 than in 1964. It is true that prediction 2, showing farmers' hypothetical short-term response to international prices did point to a substantially larger acreage in 1964 than the actual one (almost 0.2 million feddan), and to a continued high level for 1965. The acreage increase in 1965 could thus be interpreted as a delayed government overreaction to international prices, as if the authorities had reacted to international prices in much the same way as the farmers had done in the past. It appears, however, that the reactions of the authorities were based, rather, on some kind of "commodity balance" thinking. When export sales were brisk and stocks depleted

TABLE 7–4

Cotton Acreage, Export Volume, and International Prices,
1962–63 to 1968–69

	Acreage (000 feddan)		Export Volume (000 MK)[a]	Relative Output Value at International Prices (F_{cotton})[b] (Index)	Internatio Cotton Pr (£E per N
	Actual	Allotted			
1962–63	1,627	—	6,061	2.06	303
1963–64	1,627	1,850	5,835	1.97	311
1964–65	1,611	1,630	6,843	2.11	353
1965–66	1,900	1,950	6,848	1.84	345
1966–67	1,859	1,900	6,043	1.86	365
1967–68	1,626	n.a.	5,194	2.04	416
1968–69	1,464	1,600	4,783	2.20	457

NOTE: The year is the cotton year September 1–August 31. The acreage is for the crop vested at the beginning of the cotton year and sown at the middle of the preceding cotton y the figures are for acreage sown.

SOURCES: Acreage: B. Hansen and K. Nashashibi, NBER Working Paper No. 48, New Y 1975; F_{cotton}: Table A–4; international cotton price: B. Hansen and K. Nashashibi, ibid., T 17; export volume: *Economic Bulletin*, N.B.E., 1969.

a. MK = metric kantars (= 50 kg).

b. See Table A–4.

in 1964, the government reacted by expanding the cotton acreage, and a sort of "cobweb cycle" was generated during these years, with acreage lagging one year behind the export volume. Table 7–4 gives figures for acreage, export volume, relative output-value of cotton in terms of international prices (F_{cotton}), and the international cotton price itself.

While export volume, relative output value in terms of international prices, as well as the international cotton price, all could explain the acreage expansion from 1964 to 1965, only the (lagged) export volume can explain the subsequent development: a continued large allotment and cotton acreage in 1966, followed by a fall in acreage in 1967 and 1968. (We are assuming that the actual acreage in 1967–68 roughly reflect the allotments.) The allotment for cotton was cut down from the 1967 level to about 1.6 million feddan in 1968.[13] The export volume in a particular year is, in turn, determined by foreign demand, Egyptian acreage, yield, and surplus stocks. Since the Egyptian authorities are known to think in terms of commodity balances, it seems clear that we have here the basic explanation of the cotton acreage policy. More appropriate forecasting methods would clearly have led to a different acreage policy.

How suboptimal was the cotton acreage policy? Taking our prediction of the optimal area (prediction 3) at face value, it would seem that, after having been somewhat below optimal from 1962 through 1964, the actual area was about 0.4 million feddan too large in 1965 and 1966. This amounts to a misallocation of about 4 percent of the total crop area in the country. The downtrend in the predicted optimal area from 1965 on is due exclusively to the enlarged water supply. As already pointed out, our estimated response function may exaggerate the negative effects of water on the cotton acreage. The relative output-value of cotton—F_{cotton}—was about the same in 1967 as in 1962, and the same in 1968 as in 1964. We cannot exclude the possibility that the cotton acreage was again about optimal already in 1967 and that it even may have been suboptimal in 1968. All we can say with some confidence, therefore, is that the cotton acreage in 1965 and 1966 was significantly higher—perhaps more than 25 percent—than the true optimum, whereas for the other years it may not have been very different from the optimum.

RICE

Rice is the second big export crop the government was much concerned about during the sixties. Here, too, it is immediately clear from Chart 7–2

CHART 7–2

Rice: Actual versus Predicted Crop Areas

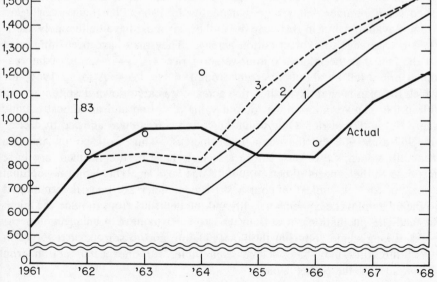

that something dramatic happened around 1965; while prediction 1 (farmers' response at actual ex-farm prices without controls) points to a strong increase that year, actual acreage fell substantially. Clearly this was an inevitable result of the increase in cotton acreage. The government could not push up the cotton acreage by 300,000 feddan without causing the acreage for other summer crops (rice and maize) to fall.

The picture is complicated by the fact that prediction 1, based on actual ex-farm prices, indicates a much lower rice acreage than the actual one from 1962 through 1964. Most probably it is again the water supply variable that causes problems. We note first (Appendix A, Table A–2) that the unlagged water coefficient in the estimated response function for rice is large, highly significant, and positive, as should be expected, while the lagged coefficient is small and insignificant. It should also be recalled that, as an indicator of water supply, we have used the monthly discharge of the Nile at Aswan in May–June. The discharge at Aswan at a given point of time may be a relatively poor indicator for the simultaneous water supply to the fields in the Delta, where most of the rice is grown (see Chapter 6, p. 146). Since the need for boosting exports began to be felt strongly already in 1961, when both the cotton and rice crops failed and exchange reserves were exhausted, the authorities were apparently able to shift the irrigation patterns to the advantage of rice cultivation—hence the high level of actual rice acreage from 1962 to 1964.[14] Note that the actual acreages in 1962 and 1963 correspond to the plans. For 1964 the plan was unrealistically high, but acreage continued to increase.[15]

All this, however, does not imply that rice cultivation should have diminished when summer water supply increased in 1965. Plan figures for 1965 are not available, but in this year the authorities must have deliberately sacrificed rice acreage to expand cotton acreage. They may have been influenced by the fact that the relative output-value of rice—F_{rice}—in terms of international prices fell by about 8 percent from 1963 to 1964. Also, in 1966, for which the plan is again available, rice acreage was kept down despite a strong fall in the relative international output-value of cotton and an almost equally sharp rise in that of rice. Only when the cotton acreage was allowed to decline in 1967 and 1968 did the rice acreage increase. Thus, both cotton and rice (as well as corn, see below) acreages seem to have been controlled largely in response to the exports of cotton, with a one year lag. This is not an optimal system of control—unless, of course, the Egyptian acreage policies were linked to the bilateral trade agreements with and the demands from the Soviet Union. In fact, the fluctuations in cotton exports seem to have been geared to the yield of long staple cotton in the Soviet Union, and to some extent Egyptian agriculture thus may have served as a buffer for unexpected cotton crop fluctuations in the Soviet Union.

How far, then, was the actual rice acreage off the optimum? If we admit that our water specification may be deficient by ignoring the storage possibilities in the Delta[16] and by exaggerating the impact of water from 1965 on,[17] there is little we can say except that the rice acreage must have been substantially below the optimum level in 1965 and 1966, and perhaps also in 1967 and 1968.

CORN

Corn is the third big summer–autumn crop to be influenced by the policy changes in 1965. We find that prediction 1, based on actual ex-farm prices, explains the actual acreage fairly well until 1964, although the direction of change is wrong. In 1965, contrary to the forecast of a continued increase, there is a substantial drop in the corn acreage, as should be expected considering the expansion in cotton acreage. It should be recalled that the authorities had good reasons for planning a decline in the production of cereals for domestic consumption from 1962 to 1965 (and perhaps even 1966). The inflow of PL480 aid reached a high level during this period, and, although American corn is not a good substitute for Egyptian "durra" as a food grain, one should certainly expect some impact on domestic production. In fact, the government planned for a sharp contraction in corn acreage already in 1964, probably related to the excessive expansion planned for rice.

The forecasts for the (total) corn acreage hide the strong shift from autumn (short season) to summer (full season) corn that took place mainly after 1964, partly made possible by the increase in water supply during the spring. The yield of summer corn is about 50 percent higher than that of

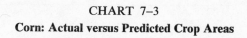

CHART 7–3
Corn: Actual versus Predicted Crop Areas

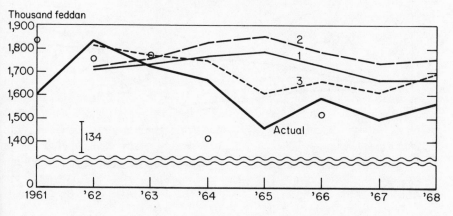

autumn corn. Our estimates for the period 1913–1961 show a negative, albeit small, impact of the greater water supply on total corn acreage, but our model does not distinguish between summer and autumn corn. Since an increase in water supply, however, raises average yield through the relative increase of summer corn, it also raises output value per feddan and thereby the F-variable. For corn, the water and the F-variable tend to be correlated, and possibly our estimate may not distribute the roles played by water supply and relative profitability correctly.

We note, nonetheless, that prediction 3 (the optimal acreage) predicts the movements of the actual acreage during the whole period fairly well, though with a slight upward drift, suggesting that government interference may have brought the acreage closer to optimum than the price mechanisms under free trade might have done.

MILLET

This subsistence food grain is mainly grown in Upper Egypt, and we should not expect cotton controls to have significant repercussions on its acreage. Actual acreage has been expanding slowly (together with labor), whereas the forecast at actual ex-farm prices first shows a slow decrease until 1965 and then a rapid increase. The actual development follows planned acreage fairly accurately and it would seem that here government interference could be the proper explanation for the increase in acreage.

CHART 7–4

Millet: Actual versus Predicted Crop Areas

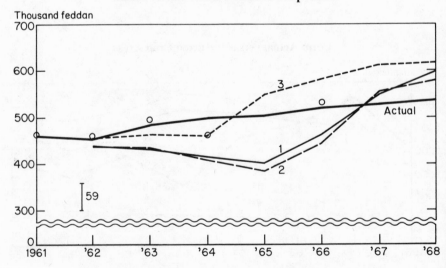

WHEAT

One would be inclined to expect that during the years of the PL480 wheat inflow government efforts were directed at limiting the wheat area and that, once PL480 aid was cut off and wheat supply suddenly became a serious problem, planning aimed at increasing the wheat area. Actually, available acreage plan figures show almost the opposite development (see Chart 7–5). Through 1963 the planned area was kept constant at 1.475 million feddan. It was increased to 1.575 million feddan for 1964—before there was any doubt about the continuation of PL480 aid. The uptrend continued to 1.672 million feddan for 1965, but here we might see the influence of deteriorating relations with the United States, although the wheat shipment agreement did not lapse until July 1965 and a six-month extension was then obtained. The plan figure for 1966 is, unfortunately, not available, but for 1967 (that is, for the wheat crop sown in November–December 1966) the planned area was cut down to 1.338 million feddan.

These developments in the planned wheat area are hard to understand, unless the Egyptian requests for PL480 shipments are seen as stemming from the shortfalls of the actual areas as compared with the planned ones and, hence, of actual as compared with planned production. But then we have to explain why the actual wheat acreage fell so sharply until 1965 and then started increasing again, thus moving opposite to the plan figures. Our model does not help us to understand this discrepancy; prediction 1 (at actual ex-

CHART 7–5

Wheat: Actual versus Predicted Crop Areas

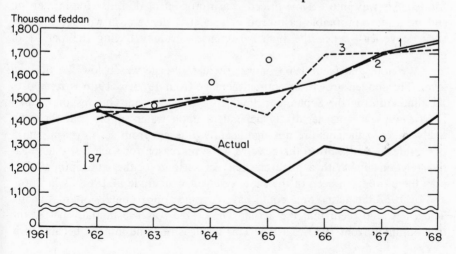

farm prices) points to a steady increase in the wheat area over the whole period from 1962 to 1968.

This is a situation where a general economist would see no problems. A glance at the relative wheat price, or, better still, the relative profitability indicator, F, in Appendix A (Table A–4) seems to explain everything fairly well. For wheat, F, calculated at ex-farm prices, fell by 25 percent from 1961 to 1964 and rose by 8 percent from 1964 to 1967. From 1962 to 1965 the acreage fell by 20 percent, and, at a short-term price elasticity of 0.8, the drop would be explained (assuming a one-year lag) by relative profitability. Profitability explains less of the increase from 1964 to 1967, unless we assume a somewhat higher short-term elasticity. A priori, such elasticities would look a bit high, but not impossible. The problem is that our econometric estimates for 1913–1961 yield a very low short-term F elasticity for wheat—0.03. It is true that the estimate for the coefficient of F is very imprecise, but even if we assume the coefficient's value to be equal to the estimate *plus* three standard deviations, the elasticity would still reach only 0.15.

This raises the question whether the elasticity of the wheat acreage with respect to F may have increased drastically from the 1913–1961 period to the prediction period. It stands to reason that over time wheat has become less and less of a subsistence crop; this in itself tends to increase elasticity. An important contributing factor might also be the compulsory delivery of wheat. During the period of prediction, farmers were obligated to deliver a certain proportion of their wheat crop to the government at relatively low fixed producer's prices. The average ex-farm price actually obtained by the farmers should reflect this arrangement for farmers who normally sold the wheat crop. But for subsistence croppers it may have also meant forced sales beyond what they would normally have contemplated. If wheat was suddenly forcibly transformed this way into a (low-priced) cash crop, it made sense for farmers to shift to a more profitable cash crop or to a subsistence crop without compulsory deliveries—hence the higher response elasticity during the period of prediction.

We note that from 1963 onward actual acreage was below the optimal level. The sudden growth in optimal acreage from 1965 to 1966 is related to the diminution in the September flow of water at Aswan. Our response functions show wheat as negatively dependent upon water supply, but the relatively large coefficients are not significantly different from zero even at the 5 percent level, and a priori there seems to be no reason for such a strong negative relationship. With a price elasticity close to zero, the true optimal area may therefore have been of the same order of magnitude in 1968 as in 1962, and by 1968 the actual area could have become approximately optimal again. Thus, it would seem that the actual wheat area was substantially below the true optimum from 1963 to 1967. This result is of some interest because it is frequently contended by specialists that wheat is an inferior crop that should not be grown in Egypt to any significant extent.[18]

The conclusion would thus appear to be that the reduction in the actual wheat acreage and its suboptimality were, indeed, a consequence of government intervention, albeit not via acreage but via compulsory deliveries at low prices. The latter, obviously intended to increase urban supply, was thus counterproductive in regard to area cultivated. The efforts to bolster wheat acreage and, at the same time, enforce deliveries at low prices were inconsistent measures, with the latter taking the upper hand in affecting actual acreage.

BARLEY

Barley is the crop for which the deficiencies of specification in the acreage response function may be most serious. To the extent that it grows on the coastal strip, it depends on rainfall rather than on Nile water. It is not generally part of the standard rotations and does not compete with other crops. Nonetheless, there is a partly significant, strongly negative influence from the

CHART 7–6
Barley: Actual versus Predicted Crop Areas

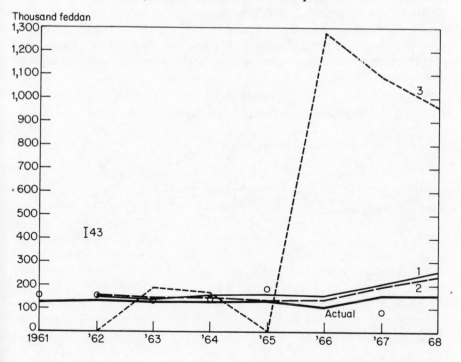

water variable. The barley acreage diminished strongly from 1913 to 1961, together with the expansion of cotton in the northern part of the Delta alongside the increase in water supply; but this historical relation does not exist any longer. Prediction 1 explains the actual acreage fairly well, although it is persistently running at a slightly higher level. This may be due to government interference—beginning with 1963, barley was banned in certain regions in the northern part of the Delta. According to prediction 3, barley should not have been grown at all in 1962 and 1965, the optimal acreage being negative for these years. From 1965 to 1966, the optimal acreage shoots up to 10 times the actual acreage. This enormous increase is exclusively related to the fall in the September flood discharge at Aswan from 1965 on. It might have been better to forecast without using the water variable after that time, in which case the optimal acreage would have become negative for all three years from 1965 to 1968. This prediction for the optimum for 1962–1968 probably correctly reflects the fate of barley in the standard rotation but cannot be true for the coastal strip, where nothing else can be grown.

WINTER ONIONS

Although onions are a secondary, albeit potentially important, export crop, the government has always been interested in promoting their cultivation. The actual acreage from 1963 to 1968 was somewhat larger than prediction 1, the difference probably indicating government interference. Plan figures are available but appear to be simple, passive forecasts. It is noteworthy that prediction 2 (farmers' hypothetical response at international prices) predicts the actual area with great precision. The optimal acreage,

CHART 7–7

Onions (Winter): Actual versus Predicted Crop Areas

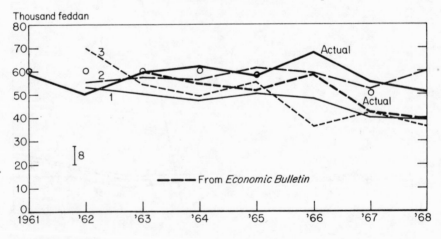

according to prediction 3, in 1962 was somewhat higher than the actual area, but then runs somewhat below it until 1965, when it drops substantially. This drop is related to the change in water supply, and once more the possibility of mis-specification has to be considered.

The estimate of the response function shows positive but insignificant coefficients for the water variable. These may be expected to have positive signs, onions being highly dependent upon water supply. They are sensitive, however, to overwatering, so that a linear specification may be wrong, and the sharp reduction in the September 1965 discharge need not necessarily imply that winter onions on land with perennial irrigation got less water than before. The decisive factor after 1965 is, rather, that basin irrigation diminished and perennial irrigation expanded, and this should have a positive effect on the onion acreage. Prediction 3 should probably be disregarded altogether for the years 1966, 1967, and 1968, when the true optimal acreage may have been increasing.

BEANS

Here is a crop with an almost perfect explanation by prediction 1 (farmers' response to actual ex-farm prices) of the actual area. This could be taken to mean that direct government intervention with the acreage has been negligible or totally unsuccessful.[19] Plan figures are available; they tend to be at the level of the actual figures, and are probably passive forecasts.

CHART 7-8

Beans: Actual versus Predicted Crop Areas

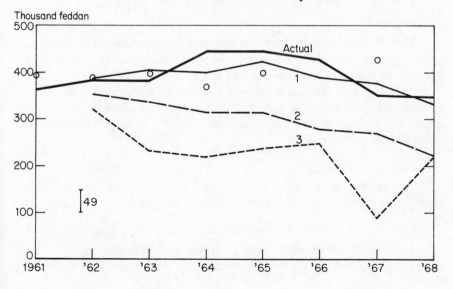

CHART 7–9

Lentils: Actual versus Predicted Crop Areas

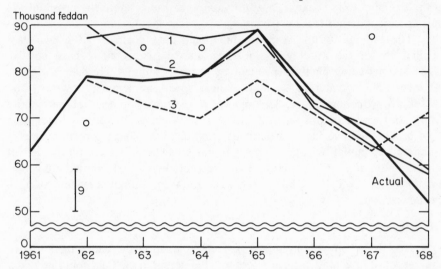

The optimal acreage, according to prediction 3, is much lower than actual acreage. Note that the estimated coefficients for the influence of water supply are very small. Thus, the predictions are little influenced by the changes in water supply.

The picture corroborates our previous findings that beans are the most strongly protected crop in Egypt.

LENTILS

The situation is much the same here as with beans; actual ex-farm prices (prediction 1) explain the actual acreage very well from 1962 to 1968, particularly the steep decline from 1965 to 1968.

The optimal acreage of prediction 3 is running substantially below actual acreage through 1967. The influence of water is considerable, but it is not clear whether there is any mis-specification here. The negative lagged effect of water is highly significant.

HELBA (fenugreek)

International prices were not available, and only prediction 1 could be used. Controls have probably been of little consequence for this small crop.

CANE

The major part of the acreage is grown under contract with the state-owned sugar factories, and the government is always able to fix upper limits

CHART 7–10

Helba: Actual versus Predicted Crop Areas

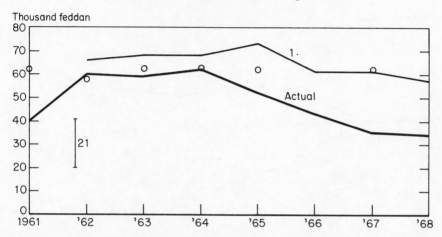

to the area cultivated. After the introduction of cooperatives, it has probably also been capable of exerting downward control over the contractual acreage, imposing upon the farmers the acreage allotted to cane in the annual plan.

Actual ex-farm prices (prediction 1) point to a declining acreage from 1962 to 1966 and to a slight rise thereafter, increasingly below the level of actual acreage. There is little doubt that the government exerts a decisive influence on acreage here.

The optimal acreage under prediction 3 reflects the violent fluctuations in the world price of sugar. At the peak of the world price in 1963, the actual area seems to have been about optimal. When world market prices, beginning in 1965, became more normal, the optimum seems to have been only some 30 to 40 thousand feddan, about one-quarter of the actual acreage. The coefficients of the water variable in the estimated response function are relatively small and there is nothing to indicate serious mis-specification for this crop.

It should be emphasized that the international prices used for cane in predictions 2 and 3 are f.o.b.-based, imputed cane prices. Had c.i.f.-based prices been used (as in the case of the ERP and DRC estimates for sugar), the optimal cane acreage would have been 10–15 percent higher (see, further, Chapter 8, p. 239).

Problems of Measuring the Loss from Misallocation.

The concepts of ERP and DRC were originally established to indicate misallocation of resources via price distortions for commodities, or the loss from misallocation. It is easy to set up a formula for the total loss assuming

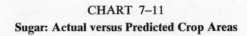

CHART 7-11

Sugar: Actual versus Predicted Crop Areas

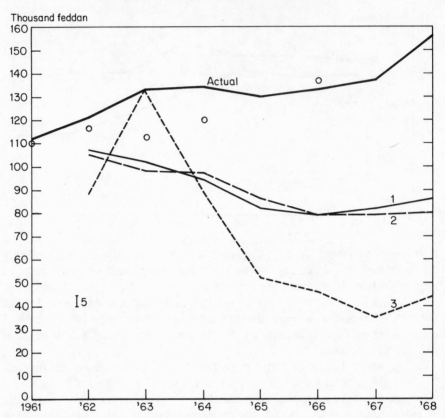

our model to be a correct specification (excluding, among other things, produced inputs).

Let f as superscript denote foreign and d domestic. The loss is then measured by

$$\Sigma p_i^f q_i^f - \Sigma p_i^f q_i^d \qquad (3)$$

where q_i and q_i are the quantities produced when producer prices equal foreign and domestic prices, respectively, and producers in both cases are assumed to maximize the total crop value at actual producer prices. Note the difference between equation (3) and the ERP, which is based on the expression

$$\Sigma p_i^d q_i^d - \Sigma p_i^f q_i^d.$$

With a well-behaved community indifference map, expression (3) will measure (at least ordinally) the potential welfare loss from price distortion.[20] (We could normalize (3) through dividing by $\Sigma p_i^f q_i^f$, but it is immaterial for what follows.)

Considering the infinitesimal case where actual domestic prices deviate from international prices by dp_i, the loss is

$$\Sigma p_i^f dq_i \qquad (4)$$

which by assumption is nonpositive, and negative if any $dq_i \neq 0$.

In our model the production functions are (see Appendix A, equation 1):

$$q_i = y_i f_i(A_i, L_i, W_i) = q_i(y_i, A_i, L_i, W_i)$$

where in optimum $A_i = A_i(F_i, A, L, W)$, $L_i = L_i(F_i, A, L, W)$ and $W_i = W_i(F_i, A, L, W)$. We have thus

$$dq_i = [q'_{iA_i} A'_{iF_i} + q'_{iL_i} L'_{iF_i} + q'_{iW_i} W'_{iF_i}] \cdot dF_i, \qquad (5)$$

assuming y_i, A, L, and W to be constant. Recalling the definition of F_i (see Appendix A), insertion of (5) into (4) leads, after some rearrangement, to the following expression for the loss:

$$\Sigma[e^{q_i}_{A_i} e^{A_i}_{F_i} + e^{q_i}_{L_i} e^{L_i}_{F_i} + e^{q_i}_{W_i} e^{W_i}_{F_i}] \, p_i^f \, q_i^f \left[\frac{dp_i}{p_i} - \frac{\Sigma w_i y_i dp_i}{\Sigma w_i y_i p_i} \right] \qquad (6)$$

where the es are partial (long-term) elasticities of the superscript with respect to the subscript. Replacing the first square bracket by $E^{q_i}_{F_i}$, the total elasticity of output with respect to relative output-value, (6) reduces to

$$\Sigma E^{q_i}_{F_i} \cdot p_i^f \, q_i^f \cdot \left[\frac{dp_i}{p_i} - \frac{\Sigma w_i y_i dp_i}{\Sigma w_i y_i p_i} \right]. \qquad (6')$$

We, thus, find the total loss by multiplying for each crop the total crop value, $p_i^f q_i^f$ (at optimum at international prices), by the (total long-term) supply elasticity, $E^{q_i}_{F_i}$, with respect to relative output-value, and by the difference between the nominal rate of protection for the crop itself and the (weighted) average nominal rate of protection for all crops. Note that the loss becomes zero when all crops enjoy the same rate of protection. An important implication is that if the only protection (negative or positive) is a general over- or undervaluation of the currency, there will be no loss from price distortion. This result is closely related to the fact that our model assumes completely flexible factor prices.

Equation (6') lends itself to quantification, but requires estimation of all supply functions; we have made no attempt to estimate supply functions and would, in any case, miss one of the more important ones, that for clover. If supply functions are not available, we could work on the basis of equation (6). The latter, however, requires estimation of both production functions for all crops and response functions for all primary inputs—land, labor, and water—which is not feasible because information about inputs by crop is available only for land.

It might be thought that total loss from acreage misallocation could be obtained as the sum of the differences between optimal area (prediction 3) and actual area multiplied by domestic values added (DVA) per feddan at international prices, assuming that the difference between total actual and total optimal area would be cultivated by clover. A crude calculation for 1963 made on this basis shows a total loss of about £E9 million, or about 2 percent of total domestic value added at international prices for the crops covered. Such a calculation is, however, entirely unreliable since it is based on *average* DVA per feddan calculated at international prices, given the *actual* distortion. There were large differences between average DVA per feddan at international prices in 1963, and it is easy to visualize a deviation from the optimal crop pattern which, with this method of calculation, would even show a total gain. A correct method of calculation would be to take the difference between (a) the sum of optimal areas multiplied by DVA per feddan at international prices and at optimal cropping and (b) the sum of actual areas multiplied by actual DVA per feddan at international prices. We do not know, however, the DVA per feddan that would prevail at optimal cropping. Hence we have to abstain from quantifying the total loss.

Ranking According to ERP, DRC, and Optimal Acreage.

As a basis for ranking crops according to effect of protection on production we might use the quantity distortion

$$\frac{dq_i}{q_i} = E_{F_i}^{q_i} \left[\frac{dp_i}{p_i} - \frac{\Sigma w_i y_i dp_i}{\Sigma w_i y_i p_i} \right] \tag{7}$$

On our assumptions here (no imported inputs), the ERP for crop i is simply dp_i/p_i. Hence, ranking is bound to be different on the two criteria, unless the supply elasticities, $E_{F_i}^{q_i}$, are very similar for all crops.

Since we do not know the supply elasticities, we limit ourselves to studying the misallocation of land on the basis of our analysis of area responses. We can proceed in various ways. For example, we can compare the optimal acreage, prediction 3, with actual acreage and use the difference (divided by the optimal acreage) as a measure of misallocation. This would yield a measure of the combined effect of price distortion and direct government interference with acreage (disregarding random errors): A in Table 7–5.

We can also compare optimal acreage, prediction 3, with farmers' response to actual ex-farm prices, prediction 1, and use the difference (divided by optimal acreage) as a measure of the misallocation related to price distortions and market imperfections: B in Table 7–5.

Finally, we can compare farmers' response to actual ex farm prices, prediction 1, with farmers' response to international prices, prediction 2, and use the difference (divided by the latter acreage) as a measure of the short-term misallocation related to price distortions: C in Table 7–5.

The ranking of misallocation according to each one of these three measures will be compared with the ranking according to ERP and DRC.[21] This will throw light upon the latter two as measures of misallocation. The only year for which we can make this comparison is 1963, and it is possible only for the ten crops listed in Table 7–5.

We note first why there is no perfect rank correlation between ERP and DRC: nontraded outputs and inputs are included, and the DRCs are calculated

TABLE 7–5

Ranking of Crops in 1963 According to ERP, DRC, and Alternative Measures of Acreage Misallocation

			Rank in Decreasing Order		
Crop	ERP[a]	DRC[a,b]	A (Actual Area − Prediction 3)/ Prediction 3	B (Prediction 1 − Prediction 3)/ Prediction 3	C (Prediction 1 − Prediction 2)/ Prediction 2
Cotton	7	7	9	6	8
Rice	9	8	8	10	10
Corn	3	5	7	5	7
Millet	4–5	2	5	8	6
Wheat	6	3	10	4	5
Barley	4–5	4	4	3	4
Onions	8	10	2	7	9
Beans	1	1	1	1	1
Lentils	2	6	3	2	2
Cane	10	9	6	9	3

NOTE: Spearman's rank correlation coefficient works out as follows, with critical levels at 1 percent and 5 percent probability at 0.76 and 0.56, respectively:

ERP−DRC	0.75	ERP−C	0.57
ERP−A	0.45	DRC−C	0.50
DRC−A	0.10	A−B	0.41
ERP−B	0.84	B−C	0.67
DRC−B	0.59	A−C	0.45

a. According to Table 7–1.
b. DRC includes trade and transport margin.

on the basis of imputed factor prices to adjust for government controls over land rentals and to allow for normal profits on capital. It is also recalled that what disturbs the rank correlation between A, on the one hand, and B and C, on the other, is direct government interference with acreages, as well as random disturbances, while the lack of perfect correlation between B and C expresses differences between short- and long-term misallocation of land.

As is to be expected, neither ERP nor DRC can be used as an indicator of the long-term misallocations related to both price distortion and direct acreage interference (including random disturbances). The correlation coefficients ERP–A and DRC–A are insignificant and very low in the latter case.

The ERP could, however, be taken as a relatively reliable indicator of long-term and a weak indicator of short-term misallocation resulting from price distortions alone. The correlation coefficient ERP–B is significant at the 1 percent level, and that of ERP–C, at the 5 percent level.

The DRC, finally, can be used as a weak indicator of long-term misallocation stemming from price distortion, with the correlation coefficient DRC–B significant at the 5 percent level.

Needless to say, these results do not lend themselves to generalizations about the relative merits of different measures of distortion. As it happens, in this case the ERPs do, in fact, give a good indication of the relative extent to which acreages are off the optimum due to price distortion. This may be because the response elasticities with respect to price are quite similar here, but it may also be related to the fact that the share of purchased produced inputs in Egyptian agriculture is so low that substitution effects are negligible; in that case the ERPs should, indeed, be correct indicators.

Conclusions.

In the preceding discussions it may not have been easy to see the woods for all the trees: there are many crops and many years. We have, therefore, tried to summarize our findings in regard to misallocation of land in Table 7–6. The table works with averages of the 1962–1968 prediction period presenting, for each individual crop (except barley, for which there are serious specification problems, and helba, for which international prices are not available), as well as for all crops taken together, averages of the absolute deviations of actual from optimal crop areas measured as a percentage of the average optimal area ("optimal" as defined by our model and as measured by prediction 3). In proceeding like this, we have obviously assumed that upward and downward deviations are equally bad, and that a deviation of two acres is twice as bad as a deviation of one acre.[22] Our model contains three factors that contribute to making actual and optimal acreages deviate, and Table 7–6 shows a breakdown of the deviations on this basis.

TABLE 7–6

Misallocation of Land, Average 1962–1968

(percent of optimal acreage)

		Deviation from Optimal Acreage			
		Due to Imperfect Market Forces	Due to Government Interference		
	Total		Total	Price Distortion	Other Intervention
Cotton	12.1	5.4	6.7	2.3	4.4
Rice	21.8	4.7	17.1	8.6	8.5
Corn	5.3	6.1	−0.8	−2.1	1.3
Millet	8.9	14.0	−5.1	−2.2	−2.9
Wheat	16.4	2.1	14.3	0.9	13.4
Beans	78.3	37.4	40.9	36.3	4.6
Onions	29.5	25.7	3.8	−12.5	16.3
Lentils	10.3	11.3	−1.0	2.2	−3.2
Cane	93.8	42.5	51.3	0.0	51.3
Total	7.9	3.5	4.4	1.2	3.2

SOURCE: Our calculations.

1. The market forces are imperfect. Farmers' responses lead assymptotically at best to the optimum in the long run, and it may take considerable time for actual acreage to reach the vicinity of the optimum. If prices and other conditions change continuously—and they do—farmers will tend to be permanently off the optimum. We measure the impact due to this factor as the average of the absolute differences between predictions 2 and 3 (as percentages of the average optimal area). Note that we are here comparing the optimal pattern with another hypothetical situation: prediction 2 estimates what the areas would have been had international prices prevailed in Egypt.

2. Government intervention in prices, however, makes ex-farm prices differ from free trade prices. The difference is the price distortion, and we are particularly interested in its impact on land allocation.[23] We measure the impact of price distortion as the average of the absolute differences between predictions 1 and 2 (as a percentage of optimal acreage), prediction 2 being equal to prediction 3 *minus* the impact due to imperfection of market forces defined under 1. above.

3. After the impacts defined under 1. and 2. have been taken into account, a residual remains (the difference between prediction 1 and actual area) that we ascribe to other kinds of government intervention (like the

cooperatives and the irrigation system). This residual is presented as "other intervention" in Table 7–6. It should be recalled that it includes stochastic disturbances, for which we have no measure. We hope that these may tend to cancel each other out, but with averages based on only seven years we cannot be sure of that.

Finally, a few remarks are in order to explain the total figures in the last row. These were calculated by adding up the absolute average deviations for the individual crops and relating them to the sum of all optimal acreages. A positive deviation from the optimal acreage for one crop must, however, have a tendency to be balanced by negative deviations for other crops (given total acreage). Since this method of calculation accordingly involves double counting, the resulting percentages were divided by two to obtain the figures in the table.

Looking first at our estimates of the total deviation from optimal acreage (first column), we find that it varies between 5 and 94 percent for individual crops and approaches 8 percent for the total area. In other words, at least 8 percent of the total crop area was planted with the wrong crops.[24] Almost half of this (3.5 percent) can be ascribed to imperfections of the market forces; the rest is due to government interference. Thus, the imperfections of the farmer and the imperfections of government seem to have been on the same order of magnitude. The trouble is that they have, on balance, been cumulative. Far from improving upon the play of market forces, the government has just made things worse in regard to land allocation. The picture is not a uniform one, however. For three crops—corn, millet, and lentils—government interference appears to have improved land allocation. But this must be fortuitous; the government paid little attention to these crops in its allocation policies.

Price distortions account for a minor part of the misallocations ascribed to government interference, only 1.2 percent out of 4.4 percent for the total area. This result is not unexpected in view of the very low price elasticities found in this study. For the individual crops, the effects of price distortion are generally small (rice, beans, and onions being the exceptions). For three crops (corn, millet, and onions) the price distortions appear to have improved the allocation of land, but, once again, this result was probably fortuitous.

The impact of "other (government) intervention," as measured here, varied much from crop to crop and appears to have improved land allocation for two crops, millet and lentils. In a previous section the question was raised whether direct acreage controls could have been used by the government for neutralizing allocational effects of price distortions made for income-distributional purposes. Effects of price distortions and other kinds of government intervention appear, indeed, to have tended to cancel each other out for three crops—corn, onions, and lentils. For two of these, however, the effects of price distortions were such as to improve land allocation, and we have no reason for supposing that the government reasoned that out in advance. Again, what happened was probably fortuitous. The important thing in this connection is, of course, that for the big export crops, together with wheat and corn, towards which the government's efforts were largely directed, "other intervention" served only to reinforce the misallocation due to price distortion.

Returning to the problem of the total loss incurred by misallocation of land (already discussed on pp. 185–188), the 8 percent misallocation of the total acreage might be taken as a starting point for conjectures about the total loss. If nothing of value had been grown on this 8 percent, the total loss would have been about 8 percent of total output (given certain assumptions of homogeneity of land), and this figure may serve as an upper limit to the possible loss. But something of value, even at international prices, was, of course, grown upon the misallocated land. Assuming, for example, that the value of what was actually grown was about half the value of what should optimally have been grown, the total loss would amount to about 4 percent of the total crop, and about half of this, 2 percent, would be due to government interference. These losses are big enough to cause serious concern for a poor country. On the national level, the equivalent of the loss, invested wisely, could have increased the growth rate of per capita income by 1 or 2 percent, or, at a given growth rate, could have served to make Egypt self-financing during the sixties—free from those foreign exchange and balance of payments problems that, to some extent, were the very excuse for introducing the controls.

A final caveat: the results obtained from this econometric exercise are, of course, no better than the model and the statistical estimates upon which it is based. In the light of all the objections we ourselves have raised against the model, the whole exercise should perhaps be viewed mainly as an illustration of a methodology for studying suboptimalities arising from price distortion and direct interference with agricultural production. Here we shall only repeat one crucial assumption, previously emphasized: that instantaneous adjustment to the long-term state at any moment would be cost-free. Hence, our identification of long-term response and optimum.

The delayed response of farmers is partly related to adjustments of price and yield expectations, partly to possible costs inherent in changing rotations suddenly. We have assumed that expectational adjustments are the dominant factor, and that ideally correct forecasts could be obtained at negligible costs. Of course, it could have been the costs of changing rotations that were the decisive factor, although we do not think so. In that case we could have, as another extreme assumption, identified the optimum with prediction 2, farmers' hypothetical short-term response at international prices. Then there would be no loss from the imperfection of market forces—indeed, the assumption would be that market forces are perfect—and there would be no room for improving land allocation through direct government intervention with acreage. It is clear that we would once again find price distortions to have been a minor factor in creating misallocation of land as compared with direct government intervention.

The truth probably lies, as usual, between the extremes—closer, in our view, to the first extreme than to the second. It would certainly be ridiculous to assume that peasants are perfect price forecasters; the costs involved in sudden changes of cropping patterns are more difficult to ascertain.

AGRICULTURAL PRICING AND INCOME DISTRIBUTION

Apart from the inevitable intervention through the management of the irrigation system, direct interference with crop rotations and acreages was largely absent in 1961, at least outside the land reform estates (about 10 percent of the cultivated area at that time). Since prices had been fairly stable for some years, it can probably be assumed that the composition of crops was roughly in equilibrium at the existing domestic prices. Thus, 1961 is a convenient year for examining the income-distributional effects of the government's agricultural pricing policies. Adjustment must be made, however, for the cotton crop failure that year.

We have already seen that, in applying an elaborate crop rotation system, most Egyptian farmers are multicroppers (cane and fruit growers being the major exceptions), but it is still possible to classify them by major crop. For example, farmers on a two-year rotation with cotton and no rice are particularly dependent upon cotton prices, while in the North farmers may grow rice every year with no cotton and are thus mainly dependent upon the rice price. To equalize agricultural income, therefore, it was a natural step for the government—on top of the land reforms—to attempt equalizing farmers' income from various crops.

The income position of the farmers, however, depends critically on whether they are owner-cultivators or tenants (sharecroppers), and on the extent to which they employ hired labor (small farmers hire less labor per feddan than big farmers). Table 7–7 shows income per feddan for owner-cultivators and tenants, with all or no labor hired, calculated on the basis of actual domestic and international prices, respectively. Income for an owner-cultivator who hires all labor is defined as the (maximum) land rental plus actual (residual) surplus to capital and management. For an owner-cultivator with no hired labor, income consists of land rental, imputed payment for the cultivator and his family's labor, *plus* actual (residual) surplus to capital and management. Income of a tenant is the same as that of an owner-cultivator

TABLE 7-7
Income in Agriculture, 1961
(£E per feddan)

Crop	Income at Actual Prices				Income at International, Imputed Prices[a]			
	Owner-Cultivated		Tenant		Owner-Cultivated		Tenant	
	All Labor Hired	No Labor Hired	All Labor Hired	No Labor Hired	All Labor Hired	No Labor Hired	All Labor Hired	No Labor Hired
Cotton[b]	45.580	56.660	24.230	35.310	44.258	55.338	15.435	26.515
Rice	18.554	26.504	6.660	14.610	25.021	32.971	13.127	21.077
Millet	21.163	27.283	13.023	19.143	14.317	20.437	3.328	9.448
Sesame	22.001	26.151	15.031	19.081	12.008	16.158	2.998	6.748
Peanuts	19.775	28.375	10.155	18.755	47.580	56.180	34.593	43.193
Corn (summer)	20.413	24.733	11.793	16.113	12.887	17.207	1.250	5.570
Corn (autumn)	11.859	16.178	3.239	7.559	6.558	10.874	-5.083	-0.763
Wheat	23.398	26.678	4.795	8.075	16.707	19.987	-1.896	1.384
Barley	18.168	20.768	5.262	7.862	17.306	19.906	4.400	7.000
Beans	21.657	24.317	9.827	12.487	9.647	12.407	-6.223	-3.563
Lentils	27.434	30.364	13.274	16.184	25.862	28.772	6.719	9.629
Onions (winter)	58.899	66.589	43.379	51.069	78.577	86.267	57.625	65.315
Chick-peas	54.274	57.394	40.134	43.254	31.333	34.453	12.244	15.364
Sugar cane	48.912	58.642	24.632	34.362	—	—	—	—

NOTE: It is difficult to give figures for income from sugar cane at international prices. Results depend upon the extent the loss or gain for the integrated industry is passed on to the sugar cane cultivators.

SOURCE: Hansen and Nashashibi, NBER Working Paper No. 48, New York, 1975, Tables 2 and 5.

a. With deduction of 10 percent trade and transport margin.

b. Calculated at normal yields of lint and seeds.

after deduction of land rental. It should be recalled that in 1961 the maximum rentals were considerably lower than hypothetical market rentals; the residual surplus to capital and management thus includes part of the true rent of land for both owner-cultivator and tenant (unless he pays black market rentals). The maximum-rental policy (with a ban on short-term tenure and other measures to give the tenant a more secure position) was designed to resolve the special income-distributional problems between tenants and owners.

All Egyptian farmers, even the smallest peasants, hire labor, but for very small peasants, whether owner-cultivators or tenants, income calculated on the assumption of no hired labor may be fairly representative. In its price policies the government certainly had the small peasants in mind; it is more difficult to know whether it was concerned with small owner-cultivators, small tenants, or both. The special measures taken to regulate the tenant-owner problem suggest that the government mainly looked to the small owner-cultivator in its price policy.

Table 7–7 shows a remarkable similarity in the income per feddan for all crops of owner-cultivators with no hired labor. Rice, millet, sesame, peanuts, summer corn, wheat, barley, beans, and lentils are all within the range of £E20–30. Cotton income was much higher, almost £E57 per feddan. Cotton, however, should be evaluated together with a one-cut crop of clover (berseem), and it should be taken into account that cotton *plus* a one-cut clover crop occupy the field for twelve months, while the crops listed above are in the fields for only about six months. On a six-month basis, cotton *plus* clover would not yield much more than £E30 per feddan. A similar argument applies to cane, which is in the fields twelve months per year; calculated on a half-yearly basis, the income from cane is £E29 per feddan. The only crops with income per feddan on a half-yearly basis that deviate substantially from the £E20–30 per feddan level are winter onions and chick-peas, occupying the fields seven to eight months and yielding an income of more than £E40 on a half-yearly basis; but these are minor crops. For tenants with no hired labor, the differences in income from various crops are more pronounced.

At international prices, incomes of owner-cultivators (and even more so, of tenants with no hired labor) *would* have differed substantially and a pronounced income inequality among the various types of growers (classified by crop) would have arisen. Rice farmers, in particular, would have gained much, but cane growers would have lost. And beans would have become a rather poor crop. Cane would have been grown (voluntarily) only on a small area at the international prices in 1961, and for tenants both beans and autumn corn would have caused losses, although these two crops might have been grown for subsistence consumption.

Thus, the introduction of international prices for efficiency reasons would have had serious consequences for income distribution among farmers. The government would probably not have been able to handle this problem by any other means (direct subsidies, for instance). It is in the light of these circumstances, together with the low response elasticities for most crops, that we should appraise the government's policies in regard to relative domestic agricultural prices. Also, its additional measures of direct and indirect interference with acreage were probably less taken with a view to efficiency than as an emergency response to compelling demands for an expansion of exports.

FINAL REMARKS

The discussion in this chapter has been concerned mainly with the relative prices of agricultural output, although costs have, to some extent, been brought into the picture as well. The emphasis has been on the effects on the allocation of land among crops. There remains the problem of the absolute level of profitability in agriculture and its implications for income distribution between rural and urban populations and for progress in agriculture. As indicated in the beginning of this chapter, the absolute level of private profitability in agriculture declined somewhat until 1964–65. From then on, the intersectoral terms of trade between agricultural and manufactured products moved definitely in favor of agriculture, yet profitability seems to have remained poor to the end of the sixties. The consequences for income distribution of this development are obvious.

It is less clear how this may have affected investment and growth in agriculture. With the present institutional setup, initiative in regard to both innovation and investment is divided between the individual farmers, the cooperatives, and the government. The individual farmers probably tend to react to profitability as in any other institutional setting, but with initiative limited by the powers given to cooperatives and government. The taxation of agriculture, typical of the price policies during most of the sixties, must have deterred both innovation and investment on the individual level. On the other hand, the government might well have had a full understanding of the higher level of profitability at international prices and, hence, promoted innovation and carried out investments to increase agricultural production. Such has, indeed, been the policy of the government: the Aswan High Dam and the piped drainage project are the most conspicuous examples, and the introduction of new varieties of cotton, corn, and wheat could also be mentioned. Yet, it is uncertain to what extent government initiative has replaced the circumscribed iniative of individual farmers. About the activities of the cooperatives little systematic information is available. Altogether, since the country has been involved in war during most of the period under review, with general detrimental effects on all development efforts, it is probably impossible to single out the effects on agricultural development of price, trade, and production regulations.

NOTES

1. Data are available for before 1961 and after 1964, but on the cost side only with classification by operation. For our purpose, classification by input category (labor, commodity, etc.) is needed, and this classification has only been published for the years 1961–1964.

2. See B. Hansen and K. Nashashibi, "Protection and Competitiveness in Egyptian Agriculture and Industry," NBER Working Paper No. 48, New York, 1975.

3. Small quantities of cane for direct consumption are, of course, traded internationally; but the price of such cane can hardly be considered significant for the crop as a whole.

4. Since we are dealing with many small producers, we can generally assume that ERPs express degrees of protection, with cotton at the alleged upper limit as possibly the only exception.

5. 1961 was a year with an exceptional cotton crop failure. Our calculations assume that cotton yields of lint and seed were normal in 1961.

6. We put the word taxation between quotation marks because the difference between average domestic and international prices has not been fully collected as revenue for the government; part of it has gone directly to consumers.

7. Something similar must hold true for all countries that normally protect food grain production.

8. This circumstance is now generally recognized in the literature on effective protection. See, for instance, J. Bhagwati and T. N. Srinivasan, "The Theory of Effective Protection and Resource Allocation," working paper, Department of Economics, M.I.T., January 1971.

9. See, for instance, E. O. Heady, N. S. Randhawa, and M. D. Skold, "Programming Models for the Planning of the Agricultural Sector," in I. Adelman and E. Thorbecke, *The Theory and Design of Economic Development,* Johns Hopkins University Press, Baltimore, 1966.

10. *Economic Bulletin,* National Bank of Egypt, Vol. 15, No. 4, 1962, p. 267; *Economic Review,* Central Bank of Egypt, Vol. 3, No. 4, 1963, p. 410.

11. *Economic Bulletin,* National Bank of Egypt, Vol. 18, 1965.

12. To account for the positive long-term effect, we would expect the lagged water supply to have a substantial positive coefficient, whereas, in fact, it has a small negative coefficient (see Appendix Table A-2).

13. There were complaints at this time that the government had difficulties in getting farmers to plant the full cotton allotment. Prediction 1 for 1968 points to an acreage of 1.4 million feddan. The allotment was about 1.6 million, with actual acreage close to 1.5 million feddan. This fact could be taken as an indirect test of the reliability of prediction 1.

14. One might wonder to what extent the relatively high short-term price elasticity for rice acreage reflects the irrigation authorities' response to rice prices back in time rather than the farmers' response. But if that were the case, prediction 1 should not have gone wrong in 1962–1964. If, however, the authorities reacted to international prices from 1961 on, which (considering the looming foreign exchange crisis) is quite

plausible, we should, perhaps, look at prediction 2 instead, which explains actual acreage perfectly from 1962 to 1964.

15. As mentioned earlier, a system of contractual rice growing with predetermined prices was introduced in the sixties. It should tend to change the lag structure of the model, but since we do not know to what extent rice has been grown on such contracts we have not been able to take it into account.

16. This possible mis-specification concerns all crops, of course, but takes on primary importance only in regard to rice.

17. The linearity of our response functions is suspect at this point.

18. W. F. Owen, "Land and Water Use in the Egyptian High Dam Era," *Land Economics,* August 1964. Note that if straw had been included in the calculation of relative output value, F_{wheat}, wheat would stand out as an even better crop.

19. Intervention with beans has mainly taken the form of legal specifications as to which varieties are to be grown in the various regions.

20. J. Bhagwati and B. Hansen, "Should Growth Rates be Evaluated at International Prices," in *Development and Planning, Essays in Honor of Paul Rosenstein-Rodan,* J. Bhagwati and R. S. Eckhaus, eds., London, 1972, pp. 53–68.

21. Equation (7) disregards costs and nontraded outputs and is based upon nominal rates of protection; this is the case also with our predictions. The estimates of ERP in Table 7–1 do take these circumstances into account. This fact is of little consequence for our comparisons, however, because the ranking of nominal rates of protection in 1963 according to Table 7–3 is identical with the ranking of ERP in 1963 according to Table 7–1, the only difference being that rice and cane are interchanged at the bottom. The rank correlation coefficient between nominal and effective rates of protection in 1963 is 0.994.

22. There are well-known objections to social welfare functions with such properties. Our assumptions, however, present a proxy description of the conditions of production in agriculture and not of any social welfare function. Around the optimum our assumptions are very reasonable.

23. See pp. 188–189 of this volume.

24. Strictly speaking we measure only the difference between totals of optimal and actual acreages. But the government might, of course, conceivably impose the correct total acreage but impose it on the wrong lands. This kind of misallocation we cannot observe by our method.

Part Three

Protection, Controls, and Competitiveness in Egyptian Industry

Chapter 8

The Traditional Industries

Part Three presents detailed studies of the competitiveness of Egypt's major modern manufacturing industries in the fifties and sixties, particularly during the years around the devaluation of 1962. Evaluation is based primarily on estimates of effective rates of protection (ERPs) and domestic resource costs (DRCs) for each individual industry.

The details of the estimates have been published elsewhere.[1] Here we shall only point out that they are based upon detailed output and cost information for the individual industries and *not* upon input-output tables and input coefficients implied by such tables. Input-output tables for less developed countries are usually quite unreliable and may not always utilize all available data; moreover, in the case of Egypt, no adequate up to date input-output table has been available to the authors. Hence, only those industries for which sufficient information about inputs and outputs could be obtained are included here. They include ten manufacturing industries, of which four are traditional and six are new. Measured by value added, they cover 26.2 percent of manufacturing industry with over ten workers per establishment and 22.8 percent of all establishments (see Table 8–1). Measured by wages and salaries paid, the coverage is 29.3 percent, and by employment, 28.1 percent (in both cases for establishments of over ten workers). While the coverage of modern manufacturing is certainly higher, we clearly cannot claim that our sample is representative. In addition, the estimates of ERPs and DRCs are of widely differing quality, indicating, for some industries, orders of magnitude at best.

The years taken for study depend entirely upon availability of data. For seven industries, years before as well as after the devaluation of 1962 could

TABLE 8–1

Employment, Wages and Salaries, and Value Added in Manufacturing Industry, 1966–67

Code	Industry	Employment (thous.)		Wages and Salaries (mill. £E)		Net Value Added (mill. £E)	
		Total	Incl. in This Study	Total	Incl. in This Study	Total	Incl. in This Study
20	Food	78.8		12.9		36.5	
207	Sugar^a		20.8		4.1		4.7
21	Beverages	5.7		1.3		3.4	
22	Tobacco	12.3		3.0		13.0	
23	Textiles	247.6		47.4		107.6	
231	Spinning and weaving, dyeing and finishing^b		113.7		22.9		46.8
24	Footwear and apparel	9.9		1.7		3.6	
25	Wood cork	3.6		0.6		0.9	
26	Furniture	8.9		1.5		2.4	
27	Paper	13.5		2.4		7.3	
271	Paper and paper pulp^c		1.4		0.3		0.7
28	Printing and publishing	13.5		3.5		5.6	
29	Leather	2.9		0.5		1.0	
30	Rubber products	4.1	1.6^d	1.5	0.5^d	2.6	2.3^d
31	Chemicals	46.1		10.9		32.0	
311	Industrial chemicals and fertilizers^e		7.3		1.6		9.1
32	Petroleum products	10.2		3.3		10.3	
33	Nonmetallic minerals	32.6		5.6		10.7	
334	Cement		5.0		1.3		3.7

Code	Industry						
34	Basic metals	23.0		6.6		9.6	
341	Iron and steel		8.8		2.5		2.5
35	Metal products	25.5		4.5		8.8	
36	Nonelectrical machinery	7.0		2.3		2.9	
37	Electrical machinery	11.2		2.7		8.8	
38	Transport equipment	19.1		4.5		4.9	
383	Automobiles		5.3		1.2		2.4
39	Miscellaneous	6.7		1.2		3.2	
	All establishments with 10 or more workers	584.3	163.9	117.3	34.4	275.1	72.2
	All establishments with fewer than 10 workers	285.1	n.a.	n.a.	n.a.	56.4[f]	n.a.
	TOTAL	869.4					

SOURCES: *Industrial Census* (ten workers and over), and *Industrial Census for Small Enterprise, 1967*, Central Agency for General Mobilization and Statistics (CAGMS), Cairo, April 1971.

a. Average 1960 and 1969–70.
b. Cotton spinning: average 1960 and 1969–70; weaving: 1965–66.
c. 1962–63.
d. 1963–64.
e. 1964–65.
f. Gross value added.

be studied; for three industries, data were available for only one year after the devaluation. Comparability is, thus, quite limited for several reasons.

In regard to interpretation, we emphasize that the industries were subject to several kinds of government intervention during the fifties and sixties, of which foreign exchange control is only one (and perhaps not even the most important one). All large industries were nationalized in 1961 or 1963, and have been exposed to both price and trade controls. Their investment programs have been designed by the government, and interference with their production programs through allocation of foreign exchange, specification of the type and source of inputs to be used, as well as the direction of output has been frequent. In addition, they were forced to increase both employment and wages in 1961 and 1962. To separate the impact of these various forces is exceedingly difficult, if not impossible.

This chapter is devoted to the traditional industries—cotton textiles (spinning and weaving), sugar, and cement—which (except sugar) were established in the early days of the country's industrialization around the turn of the century. When free trade was the prevailing dogma, particularly under British rule, they all had to struggle—and survive—with little protection, even, at times, with negative protection. Partly because of their early strength and partly because of government support, they have grown to become the largest employers and foreign exchange earners in the modern manufacturing sector.

The position of some important new industries, largely established after World War II, will be examined in Chapter 9. They represent an attempt to broaden the industrial structure toward the manufacture of basic intermediate products for which a large domestic market exists. The industries in this group are: phosphate fertilizers, nitrate fertilizers, paper, rubber tires, iron and steel, and automobiles.

The results obtained in the individual industry studies will be used in Chapter 10 for a general evaluation of resource use in manufacturing.

THE COTTON SPINNING AND WEAVING INDUSTRY

Historical Development.

Modern cotton textile manufacture in Egypt dates back to the first decades of the nineteenth century, when Mohammed Ali monopolized weaving and trading in cotton textiles and introduced large-scale cotton spinning.[2] Between 1818 and 1820 a number of cotton spinning mills were set up with European machines, together with bleaching and dyeing establishments. They were not successful, but the introduction of long staple cotton cultivation gave further stimulus to government investment in the industry. By 1833 thirty factories were in operation; at the peak of their activity in the late 1820s, they employed about 30,000 workers. Power was mostly provided by treadmills propelled by mules and buffaloes, although in some cases steam engines were imported. Jennies and looms were largely manufactured domestically, by Egyptian carpenters working under the direction of French technicians.

Appraisals of Mohammed Ali's industrialization ventures differ widely. There are reports of gross inefficiency, to which the centralized administration of the cotton mills probably contributed, but it seems that the industry was able to hold its own in the production of coarse cloth. Nominal protection was virtually nil and imports were, in principle, free (from 1820), but the armed forces provided an assured market and Mohammed Ali had the power to interfere with the importation of goods and to force his subjects to purchase domestic products. Substantial exports of yarn to Europe and of fabrics to Arab areas took place, and Indian muslins were gradually replaced by domestic products.[3] Toward the end of Mohammed Ali's reign, the industry declined. After various military defeats and the treaty of 1838 between the Powers and the Sublime Porte, which effectively removed all trade obstacles (apart from low import and export taxes) by abolishing monopolies, he was no longer able to finance the factories (which were operating at big losses). A large increase in cotton goods imports—mostly of yarn and fine cloth—ensued, and weaving and dyeing of coarse cloth adapted to domestic tastes survived only at the handicraft level, particularly in Upper Egypt.

A second attempt to establish a modern textile industry was made toward the end of the century. A spinning mill with 20,000 spindles was built in Cairo by the Egyptian Cotton Mills Company (founded in 1899), while an integrated mill, the Anglo-Egyptian Spinning and Weaving Company, was built at Alexandria.[4] Both mills had some prospects for success since they oriented their operations toward a large domestic demand for coarse yarns spun from ordinary domestic cotton from Upper Egypt, which was replaced by low-grade Indian and Syrian cotton whenever the former was considered too expensive. Moreover, the mills were protected by relatively high transportation costs and by the 8 percent customs duty applied to all imports. But no sooner had the first factory started operations in 1901 when a countervailing excise tax of 8 percent was imposed, nullifying the external tariff. The excise tax was pushed by Lord Cromer personally in the name of free trade, but probably also under pressure from the Lancashire industry. The fact that the excise tax was not imposed across the board on all import-competing industries (cement, for example) lends force to this argument.[5] Since the cotton mills had to pay duty on all imports—raw cotton as well as coal, dyes, and machinery[6]—they suffered, in effect, a negative "protection." The two companies had great difficulties to show profits and in 1907 the Egyptian Cotton Mills Company had to close down. The Anglo-Egyptian survived somewhat longer, benefiting from a five-year suspension of the excise tax granted by Cromer's successor. Nonetheless, it had to be reorganized by a German group in 1912 as the Filature Nationale d'Egypte. Contemporary observers hint at taxation as the basic difficulty of the industry. But Egypt's cottage industry, too, had difficulties in surviving. A 1909 survey of the weaving industry in Assiout notes that all the cotton yarn used there came from Europe and, in particular, from Lancashire.[7] Cotton spinning seems to have been virtually nonexistent outside the two modern mills. Moreover, hand-weaving "was declining on account of the competition from Europe. The town had only 70 looms while a few years ago it had 300."[8] It is significant that the small town of Akhmin in Upper Egypt was considered to be "the cotton center" because it provided yarn to the surrounding villages for weaving and was the recipient of their cloth.[9]

The industry prospered temporarily when trade was disrupted during World War I,[10] but stagnation returned in the early 1920s (Table 8-2). Thus, the industrial census of 1927 lists only 27,184 people as occupied in the textile industry as a whole, and mostly in fibers other than cotton. Only sixty-four establishments in cotton spinning and weaving had more than ten employees and only two were considered modern.[11] A compilation of factories founded from 1884 to 1951 does not indicate the opening of a single new textile factory during the two decades between 1907 and 1927.[12]

In addition to taxation of the industry, a law was passed in 1916 prohibiting the importation of foreign raw cotton for domestic consumption,

TABLE 8-2

Cotton Consumption by Domestic Spinning Mills and Yarn Imports

(five-year averages)

Period	Cotton Consumption (000 kantars)	Yarn Imports (tons)
1900–04	20.4	—
1905–09	25.8	—
1910–14	26.8	690
1915–19	54.4	—
1920–24	55.8	—
1925–29	55.8	720
1930–34	176.8	600
1935–39	513.4	480
1940–44	868.0	—
1945–49	1171.0	50

SOURCE: *Economic Bulletin,* National Bank of Egypt, 1951, No. 2.

allegedly to protect domestic cotton from foreign plant diseases. Whether this motivation was only a pretext for a protectionist measure or not, it certainly served the interests of the big landlords—the major cotton growers—very well. On the other hand, it dealt a severe blow to the textile industry, the main natural advantage of which lay in satisfying the mass demand for cheap cloth, for which domestic cotton was of too high a quality and hence too expensive. As far back as 1898, Egyptian spinning mills had been importing Indian short staple cotton to produce coarse cloth at competitive prices. The impact of the 1916 measure was fully realized in 1925, when the excise tax on Egyptian cotton manufactures was finally abolished. Unable to compete in the foreign market for coarse products because of high raw material costs, the industry thus became restricted to a protected market, sheltered at first by the general 8 percent tariff and eventually by higher rates when Egypt obtained tariff autonomy in 1930. In the expectation of higher tariffs, the Bank Misr founded a small factory in 1927 that later grew into a giant, with over a quarter of a million spindles: the Misr Spinning and Weaving Company at Mahalla El Kubra. More spectacular at the time, however, was the expansion of the Filature Nationale from 20,000 spindles in 1917 to 60,000 spindles in 1931.

When tariff autonomy was obtained in 1930, Egypt immediately raised the tariff on yarn and cloth from 8 to 12 percent. It was raised again on several occasions, until it reached £E10 per 100 kg. on yarn of lower counts, that is, roughly 30 percent of the import price in 1949. As a result of the tariff measures, production trebled and imports declined (Table 8–2). Value added data do not extend back to the 1930s, but the 1937 census reveals that, second only to the tobacco industry, the textile industry as a whole surpassed all other manufacturing sectors (including food) in terms of value of assets.[13] Bearing in mind differences in capital intensity, it may very well have been the leading manufacturing activity in terms of value added (at the two-digit level) in 1937.

World War II led to a further expansion of the industry, together with an enormous improvement in its financial position. Most companies were able to write off their equipment within a short period of time (six years in the case of the Misr Spinning and Weaving Company), to accumulate large stocks of raw materials and manufactured goods, and to build up their financial reserves substantially.[14] Consequently, the industry was able not only to replace its old equipment completely after the war but also to finance further new investments.[15] Thus, imports of textile machinery rose from 1,100 tons in 1940 to an annual average of 11,500 tons during the period 1946–1950.[16]

Toward the end of the 1940s a number of smaller mills had difficulties in marketing their products, particularly coarse materials. The main reason given was the excessive cost of domestic cotton in the production of coarse yarns.[17] And as the demand from the Allied Forces in Egypt petered out after the war, the industry found itself saddled with excess capacity, protected by relatively high tariffs, but unable to export. The problem raised by the high cost of producing coarse cloth on the basis of high quality domestic cotton was tackled by imposing an export tax in 1948 on all varieties of cotton. In addition, a subsidy was granted in 1949 to help local mills export their surplus production.[18]

To satisfy domestic demand for cheap cotton cloth, large spinning and weaving mills were, in addition, subjected to a system of government-fixed prices on low-grade cloth in 1950.[19] This measure, which became a permanent feature of the Egyptian economy, was one of the first direct, large-scale government interventions in the price mechanism for manufactured products after the war. The subsidy system was suspended in April 1950 on the assumption that the high export tax on raw cotton would provide sufficient protection. Textile exports fell, however, until August, but started rising again under the stimulus of the increasing world demand related to the Korean War.[20]

After the Korean boom, textile exports fell nearly to half the level reached in 1951 and concern was voiced again about the need to stimulate demand for the industry's output. In 1953 two protective measures were taken: customs duties on cotton textiles were increased, and a fund for the "consolidation of the spinning and weaving industry" was created. The fund, financed by export taxes on cotton, was aimed primarily at promoting exports by coordinating the marketing effort abroad, by reorienting production toward the specifications of foreign demand, and by granting subsidies to cotton textile exporters.[21] After the elimination of the export tax on raw cotton at the end of the fifties, the export subsidies for textiles were financed by an excise tax of 2.5 to 5 percent, later increased to 6 percent, on the value of the raw cotton consumed by the spinning mills.

Significantly, voices were now raised once again to the effect that any long-run solution to the problems of the Egyptian cotton textiles industry had to be based on permitting imports of cheap short staple cotton.[22] Although moves in this direction were taken after 1965, as we shall see below, this issue has never been squarely faced by the government. The catastrophic consequences of this on the competitiveness of the industry will be discussed in the next two sections.

Cotton Yarn and Cloth: Production and Trade.

The production of cotton yarn experienced rapid growth between 1950 and 1971, with an average annual rate of 5.5 percent (Chart 8–1). Per capita apparent consumption (production plus imports minus exports) of textiles (cotton, wool, and synthetic fibers) increased by only 0.85 or 1.8 percent annually, depending on whether the prosperous post–World-War II period or the recession years 1952–1953 are taken as a base.[23] Exports of cotton fabrics, which, supported by subsidies, began in 1948 after half a century of import substitution, provided the major stimulus for the growth in production, although the income redistribution that took place in the 1960–1971 period may have also played a role.[24]

The growth of cotton textile exports, particularly of yarn, was mainly due to the opening of a large market in Eastern Europe (Table 8–3). Yarns were exported to Romania as early as 1954, and large exports of fabrics to Eastern European countries began in 1964. Of the roughly 30,000-ton increase in yarn exports from 1957 to 1966, almost 24,000 tons went to bilateral trade

CHART 8–1

Cotton Textiles: Production and Exports, 1948–1971

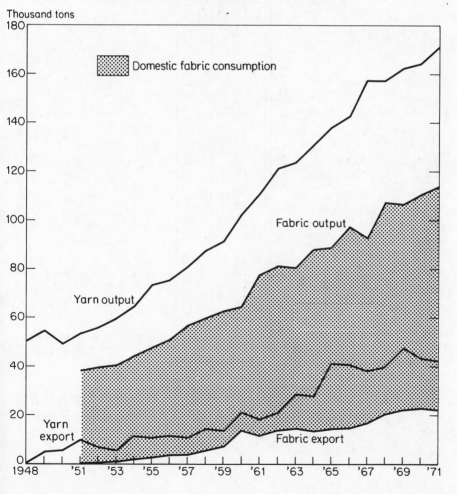

TABLE 8–3
Cotton Textile Exports

Year	Yarn				Cloth			
	Tonnage Exported (000 tons)		Unit Value (£E per ton, f.o.b.)		Tonnage Exported (000 tons)		Unit Value (£E per ton, f.o.b.)	
	Total	Convertible Currencies	OECD Countries[a]	Eastern Europe	Total	Convertible Currencies	OECD Countries[a]	Eastern Europe
1949	4.7	4.7	—	—	—	—	—	—
1950	5.3	5.3	—	—	-0.1	—	—	—
1951	9.8	9.8	—	—	0.1	0.1	—	—
1952	6.6	6.6	—	—	0.5	0.5	—	—
1953	5.4	5.4	—	—	0.6	0.6	837.0	—
1954	11.2	8.3	457.4	—	1.8	1.8	1,005.0	—
1955	10.5	5.4	443.5	—	2.5	2.5	1,429.0	—
1956	11.2	4.3	—	—	3.6	3.6	994.0	—
1957	10.7	6.6	—	—	3.7	3.5	954.0	—
1958	14.2	3.9	—	—	5.1	3.3	863.0	—
1959	13.4	5.3	463.0	—	7.0	6.6	747.0	—

1960	21.0	14.1	472.0	—	13.5	13.2	659.0	—
1961	18.1	12.4	474.0	—	11.5	11.4	637.0	—
1962	20.8	15.8	—	—	13.7	13.7	551.0	—
1963	28.7	15.3	—	—	14.7	14.5	—	—
1964	27.6	14.1	464.7	840.0	13.3	10.6	467.2	—
1965	41.1	15.5	469.2	—	14.5	11.0	499.6	—
1966	40.7	12.8	482.2	914.5	14.6	10.9	536.0	1,018.0
1967	38.0	11.1	473.9	925.1	16.9	11.4	496.4	1,110.0
1968	39.3	14.7	468.1	946.4	20.2	14.2	509.8	1,015.0
1969	47.7	23.3	511.5	1,014.9	22.0	16.0	530.2	1,117.0
1970	43.4	17.5	542.6	1,009.2	22.7	16.2	543.4	1,130.0
1971	42.1	16.7	—	1,015.8	22.4	17.0	—	—

SOURCES: *Monthly Bulletin of Foreign Trade*, CAGMS, Cairo, various issues. For c.i.f. unit values, *Supplement to the World Trade Annual*, Statistical Office of the United Nations, New York, 1968 to 1970 issues.

a. Beginning 1964, c.i.f. for OECD countries.

partners, who accounted for about 48 percent of Egypt's total exports of cotton yarn and fabrics in 1970–71. Moreover, Egypt was also able to double its exports to multilateral partners between 1957 and 1967. The growth rate of exports slackened somewhat after 1965, although a number of new markets, particularly among developing countries, were opened. From 1965 to 1971, exports to multilateral markets fluctuated strongly in response to the business cycles in the developed market economies.

While the volume of textile exports was steadily growing, unit values were at best stagnant, if not falling. In this regard, however, it is essential to distinguish between exports to multilateral and those to bilateral markets. In 1955, the unit values obtained in the two markets were virtually the same, but gradually a relative increase in prices of yarn and cloth exported to bilateral (mainly Eastern European) partners took place, particularly after the Soviet Union became a large-scale importer of Egyptian textiles in the early 1960s. Table 8–3 shows that during the period 1964 to 1970 prices obtained in the Eastern European markets for cotton yarn were almost double those in Western markets. The explanation may be quality differences. Unfortunately, we do not have a country-by-country distribution of yarn exports by count. It is reasonable to assume, however, that the Soviet Union, a major short staple cotton producer, would want to supplement its own coarse yarn production by finer yarns from Egypt, particularly because its lagging production of synthetic fibers compels it to use a relatively large proportion of long staple cotton in its textile industry. Granted that exports to the Eastern European countries are heavily weighted toward high count yarns, the trade statistics still point to artificially high prices for such imports. It seems likely that the bilateral trading arrangements have hiked the nominal Egyptian export prices, and that the real prices obtained are elusive because they depend upon the commodities (including weapons) received in exchange.[25]

Consequently, we shall take the unit values for multilateral yarn exports as representative of world prices. Table 8–3 illustrates that, while average export unit values of yarn in Egyptian currency were stagnant (or rose slightly) from the mid-1950s to 1969—with due adjustment for the 1962 devaluation and the gradual increase in quality[26]—world prices actually fell. This decline in world prices of cotton yarn is consistent with the virtual constancy of the price of short staple cotton—the usual raw material base for coarse yarns—between 1955–56 and 1970–71, with the large productivity increases achieved in major producing countries over the period and the competition from synthetic fibers. Hence, over time, Egypt has been receiving less and less per standardized unit of yarn exported.

We may note that the margin between the value of a ton of Ashmouni cotton (the main raw material used in spinning) and a ton of yarn at international prices is quite narrow, ranging between $250 and $300.[27] When the yarn price is adjusted for cotton wasted in the process of spinning,[28] even this narrow margin vanishes. Thus, the unit values received for cotton exported in the form of yarn (deducting 17 percent for waste) during the years 1964 to 1970 were approximately the same as the unit value obtained for direct exports of the raw cotton (Ashmouni) (see Chart 8–2).[29] In this sense, value added in yarn production, evaluated at international prices, appears to be quite small. This unfortunate circumstance, however, has much to do with the use of medium-long staple cotton, such as Ashmouni, in the production of coarse yarns. We shall return to this problem when the DRCs of the textile industry are discussed.

CHART 8–2

Exports of Raw Cotton and Cotton Textiles, 1950–1972

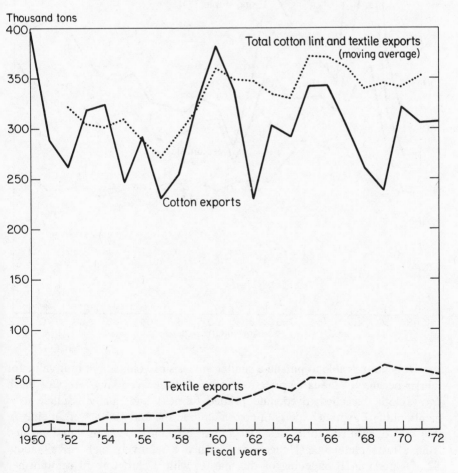

CHART 8–3

Cotton Prices, 1948–1972

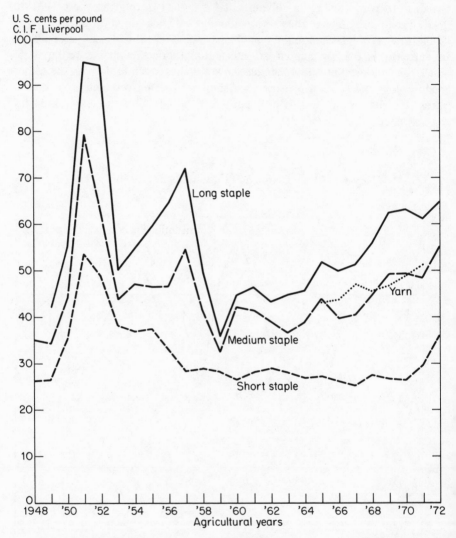

It is not possible to pursue a similar analysis of volume and unit value for fabrics because of the large price differences between various degrees of finish (gray cloth, bleached, dyed, and printed fabrics) and quality. Suffice it to mention that Egyptian exports of cotton cloth in the mid-1950s were mainly in the form of printed fabrics destined for Arab countries, where they benefited from a taste preference. Hence, they fetched a relatively high price—about $2,500 per ton. Broadening of the market with a shift toward semifinished cloth resulted in a gradual decline in unit values to an average of $1,658 in 1968–69: $1,850 in Arab countries, $2,200 in Eastern Europe, and $1,150 in other countries. Note that for fabrics, too, the price obtained in trade with Eastern Europe is remarkably high.

Since 1966 exports of cloth to bilateral trade partners has been stabilized at about 5,500 tons annually; all growth has been in the direction of other trading partners, particularly the Arab countries, North America, and members of the EFTA. But in all these markets, Egyptian textiles face stiff competition, and inability to meet specifications—however temporary—in a rapidly changing pattern of demand easily results in loss of markets. The EEC countries and African countries can be cited as examples.

Within the framework of the GATT Long-Term Agreement on Textiles, a quota of 3,600 tons for cotton cloth exports to the EEC countries in 1970–71 was set for Egypt. A quota set a few years earlier had been increasing by 4 percent annually. By 1969 only two-thirds of the quota was used, and during the following two years Egyptian exports to the EEC region were falling slightly.[30] In the markets opened by the GATT agreement (within the quota limits), lack of competitiveness must have played a part in the Egyptian lag. Also, Egypt has been unable to use up its quota in the United States, but it is not clear to what extent this may be related to the somewhat strained relations between the two countries. In any case, the GATT agreement has not served effectively as a brake on Egyptian textile exports. In this regard Egypt is in a position similar to that of India: lack of competitiveness is the basic obstacle. In Africa, which accounted for most of the exports to non-Arab developing countries, competing printed fabrics with "African" designs from Eastern Europe reduced the Egyptian share of the market substantially in such countries as Nigeria, Niger, Dahomey, and the Ivory Coast.[31]

Costs and Revenues, 1956 to 1969–70.

Evaluation of the competitiveness of the textile industry is always fraught with difficulties related to the diversity of both outputs and material inputs. The increasing integration of spinning and weaving activities makes independent evaluations of these activities more and more problematic, and, finally, the export mix may differ substantially from the general product mix. In Egypt the problems are compounded by the aggregation of cost and revenue data for all plants employing more than ten workers. At best we can obtain a picture of the average performance in the industry, but wide differences among establishments are known to exist in respect to productivity and efficiency; we have not been able to evaluate separately the profitability and competitiveness of those technologically advanced enterprises that specialize in exports and would therefore be particularly interesting from our point of view.

The available data permit us to estimate ERPs and DRCs for the joint production of yarn and cloth in 1956 and 1960, for the production of cloth in 1965–66, and for that of yarn in 1969–70. The 1956 and 1960 data are comparable. Included are establishments with more than fifty workers, primarily engaged in the production of yarn. The establishments processed about half their production of yarn into cloth in 1956 and 44 percent in 1960. For 1969–70, the same types of establishments were studied, but their number was reduced to sixteen through mergers and liquidation, and they all belonged to the public sector. The cost data published for 1969–70 claim to pertain to spinning only, and this, indeed, seems to be the case for the material inputs costs, but not for labor and capital costs. Estimating that 30 percent of labor had been occupied in weaving and other activities related to the production of fabrics, we reduced both wage and capital costs on that crude basis by 30 percent.[32] It follows that the estimates of ERPs and DRCs for 1969–70 are not fully comparable to those for 1956 and 1960, and that the estimates for the 1969–70 year are more shaky than those for the earlier two years.

For 1965–66, the data cover weaving establishments only. They include eighteen large establishments in the public sector and 223 private establishments, most of the latter having fewer than fifty workers.

On the revenue side, the main problem was to find export prices that corresponded to the product mix for the establishments included in the four years. Exported yarns do not differ significantly from those for domestic consumption in regard to degree of finish but usually have higher counts. As already mentioned, f.o.b. unit values for yarn exported to multilateral markets have been used as international prices for yarn, but they had to be adjusted for differences in average counts. Fabric prices vary widely according to degree of finish and quality, and the product mix sold for domestic consumption differs substantially from the export mix. Domestic consumption consists mainly of dyed and printed fabrics, while exports include large quantities of gray cloth in bulk. Exports to Arab countries, however, consist largely of finished fabrics similar to those marketed domestically. Hence, unit values for fabrics sold in the Arab countries may be used as an approximation for the prices that domestically marketed fabrics could obtain in multilateral exports.

It should be emphasized, therefore, that the available data do not permit accurate calculations of ERPs and DRCs; the results presented in Table 8–4 at best indicate broad orders of magnitude. The calculations for this industry are less reliable than those for the industries discussed later.

The Competitiveness of the Cotton Textile Industry.

The immediate impression from Table 8–4 is that of an industry with a low and declining competitiveness. We shall argue, however, that this im-

Rates of Return, ERPs, and DRCs in the Cotton Textile Industry

	Textile Industry				Cotton Cultivation and Spinning as an Integrated Activity		Cotton Cultivation as a Separate Activity	
	Primarily Yarn with Some Fabric		Fabrics	Yarn				
	1956	1960	1965–66	1969–70	1960	1969–70	1960	1969–70
Actual Domestic Raw Cotton Basis:								
Rate of return, percent {at actual domestic prices	12.6	9.0	13.0	20.3	—	—	—	—
{at international prices	4.9	0.9	−15.0	−10.2	—	—	—	—
Effective rate of protection, ERP, percent	31	62	68	213	—	—	—	—
Domestic resource costs, DRC, piasters per U.S. $, at rate of return: 5 percent	38.8	46.9	64.5	70.7	34.2	50.5	—	—
10 percent	46.8	55.9	69.7	85.9	36.6	55.5	—	—
15 percent	54.8	63.9	75.0	101.0	39.0	58.1	—	—
Hypothetical Foreign Raw Cotton Basis:								
Domestic resource costs, DRC, piasters per U.S. $, at rate of return: 10 percent	35.5	37.8	—	54.4	—	—	—	—
Direct Export of Raw Cotton:								
Domestic resource costs, DRC, in cultivation, "normal" returns, piasters per U.S. $: a) average for varieties exported	—	—	—	—	—	—	26.7	35.5
b) average for varieties consumed by textile mills	—	—	—	—	—	—	30.8	45.0
Official exchange rate, piasters per U.S. $	35.2	35.2	43.5	43.5	35.2	43.5	35.2	43.5

SOURCE: B. Hansen and K. Nashashibi, "Protection and Competitiveness in Egyptian Agriculture and Industry," NBER Working Paper No. 48, New York, 1975, Table 18.

pression may be misleading as a guide to the future—provided the government is prepared to permit imports of short staple cotton.

The effective rate of protection was 31 percent in 1956 and increased to 62 percent before the devaluation of 1962.[33] In 1965–66 ERP was 68 percent for fabrics and in 1969–70 213 percent for yarn. Since changes in foreign prices and productivity were relatively small between these two years, it seems clear that effective protection was much higher for yarn than for fabrics, a phenomenon that is closely related to the relatively high prices obtained for Egyptian fabrics in Arab countries. It also seems clear that a product mix similar to that underlying the ERPs for 1956 and 1960 must have enjoyed a much higher degree of effective protection after the devaluation than before.

Domestic resource costs show a similar picture. At 10 percent return to capital, DRC in 1956 was already considerably higher than the official exchange rate, 46.8 piasters for the U.S. dollar against 35.2 piasters, and in 1960 it increased to 55.9 piasters (but see footnote 33). The DRC for fabrics in 1965–66 was 69.7 piasters, and for yarn in 1969–70, 85.9 piasters. For a comparable product mix it would seem that the DRC had increased from about 55 piasters before the devaluation of 1962 to around 80 piasters in the mid-sixties. While the official devaluation in 1962 amounted to 24 percent and the effective devaluation was lower, DRC increased by 40 to 50 percent. The industry was, thus, far from competitive, even at the "realistic" rate of 61 piasters, suggested by the IMF in 1966, and its competitiveness shows deterioration.

This gloomy picture of the leading Egyptian manufacturing industry rests, of course, on the assumption that the raw material basis of the industry is domestic cotton. We have already pointed out that the competitiveness of the industry is impaired by the ban on cotton imports: the industry is forced to use expensive, high-quality cotton for producing coarse qualities of yarn and fabrics that could equally well be made with cheaper, low-quality cotton such as American Middling 15/16 or Indian cotton. To quantify the impact of this trade restriction, we include in Table 8–4 DRCs calculated on the assumption of a shift in the raw material base to foreign cotton purchased at international prices about 20 percent below those of the Egyptian varieties actually used. The improvement in the competitive position is striking: DRC in 1956 would have been about the same as the official exchange rate at that time, and only slightly higher in 1960. In 1969–70, DRC for yarn would have been considerably higher than the official exchange rate (54.4 piasters against 43.5) but considerably lower than the "realistic' rate of 61 piasters.

We note that not only would the level of the DRCs be much lower if production were based on imported cotton, but also their increase during the sixties would have been lower—44 percent against the actual increase of 54 percent. This is related to the fact that long-staple prices increased in relation to short-staple prices during the sixties, which by itself makes the substitution of short for long-staple cotton as an input more attractive. But this price trend may be reversed in the future.

It should be added that our calculations at this point are particularly crude and that they do not take into account the possible external costs that originally were the motivation (or pretext) for the ban on foreign cotton, i.e., the risk of importing new plant diseases. We are not in a position to judge how serious that risk really is, and we do not want to belittle the problem. However, the fact that the government has permitted some importation of cheap Indian and Chinese cotton as well as low-grade yarn in recent years shows a growing awareness of the possible gains from such a policy and perhaps also indicates that the risks may have been exaggerated.

If the textile industry were to base its production on foreign cotton, the domestic cotton now consumed by the industry at home would have to be exported. On that basis, in 1960 the industry would have been producing at a DRC of 37.8 piasters, with the replaced cotton produced at a DRC of 30.8 piasters (Table 8–4, col. 7); a devaluation of less than 10 percent would have sufficed to make the textile industry competitive. For 1969–70 the corresponding DRCs were 54.4 and 45.0 piasters. Even the replaced cotton would here require a slight devaluation (beyond that of 1962) to be competitive, but both textiles and replaced cotton would be highly competitive at the realistic rate of 61 piasters.

Table 8–4, finally, contains an estimate of the DRCs for cotton cultivation and spinning considered as an integrated activity. One reason for making this calculation is that there are great difficulties in gauging the international price for the low grade, medium staple varieties actually consumed by the textile industry. Were Egypt faced with a downward-sloping foreign demand curve for cotton lint, an attempt to export the cotton now used by the textile mills would result in a marginal revenue correspondingly lower than its current export price. In that case there might be an advantage in selling it in the form of textiles, if demand is more elastic for the latter than for the former. In treating cultivation and spinning as an integrated activity, we sidestep the problem of the international price of cotton. The DRCs thus obtained fall, as they should, in between the DRCs for the industry and cotton cultivation considered as separate activities. For 1960 (at a 10 percent return), the DRC was 36.6 piasters for the integrated activity and 55.9 and 30.8 piasters, respectively, for the independent activities. Hence, the integrated activity was almost competitive at the official rate.

In Table 8–5 we present the implicit tariff rates for cotton yarn, dyed and printed fabrics, and rayon yarn, calculated as the percentage difference between actual domestic and international prices. They show the nominal protection and, at the same time, give an impression of the government's domestic price policy for textiles.

TABLE 8–5

Implicit Tariff Rates for Textiles

(percent)

Commodity	1956	1960	1965–66
Cotton yarn	7.5	20.6	39.3
Dyed and printed cotton fabrics	12.2	13.0	48.5
Rayon yarn	18.2	19.8	80.2

SOURCE: Hansen and Nashashibi, NBER Working Paper No. 48, New York, 1975.

In 1956 the implicit tariff rates were quite low; at that time protection was largely provided through the export taxes on cotton. By 1960 the level of implicit tariff rates was on the rise, despite the abolition or reduction of export taxes on various varieties of cotton. By 1965–66 a very substantial increase in nominal protection had taken place, the implicit tariff rate having doubled for yarn, more than trebled for fabrics, and quadrupled for rayon yarn. This development is also reflected in the official wholesale price index, which shows a rise in the textiles subindex of 4 percent from 1955 to 1960 and of another 24 percent from 1960 to 1965. The domestic price rise was strong enough to permit an increase in the actual rate of return on capital for the industry from 12.6 percent in 1956 to 13.0 percent in 1965–66 and 20.3 percent in 1969–70 (Table 8–4).

Productivity Developments.

A look at productivity trends may throw some light on the causes which may have led to the declining competitiveness of Egypt's cotton textile industry. During the last two decades, productivity in textile manufacturing has increased rapidly throughout the world. Apart from technological developments, which have heightened the speed of ring spinning frames and looms and integrated a number of functions,[34] productivity has increased in many countries as a result of rationalizing the industry by scrapping old plants and replacing them with modern ones. Moreover, the high capital intensity associated with the new technology has meant a much higher rate of plant utilization and hence a shorter lifetime.[35] Consequently, technical innovations embodied in new equipment have been disseminated rapidly in developed Western countries and Japan, with per capita output more than doubled in the last fifteen years and operating costs drastically reduced.[36] The labor-saving innovations (such as the shuttle-less loom) may not have been to the advantage of developing countries, but they certainly improved the competitiveness of the developed countries.

In Table 8–6 we have attempted to illuminate productivity developments for labor and capital in the cotton spinning and weaving industries of Egypt. Ideally, capital productivity should be measured by output per hour of operating machines (rings). This information is not available, and since output per spindle-hour is available only as the product of capacity utilization and number of spindles installed, we prefer to simply reproduce these series. Capacity utilization in spinning has been quite high and, if the data are reliable, it exceeds that of most countries surveyed by GATT.[37] During the 1950s capacity expanded steadily, with the number of spindles doubling from 1953 to 1960 at a high rate of utilization. During the first five-year plan (1960–61 to 1964–65) and up to 1967, the industry seems to have been somewhat neglected. Capacity utilization rose to the upper limits of feasibility—in 1967 it must have actually hit the ceiling. This very high degree of capacity utilization was detrimental to efficiency, partly because obsolete machinery had to be put into operation. After 1967 a large increase in the number of spindles helped to improve the situation.

A comparison of capacity utilization and output per spindle installed indicates the impact of the introduction of new high-speed machinery. From 1966 to 1969–70, capacity utilization fell by 7 percent while output per spindle installed rose by 5 percent. This development is consistent with the increase in capital per employee.[38]

Such a development, however, implies that the industry has failed to adjust its labor requirement to the new level of machinery performance. Actually, there is evidence of substantial overstaffing, particularly during the 1960s. While labor productivity rose rapidly from 1956 to 1960, the increase seems to have been quite slow from 1960 to 1969–70. Shortcomings in the data may be partly responsible for these results, but generally the situation is similar to that in other industries with respect to overstaffing. In measuring labor productivity, the long-term trend toward production of finer yarn has not been taken into account, a circumstance that might explain the apparent slowdown of productivity growth.[39] However, in an interview with one of the authors, a high official in the Ministry of the Economy affirmed that the industry had an excess of workers amounting to 20 percent of its labor force, a situation that could not be remedied because of the resulting unemployment with all its related problems. It has been suggested publicly that wages and salaries of excess workers be shown separately in the accounts of an enterprise to reveal its true performance and possibly entitle it to compensation.

With respect to weaving, productivity trends are much more difficult to measure because of the large variety of products with different degrees of finish and quality. Measured simply as output in tons per loom installed, productivity growth has been rapid, well above that in spinning. To some extent the increase in output per loom installed was due to higher capacity utilization.

TABLE 8-6

Productivity Indicators in Egyptian Cotton Spinning and Weaving

Year	Spindles Installed (000)	Capacity Utilization (%)[a]	Output per Spindle Installed (kgs.)	Output per Man-Hour (kgs.)[b]	Capital per Employee (£E)[b]	Average Yarn Count (English)
			Spinning			
1953	593	80.8	100.1	—	—	17.7
1956	768	—	97.6	0.722	223.3	18.8
1958	1,054	—	82.6	0.754	195.7	21.2
1960	1,185	83.1	86.1	0.820	202.0	21.2
1964	1,366	90.1	93.3	—	—	23.3
1965	1,416	96.5	96.4	—	—	23.7
1966	1,477	97.0	95.0	—	—	23.7
1967	1,484	99.8	104.9	—	—	24.2
1968–69	1,545	96.9	102.0	0.841	289.2	24.6
1969–70	1,614	90.3	100.6	0.862	313.5	24.9
1971	1,762	—	97.0	—	—	25.1

TABLE 8-6 (concluded)

Year	Looms Installed (000)	Capacity Utilization (%)[a]	Output per Loom Installed (tons)	Output per Employee (000 meters)[b]	Capital per Employee (£E)[b]
		Weaving			
1953	13.7	—	1.99	—	—
1956	17.2	—	2.93	6.49	104.4
1958	19.5	—	3.20	8.97	113.0
1960	21.7	70.0	2.96	9.12	—
1964	22.8	82.0	3.85	—	—
1965	24.8	79.5	3.58	—	—
1966	25.2	81.1	3.85	12.30	231.4
1967	25.5	87.6	3.63	—	—
1968–69	25.6	—	4.06	—	—
1969–70	27.2	—	3.97	—	—
1971	29.1[c]	—	3.90	—	—

SOURCES: Rows 1, 3, 6, 7, 8, and 9: Federation of Industries, *Yearbook*, several issues, and GATT COT/W/115, Add. 1, Table III–1; rows 4 and 5: *The Cotton Spinning Industry*, CAGMS, March 1970; rows 10 and 11: *The Cotton Weaving Industry*, CAGMS, March 1968.

a. Defined as actual weight of yarn and cloth, respectively, produced in 24 hours compared to the maximum weight of yarn and cloth which could be produced. For yarn this maximum appears to be on the order of 7890 hours per spindle per year.

b. Capital is defined as the machinery in operation evaluated at historical costs.

c. In addition, there are some 22,242 hand looms spread over villages and workshops.

This certainly was the case between 1960 and 1967. But, the rise in the proportion of automatic looms (from 53 percent in 1960 to 59 percent in 1967) must also have contributed to raising output per employee and output per loom. The higher level of mechanization is evidenced by the sharp increase in the capital-labor ratio.

Public versus Private Sector.

For the weaving industry some interesting information is available that may throw some light on the retardation of productivity growth that characterized the 1960s. Data on the structure of ownership show that about 30 percent of all mechanical looms (automatic and nonautomatic) in 1971 were owned privately, mostly by 177 smaller establishments with fewer than fifty workers. At the same time, some of those with over fifty workers—representing slightly less than one-fourth of the private firms—are quite large. To be sure, the larger private establishments are tied to the public firms by permanent contracts and operate under tight supervision and with fixed prices. Comparative data for public and private enterprises have been published on the distribution of equipment, labor, and inventories in the weaving industry for the year 1965–66. Unfortunately, no information is available on the distribution of output and value of production in the two sectors. Nevertheless, the data shown in Table 8–7 suffice to reveal interesting differences between the two sectors and to give some insight into the operations of the public firms. The distribution of equipment is included mainly for descriptive purposes; we have no way of knowing which technique is optimal, given the type of cloth to be produced, levels of wages and skills, and capital costs. If the prevailing institutional constraints mean constant overstaffing in the public sector, then, it could be argued, the lower the proportion of automatic looms the better!

The breakdown of employees shows a much higher proportion of operatives in the private firms than in the public sector, which seems to be saddled with an army of administrators and service employees. Although the higher degree of mechanization in the public sector, with a higher proportion of automatic looms, may require more maintenance work, this still does not account for the large difference observed.

Finally, average monthly wages in the public sector are double those in the private sector, where the average yearly man-hours are greater. This may be justified, to some extent, by the greater skills necessary for the technological sophistication of the public sector but, again, the large difference between the two suggests higher compensation of labor in the public sector.

Inventories in the public sector were enormous: finished and semifinished goods accounted for 30 percent of total annual output in the industry. This

TABLE 8–7

Public versus Private Sectors in the Cotton Weaving Industry, 1965–66

	Public	Private
Structure of Equipment		
Hand looms	22	4,930
Mechanical looms	3,143	4,550
Automatic looms	13,157	1,153
Total	16,322	10,633
Labor		
Number of employees	36,038	10,813
Percentage of employees		
Operatives	62.1	80.7
Service employees (maintenance)	27.5 ⎫ 37.0	14.1 ⎫ 16.5
Administrators	9.5 ⎭	2.4 ⎭
Owners, directors, and experts	0.8	2.8
Average man-hour per employee per year	1,842	2,170
Average monthly wage (£E)	20.79	9.07
Fringe benefits (£E)	0.98	0.14
Inventories (000 £E)		
Finished goods	15,529.6	117.9
Semifinished goods	12,861.1	4.4
Raw materials	7,586.8	134.9
Total	35,977.4	257.2
As percentage of total fixed assets	67.3	14.5

SOURCE: *The Cotton Weaving Industry*, CAGMS, March 1968.

fact is consistent with the general inventory growth in public firms noted for 1965–66 in the follow-up and appraisal of the first five-year plan. It is true that for weaving this occurred in a period of slack demand (see Chapter 5), and private subcontractors simply had to execute orders and deliver goods to the public sector without bearing any responsibility for the marketing. Nevertheless, it reflects a failure in adjusting supply to demand: it should not be forgotten that demand was cut back deliberately to stop overheating the economy and the pressures on the balance of payments, and, under such circumstances, public enterprises should not keep production going at all cost.

To sum up, in the weaving industry, the effects of nationalization have not been beneficial, and have probably been detrimental, to productivity and general efficiency.

THE SUGAR INDUSTRY

The modern sugar industry in Egypt dates back to the last century. The collapse of cotton prices after the cotton famine of the 1860s prompted the Khedive Ismail to look for other commercial crops for the khedival domains. Cane cultivation appeared to be an appropriate alternative, since it was particularly well suited to the soil and irrigation of Upper Egypt. Under the basin irrigation system prevalent there at that time, only one (winter) crop could be planted, and where perennial irrigation existed, cotton yields were generally lower than in the North, all of which made cane cultivation attractive. However, winter temperatures in Upper Egypt are too low for the use of common high-yielding cane varieties. Hence, the sugar yield in Egypt is usually lower than that in the major growing countries.[40] Directed and financed (via foreign loans) by the Khedive, cane cultivation was expanded and a number of sugar factories were established in Upper Egypt. It was a very large investment at the time—£E6 million. When the Khedive went bankrupt and was deposed, the factories were taken over by Egyptian and French capitalists.[41]

Up to 1880 only raw or brown sugar was produced locally, and it had to be exported to Marseilles for refining. In 1881 a Franco-Belgian company built a refinery at Hawamdieh, near Cairo—the largest of its kind in the world at that time—the capacity of which exceeded local production of raw sugar and thus required imports from abroad. In 1892 it merged with the company that had taken over the sugar factories originally built by the Khedive, and in this form maintained a private monopoly on sugar production until 1961.

In 1905 the sugar company went bankrupt as a result of low prices and the absence of any kind of protection. The industry was reorganized on a smaller scale to be able to compete with imports of refined sugar; by 1910 cane acreage was reduced to 40,000 feddan from a maximum of 88,000 feddan in 1901–1902. During World War I, with sugar imports difficult to secure, the industry was revitalized, but it was threatened again during the Depression, when prices of sugar from Cuba and Java reached a low point. Consequently, the government intervened in February 1931, imposing (variable) import duties on sugar at a level sufficient to shelter domestic production. The government was also authorized to fix the sugar cane acreage, the prices to be paid by the company to cultivators, the quota of raw sugar to be imported for refining, the quantity to be exported, and, finally, the price at which the refined sugar was to be sold to consumers. "The price was to be such that after making allowance for reserves and excise duty a minimum dividend of 5 percent was guaranteed to shareholders and bondholders. Any surplus profits were to revert in part to the government on a progressive scale."[42] Ever since that time, the government has maintained its support of and close control over the sugar industry. In 1956 it was "Egyptianized" and in 1961, of course, it was nationalized.

Within the framework of the first five-year plan (1959–60 to 1964–65) and the projected expansion of cane cultivation related to the construction of the Aswan High Dam, a new government-owned sugar company was formed to undertake the construction of a factory at Edfu. Four more factories were constructed later and the old refinery at Hawamdieh was expanded. The industry branched into the production of cane and sugar derivatives—paper pulp, grain board, vinegar, acetic acid, dry yeast, and cosmetics. Altogether, £E48 million were invested in the sugar-based industry during the 1960s.

Sugar Production and Trade.

The development of raw sugar production from 1939 to 1971 is depicted in Chart 8–4. Its fluctuations depend essentially on cane area planted and yield per acre.[43] The area planted is constrained by the water supply; cane requires three times more water per acre than such alternative crops as cotton or wheat. The sugar output series (with a one-year lag) is correlated with the annual discharge of the Nile at Aswan.[44]

For almost four decades, from 1931, when sugar began receiving protection, until 1968, the sugar cane area remained roughly constant, fluctuating between 80,000 and 100,000 feddan. The government attempted to maintain the area within this range via the price mechanisms, increasing the price of cane as costs of production rose.

A significant expansion of output occurred between 1952 and 1955, which requires some explanation. Until the fall of 1952, sugar was rationed both for consumer and industrial use. The government maintained a foreign trade monopoly by imposing virtually prohibitive tariffs and taxes (exceeding 200 percent) on privately imported sugar.[45] In September 1952 it liberalized the consumption of sugar, setting a free market price that exceeded that of rationed sugar by some 50 percent. There was no incentive for domestic supply to meet the increase in demand, with prices remaining unchanged. Alarmed by the sharp rise in imports, the government increased producer prices in 1953, and the cane area was expanded by 12 percent.[46]

More significant, however, was an increase in yield by 20 percent. This was partly due to the application of more labor and greater care for the crop made possible by the higher prices. Over the whole period from 1952 onward, most progress was realized after the cane was cut; greater efficiency in sugar extraction in the factories and a shorter time span between harvesting and cane crushing had much to do with this phenomenon. A more accurate assessment of cane maturity and the treatment of cane seeds with hot water, increas-

CHART 8-4

Sugar: Production and Consumption, 1939–1971

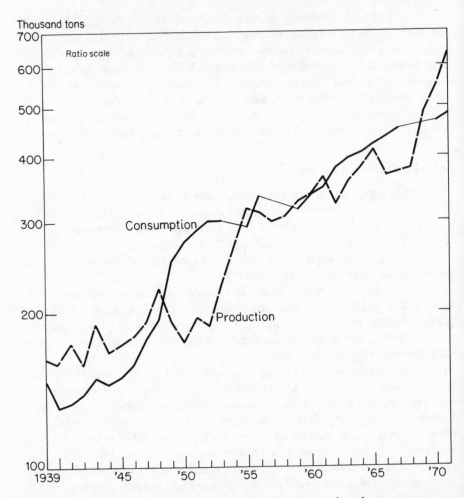

ing resistance against viruses, also contributed to increasing the average sugar content of cane from 9.29 percent in 1954 to 10.18 percent in 1960 and 11.33 percent in 1969. The completion of the Aswan Dam enabled the sugar cane area to expand in 1969 and 1970 to almost 130,000 feddan without a fall in yield.

The government's foreign trade policy in regard to sugar served two purposes: it stabilized consumption and occasionally earned foreign exchange. Fluctuations in the production of refined sugar were offset by imports of raw sugar in case of a shortfall in domestic output or by exports of refined sugar in case of overproduction. In general, imports and exports occurred at the same time, with imports consisting in raw sugar and exports, in refined sugar. The latter was sold at a premium abroad, particularly to other Arab countries, where it is in strong demand because of its higher level of sweetness than that of other sugar varieties available in the world market. This fact also explains the normally higher unit values for exports than for imports of refined sugar (Table 8–8).[47] Imported sugar was mixed (after refining) with domestic varieties and used for local consumption.

Because of the water constraint on supply and a rising population and consumption, Egypt gradually shifted its position during the fifties and sixties from net exporter of sugar to that of net importer (Chart 8–4). By 1966 net imports had reached 137,000 tons, or 24 percent of domestic consumption. However, with water supply increased as a consequence of the High Dam, sugar production rose 73 percent from 1966 to 1971, utilizing the new refining capacity created since 1964 and once again turning Egypt into a net exporter.

Sugar Prices and Costs of Production.

Prices in the world sugar market are characterized by strong fluctuations. Unless some long-term price is defined, at least within a certain range, profitability calculations, particularly for planning purposes, become intractable. Fortunately, the fluctuations shown in Table 8–8 seem to follow a cyclical pattern around a constant level. Starting in 1954, an upward movement of raw sugar prices can be discerned, with a peak in 1957. A trough occurs in 1961, with a new peak in 1963, and so on. The first two cycles are roughly of a six-year duration, although the cycle beginning in 1967 seems somewhat longer with what appears to be a peak in 1973. The average price was 3.58 U.S. cents per pound for 1955–1960, 4.03 U.S. cents for 1961–1966, and 3.76 U.S. cents for the period 1967–1972. These averages are quite similar and enable us to define a long-term price over the past eighteen years in the range of 3.5 to 4.0 U.S. cents per pound.

For purposes of profitability calculations, we chose an average of three cycle averages—3.79 U.S. cents per pound—as the world price to be measured against domestic costs of sugar production for both 1960 and 1970, the two years for which detailed information about domestic costs in processing is available. This price corresponds to £E36.73 and £E45.87 per ton, c.i.f. Alexandria, at the official rates prevailing before and after the 1962 devaluation.[48] Adding an average refining margin of $18.03 per ton,[49] we obtain the "long term" c.i.f. import prices for refined sugar of £E42.19 and £E52.00, respectively, before and after 1962. We also calculated "short term" world prices—three-year averages—confronting the industry around 1960 and 1970. These short-term world prices are £E37.45 for 1960 and £E53.12 in 1970.

TABLE 8–8
Price Series for Raw and Refined Sugar

Year	Raw Sugar				Refined Sugar		
	Price at Caribbean Ports (f.o.b., U.S. cents per lb.) (1)	Hypothetical Long-Term Import Price (c.i.f., £E per ton)[a] (2)	Import Unit Value (c.i.f., £E per ton) (3)	Domestic Unit Value (£E per ton) (4)	Hypothetical Long-Term Import Price (c.i.f., £E per ton)[b] (5)	Import Unit Value (c.i.f., £E per ton) (6)	Export Unit Value (f.o.b., £E per ton) (7)
1954	3.26	—	—[c]	—[d]	—	—[c]	—[d]
1955	3.24		—[c]	28.95		42.15	39.20
1956	3.48		—[c]	31.31		44.32	39.19
1957	5.15	34.44	38.78	30.76	44.79	56.40	—[d]
1958	3.50		33.97	30.75		41.09	44.19
1959	2.97		33.31	31.95		—[c]	30.04
1960	3.17		26.85	32.63		34.20	34.46
1961	2.91		29.89	32.21		34.15	35.62
1962	2.98		25.26	—[d]		32.49	31.54
1963	8.50	46.84	88.56	—[d]	54.68	74.75	50.99
1964	5.87		80.20	—[d]		170.27	107.52
1965	2.11		79.86	—[d]		83.09	38.58
1966	1.86		42.69	—[d]		43.49	39.14

Year						
1967	1.99	26.25	—a		32.02	39.12
1968	1.98	38.55	—a		32.35	35.17
1969	3.37	—c	37.06		29.57	33.14
1970	3.71	—c	—a		27.62	45.87
1971	4.49	—c	—a		—c	59.02
1972	7.04	—d	—a		—d	—d

Braces: 44.28; 52.12

SOURCES: Col. (1): FAO, *Production Yearbook*, various issues, and *Monthly Bulletin of Agricultural Economics and Statistics*, various issues; col. (3): Federation of Industries, *Yearbook*, various issues; col. (4): CAGMS, *The Sugar Industry*, May 1963 and, for 1969, *Industrial Statistics by Commodity, 1969*; cols. (6) and (7): Federation of Industries, *Yearbook*, various issues.

a. Average unit value over corresponding years in col. 1 *plus* freight margin at $18.90 per ton converted at official rates of exchange.
b. Plus refining margins of $18.03 per ton.
c. No imports.
d. Not available.

Unlike the long-term world price, which has shown no clear trend over the cycles during this period, domestic costs of sugar production in Egypt have tended to rise both for cane cultivation and for processing. Since cane has no international price, we have treated the sugar industry as an integrated activity from cane cultivation to sugar refining.

Cost of Land, Capital, and Depreciation.

The competitiveness of the integrated sugar industry, from cane cultivation to refining, is gauged on the basis of effective rates of protection and domestic resource costs per U.S. dollar. In calculating the DRCs, certain problems arise in connection with costs of land and capital services that are worth noting.

To make comparisons among alternative uses of land, rents must be evaluated as if they were not subject to control (see Chapter 7, p. 196). In Chapter 7 the assumption was made that, without controls, rents would have increased in proportion to output value since 1949. On that basis, the imputed rent for cane in 1961 was calculated to be £E32.78 per feddan, compared with the official average maximum rent of £E24.28, and on the same grounds the imputed rent should be about £E32.00 for 1960. In 1967, the last year for which cost data are available, average official rent for cane land was £E23.00, that is, slightly lower than in 1960,[50] and, in line with the policy of keeping land rentals unchanged, must have remained at about that level till 1970, when actual (official) rent per feddan may be assumed to have been £E24.00. The assumption that market rents follow output value cannot be upheld for such long periods, however, for in the long run rents do not fully rise in proportion to agricultural value added. Total agricultural value added increased by 85 percent from 1960–61 to 1969–70. Assuming the share of rents to run along its historical trend,[51] we could expect an increase in rent by about 60 percent over the same period in the absence of controls. On that basis, we are working with an imputed rent of £E51.00 per feddan for 1970. Summarizing, we thus assume:

	1960	1970
Average actual (official) rent per feddan (£E)	23.85	24.00
Imputed market rent per feddan (£E)	32.00	51.00

In regard to returns to management and capital, the problem is to choose "normal" returns for both 1960 and 1970. In the processing stage we work alternatively, as elsewhere, with 5, 10, and 15 percent on capital invested. For 1960 cultivation we use Chapter 7's assumption of a "normal" return of

£E12.00 per feddan per year, and for 1970 we assume, somewhat arbitrarily, a rise to £E18.00 per feddan per year. It must be emphasized that this assumption implies some double counting because plowing and other operations are often carried out with the assistance of factory-owned equipment that is counted as capital in the processing stage.

The evaluation of the industry's fixed assets consists in adjusting the highly understated investment at historical cost for 1960 and adding to it the value of the fixed assets created between 1960 and 1970 (which actually went into production), yielding capital figures of £E22.3 million and £E56.6 million for 1960 and 1970, respectively. We suspect that these estimates understate the value of the industry's capital at replacement cost and hence should be viewed with caution.

Depreciation charges, also estimated for 1970 on the order of £E5 million, substantially exceeded the actual capital replacement funds appropriated by the Ministry of Industry to the sugar industry. In this respect it is interesting to note that, while the Ministry of Industry was expanding the capacity of the sugar industry by the addition of new plants in the second half of the 1960s, it was seriously neglecting the capital replacement and modernization needs of the industry's older factories.

Appropriations actually disbursed by the Ministry of Industry to the sugar sector (including paper pulp and all sugar derivative industries) for capital replacement were as follows:

	Domestic Currency (000 £E)	Foreign Currency (000 £E)	Total (000 £E)
1967–68	0	0	0
1968–69	384	0	384
1969–70	548	221	769
1970–71	70	0	70
1971–72	150	322	473
1973	50	381	431

In none of the years shown did the actual allocation even approach our estimated requirement. The 1967 war eliminated replacements altogether for 1967–68, and significant appropriation in foreign exchange only occurred after 1969. Moreover, while roughly two-thirds of depreciation charges should be allocated to imported replacement equipment (since the import content of depreciation expenditures is equivalent to two-thirds) and hence requires foreign exchange, only one-third of the appropriations was made in foreign exchange. The impression is clearly conveyed that capital replacement commands a low priority in the Ministry of Industry's overall exchange allocations and hence is subject to the vagaries of foreign exchange availability after the requirements for current production and new investments have been met. Comparable information obtained on other sectors of production (see Chapter 10) suggests that the treatment of capital replacement in the sugar industry may be quite typical.

The Competitiveness of the Integrated Sugar Industry, 1960 and 1970.

Considering first the long-term position, Table 8–9 shows some negative protection (−5 percent) for 1960, but positive protection (14 percent) for 1970. The ERPs estimated in Chapter 7, Table 7–1 on the basis of current prices for the years 1961, 1963, and 1964 average out at −19.6 percent.

At a 10 percent return to capital in the industry, the 1960 DRC was 34.1 piasters per U.S. dollar against the official exchange rate of 35.2. The average for 1961, 1963, and 1964 (Table 7–1) was 40.0 piasters. Our calculations, however, as already emphasized, may contain some double counting of resource costs. Disregarding capital costs in cultivation completely (which, on the other hand, means an underestimation of total capital costs), the DRC in 1960 was considerably lower than the official exchange rate (at a 10 percent return), and may have been lower even at a 15 percent return. We can conclude that the sugar industry was competitive in the long term at the official exchange rate before the devaluation of 1962.

In 1970, at 10 percent return, the DRC had increased to 53.6 piasters per U.S. dollar. The official rate was then 43.5, and thus sugar was no longer competitive in the long term at the official rate, even when allowance is made for some double counting of resource costs. It was the sharp rise in wage costs that was largely responsible for the deterioration of the competitive position of sugar. While both total (imputed) land rent and capital costs increased by 130 percent from 1960 to 1970, total wage costs rose by 217 percent. The relatively strong wage increase is related to the rural location of the sugar factories. Rural wages increased much more than urban industrial wages during the 1960s.

Thus, the industry was in good shape in 1960. From a long-term point of view, it was competitive at the official exchange rate. Without the inflation and wage increases, the heavy investments made in the industry during the 1960s would have been fully justified at the exchange rate in effect after the devaluation of 1962. We note also that at the exchange rate of 61 piasters per U.S. dollar the industry would, ceteris paribus, have been highly competitive in the long term in 1970, despite the wage increases.

The position in the short term was different. On the basis of the three-year averages of the world prices for refined sugar, the ERP was 17.4 percent in 1960 and slightly lower, at 12.2 percent, in 1970. In Chapter 7 we found an ERP of 37 percent for 1961 (Table 7–1), when the international price

TABLE 8–9

ERPs and DRCs in the Integrated Sugar Industry

Year	ERP (%)	DRC			Official Exchange Rate (piasters per U.S. $)
		At 5% Rate of Return (%)	At 10% Rate of Return (%)	At 15% Rate of Return (%)	
1960					
At long-term average price of refined sugar	−4.7	30.4	34.1	37.7	35.2
At three-year average price of refined sugar	17.4	36.6	40.9	45.3	35.2
1970					
At long-term average price of refined sugar	14.0	48.4	53.6	58.8	43.5
At three-year average price of refined sugar	12.2	47.0	52.1	57.2	43.5

SOURCE: Hansen and Nashashibi, NBER Working Paper No. 48, New York, 1975, Table 19.

was somewhat lower. The DRC (at a 10 percent return) was 40.9 piasters per U.S. dollar in 1960, and sugar was clearly noncompetitive at the actually ruling exchange rate. In Chapter 7 (Table 7–1) the DRC for 1961 was found to be 60 piasters. It should be emphasized, however, that the short-term non-competitiveness in 1960, according to this calculation, does not justify shifting away from sugar, even from a short-term point of view. For in the short term, the opportunity costs of capital in processing are zero, and at a 0 percent rate of return, the short-term DRC would have been much lower than the official exchange rate. By 1970, despite a substantial increase in the short-term international price, the DRCs increased, too, and a slight deterioration occurred in the industry's competitive position (relative to the new exchange rate) compared to 1960.

Domestic sugar prices lagged behind the uptrend in short-term international prices between 1960 and 1970. Most of the domestic price increase to the consumer took the form of higher excise taxes. Consequently, the industry incurred consecutive losses during that period, averaging £E2 million per year. In 1970–71 the industry disbursed £E43.6 million to the Treasury in various excise taxes. Since it also received a number of "compensation" payments, its net contribution was somewhat lower. Hence the industry's consecutive losses should have little meaning as an allocative criteria. On the other hand, by reducing the capital reserves available to it, they have certainly hampered the company's capital replacement program.[52]

Here again we run into the problem of centrally prescribed prices and the distortive effects they have on the distribution of production and, indirectly, of investments. To take the sugar industry as an example, the ex-factory price has hardly been changed in twenty years, while the costs of all inputs have naturally risen. In addition, the retail sale of sugar operates on two price levels: a free market price and a lower price for rationed sugar. Consequently, the sugar industry is paying four different excise taxes and sales taxes to the Treasury and is receiving five kinds of subsidies.[53] The net result is that the sugar industry is incurring losses on its sugar operations but making profits on the sugar derivatives. A similar situation prevails in the case of steel, textiles, and paper, among others.

In view of the important role of rising wage costs in the deterioration of competitiveness, it would be important to evaluate labor productivity and its development in the factories during this period, but attempts in this direction have been frustrating. Scanty reliable information on employment is available other than the total number of workers employed in 1960 and 1970, and it is not clear what categories of seasonal labor are included. Moreover, it is uncertain to what extent the shorter working hours in industry after 1961 were applied to this rural industry, with its 150-day working season. Assuming shorter hours worked and comparability of data for the two years involved, labor productivity measured by tons of sugar per man-year (the number of workers employed in a year) increased by 37 percent from 1960 to 1970, compared with an increase of only 17 percent with an assumption of unchanged hours. In any case, the growth in productivity was small relative to the rise in wage rates.

Sugar versus Other Crops.

Even if it were competitive in the long run at the official rate, sugar does not necessarily have a comparative advantage vis-à-vis crops that could alternatively be grown on the same land. Actually, these might conceivably be more competitive. This is the problem we are examining in the following pages.

In Chapter 7 (see Chart 7–11) an ambitious attempt was made to predict the optimal cane acreage for the years 1962 to 1968. The optimum was defined as the hypothetical long-term response of cane cultivators to current international f.o.b. prices, with fluctuations in the predicted optimal area due to fluctuations in international prices for sugar and other crops. For the period 1962 to 1968, the average predicted optimum was about 70,000 feddan, but the average international sugar price was 3.6 U.S. cents per pound f.o.b., while the long-term f.o.b. price is here assumed to be 3.8 cents, or 5.3 percent higher. At a 5 percent higher F-value for sugar (see Appendix A, Table A–4), the optimal acreage would be about 73,000 feddan. In addition, we have to allow for the difference between c.i.f. and f.o.b. prices—on average about 15 percent (see above). At c.i.f. prices, the optimal acreage would be about 82,000 feddan. This acreage should be compared with total actual cane acreage, including land planted with cane for delivery to private molasses production. The average total acreage was 115,000 feddan for these years, and the average optimum at the long-term price should have been about 61 percent of the actual acreage. Carried over to the area cultivated under contract with the factories, this would imply an optimal area of about 58,000 feddan, as compared with an actual average of about 95,000 feddan. In terms of sugar production, this means a reduction to about two-thirds of actual production.

The analysis in Chapter 7, however, was based on national aggregates and assumed that all crops competed equally against each other. This assumption conceals the fact that cane is grown almost exclusively in the southernmost part of the valley, where cotton is less profitable (yield is lower and only lower-priced medium staple varieties can be grown) than in the Delta and the northern part of the valley, and where rice is not grown at all. We thus have to compare with a feasible alternative crop rotation, and this comparison will probably show sugar in a more favorable light.

One of the most profitable rotations in Upper Egypt (according to a special survey made by the Ministry of Agriculture) is shown in Table 8–10. It

TABLE 8-10

Full Three-Year Rotations: Sugar and Alternative Rotation

(£E per feddan)

	Alternative Rotation, 1961			Sugar, Three Years			
	Income to Owner-Cultivator without Hired Labor, at Domestic Prices	DRC	Domestic Value Added at International Prices	Income to Owner-Cultivator without Hired Labor, 1961, at Domestic Prices	DRC, Cultivation and Processing at 10% Return, 1960	Domestic Value Added, at International Prices Refined Sugar, 1960, Based on	
						Long-Term Average Price	Three-Year Average Price (1959–61)
Year / Crop (1)	(2)	(3)	(4)	(5)	(6)	(7)	(8)
1 Clover	n.a.	n.a.	n.a.	58.6	119.4	124.5	103.6
Cotton[a]	56.7	65.2	70.7				
2 Wheat	26.7	26.1	18.2	58.6	119.4	124.5	103.6
Millet	27.6	28.5	24.8				
3 Onions	66.6	53.7	103.3	58.6	119.4	124.5	103.6
Millet	27.6	28.5	24.8				
Years 1–3, Total	205.2	202.0	241.8	175.8	358.2	373.5	310.8
DRC in piasters per U.S. $[b]		29.4				34.1	40.9

SOURCES: Cols. (2) and (5), Table 7–1. All others, B. Hansen and K. Nashashibi, NBER Working Paper No. 48, New York, 1975.

a. Based on normal crop.

b. Calculated by dividing DRC by domestic value added at international prices and multiplying by the official exchange rate of 35.2 piasters per U.S. dollar.

assumes perennial irrigation. In the third year of this rotation, lentils or beans might be substituted for onions, but while either of these two crops may be more profitable in terms of domestic prices, onions have by far the lowest DRC in terms of international prices, at least for the period 1961 to 1964 studied in Chapter 7 (see Table 7–1). Hence, we have chosen to compare sugar with a rotation that includes one crop of onions.

Columns 2 and 5 compare income going to owner-cultivators with no hired labor and at actual domestic prices under the two systems. Accordingly, cane growing was almost as attractive as the alternative rotation; indeed, the government fixed domestic cane prices so as to achieve competitiveness domestically. It is true that the alternative rotation shows a somewhat higher income than that from cane growing—£E205.2 as against £E175.8 over three years—but this figure exaggerates income, despite the exclusion of clover, insofar as cotton yields a much lower income per feddan in the southern parts of the valley than the national average on which Table 8–10 is based. Moreover, the calculation of income from cane does not consider that, as mentioned before, part of the costs of plowing and irrigation is carried by the factories. Finally, it should be recalled that the alternative rotation in question is the best possible one we could find. It can be concluded, therefore, that at domestic prices, cane and the alternative rotation were approximately equally attractive from the farmers' point of view.

The DRC for the alternative rotation in 1961 was 29.4 piasters per U.S. dollar, against the official rate of 35.2. At the long-term average world price for refined sugar, the DRC for sugar (at a 10 percent return) including cultivation was 34.1 in 1960. But, in view of the double counting of resource costs for sugar (which brings the sugar DRC further down) and the exaggeration of income from cotton (which may bring the DRC for the alternative rotation further up), we have no clear answer to our question about the comparative advantage of sugar versus the alternative rotation. The two may have been about equal.

It should not be overlooked, either, that we are making a comparison between DRCs at an (allegedly) long-term international price for sugar and at the actual international price for the alternative crops in 1961; short-term fluctuations in the latter could, of course, change the picture. We have not found it feasible, however, to calculate long-term prices for the alternative crops, but their international prices (in foreign currency) generally did not increase from 1962 to 1968. Finally, we should also take into account that the alternative rotation becomes more profitable the further north in Upper Egypt the cultivation is located. It might therefore be argued that, at best, it is only in the southernmost parts of the valley, at Aswan and Qena, that cane may have a long-term comparative advantage over the alternative rotation. Most of the expansion in the 1960s did take place in Aswan and Qena, but the government also built two new raw sugar factories further to the north, in Sohag, and it is doubtful whether this particular investment was justified.

If, therefore, we conclude that the major part of cane cultivation was economically justified in 1960 but that some of it should have been eliminated, we are quite in line with the predictions made in Chapter 7.

Employment and Other Aspects.

An assessment of the sugar industry must also take employment effects into account. All our calculations assume that opportunity costs for labor are equal to actual wages, with the implicit assumption that labor employed in the sugar industry could find alternative employment at these wages over the long term. If this assumption is not substantiated, the DRC of sugar falls in relation to that of the alternative rotation, because sugar (including processing) is much more labor-intensive than the other rotation.

The sugar industry (processing) is the second largest industrial employer, textiles being the largest. It employs approximately 26,000 regular workers in its factories and refineries and a much larger working force during the short cane-crushing season, drawn mainly from rural areas and partly during slack agricultural seasons (December to May). Thus it combines a number of advantages often emphasized in development strategies: a high rate of labor absorption per unit of capital invested and income created mainly in rural areas—even in the least developed ones in Egypt—during slack seasons.

Another circumstance is the increasing demand for the by-products of the industry, related to the development of manufacturing industry in general. Products such as acetic acid, alcohol, carbon dioxide, and yeast can be derived from molasses. In addition, the cane residual, or bagasse, can be used for manufacturing grain board and paper pulp, where it has a large potential if other cellulosic raw materials become scarcer, unless oil becomes dearer as a substitute in the factory furnaces. Calculations of the maximum price the paper industry could pay for bagasse reveal a net gain to the sugar industry over and above its fuel opportunity cost of £E1.82 per ton of bagasse used for paper pulp. If 300,000 tons of bagasse were taken up by the paper industry (roughly representing its potential demand), it would reduce the sugar industry's DRC by approximately 1 piaster per U.S. dollar.[54]

THE CEMENT INDUSTRY

The manufacture of cement was started in Egypt in 1900, when the Société Anonyme des Ciments d'Egypte (a Belgian venture) built a factory near Cairo. Based on large deposits of raw materials in the vicinity of the major consuming center, the new industry was induced by the demand for cement

THE TRADITIONAL INDUSTRIES

from the first Aswan Dam. Up until World War II, its major source of energy was imported Cardiff or German coal; World War II forced a shift to liquid fuel.

During its first two decades the cement industry had great difficulties to survive. Up to World War I it had to compete with foreign cement without special protection (apart from the high cost of transport, of course), and during the war fuel supplies were cut off. Although still without special protection during the 1920s, the industry captured a significant share of the domestic market in competition with imported cement. At that time two of the four cement companies in existence today were founded.[55] Yet, until the Great Depression, the industry's share of the domestic market did not exceed 20 percent.

In 1930 a 15 percent import tariff was imposed on cement; it led to the disappearance of cement imports during the thirties. At the outbreak of World War II, an excise tax of £E0.70 per ton (43 percent of the domestic ex-factory price) was imposed on cement. The excise tax remained in force after the war, but by that time the industry had obtained a definite comparative advantage. Despite the fact that the excise tax—imposed only on domestic production—exceeded the import tariff and that the currency was probably overvalued (see Chapter 3, pp. 67–68), the domestic ex-factory price was low enough to eliminate imports. With the exemption of exported cement from the excise tax in 1952, exports rapidly increased and had already reached a level of 500,000 tons by 1958.

The expanded capacity was not enough to meet both domestic and foreign demand during the years of the first Five-Year Plan, 1960–61 to 1964–65, when large construction projects (particularly the Aswan High Dam) temporarily diverted exported cement to domestic consumption (see Chart 8–5 and Table 8–11) and cement imports became necessary. With the reduction of investments after 1965 (see Chapter 5), the situation changed again and the industry is now an important foreign exchange earner, second only to cotton textiles among manufactured exports. Its net foreign exchange earnings increased when two of its major imported inputs (fuel oil and paper) were replaced by domestic products, increasing the proportion of domestically produced inputs in cement from 20 percent in 1954 to 88 percent in 1965–66. At the same time, the industry diversified into the production of special varieties of cement, first as import substitutes and later, as in the case of white cement, as exports.

Costs, Revenues, and Competitiveness, 1954 to 1965–66.

Data on the industry's revenue and cost structure have been compiled for 1954, 1957, 1960, and 1965–66 from the consolidated accounts of the exist-

CHART 8–5

Cement: Production and Trade, 1925–1970

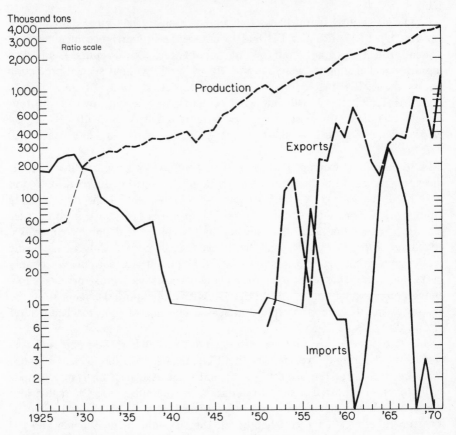

ing four cement companies.[56] On the basis of these data, estimates of the industry's effective rate of protection and resource costs per dollar were made at current and constant international prices (see Table 8–12, where indices of variable input costs and productivity of labor and capital are also shown).

We have chosen to use the average export prices f.o.b. in all revenue estimates at international prices. As Table 8–11 indicates, the average export price tended to fall as the quantity exported increased, while the unit value obtained from neighboring countries, represented by Saudi Arabia, remained roughly constant over the entire period. Since the increase in exports was achieved mostly through expansion to more remote areas (such as West African countries), the f.o.b. price had to be lowered to absorb freight costs and to assure competitiveness on a c.i.f. basis with alternative suppliers.

TABLE 8–11
Exports of Egyptian Cement: Tonnage and Prices
(three-year averages)

	Quantity (000 MT)	All Exports, Unit Value		Exports to Saudi Arabia, Unit Value (f.o.b., U.S. $)	Effective Exchange Rate (piasters per U.S. $)
		(f.o.b., £E)	(f.o.b., U.S. $)		
1953	118	5.4	14.3	14.2	36.5
1957	228	5.9	15.5	—	38.2
1961	689	4.1	10.7	12.2	38.3
1964	157	6.4	14.7	11.8	43.5
1971	1,340	4.2	9.7	13.4	43.5

SOURCE: Federation of Industries, *Yearbook*, various issues.

TABLE 8-12

**Cement Industry: ERPs, DRCs, Return to Capital, and
Performance Indicators**

	Rate of Return to Capital			DRC at Current International Prices, f.o.b. (piasters per U.S. $)		
	At Actual Domestic Prices (%)	At International Prices (%)	ERP (%)	5% Rate of Return	10% Rate of Return	15% Rate of Return
1954	18.0	34.7	−30.8	16.4	19.8	23.2
1957	10.2	35.6	−45.5	17.3	20.7	24.2
1960	7.6	19.6	−34.6	22.2	27.7	33.2
1965–66	10.9	22.5	−27.6	26.5	31.3	36.2

Indexes of Performance
(1954 = 100)

	Labor Productivity (per hour)		Capital Productivity (per £E of equipment)		
	Value Added at Constant Internatl. Prices	Output (tons of cement)	Value Added at Constant Internatl. Prices	Output (tons of cement)	Output (unit value)
1954	100	100	100	100	100
1957	102 (122[a])	104	57 (68[a])	55	91
1960	138	137	60	60	93
1965–66	117	114	88	90	132

SOURCE: Hansen and Nashashibi, NBER Working Paper No. 48, New York, 1975, and official statistics.
   a. Adjusted to 90% capacity utilization.
   b. The definition of maximum capacity assumes a certain number of days per year set aside for repair and maintenance.

During the period under review here, the profitability of the cement industry suffered from a gradual erosion through adverse price developments for outputs and inputs. The unit value of total output at domestic prices fell in 1957 and recovered only slightly by 1960. Quantifiable material input prices remained constant, but other inputs, such as services and spare parts, probably increased in price. The price squeeze was accentuated in 1962 because of the devaluation, and even more so during the period of price increases in 1965 and 1966. By 1966, ex-factory cement unit values had risen by only 16 percent over 1954, against a 40 percent increase in the prices of major inputs.

TABLE 8–12 (concluded)

DRC at Constant International Prices, f.o.b. (piasters per U.S. $)			Exchange Rates (piasters per U.S. $)		
5% Rate of Return	10% Rate of Return	15% Rate of Return	Official Buying Rate	Effective Rate	Capacity Utilization (%)
16.4	19.8	23.2	34.9	36.5	89
19.0[a]	22.4[a]	25.7[a]	34.9	38.3	75
16.4	20.7	25.2	34.9	38.3	91
21.9	26.8	31.9	43.5	43.5	107[b]

Indexes of Performance
(1954 = 100)

Material Inputs (unit value)					Total
at Domestic Prices	at Current Internatl. Prices	Hourly Wages	Total Output Volume	Total Number of Employees	Number of Hours Worked
100	100	100	100	100	100
102	102	131	116	111	110
100	100	146	167	124	122
140	137	142	211	200	185

(The unit price of total output was, however, 32 percent higher than in 1954.) The price increase in inputs was particularly notable for limestone and clay, packing materials, and fuel oil. Hourly wages increased sharply from 1954 to 1960, but then, remarkably enough, seem to have fallen slightly between 1960 and 1966 (had we included pension and social insurance contributions, a slight increase in wages would have been found). The cement industry thus follows a pattern found in other Egyptian industries (see Chapter 4, p. 95): the government's control over prices and its concern about keeping domestic prices low despite rising input prices (particularly for imported inputs) has lowered profits.

The industry's net value added evaluated at international prices is much higher than at actual domestic prices. Export prices exceed domestic prices, and tariff rates and premiums were gradually increased on imported materials like spare parts and kraft paper bags. Two important traded inputs, fuel oil and packing materials, were replaced by domestic substitutes during the period under review. For packing materials, domestic prices exceeded import prices. Domestic production of fuel oil was expanding rapidly, and what had been an import item until 1960 became an export item by 1965–66; in our calculations we had to shift from c.i.f. prices to f.o.b. prices for fuel oil. This circumstance partly explains the drop in fuel oil costs at international prices, and was a factor in preserving the competitiveness of the cement industry.

Profitability—net profit (before income taxes) as a percentage of capital[57]—was also much higher when calculated at international prices during the whole period. At actual domestic prices, profitability fell from 18.0 percent in 1954 to 7.6 percent in 1960, after which it recovered to 10.9 percent in 1965–66 (13 percent, if interest and rent payments are included in net profits). At current international prices, profitability was 34.3 percent in 1954, fell to 19.6 percent in 1960, and rose again to 22.5 percent in 1965–66. We must add that, when exports were vigorously expanded in 1969 at a considerable decline in export prices due to longer transports, profitability at international prices still remained at 11.6 percent (and somewhat higher if interest and rent payments were included in net profits). It would thus seem that the industry during the whole period was socially profitable, although profitability shows a downward trend.

The highly "taxed" position of the cement industry as compared with a free trade situation is reflected in the negative ERPs shown in Table 8–12. The ERPs fluctuated between −28 and −45 percent. Similarly, the DRCs were much lower than both the official and the effective exchange rates, even at an imputed rate of return to capital of 15 percent. After a more than 50 percent rise from 1954 to 1965–66, DRC still did not exceed the level of the effective rate of exchange in 1954.

Thus, during the whole period, the industry was highly competitive (even at an overvalued exchange rate) and it is one of the failings of Egyptian investment policies during the first Five-Year Plan (1960–1965) to have permitted cement exports to slip back from almost 700,000 MT in 1961 to slightly above 150,000 MT in 1964. Expansion of capacity could have anticipated the High Dam requirements, and reduced domestic demand after the Dam's completion would have been offset by larger exports. In fact, the level of exports attained in 1971 was almost twice as high as the peak reached in 1961.

Productivity.

To appraise productivity of factors, Table 8–12 shows index numbers (1954 = 100) of physical output and net value added at constant 1954 international prices, both per unit of factor input (labor and capital).

Labor productivity increased slightly, from 100 to 102, between 1954 and 1957, when the industry was expanding its capacity. The capacity expansion was accompanied by a decline in capacity utilization and a sharp drop, from 100 to 57, in productivity of capital by 1957. Note that, with value added in 1957 adjusted to the level of capacity utilization prevailing in 1954 and 1960, labor productivity increases from 102 to 122 and capital productivity, from 57 to 68. Between 1957 and 1960, labor productivity rose further to 138 (in terms of value added), with capital productivity remaining at 60. These opposite changes are, of course, perfectly natural in an industry that relies on a standard technology with little technical progress; it simply indicates that capital intensity has increased and has served to increase productivity of labor. The increase in labor productivity (over 6 percent per year) is noteworthy; it exceeded the average of 4 percent rate of increase achieved for all industry during that period.[58] Nonetheless, it was outstripped by an even steeper rise in wages, which exceeded the average for all industry. The cement industry seems to have experienced an improving quality of labor through a relative increase of professional staff and qualified workers. The proportion of employees holding academic degrees grew from 1.4 percent in 1954 to 2.4 percent in 1960, that of middle management and technical staff, from 2.3 percent to 4.2 percent, while that of unskilled workers fell over the same period.

During the period 1960 to 1965–66, the trend was reversed. Labor productivity fell by 17 percent, while capital productivity rose by 50 percent. In this connection, we must remember that after the nationalization of the industry in 1961 a general employment drive took place, with increased employment and reduced working hours per week. This employment drive did not spare the cement industry, causing labor productivity to decline. While output increased by over 26 percent from 1960 to 1965–66, the number of employees increased by 64 percent and man-hours, by 52 percent. Alongside the decline in labor productivity, an increase in capacity utilization beyond its optimal theoretical maximum (the definition of maximum capacity assumes a certain number of days per year set aside for repair and maintenance) contributed to the productivity growth of capital and may have negatively affected labor productivity.

As labor productivity fell, wages per worker also declined. This fact is difficult to explain, considering the general rise in wages and the improvement in skill distribution during that period. It is possible that the industry was able to reduce the average earnings of unskilled workers through a cut in overtime work. There seems to have been an attempt to bring the level of wages into line with productivity, and with the increased capacity utilization the industry succeeded in preventing the profit rate from shrinking further.

Clearly, the cement industry's performance during the period 1960 to

1965–66 was inferior to that of the preceding period. It is not obvious how much this had to do with the change from private to public ownership. The cause was, rather, the misconceived employment policy imposed on all big industries. Had the cement industry remained in private hands, it probably would have had to conform to the employment policy. There is nothing to indicate that the industry suffered from shortages related to foreign exchange controls. Production did suffer (see Chart 8–5), but this can be explained by the falling off in the cement requirements of the Aswan High Dam construction, as well as the deflation that took place in 1965–66. (See Chapter 5, pp. 112–121).

In a more indirect way, the industry seems to have been adversely affected by the centralization of investment decisions into the ministry and away from company managers. Capacity seems to have been better geared to domestic *and* foreign demand during the 1950s than during the 1960s. Net exports reached a peak in 1961 and declined thereafter until 1964. Central planning failed, but it is not clear why. It is true that a decision to speed up construction of the Aswan High Dam, and thus increase domestic demand, was taken after the first Five-Year Plan had been worked out, but there should have been sufficient time to revise the investment plans for the cement industry accordingly. Did the planners deliberately sacrifice exports? Or was the whole problem simply ignored? With free trade, decentralized investment decisions, and profit maximization, this would probably not have happened; it would not have been overlooked that exports were more profitable than sales to the domestic market. It would seem that the planners ignored, or were ignorant of, this basic fact.

But when viewed over a longer term—the period between 1950 and 1971, for example—the overall performance of the industry is quite satisfactory. The increase in the DRCs between 1954 and 1965–66 at constant prices was relatively small considering the organizational changes that took place after 1961 and the labor policy adopted by the government. The productivity of capital increased rapidly between 1957 and 1965–66 (even after adjustment for capacity utilization) and the industry remained highly competitive and profitable. Its major strength, as revealed by intercountry comparisons of the relative cost components in this industry, derives from a higher quality of labor available to it—for a given level of wages and capital stock—than to some of its competitors.[59] And while its competitiveness may have declined somewhat from 1960 to 1965, the tighter organizational controls that followed the 1967 war and the greater cost-consciousness of the government may have reversed the situation.

NOTES

1. Bent Hansen and Karim Nashashibi, *Protection and Competitiveness in Egyptian Agriculture and Industry,* NBER Working Paper No. 48, New York, 1975.

2. This and the following paragraph are based on E. R. J. Owen, *Cotton and the Egyptian Economy, 1820–1914,* Oxford, 1969. See also H. A. B. Rivlin, *The Agricultural Policy of Muhammad Ali in Egypt,* Cambridge, Mass., 1961, and Moustafa Fahmy, *La Révolution de l'industrie en Egypte et ses conséquences sociales au 19ᵉ siècle, 1800– 1850,* Leiden, 1954.

3. Owen, op. cit., pp. 46–47, and Fahmy, op. cit., pp. 26–27.

4. By 1906 the Anglo-Egyptian had 20,000 spindles with 400 looms. See Owen, op. cit., p. 224.

5. Owen, op. cit., pp. 302–303 and 383–385; and R. L. Tignor, *Modernization and British Colonial Rule in Egypt, 1882–1914,* Princeton, 1966, pp. 364–365, particularly notes 11 and 12. The only other domestically produced commodities to bear the tax were sugar and salt. See also E. R. J. Owen, "Lord Cromer and the Development of Egyptian Industry, 1883–1970," *Middle Eastern Studies,* London, Vol. II, No. 4, July 1966, pp. 282–301.

6. Either directly for metal machinery imported or indirectly on the wooden machinery produced domestically. Insofar as the import duty exceeded the price differential between ordinary Egyptian cotton and Indian cotton, it may have shifted the domestic consumption of cotton toward local varieties.

7. W. V. Shearer, "The Weaving Industry in Asyout," *L'Egypte contemporaine,* Cairo, No. 1, 1910, p. 184.

8. Ibid., p. 185.

9. Hand-weaving after Mohammed Ali took place mainly in Upper Egypt, where basin irrigation imposed a long idle period on the peasantry, which it used in textile handicrafts to supplement its meager one-crop income. Before Mohammed Ali there was a flourishing weaving industry in the Delta. It was killed off by Mohammed Ali's monopoly and was never revived after its abolition because the concurrent change to perennial irrigation in the Delta led to a strong increase in labor demand for agriculture during the previously idle summer season that weaving could not compete with.

10. El-Gritly notes that the Filature Nationale was able to treble its capital by plowing back the profits of the financial year 1917–1918. See A. I. El-Gritly, "The Structure of Modern Industry in Egypt," *L'Egypte contemporaine,* November-December 1947.

11. 1927 was the year of the first industrial census; it covered all establishments without lower limits as to the number of employees. Unfortunately, its objectives were misinterpreted by the press, which circulated rumors about the establishment of an income tax in the country. Consequently, all details reported on inputs, wages, and value added were considered totally misleading and left unpublished. *Industrial Census,* March 1927, Cairo, Government Press, 1931.

12. K. M. Barbour, *Growth, Location, and Structure of Industry in Egypt,* New York, 1972, pp. 59–69.

13. *Industrial and Commercial Census, 1937,* Cairo, Government Press, 1942, p. 338.

14. Misr Spinning and Weaving Co. was able to increase its reserves tenfold. The other big company, Filature Nationale, increased its dividends from 45 piasters per share in 1938 to 130 piasters in the postwar years. See *Economic Bulletin,* National Bank of Egypt, 1951, p. 100.

15. In our DRC calculations, therefore, we have considered the postwar years as the starting point in the life of capital equipment.

16. *Economic Bulletin,* N.B.E., 1951, p. 98.

17. Ibid., pp. 100–101.

18. The subsidy was based on the current price difference between Ashmouni G/FG and Indian and American cotton. It amounted to 21 percent of the cost of Egyptian cotton in 1949. Applying this percentage to the respective shares of cotton costs in yarn and cloth, we obtain the ad valorem subsidy on yarn and cloth exported. See Federation of Industries, *Yearbook,* Cairo, 1950–1951, p. 36, and *Economic Bulletin,* ibid., pp. 101–102.

19. The fixed price did not apply to small establishments. One reason might be their higher cost of production, but most probably the exemption was related to difficulties in controlling small establishments.

20. Federation of Industries, *Yearbook,* Cairo, 1950–1951, p. 37.

21. Federation of Industries, *Yearbook,* Cairo, 1953–1954. See also GATT document L/1816, pp. 46–47. On the supply side, a series of measures, mostly compulsory, were directed to assure an adequate supply of domestic cotton to the textile mills. In the 1949–50 season the government decided to restrict the acreage planted under long staple cotton to expand medium staple varieties (*Economic Bulletin,* N.B.E., 1949, p. 214). During the Korean boom (the 1950–51 season) the government first entered the market as a buyer of medium staples, Ashmouni, Giza 30, and Zagora, of low grades, to meet the requirements of local spinners. Then, in December, it issued a decree requisitioning cotton at fixed prices. (*Economic Bulletin,* N.B.E., 1950, p. 261). In 1953–54 an outright ban on exports of Ashmouni and Żagora (up to grade "Good" + 1/4) was decreed. (*Economic Bulletin,* N.B.E., 1954, p. 27). This was the case again in 1959 for all medium staples (including Denderah and Giza 47). And when export taxes for other varieties were abandoned in 1958 and 1959, they were maintained for Ashmouni. In 1960 Ashmouni became subject to an export quota of 800,000 kantars. (*Economic Bulletin,* N.B.E., 1960, No. 1, p. 26). Finally, after the cotton trade monopolization by the government in 1961, exports were treated as a residual after the local mills had determined their requirements. Gradually, exports of medium staple cotton declined and the production of Ashmouni and Giza 66, which amounted to 2 million kantars in 1969, was totally absorbed by domestic spinning mills.

22. *Economic Bulletin,* N.B.E., 1951, pp. 100–102.

23. Cotton fabric consumption accounts for 87 percent of the total, with 12 percent for artificial fiber and 1 percent for wool.

24. Per capita consumption grew at a rate of 1.6 percent during the years 1958 to 1971.

25. K. Nashashibi, "Bilateral Trade as a Development Instrument under Global Trade Restrictions," NBER Working Paper 54, New York, 1975.

26. The average count of yarn exported went up from 17.7 in 1956 to 27.3 in 1962–63 and to 30.5 in 1970–71. While the Consolidation Fund attempted to adjust Egyptian export prices to those prevailing in European markets, Egyptian yarns, nonetheless, often failed to compete with Japanese and Polish products on the German, Dutch, and Belgian markets. GATT document L/1816, pp. 47–49.

27. The margin between gray yarn and gray cloth is even narrower—it averages $57 per ton, or roughly 5 percent of the price of yarn.

28. See footnote 29.

29. Part of the waste is recovered at a much lower unit value and reused. However, this cost reduction is probably more than offset by the use of finer varieties than Ashmouni in the cotton exported.

30. In 1966 the quota must have been around 3,000 tons. Exports to the Common Market amounted to 1,500 tons. See Federation of Industries, *Yearbook,* 1970, 1971, and 1972 issues.

31. Federation of Industries, *Yearbook,* 1972, p. 62.

32. Estimates were derived from separate data on weaving operations in 1960.

33. Our calculation may exaggerate competitiveness in 1956 and underestimate it for 1960. Thus, the decline in competitiveness from 1956 to 1960 may be more apparent than real.

34. Direct feeding of the cards from the bale-opening machinery and direct spinning from the drawing-frames (ultra high drafting system, for example). See *The Textile Industry,* United Nations Industrial Development Organization, New York, 1969.

35. *Modern Cotton Industry,* OECD, Paris, 1965.

36. *The Textile Industry,* UNIDO, New York, 1971, pp. 13–24. Also *Modern Cotton Industry,* op. cit., pp. 95–107.

37. GATT, *A Study in Cotton Textiles,* Geneva, 1966, and the follow-up report *Cotton Textiles, 1962–1963,* UNIDO, COT/W/115, Tables I and IV.

38. Here again we are faced with consistency problems, since the data collected in the 1968–1970 period differed in method and coverage from the data collected in 1956–1960.

39. Thus, yarns up to count 30 may only be carded, while yarns with higher counts have to be combed.

40. "La culture de la canne à sucre en Egypte," Société d'Entreprises Commerciales en Egypte, 1952, pp. 25–27.

41. *Economic Bulletin,* N.B.E., 1950, p. 11.

42. Ibid., p. 12.

43. As mentioned in Chapter 6, cane is also planted for sale to small private molasses factories. In the following, "area" refers to area planted under contract with the sugar factories and does not include areas planted for other sales.

44. Sugar cane is harvested in December and sugar factories are at work over a 150-day season from January to May. For the discharge of the Nile at Aswan, see Hansen and Nashashibi, NBER Working Paper No. 48, Table 14.

45. Federation of Industries, *Yearbook,* 1952–1953, p. 75.

46. Federation of Industries, *Yearbook,* 1953–1954, p. 63.

47. Since the price response of exports to world price developments seems to lag behind imports, periods of sharp price fluctuations (1962–1966) may reverse this relationship.

48. Food imports were not subjected to any premiums prior to the devaluation of 1962. Hence the official rate of exchange was used to convert U.S. dollar sugar prices to Egyptian currency. To the f.o.b. price at Caribbean ports a freight margin covering transportation to the Mediterranean was added. FAO, *Production Yearbook,* several issues.

49. Obtained by taking the difference between export prices of raw and refined sugar at Caribbean ports. FAO, ibid.

50. *Agricultural Economics* [*El iqtisad el zirai*], Ministry of Agriculture, Cairo, April 1969, p. 186.

51. Bent Hansen, "The Distributive Shares in Egyptian Agriculture, 1897–1961," *International Economic Review,* Vol. 9, No. 2, June 1968.

52. *Al Talia,* August 1973, pp. 52–60.

53. "Report of the Committee on Planning and Balance on the Egyptian Sugar and Refining Company," *Al Talia,* Cairo, August 1973, pp. 55–56. The subsidies are illustrative of the problems encountered in attempting to stabilize prices and influence income

254 PROTECTION, CONTROLS, AND COMPETITIVENESS IN INDUSTRY

distribution: (1) When in July 1959 the government reduced the price of rationed sugar, it committed itself to compensate the sugar company for the price difference. (2) When the government raised the purchase price of cane from the farmers (February 1965) it disbursed to the sugar company the difference in price. (3) The increase in the import price of jute bags was partially compensated by the government. (4) It was decided in July 1967 to grant a subsidy to the sugar company of £E3.956 per ton of sugar to compensate it for a general increase in input costs. (5) When the Egyptian railroad abolished the preferential rates it had granted the sugar company, the government compensated it for the difference in rates. Needless to say, each subsidy entailed the creation of a number of committees, investigations, and reports.

54. Hansen and Nashashibi, op. cit.

55. The Société Egyptienne de Ciment (1927), which absorbed the Helwan Portland Cement Co. (1929) and the Société Anonyme de Ciment (1931). In addition, two other companies were founded after World War II.

56. Hansen and Nashashibi, op. cit.

57. Capital is here taken at actual historical value, which presumably implies an exaggeration of the increase in the rate of return from 1960 to 1965–66.

58. B. Hansen and G. A. Marzouk, Development and Economic Policy in the U.A.R. (Egypt), Amsterdam, 1965, p. 133.

59. Hansen and Nashashibi, op. cit.

Chapter 9

Efforts to Broaden the Industrial Structure: The New Industries

FERTILIZERS

In Chapter 6 we mentioned the change from basin to perennial irrigation that took place in the second half of the nineteenth century and the increased need for fertilizer inputs that accompanied it, further intensified in the 1960s by the Aswan High Dam. As early as 1911, Egypt imported 60,000 tons of fertilizers, and by 1960 her consumption of fertilizer per acre of cultivated land surpassed all developing countries except Taiwan and South Korea.[1] Thus, there is a very substantial domestic market for chemical fertilizers in Egypt. The demand is concentrated on phosphate and nitrogen fertilizers; potash is of secondary importance.

Since phosphate and nitrogen fertilizers are produced by two distinct industries in Egypt, they will be discussed separately.

The Phosphate Fertilizer Industry.

The phosphate fertilizer industry had a relatively early start in Egypt—the combined result of strong domestic demand and abundant domestic deposits of phosphate rock. The demand for phosphate fertilizers arose from the cultivation of beans and clover, in particular. Large deposits of relatively low-grade phosphate rock were discovered in the Red Sea area and near Esna, and earlier some of the rock seems to have been used directly in areas with sufficient soil acidity. In the beginning, most of the phosphate rock was exported to Japan. By 1936 total exports of phosphate rock had reached half a million

255

tons. But it is obvious that Egypt had natural advantages in producing super-phosphates herself.

The first superphosphate factory was established in 1937 at Kafr-El-Zayat in the Nile Delta, with a small annual capacity of 25,000 tons. It was followed by a second plant, with a capacity of 35,000 tons, at Abu Zaabal in 1948. Both got their phosphate rock by rail from the Esna deposits some 500 miles away. The location of the factories, combined with the seasonal nature of the de-mand, resulted in severe transportation problems. As capacity and scale of production were expanded, the single-track, narrow-gauge rail line responsible for part of the transportation became overburdened. Eventually this led to disruption of production in the years 1961–1964 (see Chart 9–1). Recently, a new plant with a 200,000-ton capacity was built at Assiout, much closer to the phosphate rock deposits.[2]

The sulphuric acid needed as a catalyst was originally derived from roast-ing pyrites imported from Cyprus. This technology is capital-intensive and was

CHART 9–1

Phosphate Fertilizers: Production and Trade, 1947–1971

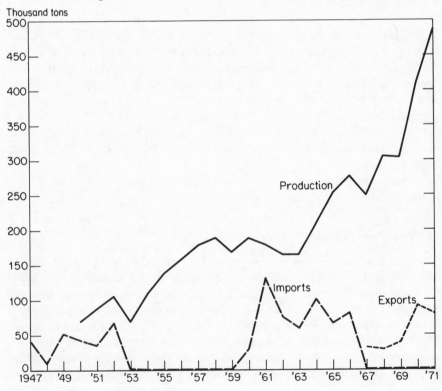

probably less economical than the one based on elemental sulphur, but may have been justified at the time because of favorable special arrangements made with the suppliers regarding prices and quantities to be delivered. The Korean boom and the growth in Egypt's pyrite requirements led to the abrogation of these arrangements, and the import price of pyrites rose from $8 per ton in 1950 to $15.50 per ton in 1953 and remained at that level thereafter.

In the early 1950s Egyptian superphosphates emerged as a powerful import substitute, although the rate of protection against imported fertilizers did not exceed 10 to 15 percent of the c.i.f. price. By 1954, domestic production was sufficient to satisfy domestic demand, and a ban on imports was imposed. In 1960, however, when production fell short of demand, imports reappeared, partly because of the transportation problems mentioned above. They fell again drastically after 1964 and Egypt emerged as an exporter of superphosphates. From 1965 to 1968 exports amounted to about 30,000 tons annually, going mainly to Arab countries. In 1970 a level of 93,000 tons was reached.

COST AND REVENUE DATA

Cost data on superphosphates, derived from the operations of the same two factories, are available for 1954, 1957, and 1964–65.[3] While the comparability of the results is enhanced by the homogeneity of the output, a change in technology between 1957 and 1964–65 that substituted elemental sulphur for pyrites in the production of sulphuric acid[4] posed some problems in interpreting cost trends.[5]

In the calculations for 1954, an adjustment to 90 percent capacity utilization (the level of utilization actually prevailing in the other years studied here) was made. Domestic resource costs were calculated on the basis of import prices c.i.f. (see Table 9–1). For 1964–65, however, we have computed resource costs also on the basis of two alternative f.o.b. export prices: the export unit value actually realized in 1964–65 and the average export unit value realized in 1969 and 1970. Comparison makes it possible for us to assess the profitability of the industry, both as an import-substituting and as an exporting activity.

THE COMPETITIVENESS OF EGYPTIAN SUPERPHOSPHATES

The industry initially looked like an inefficient attempt at import substitution: it was designed to operate at a low and uneconomical scale; it relied on low-grade phosphate deposits with unreliable and expensive transportation to the plant; and it resorted to the derivation of sulphuric acid via pyrites, normally a relatively expensive method, based on a short-lived favorable price arrangement. On the other hand, the industry benefited from cheap labor and engineering skills and was, as an import substitute, naturally "protected" by a

TABLE 9-1

Phosphate Fertilizer Industry: ERPs, DRCs, and Performance Indicators

	1954 At Actual Plant Utilization of 53% (at import prices c.i.f.)	1954 At Full Capacity Utilization of 90% (at import prices c.i.f.)	1957 At Actual Plant Utilization of 90% (at import prices c.i.f.)	1964–65 At Actual Plant Utilization of 90% (at import prices c.i.f.)	1964–65 At Actual Plant Utilization of 90% (at export prices f.o.b. of 1964–65)	1964–65 At Actual Plant Utilization of 90% (at export prices f.o.b. of 1969–70)
ERP (percent)	14.6	—	34.4	7.5	0.0	0.0
DRC at current internatl. prices (piasters per U.S. $) at rate of return of						
5 percent	31.3	23.4	35.6	27.0	30.1	40.9
10 percent	38.5	27.4	36.2	32.8	36.4	49.5
15 percent	45.8	31.4	42.2	38.6	42.8	58.1
DRC at constant internatl. prices (piasters per U.S. $) at rate of return of						
5 percent	29.7	22.2	27.7	24.3	—	—
10 percent	36.7	26.1	32.5	29.7	—	—
15 percent	43.5	29.8	37.3	35.1	—	—

Effective exchange rate (piasters per U.S. $)	37.0	37.0	38.5	43.5	43.5	43.5
Rate of return to capital (percent)						
at actual domestic prices	17.6	—	16.5	21.8	—	—
at internatl. prices	8.9	—	7.4	19.3	—	—
Performance indicators (1954=100)						
Physical labor productivity[a]	100	—	132	—	190	—
Physical capital productivity[b]	100	—	170	—	190	—
Hourly wages	100	—	130	—	214	—

SOURCE: B. Hansen and K. Nashashibi, NBER Working Paper No. 48, New York, 1975, Tables 23 and 25.
a. Tons per man-hour.
b. Tons per unit of equipment value.

large freight margin—15 to 20 percent of the import price of the final product and 40 to 50 percent of the import price of phosphate rock.

By 1954, the industry had seventeen years of experience, including a difficult period during World War II. With a domestic price 14 percent above the average import price c.i.f., the industry's rate of return on capital was 17.6 percent at a capacity utilization of 53 percent. Evaluated at import prices, the industry was competitive at a rate of return on capital of 8.9 percent, even at this low utilization of capacity. At a 10 percent rate of return, the resource costs were only slightly higher than the official exchange rate. Had the industry operated at full capacity, it would have been competitive in exports as well. Conditions were thus sufficiently favorable to offset the initial drawbacks and to make the industry profitable and competitive.

In 1964–65, the industry was efficient both as an import substitute and in exports. Its domestic resource cost, based on that year's export price and a 10 percent rate of return on capital, was 36.4 piasters, well below the official exchange rate of 43.5 piasters per U.S. dollar. At the much lower export price realized in the 1969–70 period, the resource cost per U.S. dollar earned in 1964–65 would have been 49.5 piasters, somewhat higher than the official exchange rate but substantially lower than the exchange rate of 61 piasters per U.S. dollar suggested by the IMF to the Egyptian government in 1966. The latter exchange rate would make the industry as profitable in exports (and a fortiori as an import substitute) in 1969–70 despite the international price decline.

In discussing the development of the industry's efficiency and profitability, our first focus is on the price developments in its output and input.

Over the last two decades, domestic prices for superphosphates, both at factory gate and delivered to the farmer, have remained relatively stable. Most of the time the ex-factory price has stood at about £E10.0 per ton, with the farmer paying about £E11.5 per ton.[6] During this twenty-year period, the import unit values, albeit less stable, have fluctuated around an average of £E10.0 per ton.[7] On the other hand, export unit values have been falling since 1964, possibly as a result of attempts to reach new markets and expand exports.

In contrast to the relative stability of the output prices, raw materials prices rose, particularly those of rock phosphate and packing material. Over the 1954–1957 period, however, this rise in cost was offset by a higher capacity utilization, which prevented the rate of return from falling. Profitability, measured at actual prices, was only slightly lower in 1957 than in 1954. In terms of international prices, it shows a similar development, falling from 8.9 percent in 1954 to 7.4 percent in 1957. The calculations at constant international prices and full capacity indicate that productive efficiency was higher in 1954 than in 1957. This decline in efficiency is also reflected in higher physical input coefficients.

Input prices continued to increase between 1957 and 1964–65. At the same time, wage increases exceeded the rate of productivity growth, the typical pattern for manufacturing industry (Chapter 4). However, while in the cement industry labor productivity fell, in the phosphate industry it increased substantially. An improvement in the quality of labor may have contributed to this development, but it is also a result of the "embodied" technical progress related to the expansion of capacity described above. Productivity of capital increased, although the value of the machinery and equipment installed doubled between 1957 and 1964–65. Evaluated at constant prices, domestic resource costs declined from 32.5 piasters to 29.7 piasters. On balance, the growth in labor productivity and a rise in the import price of phosphates more than offset the rise in wages and material input prices, resulting in an improvement in the competitive position of superphosphates in 1964–65 over 1957. Moreover, there is no firm evidence that production was physically less efficient in 1964–65 than a decade earlier. A hypothetical computation of resource costs at a 90 percent capacity utilization in 1954 yields a DRC of 26.1 against 29.7 in 1964–65 at a 10 percent rate of return and constant prices.

Once labor's share in value added has returned to the level prevailing before 1961, as it appears to have done by all indications in the early 1970s, the industry should be more efficient than it was in 1955 and should be highly profitable as an export activity. A comparison of its 1964–65 cost shares (relative to the international output price) to that of a Yugoslavian plant shows that Egypt derives some advantage from its labor costs, although these represent only a small share of the total. More important is the marked advantage it reaps from low raw materials costs.[8] The recent discovery of new deposits of phosphates should further strengthen the competitiveness of the industry.

The Nitrogen Fertilizer Industry.

Nitrogen fertilizer production began in 1951. The product was calcium nitrate (15.5 nitrogen) based on gases emerging as a by-product of the two petroleum refineries in Suez. Until 1961 calcium nitrate was the only nitrogenous fertilizer produced in Egypt. It was well suited to the high acidity of Egyptian soils but had a low nitrogen content and required large amounts of inert matter; transportation costs were therefore high and it was highly subject to leaching.

Imports of calcium ammonium nitrates increased rapidly during the fifties, and in 1954 it was decided to produce ammonium nitrates domestically. This type of nitrogen fertilizer is particularly appropriate for Egyptian soil: it allows for a much higher nitrogen concentration and is resistant to leaching. Moreover, the domestic demand for this type of fertilizer was sufficient to justify production on a scale large enough to attain productive efficiency. The location of the plant, however, posed certain problems. The Suez refineries supplied all their gases to the existing calcium nitrate plant and could not accommodate a greater capacity. Appreciable reserves of natural gas had not yet been discovered, and oil production satisfied only two-thirds of domestic demand. It was therefore decided to carry out an old plan elaborated after the second raising of the old Aswan Dam in 1934 for electrifying the dam and using an electrolytic process to obtain the required hydrogen.[9] The weaknesses of the original plan at the time were the relatively low economies of scale associated with the technology, the lack of demand for the oxygen by-product, and the high costs of transporting the fertilizer to the Delta, which consumes a large share of the output. The production cost of the fertilizers depended critically, of course, on the pricing of electricity. On the face of it, the price paid by the fertilizer plant for electricity seemed quite low (at 1.178 milliemes per kwh)— only one-sixth of the next lowest price paid by an industrial undertaking (cement). However, information on the costs of electrifying the dam indicate that the pricing of electricity to the fertilizer plant did assure a normal return (8 to 10 percent) on the electrification investment and hence did not conceal a subsidy for the fertilizer industry.[10] Given the large difference in the social costs of producing electricity at Aswan and in lower Egypt, the increasing demand for fertilizer in upper Egypt, with its conversion to perennial irrigation, and the rise in fuel and gas costs at the end of the 1960s, the decision to use an electrolytic process seems to have been correct. The Aswan plant, KIMA, the construction of which was well coordinated with the electrification of the dam, began production in 1961 and reached an annual output of 600,000 tons of ammonium nitrate fertilizers (20.5 percent N) by 1964.

In addition to the demand for ammonium nitrates, the government anticipated a strong increase in the demand for ammonium sulphates as a consequence of the construction of the Aswan High Dam. The two large consumers of this fertilizer are rice and sugar cane, which were to be the main beneficiaries of the increased water supply. The government decided, therefore, to build a 100,000-ton unit adjacent to the Suez plant, based on sulphur and gases from the expanded Suez refineries. This unit started production in 1963, and Suez was now developing into a petrochemical complex where all the by-products of oil refining were being gradually put to use.

The KIMA factory at Aswan suffered from the same kind of transportation difficulties that faced the phosphate industry on the long haul between Aswan and the Lower Egypt consuming areas—long shipping delays, accumulation of inventories, and spoilage of the fertilizer through moisture absorption.[11] It did not, on the other hand, depend upon long shipments of bulky raw materials. Thus, while the consumers felt the inconvenience of the transportation problems, the production process itself did not suffer from the serious interruptions that plagued the phosphate industry; this explains much of the difference between the growth performance of the two industries during the 1960–1963 period (Charts 9.1 and 9.2).

Moreover, transportation costs per unit of nutrient diminished through the output's increasing nitrogen content. In 1964 the production of the 20.5 percent nitrogen variety was abandoned in favor of a 26 percent variety, and in 1968 the latter was discontinued in favor of a 31 percent variety.[12] Apart from achieving economies in transportation costs, the higher nitrogen concentration also reduces the costs of other materials, such as limestone.

CHART 9–2

Nitrogenous Fertilizers: Production and Imports, 1950–1971

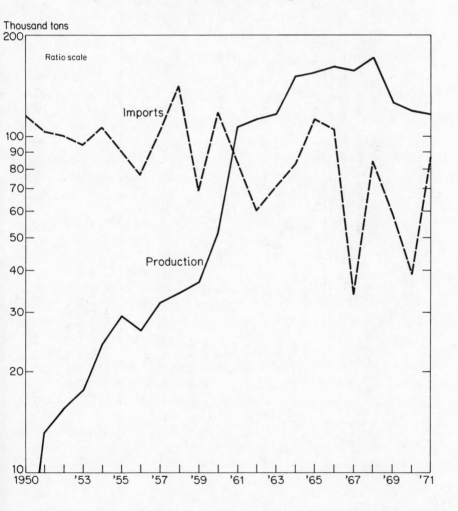

TABLE 9-2
Nitrogenous Fertilizer Prices, 1951–1968
(£E per ton of equivalent nutrient)

	1951	1953	1955	1957	1960	1963	1965	1966	1968
Calcium nitrate	31.0[a]	28.5[a]	26.8[a]	28.5[a]	25.0[a]	23.0[a]	22.6[a]	—	21.3[a]
	21.0[b]	—	20.0[b]	14.2[b]	19.1[b]	16.8[b]	19.7[b]	—	—
Ammonium sulphates	—	—	—	—	—	27.5[a]	27.5[a]	27.5[a]	26.2[a]
	—	—	—	—	—	20.2[b]	14.5[b]	19.9[b]	15.7[b]
Calcium ammonium nitrates 20.5	—	—	—	—	—	25.3[a]	25.2[a]	—	—
	—	—	—	—	—	—	18.6[c]	—	—
Calcium ammonium nitrates 26.0	—	—	—	—	—	—	31.3[a]	31.3[a]	31.3[a]
	—	—	—	—	—	—	—	22.8[c]	—

SOURCE: Federation of Industries, *Yearbook*, various issues.
a. Domestic price, ex-factory.
b. Import price, c.i.f.
c. Export price, f.o.b.

The high rate of investments in the industry together with the large domestic market explain the steepness of the production curve in the 1951–61 period (Chart 9.2). The potential demand for fertilizers in Egypt at low prices and the allocation of investment funds to the expansion of the industry could undoubtedly have maintained this rate of growth for a number of years. The 1967 War, however, resulted in the destruction of both the Suez petroleum refineries and the adjacent fertilizer plants. By 1970 the production of calcium nitrates and ammonium sulphates had completely ceased, reducing output of nitrogenous fertilizer by 30 percent.[13] Nevertheless, in spite of these setbacks, the industry should resume its growth with the inauguration in 1971 of a fertilizer plant in the Cairo area. It feeds upon the gases of the coking plant that serves the requirements of the Helwan steel mill, and its capacity is planned to reach 800,000 tons per year from the present total of 400,000 tons by 1975. The government has shown a strong and sustained commitment to both fertilizer industries to expand capacity well beyond projected consumption in the expectation of exploiting a growing export market.

COSTS AND REVENUES

Cost data are available for 1954, 1957 and 1964–65. However, it should be clear from our historical introduction that the data are strictly comparable only for 1954 and 1957; in these two years they pertain to the same product and production unit. By 1964–65 the industry had expanded into additional products and production units, and the cost data include all plants. Nevertheless, the final output may be considered the same, namely, nitrogen nutrients. The changes in nutrient concentrations, the introduction of new techniques with different inputs and by-products may all be considered technological innovations that aim at improving the performance of the industry. What matters is the competitiveness of the output-mix produced in 1964–65 as compared with the output-mix (in our case a single product) produced in the years 1954 and 1957. It can be determined by estimating the resource cost of the domestic fertilizer-mix in terms of import prices of equivalent fertilizer varieties.

In Table 9–3 we have estimated effective rates of protection and domestic resource costs in both current and constant international prices. As the industry was operating at various levels of capacity in the three years, we have also calculated resource costs at 90 percent "full capacity" utilization.

The choice of international prices causes some problems in this industry. Although Egypt has both exported and imported fertilizers, it was decided to use c.i.f. import prices. Therefore, c.i.f. prices for fertilizers with equivalent concentrations had to be found. These were readily available for calcium nitrates and ammonium sulphates because concentrations here are standardized. However, ammonium nitrates were imported in mixed concentrations during the early 1960s and this precluded the derivation of import prices by

TABLE 9–3
Nitrogenous Fertilizer Industry: ERPs, DRCs, and Performance Indicators

	1954		1957		1964–65	
	Actual Plant Utilization (64%)	Full Capacity Utilization (90%)	Actual Plant Utilization (83%)	Full Capacity Utilization (90%)	Actual Plant Utilization (80%)	Full Capacity Utilization (90%)
ERP (percent)	24.7	—	48.3	—	12.4	—
DRC (piasters per U.S. dollar) At current international prices, c.i.f.						
5% rate of return	43.3	34.4	51.7	49.1	43.3	39.2
10% rate of return	52.4	40.4	61.1	57.6	52.3	47.1
15% rate of return	61.5	46.3	70.6	66.2	61.3	55.0
DRC, at constant international prices, c.i.f. (piasters per U.S. dollar)						
5% rate of return	40.7	34.8	38.0	36.3	32.3	30.5
10% rate of return	49.8	40.8	45.4	43.0	39.3	36.7
15% rate of return	58.5	46.7	52.8	49.7	46.4	42.8
Effective exchange rate	37.0	37.0	38.5	38.5	43.5	43.5
Rate of return to capital (percent)						
at actual domestic prices	9.4	—	14.6	—	13.5	—
at international prices	1.5	—	−2.0	—	5.5	—

Performance Indicators
(1954 = 100)

Labor productivity per man-hour					
Output (in terms of pure nitrogen nutrient)	100	—	118	—	176
Value added at domestic prices	100	—	143	—	147
Value added at international prices	100	—	103	—	174
Physical capital productivity (in terms of pure nitrogen nutrient per unit value of machinery and equipment)	100	—	125	—	185
Hourly wages	100	—	132	—	193

SOURCE: B. Hansen and K. Nashashibi, NBER Working Paper No. 48, New York, 1975, Tables 24 and 25.

variety. Fortunately, both of the Egyptian varieties were exported, and through the addition of a freight margin, hypothetical import prices were calculated. Domestic and foreign prices are set out in Table 9–2.

THE COMPETITIVENESS OF THE NITROGEN FERTILIZER INDUSTRY, 1954 TO 1964–65

In its first year of production (1951) the fertilizer industry priced its calcium nitrates at £E31 per ton. The equivalent import price was £E21.0. The price difference amounted to a nominal rate of protection of 48 percent. The domestic price was then gradually reduced, with temporary increases in 1957 and 1958, to £E21.3 in 1968. The import price also declined, albeit more moderately, with the result that the nominal rate of protection was reduced to 15 percent in 1965 and perhaps to less in 1968. The degree of protection of those nitrogen fertilizers that were introduced in the 1960s was substantially higher. With each weighted by its nitrogen content, the average degree of protection in 1964–65 amounted to 29 percent. Nevertheless, small quantities of ammonium nitrates were exported in 1965 and 1966, and the intention behind the additional investments, allocated to the industry, was to create a substantial export surplus and to transform the industry into a foreign exchange earner.

Of course, it is entirely possible for an industry to be both protected in the sense that the domestic price is higher than the c.i.f. import price and to be an efficient foreign exchange earner. The necessary conditions are a domestic monopoly (the condition is fulfilled when production as well as trade are nationalized) and costs of production falling short of the c.i.f. import price by a sufficient margin to absorb freight and yielding a marginal revenue on exports equal to or larger than marginal costs.[14] We shall investigate whether these conditions were fulfilled by the Egyptian nitrogenous fertilizer industry.

Let us first look at the data for 1954 and 1957 as given in Table 9–3. In terms of domestic prices, the rate of return increased from 9.4 percent in 1954 to 14.6 percent in 1957. The general price increase that occurred after 1956 (see Chapter 3) included fertilizers.[15] This price increase helped to secure higher profitability in terms of domestic prices despite a general increase in input prices, particularly for fuel oil and refinery gases. In terms of international prices, profitability declined, however, from 1.5 to −2.0 percent, because the c.i.f. price of calcium nitrates fell. As a result, resource costs (at 10 percent rate of return) increased from 52.4 piasters in 1954 to 61.1 piasters in 1957, in spite of higher capacity utilization. At hypothetical full capacity utilization, the competitive position of the industry in 1954 and 1957 was better, of course, but the decline of competitiveness was enhanced. The ERP increased from 24.7 percent to 48.3 percent. Thus, after several years of operation, in 1957 the nitrogen fertilizer industry was in greater need of protection than in its earlier years. Prices of fertilizers abroad fell, while the domestic industry, with the given scale and technique of production, was faced with rising input prices and costs.

In terms of *constant prices*, the industry shows a lower resource cost in 1957 than in 1954, but this is attributable to the higher capacity utilization. At hypothetical full capacity utilization, the resource costs are virtually at the same level, some 20 percent above the official exchange rate.

Wage developments are not of much direct importance for the industry; wages do not exceed 10 percent of the total cost of production (at international prices). The bulk of production costs consists of payments for three inputs: fuel, refinery gases, and packing. Any substantial improvement in the industry's competitiveness depends upon cost reduction for these inputs, or on major changes in production techniques. Substantial fuel cost reductions were, indeed, achieved (in terms of international prices) through the falling oil prices during the 1960s and the shift in Egypt's position from a net importer to a net exporter of oil, with the resulting change of opportunity cost of oil from a c.i.f. basis to an f.o.b. basis. The introduction of a new packing material promised cost savings. At the end of the 1960s the industry introduced the use of plastic bags—a by-product of the domestic petroleum industry—in lieu of paper or jute bags. In addition to the advantages of lower costs and a low import content, plastic bags also protect the fertilizer from moisture. Finally, refinery gases became relatively cheaper. In the late 1940s the gases—mainly butane and methane—were wasted. Eventually, butane was marketed on a large scale for household use. This may explain a sharp price increase between 1954 and 1957. Later, however, the expansion of refining capacity and the discovery of commercial quantities of natural gas exerted a downward pressure on the price.

These favorable developments in input prices during the sixties improved the competitiveness of the Suez plant, particularly after the ammonium sulphate unit was added to the basic facilities, resulting in lower capital charges per unit of output.[16] However, the major reductions in costs were related to new techniques of production and new output mixes. Moreover, since capital invested usually increases with capacity expansion by a factor of only 0.71,[17] the large scale of production at the KIMA plant and the increased scale at the Suez plant led to more economical levels of operations.

The beneficial effects of these changes are reflected in lower resource costs, even though the average import price of nitrogen nutrients fell by 20 percent between 1957 and 1964,[18] and the industry suffered from the inflationary developments afflicting all manufacturing industry (see Chapter 4). At current international prices and actual capacity utilization, resource costs fell from 61.1 piasters in 1957 to 52.3 piasters in 1964–65 at a 10 percent rate of return, while the official exchange rate increased from 35 piasters to 43.5 piasters. Had the industry in 1964–65 been operating at full capacity (90 percent), it would almost have been competitive as an import substitute at the official exchange rate and a 10 percent rate of return. With a freight margin of £E1.20 per ton to allow for exports, resource costs in production for export in 1964–65 would have been 56.9 piasters at actual capacity and 52.0 piasters at hypothetical full capacity utilization. This is somewhat above the official exchange rate but well below the rate of 61 piasters suggested by the IMF in 1966. At this latter rate the industry would seem to be competitive in exports to neighboring Middle Eastern and African markets, where Egypt has a freight advantage over alternative suppliers.

In 1964–65 the nitrogenous fertilizer industry had thus almost reached trade efficiency as an import-substitute industry at the existing official exchange rate and as an export industry at a "realistic" exchange rate of 61 piasters per U.S. dollar, provided only that it worked at full capacity. As mentioned earlier, however, the weighted average ex-factory price that year implied a nominal rate of protection of 29 percent. The industry was really no longer in need of this protection. Indeed, at the "realistic" exchange rate and at full capacity utilization, the rate of return to capital would have exceeded 20 percent. It is clear, therefore, that the current capacity expansion aiming at export markets is correct despite the somewhat lower prices that this would bring. Also, nitrogenous fertilizers are overpriced domestically, and it is noteworthy that even at the relatively high domestic prices, optimal requirements are believed to be much higher than actual consumption. At current prices, nitrogen requirements of agriculture have been estimated at 737,000 tons, while total consumption in 1966 reached only 262,000 tons.[19] Thus, both external and internal reasons would argue in favor of expanding the nitrogenous fertilizer industry.

DETERMINANTS OF THE INDUSTRY'S COMPETITIVENESS

The transition from a heavily protected industry to an almost efficient import substitute and—at a "realistic" exchange rate—possibly even to a profitable export industry is the result of a number of factors. Of prime importance is the shift to a higher concentration of nitrogen and the exploitation of economies of scale.

Table 9–3 shows a strong increase in capital productivity. Between 1954 and 1957 it was essentially due to higher capacity utilization. In 1964–65 capacity utilization was at about the same level (80 percent) as in 1957, yet capital productivity increased by nearly 50 percent—the consequence of the adoption of more efficient production techniques. Physical labor productivity rose by almost the same percentage as capital productivity. And—for the first time among the industries reviewed so far—we find a growth in labor productivity (both physical and in terms of value added) that exceeds wage increases during the sixties.

The improvement in the industry's competitiveness was also related to the fact that it became relatively more labor-intensive (with a greater share of wages in total costs of production) and less capital-intensive. It should be emphasized that this technologically sophisticated industry could draw upon a large pool of domestic engineering skills, without which it could not have achieved the growth rate it did or succeeded in the adaptation and learning processes that transformed it into a viable undertaking.

Conclusions.

Both phosphate and nitrate fertilizer industries appear to have attained productive efficiency and were on their way to becoming profitable export ventures in 1964–65. The phosphate fertilizer industry was profitable from the outset because it could draw on a large natural resource base and needed only to operate at optimum capacity and to solve its transport problems. The nitrate fertilizer industry, by contrast, went through a trial period characterized by heavy protection and high costs of production. It finally succeeded in finding the choice of technique, product-mix, and scale of production best suited to its relative input costs. International cost comparisons for the two fertilizer industries reveal that Egypt derived a comparative advantage mostly because of the low cost of rock phosphate and electricity. Low labor costs and abundant availability of engineering skills also contributed to the competitiveness of the industry.[20]

The initial protection thus seems to have been justified by later developments, and here we have what looks like a case of a successful infant industry policy. Investment allocation to the industry's ancillary services, particularly in transportation, distribution, and storage should have been larger, but there is no indication that foreign exchange controls have directly hampered the industry. Finally, recent natural gas finds in Lower Egypt promise further development in even more competitive technologies.

THE RUBBER TIRE INDUSTRY

The development of the tire industry in Egypt originated in the early 1950s, when private entrepreneurial interests, encouraged by the government's commitment to industrialization, obtained guarantees that a domestic tire industry would be adequately protected from foreign competition. From the outset, the project appeared as a purely import-substituting venture without much prospect for developing a comparative advantage and expanding its activities into the export field.

Demand for tires and tubes amounted to 4,000 tons in 1951 and, while it declined because of the recession following the end of the Korean boom (see Chapter 2), demand projections were encouraging. The size of the existing stock of motor vehicles, its rate of increase, the extension of the road network, and plans pertaining to the establishment of an automobile industry were all cited in favor of the project. In 1953 the Transport and Engineering Company presented the Permanent Production Council with a proposal for the construction of a 5,000-ton tire plant to be expanded to a capacity of 10,000 tons within six years.[21] This is a small plant by world standards, but economies of scale in this industry are not very important over a broad range of output.[22]

On the supply side, the situation appeared less favorable. Unlike other industries considered in this chapter, the tire industry did not have any domestic raw material base that might have given it a cost advantage (equal to freight). It had to rely almost entirely on imported raw materials. A theoretical possibility of domestic substitution for some of the inputs does exist, such as synthetic rubber and nylon cord from petroleum feedstock, and steel beads and wires from the domestic iron and steel industry. The first is practically excluded, however, because of the large size of the minimum efficient plant (27,000 tons as compared with a domestic demand of 2,000 tons for synthetic rubber in 1963–64),[23] and the latter is still only a remote possibility. The cost data for 1963–64 reveal that, after eight years of operation, 92 percent of the total material inputs (including services) were still imported.

In approving the project, the Permanent Production Council subscribed to 25 percent of the original capital raised and recommended a number of protective measures:[24] (a) waiving of customs duties on imported raw materials and machinery and the imposition of adequate duties on imported tires, (b) assuring the firm of sufficient foreign exchange for imported raw materials, and (c) a government guarantee to purchase its tire requirements from the plant for five years at a price equal to production costs plus a 10 percent margin, provided the price would not exceed the price paid by the U.S. government for its tire requirements plus freight and insurance costs.

Production and Trade.

The tariff recommendations were adopted in May 1954. Information about their immediate impact on tire prices is not available, but tire prices went up by 21 percent from 1955 to 1957. The factory went into operation in 1956, and production expanded smoothly (by 12.5 percent a year) over the period from 1956 to 1970, hardly affected by raw material shortages except, for a brief period, as an aftermath of the 1967 War (Chart 9–3).

Imports declined steadily from 1957 to 1964, while exports increased rapidly from 1959 on and surpassed imports by 1961. The continued flow of

CHART 9–3
Rubber Tires: Production and Trade, 1956–1970

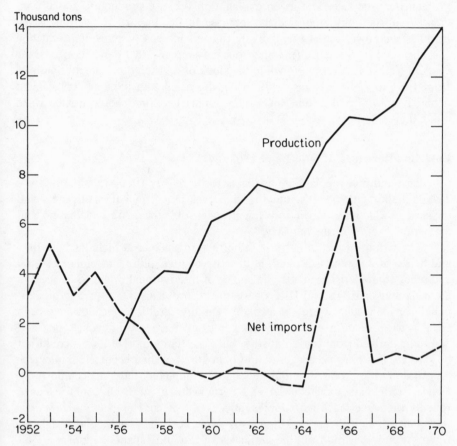

imports is partly due to the limited production program of the factory. In 1965 exports fell to almost nothing while imports soared from about 650 tons in 1964 to 7,000 tons in 1966, with a production of about 10,000 tons. In 1967 imports fell back to their earlier level, and in 1968 exports began to recover. In 1969 and 1970 the situation was quite similar to that of the years 1963 and 1964, with production, imports, and exports all running at somewhat higher levels. In the post-1967 period, net imports were restricted by a system of domestic rationing.[25]

We have no satisfactory explanation for the peculiar movements of trade between 1965 and 1967. Inventories increased from 1964 to 1965, but that can explain only a minor part of the apparent increase in consumption. Since there was a simultaneous rise in imports and drop in exports, with the rise in imports greatly exceeding the fall in exports, it would be natural to look for an explanation in the development of domestic demand. Domestic production problems can be ruled out as an explanation because production actually increased substantially alongside the increase in tire imports. Government demand is unknown, but it seems likely that an increased share of production was absorbed by the army (possibly to satisfy replacement demand after three years in Yemen). A rapid growth in the stock of registered private automobiles from 1961 to 1963 may also, with a lag, have led to a burst of replacement demand in 1965 and 1966. But erratic import licensing should not be ruled out, either.

Costs and Revenues, 1960–61 and 1963–64.

Cost and revenue data are available for the years 1960–61 and 1963–64. This is a short interval for studying the development of competitiveness and physical productivity, but it conveniently straddles the 1962 devaluation and the nationalization of the industry.

The output of this industry is rather heterogeneous. It includes both tires and tubes, of different sizes, and, in the case of tires, different number of plies and other characteristics. Thus, the choice of international prices to be used in the estimates of ERPs and DRCs gave rise to problems. C.i.f. prices for individual tires and tubes were not available (in any case, it would not have been feasible to work on a completely disaggregated basis). C.i.f. values per unit had to be derived from trade statistics, but Egyptian import statistics could not be used for this purpose because imports in 1960–61 had become complementary to domestic production and thus had a completely different composition. Hence, trade data for Lebanon and Syria were used. Both countries have roughly the same truck-automobile ratio as Egypt, and both import all their tires and tubes, with approximately the same cost, insurance, and freight as Egypt when importing from the major European and Japanese suppliers. Unit values were almost constant for both Lebanon and Syria during these years, with the average c.i.f. unit value equal to U.S. $1.04 per kilogram. We have applied this c.i.f. price to Egyptian production for both 1960–61 and 1963–64. In doing this, we ignore the fact that Egypt did not produce all of its consumption, but in 1960–61 imports amounted to only about 10 percent of total consumption (by weight). The remaining imports consisted partly of automobile tires for special purposes, but contained also motorcycle and bicycle tires. It is difficult to say, therefore, whether our choice of c.i.f. unit value exaggerates or underestimates the international value of Egyptian production. We also call the reader's attention to the possibility of quality differences between the imports of Lebanon and Syria and Egyptian output: most probably the Egyptian product's quality was lower than that of European tires. In regard to f.o.b.

prices, we had no choice but to use the unit value of Egyptian exports. It may be too high for our purposes because all Egyptian exports were made under bilateral agreements, and these may tend to inflate prices.

Competitiveness of the Industry, 1960–61 and 1963–64.

Table 9–4 summarizes the main results of our estimates. We note first that the profitability of the industry at actual domestic prices and costs was extraordinarily high. In 1960–61, the rate of net profit (before payment of

TABLE 9–4

Tire Industry: Rates of Return, ERPs, and DRCs

	1960–61 (at c.i.f. prices)	1963–64		
		(at constant 1960–61 c.i.f. prices and effective rates)	(at c.i.f. prices)	(at f.o.b. prices)
Rate of return (%)				
at actual domestic prices	71.5	69.9	59.8[a]	
at internatl. prices				
actual effective rates	8.1	6.3	2.5[a]	
official rates	−0.1			
ERP (%)				
at actual effective rates	239.9	235.9	261.9[a]	
at official rates	427.4			
DRC (piasters per U.S. $)				
at 5% rate of return	48.2	37.7	48.5	51.7
at 10% rate of return	58.5	46.5	58.5	62.2
at 15% rate of return	68.9	55.4	68.4	72.8

	1960–61	1963–64
Exchange rates (piasters per U.S. $)		
official	35.2	43.5
effective (including premiums)		
outputs	41.9	41.9
inputs	38.7	38.7

SOURCE: B. Hansen and K. Nashashibi, NBER Working Paper No. 48, New York, 1975, Table 26.

a. At official rate.

interests, rents, and taxes) on capital invested was 71.5 percent. In 1963–64, after the devaluation, nationalization, and wage increases, profitability was lower but remained as high as 59.8 percent (an attempt to calculate returns on capital at replacement costs might lower this figure to about 50 percent). The industry was given a virtual monopoly, and government price fixing did not prevent the emergence of huge monopoly profits.

The decline in the net rate of return during the period under review was partly the result of the shift from multiple to uniform exchange rates that accompanied the 1962 devaluation. In 1960–61 a multiple rate system had been in effect, with an exchange premium of 20 percent applied to imports of tires and tubes. For imported raw materials the premium was only 10 percent and for imported machinery and spare parts it was usually waived. The multiple rate system thus implied a subsidy to the industry. It disappeared with the devaluation, which, on balance, was unfavorable to the industry.

The implicit nominal tariff protection for tires (expressed by the difference between domestic output price and c.i.f. price at actually applied exchange rates) was 67 percent in both years under study. The ERP in 1960–61, however, was 239.9 percent at actual exchange rates (including premium) and 427.4 percent at the official exchange rate. These high ERPs are, of course, related to the high import content of production and the low tariffs on imported inputs.

At international prices, the monopolistic profit would, of course, disappear, but it is interesting that there would still be a profit left in 1960–61, close to "normal" (8.1 percent), at least at the actual multiple exchange rates. At the official rate and international prices, however, the rate of return would be about zero. The difference indicates the subsidy that the multiple exchange rate system implies for this industry.

The DRC in 1960–61, at 10 percent return to capital, was 58.5 piasters per U.S. dollar and was thus much higher than the official rate of 35.2, as well as considerably higher than the exchange rates actually applied to the industry—41.9 for outputs and 38.7 for inputs. The apparent contradiction—that the industry would be almost "normally" profitable with a rate of return of 8.1 percent at international prices and actual exchange rates but that, nonetheless, the resource costs at 10 percent return would be much higher than the level of the actual rates—is related to the fact that the actual exchange rate for output was higher than for inputs (see above).

In 1963–64 the official exchange rate applied to the industry was 43.5. The ERP was now 261.9 percent, somewhat higher than at the actual rates in 1960–61, but much lower than at the official rate that year. The DRC at 10 percent return to capital remained unchanged from 1960–61 at 58.5. Thus, the industry continued to be noncompetitive, but the situation was clearly much better than in 1960–61, and the industry would have been competitive at the rate of 61 suggested by the IMF in 1966. For 1963–64 we have also calculated the DRC on the basis of f.o.b. prices for output. At 10 percent return on capital, the DRC in export was 62.2, quite close to being competitive at the rate of 61 just mentioned.

Since wage costs increased very considerably during the three-year period, the unchanged DRC indicates that productive efficiency must have improved substantially. To illuminate this aspect of the problem, we have calculated the DRC for 1963–64 at constant 1960–61 prices and effective exchange rates. At 10 percent return to capital, the DRC thus calculated was 46.5, compared with 58.5 for 1960–61. Productivity of primary factors thus increased by about 20 percent over three years. This increase in productivity was partly due to a shift from natural rubber to cheaper synthetic rubber as the basic raw material. The major strength of the industry as revealed by a comparison of its costs with those of other countries lies in its low labor costs. This, combined with a relatively labor-intensive technology, allowed the industry to offset to a large extent the high cost of its imported raw materials. Despite nationalization, the industry thus fared quite well during these years, and to some extent began to prove itself a successful infant industry.

THE PULP AND PAPER INDUSTRY

This industry started in the early 1930s as a direct, private response to the protective policy instituted by the tariff reform of 1930. The industry was operating on a very small scale, almost on a handicraft basis: in 1951, seven private firms were producing a total of about 20,000 tons of paper and cardboard, and their aggregate investment did not exceed £E1.5 million.[26] Their operations were limited to the most labor-intensive stages of production, such as cutting the raw material (mostly paper waste) and reducing it to pulp. More elaborate and technically demanding processes, such as bleaching and glazing, were not attempted. Consequently, only crude packing paper and crude varieties of cardboard were produced, while imports satisfied the demand for finer qualities, particularly printing and writing paper. Both production and imports increased rapidly during the 1950s as consumption expanded. The demand for finer quality paper, used for direct consumption and as an input in the printing industry, and for kraft packing paper, particularly by the cement and fertilizer industries, became sufficiently large to encourage the establishment of modern integrated paper mills (Chart 9–4).

Technical Characteristics of the Modern Establishments.

As was the case with tires and steel (see below), the Production Council also played a crucial role in the development of the modern paper industry. In 1953 the Council made a survey of agricultural waste in Egypt to ascertain

CHART 9–4
Paper: Production and Imports, 1950–1970

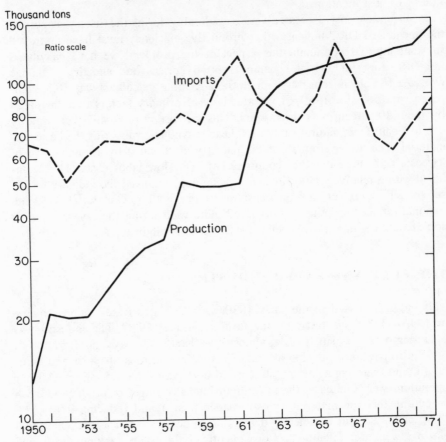

its possible use as the raw material basis for various varieties of paper pulp and sent missions abroad to solicit tenders for integrated paper plants in Egypt.[27] A pulp and paper mill was established in 1958 at Alexandria (RAKTA) with a capacity of 24,000 tons,[28] and in 1960 a kraft paper mill was established at Suez with a capacity of 20,000 tons. Production in the two mills began in 1961 and 1963, respectively.

These plants were located near sources of bulky raw material. The production of writing and printing paper in the Alexandria plant was based on rice straw from the northern part of the Delta. The kraft paper mill was divided into two units: one, producing pulp from bagasse, was located near the sugar factory at Edfu, while the other, the paper plant, was located at Suez next door to the fertilizer factories that were to receive a large part of its output.

The plants were quite satisfactory as regards linkage effects: they provided a market for the growing chemicals industry (using caustic soda and chlorine as inputs) and for by-products from sugar and rice production with a very low opportunity cost. By 1970 the importation of inputs was limited to some wood pulp and spare parts, whose share of total input value did not exceed 30 percent. On the other hand, the capital intensity of these plants exceeded that of any other manufacturing industry in Egypt.

Despite large investment outlays—£E17.1 million—the scale of operations seems to have been uneconomical. Paper production of acceptable quality is subject to large economies of scale with respect to fixed capital. For instance, a 500-ton-per-day paper mill would have required U.S. $120,000 in equipment per ton of daily output, while a 250-ton-per-day plant would require U.S. $180,000.[29] Doubling of plant size would thus reduce capital costs per unit of output by about one-third. The printing paper plant at Alexandria was designed to produce only 66 tons of paper per day. At full capacity, its capital per ton of output at the official exchange rate amounted to U.S. $740,260, with capital charges alone amounting to 24 percent of output value (at full employment and 10 percent interest). The kraft paper plant required similar capital investments. To be sure, additional lines of production can always be added in tandem with existing facilities as the market expands. This was done at the Alexandria plant in 1965, when a cardboard unit was added, and in 1968, when the printing paper capacity was expanded. But it is mainly administrative labor that is saved by this piecemeal approach. Capital requirements are by and large the same, and generally there is no large-scale advantage in regard to variable costs.

The planned small scale of production was not based on any accurate forecast of demand. Within a few years, as we shall see, excess demand was reflected in a general shortage of paper and rising imports.

Import Substitution.

Table 9–5 shows production, imports, and prices (domestic and international) of paper over nearly two decades (1953–1970). During this period domestic production increased at an annual average of 12 percent, reducing the share of imports in total consumption, which increased at an annual average of 4.7 percent (that is, roughly in line with GNP).

Reports from industries depending upon the output of the paper industry make it abundantly clear, however, that supply did not always meet demand, so that at times paper shortages emerged. Such shortages appeared for the first time in the aftermath of the 1956 Suez War, when imports were disrupted.[30] Together with the higher level of protection that the government deliberately afforded to industry at that time (higher tariffs and tighter import

TABLE 9–5

Paper Industry: Production, Imports, and Prices

Year	Domestic Production of Paper and Cardboard (000 tons)	Domestic Production of Printing and Writing Paper (000 tons)	Paper, Domestic Wholesale Price Index (1939 = 100)	Paper, Export Price f.o.b. (U.S.$ per ton)[a]	Imports of Paper and Cardboard (000 tons)	Imports of Printing and Writing Paper (000 tons)	Import Unit Value of Printing and Writing Paper (£E per ton)
1953	20.3	b	502	140	60.3	n.a.	n.a.
1954	24.2	b	465	144	67.0	25.0	75.7
1955	28.8	b	466	149	66.7	26.2	79.4
1956	32.3	2.1	496	156	65.5	25.0	82.5
1957	34.1	1.2	519	150	70.5	30.9	84.8
1958	50.5	3.4	555	145	80.3	21.9	85.3
1959	48.7	4.0	567	145	74.2	23.7	83.6
1960	48.6	6.8	514	145	99.7	34.1	84.0
1961	49.6	5.4	511	143	117.8	39.6	81.7
1962	82.9	23.2	508	138	87.7	16.3	87.7
1963	95.5	25.7	543	137	79.7	5.4	112.8
1964	104.1	29.5	534	141	74.4	1.4	125.5
1965	107.2	27.1	533	145	86.8	8.9	106.2
1966	111.7	25.2	533	152	127.4	28.8	108.2
1967	112.7	28.4	534	152	99.0	13.2	108.4
1968	116.0	32.7	534	146	67.3	4.8	94.5
1969	122.0	36.1	560	153	61.5	3.5	101.0
1970	124.8	43.2	n.a.	167	73.3	2.3	127.0

SOURCES: Federation of Industries, *Yearbook*, various issues; FAO, *Production Yearbook*, various issues.
a. Finland, kraft paper, export unit value.
b. Insignificant quantities.

controls, as explained in Chapter 2, the shortages contributed to a rise in prices which, in turn, induced an expansion of production. The average return on invested capital in the industry jumped from 7 percent in 1954 to 22.6 percent in 1957,[31] and one of the enterprises embarkęd upon production of printing and writing paper, albeit on a small scale (6,000 tons at full capacity). Imports were subsequently increased and demand satisfied. But the price rises that had taken place caused concern on the part of both the government and the printing industry (the latter being much more important than the small paper industry). In 1960, therefore, the government stepped in; it ordered price reductions by 15 percent on average for domestic paper and limited profit margins for imported paper.[32] The price cuts resulted in stagnation of domestic production, and the authorities had to permit a sharp increase in imports. Domestic costs of production—suffering from both a primitive technology and rising prices for produced inputs, domestic as well as imported—were rapidly moving out of line with the falling world market prices, and increased protection was required if private industry was to maintain, let alone increase, its share of domestic consumption.

The situation changed with the nationalizations of 1961, on the one hand, and production starting, on the other, in the Alexandria and Suez plants in 1961 and 1963, respectively. Production expanded and profitability was no longer a condition for increased domestic output. After four years of stagnation, production in 1962 was back on the growth path followed from 1950 to 1958. Imports were cut back somewhat but total supply had increased, and in the aggregate, equilibrium between demand and supply was probably established for the moment, although shortages could still occur for particular types of paper.

The 1962 devaluation did not lead to changes in the quoted prices for many varieties of paper, domestic as well as imported. This may be understandable in some cases where the import premiums, replaced by the devaluation, had exceeded the devaluation. Input prices, on the other hand, rose by about 10 percent as a result of the devaluation, and the general effect on profits was adverse:[33] in this regard the paper industry shared the general fate of manufacturing industry during these years (see Chapter 4). For the new production of printing and writing paper from the RAKTA mill, prices were brought into line with the prevailing domestic prices for imported paper, or some 50 percent above the c.i.f. prices, a level at which they remained until 1968. Considering the price cuts in 1960 and the price policies at the time of the 1962 devaluation, the overall degree of protection of domestic production may not have increased from 1954 to 1969 despite rising domestic production costs. Domestic wholesale prices for paper increased by 20 percent from 1954 to 1969, while world prices went up about 6 percent (Table 9–4) and the official devaluation in 1962 amounted to 24 percent.

In 1965 the RAKTA mill reached full capacity of production, but, with imports of paper varieties similar to those produced at RAKTA prohibited, shortages had again become serious and a black market emerged. The shortage of paper in the market was estimated to be about 37,000 tons that year, or some 20 percent of actual supply, and was attributed to the low foreign exchange quota allocated to the industry by the trade authorities.[34] In addition, repeated complaints were voiced that the distribution of imports by paper variety did not correspond to actual demand, and that domestic varieties more often than not failed to meet minimum specifications in regard to quality.[35] A sharp increase in imports in 1965 and 1966 alleviated these shortages, but supply was disrupted again by the 1967 War. In that year a new line of cardboard production with a capacity of 15,000 tons was opened at the RAKTA mill. This expansion was offset, however, by the partial destruction of the Suez kraft paper plant by Israeli attacks.[36] New paper shortages appeared in the immediate aftermath of the war as imports were disrupted. In the following year imports remained inadequate and black markets in certain types of paper prevailed, although prices were increased and productive capacity was further expanded in 1969 by the addition of a new printing paper line in the RAKTA mill.[37]

While paper imports were reduced to only one-third of domestic consumption, their absolute level remained virtually the same from 1950 to 1970; and although their product-mix changed toward finer qualities, import substitution was incomplete, particularly in the case of newsprint, which could not have been produced solely on the basis of bagasse pulp. To judge from the increase in demand, the Alexandria RAKTA plant could have been designed for a much larger capacity of production, possibly twice the actual capacity. However, there may have been some rational arguments for keeping the new industry at a low scale of production despite high fixed costs: lack of skilled workers, difficulties in mobilizing sufficient domestic raw materials, and, particularly, the necessity of gaining experience before even larger capital outlays were sunk in the industry.

Costs and Revenues: Competitiveness.

The large diversity of paper varieties produced in Egypt and the difficulty of obtaining the corresponding import price data precludes an analysis of the competitiveness of the industry as a whole. Fortunately, cost of production data were available for the operations of an important modern segment of the industry—the integrated paper and pulp RAKTA mill, which produces printing and writing paper only. The data cover the fiscal year 1962–63, immediately following the devaluation. Note that at that time there were still some starting-up expenses and capacity utilization was less than full; thus, we are studying an industry in its infant stage. Prices ex-factory were fixed at

£E151.5 and £E142.3 per ton for writing and printing paper, respectively, well above the corresponding c.i.f. prices of £E96.0 and £E90.0 per ton for allegedly equivalent varieties at the official exchange rate.[38] The price differential corresponds to a de facto nominal protection of 58 percent, but does not take into account the possibility that the quality of domestic paper may have been inferior to that of imported paper.

Costs of production at domestic and international prices are shown elsewhere.[39] As in the case of iron and steel (see below), at international prices, costs of traded inputs are close to the value of output, while total input costs (both traded and nontraded) even exceed output value. Thus, at international prices we have negative value added, defined in terms of return to primary factors of production. However, capacity utilization was only 78 percent, which, for a highly capital-intensive industry, is important. Since full capacity utilization was actually reached a few years later, we have computed DRCs for 1962–63 both at actual and at hypothetical full capacity utilization. The results are shown in Table 9–6 (see p. 284).

At a 10 percent rate of return, the DRC at actual capacity utilization exceeds 200 piasters per U.S. dollar, almost five times the official exchange rate; adjusted to full capacity utilization, it falls to 141 piasters but is still more·than three times the official foreign exchange rate. The DRCs evaluated at a 5 percent rate of return are very much lower because of the high capital charges, but even at this low rate of return the industry would be far from competitive. Cost comparisons with Indian, Mexican, and European plants show an extremely low labor productivity in Egypt for this industry, and even though wage costs hardly exceed 15 percent of total costs in this industry, unskilled labor may have increased overall costs through wastage of raw materials and an output that failed to meet the required specifications.[40]

The development of world prices since 1962–63 may have helped to increase the competitiveness of the industry. Stable until 1969, they rose some 20 percent in 1970 and 1971, and another 14 percent in 1973.[41] On the domestic front, costs of production were relatively stable during the period from 1962 to 1967, but seem to have moved up from 1967 to 1971. Domestic prices were raised from £E146 per ton for printing paper in 1967 to £E164 in 1970.[42] Since the subsequent international price trends resulted in a substantial increase in the import price of paper relative to the rise in domestic costs, it is likely that resource costs were favorably affected.

THE IRON AND STEEL INDUSTRY

As one of the big battlefronts of World War II, Egypt became a burial ground for large quantities of military equipment, iron reinforcements, and shell frag-

TABLE 9-6
Paper Industry: Rates of Return, ERPs, and DRCs, 1962–63

(percent)	
Rate of return	
at domestic prices	4.9
at international prices, c.i.f.	−3.8
ERP	239.6

(piasters per U.S. dollar)	
DRC, 5% rate of return	
at actual capacity utilization	148.4
at full capacity utilization	101.9
DRC, 10% rate of return	
at actual capacity utilization	207.7
at full capacity utilization	140.7
DRC, 15% rate of return	
at actual capacity utilization	266.9
at full capacity utilization	179.5
Official exchange rate	43.5

NOTE: DRC at full capacity utilization evaluated on the assumption that no increase in labor employed would take place. Other produced inputs and services were extrapolated on a pro rata basis.
SOURCE: Hansen and Nashashibi, NBER Working Paper No. 48, 1975, Table 27.

ments. These added to the domestic supply of iron scrap which had been exported before the war at a rate of 4,000 tons a year. The increased supply prompted domestic entrepreneurs to push for the prohibition of scrap metal exports and the establishment of a domestic iron and steel industry. At that time the annual domestic steel consumption was only about 180,000 tons, mostly beams for reinforced concrete, but consumption was expected to rise rapidly with industrialization.[43]

With domestic scrap as their source of raw material, three steel plants were established by competing firms in 1948–1949.[44] They were small, and had electrical furnaces or open-hearth furnaces fired by fuel oil; the rolling mills had an annual capacity of production of 30,000 tons each. These plants seem to have been well-managed, and they benefited from low wage rates and a price of steel scrap in line with the United Kingdom f.o.b. price. Excess demand for steel in Europe during the first postwar years contributed to the enhancement of local competitiveness by inflating international steel prices. Moreover, the major technological innovations that later resulted in large spurts in productivity and output in Europe and Japan had not yet been generally adopted. Egyptian domestic prices were about the same as average import unit values from 1952 to 1954 (Table 9–7), and could have been even lower had the government abolished the tariffs on imported inputs (coke, ferromanganese, and ferrosilicon).[45]

The three steel mills were using up more scrap than the economy was currently generating, and the stock of scrap, estimated in 1953 at 200,000 tons, was being rapidly depleted. Thus, as early as 1951 the Industrial Chamber for the Iron and Steel Industry exerted pressure upon the government to provide the necessary protection and guarantees for the creation of a fully integrated, domestic steel plant on the basis of iron ore deposits discovered at Aswan.[46] The iron content of the ore was mediocre (29 to 44 percent) and the deposits would be depleted in thirty years, but they had the advantage of being close to river and rail transportation. The much larger and richer deposits (60 percent iron) known to exist in the Western Desert at the Bahariya Oasis were left out of consideration, for they were located more than 200 kilometers from the Nile Valley and thus required large investments in transport.[47]

In 1954 the Permanent Production Council approved the project of an integrated steel plant at Helwan (a Cairo suburb) as presented by a consortium of major Egyptian firms (the Misr Group) and the German firm Demag. The Egyptian Iron and Steel Co. was established with the government and its various agencies as a major contributor to the initial capital issued and the Misr Group as a minority participant. Demag limited its participation to 20 percent of the value of the machinery and equipment it supplied up to a limit of £E2 million. Subsequent increments of capital were offered to the public with a minimum return of 4 percent guaranteed by the government.[48]

The plant was to have an annual capacity of 300,000 tons of crude steel, produced by Thomas and electrical converters. Demag undertook to deliver and install the equipment and to operate the plant in association with Egyptian managers appointed by the shareholders.[49] Top management was composed mostly of engineers. Price estimates for various steel products, submitted by the company to the Production Council, were between 12 and 36 percent below import prices, conveying the impression to the government that the plant would be competitive and would have an export potential.[50] It appears that the Helwan Steel Plant was promoted by the small rolling mills, which saw their scrap supplies dwindling and did not want to depend on imported raw materials. An integrated iron and steel plant would guarantee them a constant supply of steel ingots and semifinished products.

TABLE 9–7

Domestic and Import Prices of Steel Products

	Merchant Bars					Heavy Plates				
Year	Domestic Prices (£E per ton) (1)	Actual Import Unit Values, c.i.f. (£E per ton) (2)	Hypothetical Import Prices, c.i.f. (£E per ton) (3)	Export Prices, f.o.b. Antwerp, 4-year Moving Average (U.S.$ per ton) (4)	Average Nominal Protection (%) (5)	Domestic Prices (£E per ton) (6)	Actual Import Unit Values, c.i.f. (£E per ton) (7)	Hypothetical Import Prices, c.i.f. (£E per ton) (8)	Actual Export Prices, f.o.b. Antwerp, 4-year Moving Average (U.S.$ per ton) (9)	Average Nominal Protection (%) (10)
1952	44.0	41.8	57.9	—	—	—	—	—	—	—
1953	42.0	43.2	43.6	—	—	—	—	56.7	—	—
1954	34.2	36.2	39.0	—	—	—	—	44.4	—	—0
1955	47.0	39.9	46.3	110	—1	49.9	—	48.6	124	55
1956	50.0	42.7	46.1	103	14	77.6	—	51.1	120	65
1957	54.0	—	46.1	105	22	81.5	—	53.8	116	67
1958	57.8	—	37.9	108	31	81.5	—	42.1	115	74
1959	57.9	—	41.7	101	35	81.5	—	40.9	110	98
1960	57.9	—	43.2	99	37	89.4	—	43.9	105	113
1961	58.0	—	42.4	97	38	89.4	—	41.6	99	

Year	(1)	(2)	(3)	(4)	(5)	(6)	(7)	(8)	(9)	(10)
1962	—	—	47.7	97	—	89.9	—	46.3	98	107
1963	—	—	39.7	93	—	89.4	—	42.3	96	105
1964	—	—	44.5	90	—	89.4	—	51.4	97	97
1965	64.3	—	43.6	88	47	89.4	—	44.5	96	94
1966	64.3	45.6	41.4	87	56	—	59.3	42.7	94	—
1967	64.3	44.0	39.2	87	57	—	59.2	42.7	94	—
1968	65.0	44.2	38.8	84	60	94.4	60.6	42.3	89	110
1969	66.2	44.5	51.1	87	55	94.4	61.4	66.7	101	94
1970	82.9	69.4	56.7	96	60	114.3	83.8	66.0	115	110
1971	87.5	62.2	50.0	103	78	114.3	69.9	61.5	125	93

NOTE: Cols. (1) and (6): 1952–1955, Federation of Industries, *Yearbook;* col. (1), 1955–1967 and col. (6), 1955–1959, Domestic Price Index; col. (6), 1960–1965, Egyptian Iron and Steel Company records; 1968–1969, *Industrial Statistics by Commodity,* 1968–1969 and October 1970; 1970–1971, *Semi-Annual Bulletin for Prices of Industrial Commodities,* January 1971.

Cols. (2) and (7): Unit values from Trade Statistics in Federation of Industries, *Yearbook.* For col. (7) more expensive sheets are combined with plates in the statistics, which raises the average price somewhat.

Cols. (3) and (8): European export prices from *The European Steel Market,* United Nations Economic Commission for Europe. U.S. dollar prices were converted at a rate of $2.60 per £E until 1962, and at a rate of $2.30 thereafter. To convert prices to c.i.f., a freight margin of $11.50 per ton was added on the basis of *AMELITE Freight Conference of 1968.*

Cols. (4) and (9): Four-year moving average of f.o.b. export prices from *European Steel Market,* United Nations Economic Commission for Europe.

Cols. (5) and (10): Difference between domestic price and four-year moving average of c.i.f. import price as percent of the latter.

By the time the plant went into operation in the middle of 1958, £E19 million had been invested in ore extraction and production of steel. It was the single largest investment in the 1950s, but it was not large enough: there were substantial diseconomies of scale at that level of production and its capacity fell far short of actual and projected demand by the time it went into full operation. Whether the investment should have been made at all is another question, which we shall attempt to answer in the following section.

Steel Production, Trade, and Prices, 1951–1970.

Chart 9–5 shows production of steel and imports of finished products, as well as apparent steel consumption, from 1952 to 1970. Exports are not shown; they remained below 10,000 tons.[51] Apparent consumption equals the sum of domestic production and imports; stock figures are not available. In addition, we have constructed domestic and import price series for merchant bars, produced mainly by the three small plants, and for heavy plates, produced by the Helwan plant (Table 9–7). Two import price series are shown: unit values (from Egyptian foreign trade statistics) and export prices obtained at Antwerp by European countries (as quoted by the European Steel and Coal Community) to which we have added a c.i.f. margin.[52] European export prices are given as a four-year moving average to smooth the sharp short-run fluctuations characteristic of steel products.

Up to 1956, the actual Egyptian c.i.f. unit value for merchant bars coincides roughly with the hypothetical c.i.f. series derived from the Antwerp f.o.b. export prices. For the period 1965–1970, the hypothetical c.i.f. prices are somewhat lower than the actual unit values (columns 3 and 2); the composition of imports became complementary to domestic production, and hence the import-mix became more expensive than the domestic output-mix. This was particularly evident for plates and sheets, where price differences according to quality and size are much broader than for merchant bars. Finally, we derived a series showing de facto protection defined as the difference between domestic and average import prices as a percentage of average import prices.

The recession from 1952 to 1954 was marked by a stagnation in the domestic demand for steel; investment in residential building fell, and industry was saddled with excess capacity. At that time merchant bars, used mainly in residential construction, accounted for 80 percent of total steel consumption. The increasing domestic production of merchant bars by the three small mills was rapidly replacing imports. Domestic prices were almost competitive with c.i.f. import prices, and the actual degree of protection did not exceed 5 percent. In spite of their uneconomical scale of operations, the small steel plants were able to compete with imports, while the integrated steel plant in Helwan eventually proved to be highly inefficient. While this was partly due

CHART 9–5

Iron and Steel Products: Production, Consumption, and Imports, 1950–1971

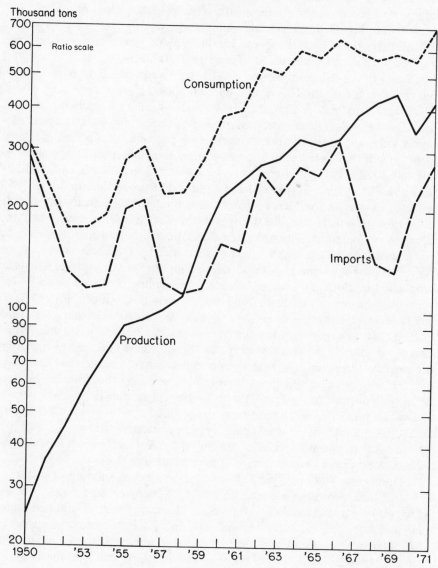

to more efficient management of the small plants, perhaps a more important reason is that the Helwan steel plant suffered much more from its relatively small scale of operation than did the smaller plants. Economies of scale are largest for blast furnaces producing the basic pig iron. The small plants dispensed with this stage of production altogether by using steel scrap and ingot.

Between 1954 and 1956 both production and imports rose in response to a recovery in economic activity (Chapter 1, Table 1–10). Imports of steel rose faster than production inputs, and the steel mills may have been close to full capacity utilization. This caused domestic prices to rise above c.i.f. prices, which remained steady; European f.o.b. prices were even declining slightly.

The 1956 Suez War disrupted steel importation and slowed down economic activity temporarily. It also marked the beginning of a period of investment growth that lasted until the mid-sixties. Demand from both residential and industrial construction rose sharply until 1962 and then more modestly until 1966, after which it turned down slightly. The production upturn in 1958 reflects the start of the Helwan plant's operation. Imports increased slightly until 1960. By that time, the Helwan plant was in full operation and the expansion in output decelerated. Domestic demand, meanwhile, propelled by the investments of the first Five-Year Plan and by the construction of the Aswan High Dam, caused a rapid rise in imports, which equaled domestic production in 1962. To be sure, growth in consumption slowed down somewhat with the demand curbs of 1965–66 and the aftermath of the 1967 War, but it resumed its tempo again in the early 1970s. At that time it became evident that the capacity of the new steelworks was far below demand. While import substitution in steel was only partial and failed to save much foreign exchange, it served to raise the prices of finished steel products substantially.

The degree of nominal protection of merchant bars rose from an average of 19 percent prior to the Suez War to 36 percent for the 1958–1961 period. This was a protective measure in favor of the three small producers, who were facing rising scrap prices. World export prices of steel, on the other hand, had been moving downward ever since the end of the Korean boom. Thus, domestic and world prices were now moving in opposite directions.

During the 1960s, the gap between domestic prices and import prices increased further, with the nominal level of protection reaching 50 percent for merchant bars and more than 100 percent for plates. Costs of imported materials rose after the 1962 devaluation, and prices were adjusted upwards. In 1970, unit values for imported steel increased sharply, and the Egyptian government raised domestic prices on merchant bars and other products by 25 percent; it increased the degree of protection when world prices eased off again in 1971. The protective position in that year vis-à-vis the hypothetical average import prices was 70 percent on merchant bars and 93 percent on plates. With respect to actual unit values, assuming the same quality and specifications for imported as for domestic products, the protection would have been 40 percent and 63 percent, respectively, for bars and plates. Significantly, the degree of protection was much smaller for merchant bars produced mainly by the small steel mills than for heavy plates produced exclusively by the Helwan plant. With respect to light sections (merchant and reinforced concrete bars), the Helwan plant had to follow the prices of the smaller plants. Protection for products not produced by the three steel mills was tailored to the high costs of the Helwan plant—hence a somewhat distorted structure of domestic prices.

The import substitution program for the steel industry brought Egypt into the company of various other small and medium-sized developing countries that attempted to create a national steel industry and ended up with high levels of protection (Peru, 106 percent; Columbia, 74 percent; Chile, 68 percent; Mexico, 46 percent; and Venezuela, 37 percent).[53] However, the result might have been more favorable had the Helwan Steel Plant been differently conceived, as we shall show in the following section.

Finally, as a supplier of inputs to other industries, including crude iron to the small steel mills, the Helwan plant must have been a source of severe disruption. Users of steel products (finished and semifinished) had difficulties in obtaining import licenses for them because foreign exchange authorities anticipated a greater domestic steel output. But the Helwan plant constantly failed to achieve its output targets, with production even falling in 1964–65 and in 1965–66.

Costs and Revenues of the Helwan Plant: Competitiveness.

Cost and revenue data obtained for the steel industry refer exclusively to the steelworks at Helwan for the year 1964–65. Unfortunately, no information is available for the three small, apparently much more efficient mills. Nonetheless, we have here the records of the "modern" and integrated sector of the industry that accounts for two-thirds of Egypt's output of steel products. 1964–65 was the sixth year of plant operations; it shows costs and productivity at a time when initial difficulties should have been overcome. Complete data are lacking for any earlier year, but data are available on output-mix and material inputs for 1959–60, so that a comparison of input coefficients would be possible. A record of profits and losses for the firm is available for the whole period.

Our ERP and DRC estimates, with some productivity indicators, are presented in Table 9–8. The Helwan plant was operating at two-thirds capacity in 1964–65. The data were not adjusted to full capacity utilization because the shortfall in production did not result from lack of demand but from difficulties in operating the plant, preventing the planned production and output-mix from being achieved.[54]

TABLE 9–8

**Value Added, Profits, DRC, and ERP
at the Helwan Steel Plant, 1964–65**

	(000 £E)
Net domestic value added	
(incl. nontraded inputs)	
at domestic prices	5,103.8
at international prices	851.5
Net value added	
at domestic prices	2,459.0
at international prices	−2,091.0
Wages and salaries (incl. fringe benefits)	2,757.0
Net profits	
at domestic prices	−298.0
at international prices	−4,848.3
Total capital	
(historical costs)	40,000.0

	(piasters per U.S. dollar)
DRC	
5% rate of return	378.0
10% rate of return	480.0
15% rate of return	582.0
Official exchange rate	43.5

	(percent)
ERP	599.4

Source: Hansen and Nashashibi, NBER Working Paper No. 48, New York, 1975, Table 28.

Table 9–8 reveals the industry subject to losses not only in terms of international prices but also in terms of domestic prices, even though the domestic, weighted average ex-factory price of its output-mix exceeded international prices by 66 percent. It is also striking that domestic value added, defined as the value of output minus the value of traded inputs, was positive at international prices (albeit with an ERP of almost 600 percent), but negative in terms of the conventional definition of value added (value of output minus value of all material inputs and services). The high costs of nontraded inputs (ore) are also reflected in the DRCs, which were about ten times the official exchange rate (at 10 percent rate of return).

From Table 9–9 it is evident, moreover, that productivity in the Helwan plant was very low compared with steel plants in other countries, be they underdeveloped or highly developed, and that productivity deteriorated with the passage of time, culminating in a particularly poor performance in 1964–65.

The first two years of operations were marked by losses (£E1.7 million), followed by a short-lived period of recovery. In 1961–1962 the firm even managed to break even. The devaluation of July 1962, however, raised the prices of coke, imported ore, ferrosilicone, and spare parts—without immediate domestic output-price compensation. Furthermore, there was a sharp increase in the coke coefficient (see Table 9–9). The result was a series of losses and worsening of productivity indices. Production reached a peak in 1963–64, with 144,032 tons of steel products, and fell thereafter to 137,970 tons in 1964–65 and 121,270 tons in 1965–66, as input coefficients rose abnormally, labor productivity declined, and a succession of breakdowns occurred. By 1964–65, investment in the industry (fixed and circulating capital) amounted to £E40 million, to which another £E10 million could be added in start-up expenses and accumulated losses over the 1959–1965 period. Between 1963 and 1965 the plant was absorbing more resources than it was generating; there were hardly any savings in foreign exchange, with net domestic value added at international prices at only £E851,000 in 1964–65, and if an international price had been attached to nontraded goods, there would have been rather large foreign exchange losses.

Causes of the Helwan Plant's Inefficiency.

One of the major reasons usually offered for the deteriorating performance is the declining quality of the iron ore. The Aswan ore deposits, estimated to be only about 25 million tons, are shallow, have a high silicone content, and are spread over a large area with a low iron content ranging between 29 and 44 percent. The richer ores were depleted first and a gradual lowering of the iron content occurred, necessitating higher coke inputs. The rate of coke consumption in 1959 was almost normal by international standards; it rose to more than 1,200 kg by 1963–64 and within one more year to 1,600 kg. No attempt was made to enrich the iron ore charge, which would have reduced transportation costs and coke inputs considerably while increasing the productivity of the blast furnace. Moreover, the blast furnace charges appeared to be quite heterogeneous, and eventually a sintering plant was installed to remedy the situation. Nevertheless, the performance did not improve significantly.

The low and changing quality of the iron ore is at most only a partial explanation. First, ore consumption per ton of steel did not increase much. Moreover, European plants have been using ores with iron contents not exceeding 40 percent for decades, yet they have not reached such high levels of coke consumption. Table 9–9 shows that inputs of both iron ore and coke were much lower in Western European countries than in Egypt.

A more general explanation might be the inexperience of Egyptian management and labor in the operation of an integrated steel plant demanding a high degree of coordination and skill. Unlike industries (such as cement or fertilizers) that have constant output specifications and produce in a continuous flow (hence with a minimum of coordinating operations), steel shapes have to be individually handled by labor, which ultimately bears a large share of the responsibility for its quality. Moreover, tight coordination between departments (blast furnace, converter, rolling mill) is essential for maintaining efficiency and depends largely on the ability of labor and the engineering staff to maintain consistent and uniform rates of production in each department.

In the light of these requirements, the labor skill structure in the plant was totally inadequate. A consulting firm, hired to diagnose the factory's ills ascribed much of the difficulties to the structure of the labor force.[55] It found that 35 percent of the workers were recruited from neighboring villages, had never before worked in a factory, and continued to pursue their rural occupations. A substantial 78 percent of the workers had no technical training in metal industries. Moreover, although substantial overstaffing was reported in 1963, employment continued to increase until February, 1965, yet output was falling—hence, the low labor productivity (see Table 9–9) and the high labor costs as compared with the United Kingdom and other Western European countries.

Low labor skills and faulty installation of some production units resulted in numerous breakdowns and work stoppages. The premature wearing-out of the linings in one of the blast furnaces and in the Thomas converters as well as numerous electrical power failures affecting the electrical converters may serve as examples.[56] Continual repairs explain the large expenses for spare parts, which amounted to £E4.5 million in 1963–1965, or 16 percent of production costs.

In addition to the poor quality of the raw material and inexperience of the labor force, serious criticism may be directed against the whole conception of the project. For one thing, the location of the ore deposits and that of the plant virtually nullified Egypt's initial advantage in having domestic ore deposits. Given the location of the deposits 900 kilometers south of Cairo, high transport costs would result whatever the location of the plant. Shipping

TABLE 9–9

Steel Industry: Costs and Performance Indicators in Egypt and Other Countries, Selected Years

| | Cost Distribution (% output value at internatl. prices) | | Performance Indicators | | | | |
	Raw Materials and Fuel	Labor	Coke Consumption (per ton of finished steel)	Ore Consumption (per ton of finished steel)	Labor Productivity (tons of finished steel per man-year)	Capacity Utilization (%)	Profits (000 £E)
Egypt (Helwan)							
1959–60	—	—	1.036	2.320	—	45	−852.9
1963–64	—	—	1.251	2.375	30	75	−1,837.7
1964–65	75.7	32.8	1.593	2.386	27	77	−1,472.2
Other Countries							
1955	34.0[a]	17.5[a]	(0.723[b] (0.881[c] (0.915[d]	(0.824[b] (1.633[c] (1.510[d]	(45[c] (90[a] (156[d]	— — —	— — —

SOURCES: Data for countries other than Egypt: *Long-Term Trends and Problems of the European Steel Industry*, United Nations Economic Commission for Europe, 1959, pp. 73, 80. Data for Egypt: for 1959–60, *Annual Report*, Iron and Steel Company, as quoted in Mohamed Metwalli, *Factors Affecting the Establishment of the Iron and Steel Industry in the U.A.R.*, 1964–65; for 1964–65, F. A. El Bahai, "The Economics of the Iron and Steel Industry: the Egyptian Iron and Steel Company," Institute of National Planning, Cairo, 1966–67.

a. UK, 1950.

b. Japan. Ore consumption includes sinter. Also, steel scrap may have been added directly to the blast furnaces.

c. India.

d. Average of nine western European countries. The ore figure includes an average of 772 kg. of sinter.

the ore by rail to the Cairo area was very expensive and exceeded the existent railroad capacity. Moreover, a new bridge across the Nile had to be built at Helwan. Shipping the ore by barge on the Nile would have meant heavy investments in ports, barges, and tow boats, and, for deep-going barges, navigability is not always safe. To locate the plant at Aswan would have entailed shipping the finished product to the Delta region and coke from Alexandria to Aswan, or from a Red Sea port. In the latter case, heavy investments in port and rail facilities would have been necessary. As a result of the high domestic transportation costs, the Helwan plant was paying the same price—and often more—(per unit of iron content) for the Aswan ore as for imported ore (c.i.f.). Hence it did not benefit from any natural advantages.

The plant also suffered from an inefficient scale of operations. It was designed to produce 300,000 tons of steel products per year, and its two blast furnaces (where economies of scale offer the greatest potential) had a capacity of 400 tons per day. For that reason alone, compared with the minimum efficient plant size at the various stages of production, costs per ton of steel would be 50 percent above those of an efficient European plant.[57] This is a general problem that tends to make steel production uneconomical in developing countries, where domestic demand is often well below the efficient scale of operations.[58]

Whether Egypt could possibly have planned for a larger capacity when the construction of the plant began back in 1956 is another question. In 1962, when the plant had operated for two years, the country's apparent total consumption was about 550,000 tons. The production of the three small plants (already existent in 1956) was about 90,000 tons. About 250,000 tons more were of a specification and quality that could not be produced in Egypt. Thus, the demand at that time for products from the Helwan plant was about 200,000 tons, in contrast to planned production of 300,000 tons at full capacity. When it reached its peak in 1966, apparent consumption was still less than 650,000 tons, implying a demand for products from the Helwan plant of less than 300,000 tons. Had developments been correctly foreseen up to 1970, there would have been no need for building a larger capacity than 300,000 tons, unless the country had planned for steel exports. It could, of course, be argued that, with more effective demand management and foreign exchange policies—and disregarding the 1967 War—investment and steel consumption could have continued their growth after 1966; in that case the capacity of the Helwan plant would certainly have been too small by 1970.

Could actual developments have been foreseen at all in 1956? To some extent, yes. A very substantial part of the investments undertaken during the years 1958 to 1962, together with the Aswan High Dam project, were in fact approved by the Production Council as early as 1954. To extrapolate a certain growth of investment beyond 1962 would not have required too much imagination. However, investing for future demand means increased unutilized capacity during the first years of operation; what is gained on the swings may thus be lost on the roundabouts. Moreover, the risk of loss from technical obsolescence would increase.

In fact, the Helwan plant did not benefit from various innovations introduced in some European plants during the 1950s. It did not use the LD oxygen converters, in particular, which would have resulted in a much higher quality of steel and a lower coke coefficient, nor did it adopt the continuous casting process that reduces the capital-output ratio in the forge as well as wage costs. And because of the low skill of labor, the use of automation to ensure quality control and coordination among the various shops might have enhanced productivity substantially despite the small scale of operations. To be sure, it is not clear whether any of these innovations could have been incorporated in the Egyptian steelworks in 1957–58. The most widely used innovation in Europe at that time was the oxygen converter, but not until 1960 was it applied in developing countries; continuous casting and computer-controlled rolling mills did not spread until the 1960s.[59] The Helwan plant was constructed at a time of technological transition, and by 1960, when it went into full operation, it was already obsolete. In this sense, it is a blessing that it was planned with a relatively small capacity.

Aside from the government's heavy responsibility in the failure of the project, one may also question the role of the German firm Demag. On the face of it, as a participant in the investment, the firm may have miscalculated the costs of production and subsequently incurred heavy losses. For instance, it may have substantially overestimated the capacity of Egyptian labor and management in running the plant. But conditions of raw material supply, quality, and location, as well as the size and technology of the plant, should have been sufficient grounds for turning down the project. As for the firm's participation in the financing, it could have easily been recouped through the deliveries of plant and equipment. Even assuming that the firm did invest up to the maximum agreed (see above), its financial commitment amounted to only a small part of the value of plant and equipment supplied.[60] A moderate overpricing of its deliveries would have sufficed to recoup the capital invested—a possibility which has suggested to some that this may be yet another instance of questionable behavior on the part of foreign enterprises in the industrialization of developing countries.

The new steel complex currently under construction with Soviet assistance attempts to remedy the ills that afflicted the old plant. It will incorporate both oxygen converters and continuous casting, and will resort to the richer and closer ore deposits of the Western Desert. Its major operations will be computerized, and it will be built at an efficient scale of operations (1.5 million tons) based on exports to the Soviet Union, partly as repayment of loans, partly in exchange for steel types that cannot be produced in Egypt. It remains to be seen whether the new plant will prove more economical.[61]

THE AUTOMOBILE INDUSTRY

After World War II, Egypt could not resist setting up an automobile industry. In doing so it followed the example of other relatively industrialized developing countries without avoiding the problems that characterize the industry in such countries: diseconomies related to small-scale production and a high foreign exchange content.[62] Other consumer durables industries (refrigerators, air-conditioning units, TV sets, et cetera) set up in Egypt after World War II seem to suffer from the same problems as the automobile industry.

It is difficult to see why the automobile industry should be given a high priority in Egypt. The relatively dense railroad system, particularly convenient in a flat country, the large possibilities for water transportation, and the low per capita income should tend to relegate road transportation to a secondary level of priority. The allegedly egalitarian ideals of the régime speak strongly against sacrificing resources for the higher income brackets' luxury goods. Moreover, the continuous diminution in the share of exports in GNP until the end of the 1960s would hardly warrant large expenditures in convertible currencies to set up an automobile industry and keep it going. Finally, the rudimentary steel and engineering industries could not sustain a rapid process of import substitution in automobile components or secure a dissemination of knowledge and skills to lower stages of production. The backward linkages simply were not there.

Imports and Production of Automobiles.

While imports of private automobiles were licensed and restricted through high customs duties (66 percent) during most of the 1950s, trucks and buses were imported relatively freely, with only a 10 percent duty on chassis without bodies. A case can be made for the domestic assembly of trucks and buses because freight costs are much higher when they are imported assembled than when they are imported in parts. It was on this basis that the Ford Motor Company (the British subsidiary) set up an assembly plant for trucks in Alexandria. It was a small enterprise with a capital of £E500,000 and 200 workers, based on importation of all parts. Output did not exceed 1,000 units per year. The production of trucks was discontinued after the Suez War, when the company was Egyptianized, but its predominant activity—the construction of bodies for trucks and buses—continued, although the latter was discouraged because the Cairo municipality insisted that bus line concessionaires import complete buses.[63]

In 1959 a new attempt was made to develop an automobile industry that would gradually increase its use of domestic components; in this connection agreements were reached between Egyptian firms and Deutz (Germany) concerning production of trucks, and Fiat (Italy) and NSU (Germany), concerning production of passenger cars. Deutz and Fiat were to deliver all tools and parts. The agreement with NSU was limited to the supply of small engines and some parts for the production of a "popular" car—the Ramses—which represented a genuine attempt to develop an indigenous, labor-intensive technology for the production of a cheap, Jeep-like automobile with an engine hardly exceeding the horsepower of a motorcycle.

All three firms received preferential customs treatment, which reduced imports of other automobiles substantially. Customs duties on fully manufactured cars were raised to 70 percent, while duties on parts were lowered to 25 percent.[64] Likewise, duties on assembled chassis of trucks and buses were raised to 30 and 50 percent, respectively, while duties on components were set at 15 percent.[65] The production capacity of these firms was small: 24,000 Fiat cars and 3,700 trucks and buses a year; the capacity of the Ramses plant is not known to us, but it was a very small enterprise.

Table 9–10 shows the growth of automobile production together with the total value of automobile imports, including all parts. Typically, the importation of finished cars and trucks drops when domestic assembly takes place; if imports of parts and tools were not included, the real foreign exchange outlays on motor vehicle consumption would be disguised.

From 1953 to 1955, the annual demand for new passenger cars amounted to about 5,000 units, and for trucks and buses, to about 1,000 to 1,200 units. After the Suez War, imports of automobiles were restricted through both quotas and high customs duties (the former being the effective limitation), while imports of trucks and buses were allowed to grow. These measures reduced foreign expenditures for private automobiles and parts and stabilized them for all vehicles and parts at around £E 10 million (roughly 5 percent of total imports) between 1955 and 1961.

1960 saw the start of production of both the Ramses and the Deutz trucks, and in 1962 the first Fiat ("Nasr") automobiles were produced. In 1962, over 2,500 vehicles were assembled, and the total import value of finished parts and vehicles immediately doubled to about £E20 million. Part of the increase can be ascribed to the devaluation, and some of it may have been due to replenishment of stocks of materials and spare parts that were in short supply during the 1956–1960 period. A much larger amount of foreign exchange, however, was clearly allocated to the importation of private cars and parts, which can only be interpreted as a liberalization of the private automobile policy as compared with the years from 1956 to 1960. This tendency was further strengthened in 1963 and 1964, when total import expenditure on motor vehicles and parts rose to £E30 million and the industry

TABLE 9-10
Automobile Industry: Production and Imports, 1954-1971

Year	Production: Passenger Cars Output (units) Ramses	Fiat (Nasr)	Passenger Cars Capacity Utilization (%)	Trucks and Buses Output (units)	Trucks and Buses Capacity Utilization (%)	Imports (mill. £E) Finished and Unassembled Vehicles and Components	of Which Finished Passenger Cars	of Which Finished Trucks and Buses
1954	—	—	—	544[a]	n.a.	5.0	1.6	0.9
1955	—	—	—	n.a.	n.a.	11.5	3.3	1.8
1956	—	—	—	n.a.	n.a.	10.5	2.0	1.1
1957	—	—	—	454[a]	n.a.	5.9	1.0	0.6
1958	—	—	—	913[a]	n.a.	10.3	0.9	1.5
1959	—	—	—	n.a.	n.a.	13.2	1.4	2.3
1960	240	—	n.a.	867	23.4	10.7	1.4	1.9
1961	211	—	n.a.	1077	29.1	10.1	1.9	1.3
1962	144	863	4.1	1549	41.8	19.8	0.9	2.3
1963	209	3806	16.8	1927	52.1	30.4	3.4	1.8
1964	449	4527	20.7	1045	44.4	31.5	2.1	3.3
1965	264	4004	17.8	1345	36.6	22.4	2.3	4.0
1966	192	1615	7.5	916[b]	24.7	26.4	7.0	2.8
1967	—	108	0.4	712[c]	19.2	13.8	0.9	1.3
1968	—	758	3.1	1232	33.3	15.0	1.3	1.7
1969	—	2325	9.7	1340	36.2	18.3	2.3	3.2
1970	—	3590	14.9	1533	41.4	20.8	6.9	5.3
1971	—	5750	23.9	1833	49.5	31.7	11.1	8.2

SOURCES: Output and capacity utilization: Federation of Industries, *Yearbook*, and CAGMS, *The Production of the Automobile Industry*, various issues.

Imports: United Nations, *Yearbook of International Trade Statistics*, various issues; Federation of Industries, *Yearbook*, 1970 and 1971.

a. Assembly only in Ford Plant.

b. 1966-67

reached the peak of its operations. Yet, capacity utilization did not exceed one-fifth for passenger cars and one-half for trucks and buses. By then, however, the government seems to have realized the implications for foreign exchange expenditures of pushing the domestic car industry to full capacity. Full capacity utilization of the three factories would have entailed foreign exchange expenditures of at least £E60 million, amounting to one-fifth of the total value of imports. In 1965, the foreign exchange crisis forced a cutback in the operation of all the plants, and in 1966 the capacity utilization of the automobile and truck plants fell to 8 and 25 percent, respectively. The cutbacks were more severe for passenger cars than for trucks and buses: like a number of other industries producing consumer durables with high import contents, the automobile industry became a buffer where cuts in foreign exchange appropriations could be made without much consequence for other producing sectors; also, employees were not laid off despite the fall in production.

In the absence of information about the decisions that led to the establishment of the domestic car and truck industry, one may speculate on the causes for this total breakdown of planned performance. It does not seem likely that the government would ever have planned to allocate £E60 million in foreign exchange to these enterprises under the illusion of export possibilities. It appears that it envisioned a rapid process of import substitution whereby domestic components would be substituted for imported ones. Thus, the Deutz Company submitted a time schedule according to which 27 percent of the truck components would be of domestic origin by the fifth year and 44 percent, by the eighth year.[66] The Five-Year Plan visualized an increase in domestic production of means of transportation from £E14.3 million to £E41.4 million, with an increase in imports from £E14.3 million to only £E17.2 million.[67] As it turned out, the local components used in the early 1960s included only upholstery, side windows, paint, brake lining, clutches, batteries, and tires. Nor was there any realistic prospect that additional simple components such as radiators and mufflers could be manufactured domestically, simply because no plants were planned for this purpose.

In a sense, the Ramses car came closest to being a domestic product, because it partly used domestically produced metal sheets. But the crudeness of the result, the many technical difficulties surrounding it, its unconventional design, and the emergence of the more glamorous Fiat project (making cars with status value) resulted in a gradual neglect of the enterprise.

The scarcity of foreign exchange in 1966 and the war of June 1967 virtually stopped production of passenger cars, while the production of trucks fell to about one-third the peak reached in 1963. Finally, in 1968–69 it became clear to the government that the agreement with the Italian Fiat Company could not be continued, considering the very large convertible currency expenditures involved. While alternatives were studied, cars were delivered only to private persons who could finance the purchase through convertible currency deposited to the account of the Egyptian company in Beirut. The solution finally reached was to resume production on the basis of Fiat components manufactured in Poland and delivered under barter arrangements against Egyptian exports. To relieve the domestic demand pressure, the government liberalized imports of finished cars purchased abroad by residents who could manage to earn convertible currencies, albeit with an increase in the customs duty to 100 percent.

The Competitiveness of the Automobile Industry.

Revenue and cost data of the industry for 1963–64 are published elsewhere.[68] In calculating the effective rate of protection, we have had to take into account the fact that ex-factory prices of finished products were far below domestic market prices. At the official ex-factory prices, the ERP is relatively modest—82.7 percent. However, private cars could be obtained only after long waiting periods, through favoritism, or from the black market. In the latter case, the prices are known to have been roughly twice the official quotations; they were probably somewhat below what the cars would have fetched at open auction. Note that black market profits accrued to purchasers who had obtained the cars at the official prices, not to the factory. Trucks were delivered to nationalized transport companies and industry at factory prices, and it is not known what their open market prices might have been. On the rough assumption that market prices of passenger cars were twice their official quotations, and using the official truck prices, the ERP amounts to 283 percent (Table 9–11).[69] The ERP would probably be higher if market equilibrium prices could be assigned to both trucks and passenger cars.

Fortunately, the domestic market price is immaterial in an evaluation of the DRCs, which are also shown in Table 9–11. At a 10 percent rate of return, the DRC is estimated at 113 piasters per U.S. dollar, and at the 5 percent rate of return level, at 83 piasters. Considering that the factories were operating at only 21 and 44 percent capacity for cars and trucks, respectively, that year, it is surprising that the production was not more inefficient. Indeed, the DRC falls well below that found for the steel industry, and is also below that for paper production.

Here is a possible explanation. Unlike the steel and paper industries, where large amounts of raw materials have to be shipped, handled, and transformed into final products, there are no "raw" materials in the automobile industry. With the exception of the few domestic inputs already mentioned, all of the produced inputs are imported components that fulfill required specifications and simply have to be assembled. This circumstance virtually ex-

TABLE 9–11

Automobile Industry: Rates of Return, ERPs, and DRCs, 1963–64

(percent)	
Rate of return	
At actual, official domestic prices	3.4
At international prices	−0.9
ERP	
At official prices	64.0
At black market prices for passenger cars	283.0
(piasters per U.S. dollar)	
DRC	
5% rate of return	82.7
10% rate of return	113.1
15% rate of return	144.3
Official exchange rate	43.5

Source: Hansen and Nashashibi, NBER Working Paper No. 48, New York, 1975, Table 29.

cludes raw materials waste (not even the metal sheets were tooled domestically) and does not allow for the breakdown of expensive equipment. To be sure, serious inefficiency in workmanship was reported at the welding stages—reflecting Egyptian labor's lack of experience with mechanical industries—and slowdowns in production were also encountered due to erratic (domestic) supplies of tires and batteries.[70] But domestic resource input, including labor, is low, and small defects in workmanship and domestic parts are not reflected in prices or costs but are borne by the consumer. Interestingly enough, developing countries with more advanced automobile industries than Egypt (in the sense of a higher *domestic* value added content) suffer from far greater inefficiency, mainly because their domestic supply of components often fails to meet required specifications.[71] Another reason for the relatively low degree of inefficiency in Egypt appears to be the low prices charged by the Italian Fiat Company for the unassembled cars. The 1,000 cc model was quoted ex-factory in Egypt at £E700, or U.S. $1,510 at the official rate of exchange, and while the import price of unassembled cars is not available to us, it seems to have been around £E600.[72] This seems to be a low price by international standards, and may be explained by the "bulk" nature of the agreement and by the fact that it concerned automobile components for models that were being discontinued in Italy.

There is no doubt that the conception and the development of the automobile industry, particularly the passenger car division, constituted a serious misallocation of resources. It is a good example of bad "planning"; supply linkages seem to have been completely left out of the picture, and foreign exchange requirements were grossly underestimated. But the initial misallocation did not cumulate because the regime was unwilling to devote further resources to save the industry—something which could have been done only at the expense of other, economically sounder projects. Ironically, the very underdeveloped state of the industry helped minimize the social losses through the almost total reliance on foreign-made components. Given the capital investment already sunk into the project, the resource cost of current operations does not exceed 50 piasters per U.S. dollar. Thus, it is probably worthwhile to pursue production until the existent fixed capital is worn out, as, indeed, appears likely.[73]

NOTES

1. Food and Agriculture Organization of the United Nations, *Fertilizer: An Annual Review of World Production, Consumption, and Trade,* 1962, Table 17.

2. Federation of Industries, *Yearbook,* Cairo, 1968, p. 98.

3. *The Chemicals Industries: Phosphate Fertilizer,* Central Agency for General Mobilization and Statistics, Cairo, 1968. See B. Hansen and K. Nashashibi, "Protection and Competitiveness in Egyptian Agriculture and Industry," NBER Working Paper No. 48, New York, 1975, Tables 23 and 25.

4. *The Reduction of Sulphur Needs in Fertilizer Manufacture,* United Nations, New York, 1969, pp. 4–6, 20. Also *Fertilizer Manual,* United Nations, New York, 1967, pp. 117–136. This technology was introduced in the 1960s in sulphuric acid production from both sulphur and pyrites. The decline in fuel consumption side by side with the increased volume of electricity generated in line with the expansion of phosphate output may be due to a change in technology. The capacity expansion which occurred between 1957 and 1964–65 seems to have embodied processes capable of recovering the heat produced from roasting pyrites or sulphur, thus providing some of the power needed by the plant. It has resulted in a substantial increase in productive efficiency and partly explains the steady decline in the "real" world prices of superphosphates that has been taking place over the last two decades.

5. See Hansen and Nashashibi, op. cit.

6. The difference between the two prices reflects transport costs to the consumption stations as well as storage charges.

7. Wholesale prices in the main producing centers of the world (France, Italy, United Kingdom) were declining between 1954 and 1962, rising till 1968, and declining again without any perceivable overall trend. (See FAO, *Production Yearbook,* various issues.)

8. See Hansen and Nashashibi, op. cit.

9. In 1937, at the initiative of the government, the English Electric Company submitted a proposal for the electrification of the dam for £E6.9 million. The project, which only needed the approval of Parliament, was shelved, probably because of the outbreak of the war. See National Bank of Egypt, *Report for February 1937*, p. 11, and *Report for April 1937*, p. 16.

10. Conversely, if the cost of electrification is integrated in the fertilizer plant investment and the electricity sold to other users is treated as a joint product, the DRC of producing fertilizers at the 10 percent of return level would hardly change. On the other hand, the DRC at the 15 percent rate of return would be higher. These estimates are based on the cost of electrification (£E27.5 million, however, it is not clear whether this also includes the cost of transmission lines to the Aswan and Kena governorates); the electricity consumption by the plant (1.4 billion kwh out of 1.9 billion kwh generated); and the conservative assumption that the electricity distributed to other users in the Aswan area would bear the same price as that charged to the fertilizer plant. We have also assumed that other material and factor inputs in the production of electricity are small. See *Industry after the Revolution and the Five-Year Plan*, Ministry of Industry, Cairo, July 1957, pp. 11–12.

11. Jute bags were used. These do not protect the fertilizers against humidity.

12. This latter fertilizer is not a perfect substitute for the former ones. It seems to lack the lime content beneficial to Egyptian soil.

13. Substitute projects are now being constructed in Alexandria and Talkah.

14. This situation implies a high rate of return on domestic sales and distortion of domestic fertilizer consumption. The situation becomes less extreme with an overvalued currency. Under such circumstances the shadow import and export prices may even exceed the domestic price.

15. This price increase was later reversed and the ban on imports of calcium nitrates lifted.

16. Had the data on the Suez facility been available to us separately from the overall returns, some of these cost developments would have appeared as early as 1964–65.

17. Factor derived for a particular plant with natural gas feedstock on U.S. Gulf Coast. See Picciotto and Sweeney, "Ammonium Manufacture from Petroleum Feedstock," *Studies in Petrochemicals*, United Nations Industrial Development Organization, New York, 1966–1967, Vol. II, p. 373.

18. For trends in fertilizer prices, see also FAO, *Production Yearbook*, various issues.

19. *Profile of Manufacturing Establishments*, United Nations Industrial Development Organization, New York, 1968, Vol. II, pp. 524–525.

20. See Hansen and Nashashibi, op. cit.

21. The construction was to be performed with the assistance of the American firm Mansfield. See Economic Development Organization, *2d Annual Report*, Cairo, 1958–1959, p. 166.

22. See Joseph S. Bain, "Economies of Scale, Concentration and the Conditions of Entry in Twenty Manufacturing Industries," *American Economic Review*, 1954, pp. 23–25; and U.S. Department of Commerce, *Census of Manufactures*, 1947 and 1958, Vol. II.

23. "Synthetic Rubbers," *Studies in Petrochemicals*, op. cit., Vol. II, p. 640. Rayon fibers are produced in Egypt but on the basis of imported woodpulp; a nylon plant producing cord suitable for tires is presently under construction.

24. Federation of Industries, *Yearbook*, 1955–1956, pp. 182–186.

25. Thus, in the period 1969–73, valid license holders were allowed to purchase one set of tires per year for private car use, and taxis were allocated two sets per year. Official prices for small tires (for Fiat cars) were £E11 per tire.

26. See Federation of Industries, *Yearbook*, 1963, pp. 225–226. See also United Nations, *Pulp and Paper Development in Africa and the Near East*, 1965, pp. 428–429.

27. Permanent Production Council, *Major Production Projects*, Cairo, July 1954, pp. 57–58.

28. The RAKTA plant was built by a West German group led by the Krupp firm for £E 4.3 million. As in the case of other industries established in this period, the Economic Development Organization subscribed to a large share of the capital, ranging from 25 to 41 per cent of paid up capital. See Economic Development Organization, op. cit., pp. 160–163.

29. "Estimation of managerial and technical personnel requirements," ibid., p. 83.

30. Federation of Industries, *Yearbook*, 1956–1957, p. 210.

31. *The Paper Industry*, CAGMS, Cairo, 1960.

32. Federation of Industries, *Yearbook*, 1960, p. 205.

33. Rates of return fell after 1962 to about 5–10 percent. See A. Moneim Ali Soliman, *The RAKTA Paper Industry*, Institute of National Planning, Cairo, 1964.

34. Federation of Industries, *Yearbook*, 1966, p. 306.

35. Federation of Industries, *Yearbook*, 1969, p. 142; and 1971, p. 110.

36. Production of kraft paper fell from 24,000 tons in 1966 to 3,400 tons in 1967, reflecting a temporary shutdown of the Suez plant. Production partially recovered in 1968 to 13,900 tons, but fell again in 1969 to 5,800. The plant was destroyed in 1970.

37. Federation of Industries, *Yearbook*, 1971, p. 109.

38. Prices for medium-grade paper reported to one of the authors by the Nasr Trading Organization. They are in line with the unit values in Table 9–5, which rose from an average of £E83 in 1959–1961 to £E113 in 1963. The increase reflects both the rise in domestic prices of imported paper due to the devaluation and a shift of imports to higher qualities of paper not produced at the RAKTA plant.

39. Hansen and Nashashibi, op. cit.

40. Ibid.

41. See FAO, *Commodity Review and Outlook*, 1971–1972, various issues.

42. *Semi-Annual Report on Prices of Manufactured Products*, CAGMS, Cairo, April 1971.

43. By 1962 per capita consumption had more than doubled, to 19 kg. In comparison, India and China consumed in 1963 roughly 16 kg. per capita, and Latin American countries consumed on average 43 kg. per capita. See United Nations, *World Trade in Steel and Steel Demand in Developing Countries*, Economic Commission for Europe, 1965, p. 88.

44. The Egyptian Copper Works (1948), the Delta Steel Mills (1948), and the National Metal Industries (1949). See Federation of Industries, *Yearbook*, 1951 and 1952.

45. In 1951 tariffs were waived, but only for imported machinery and spare parts.

46. Federation of Industries, *Yearbook*, 1951–1952, p. 88.

47. The Permanent Production Council, *The Iron and Steel Industry*, Cairo, July 1954, pp. 18–19 (in Arabic).

48. The original distribution of the capital invested was: Government—£E 1 million; Permanent Production Council—£E1 million; Demag—20 percent of equipment up to a limit of £E2 million; Bank Misr—½ million; Industrial Bank—¼ million; Misr Insurance Co.—¼ million; Misr Spinning and Weaving Company—¼ million. In

addition, these firms subscribed to increase the capital with roughly the same shares as their initial participation. Permanent Production Council, ibid., pp. 43–45.

49. Demag was represented by two members on the Board of Directors. In addition, it provided the services of about 250 German engineers and technicians in association with 300 Egyptian engineers. Sixty Egyptian foremen were sent to Germany for training before the plant opened. See F. Harbison and I. A. Ibrahim, *Human Resources for Egyptian Enterprises,* New York, 1958, pp. 63–64.

50. Permanent Production Council, op. cit., p. 22.

51. The exception is 1969, when 45,100 tons were exported.

52. We may have underestimated the transport margin; the c.i.f. applied here covers only shipping charges between Mediterranean ports.

53. Excess of domestic prices in 1963 over world export prices of merchant bars. *The Iron and Steel Industry,* United Nations, New York, 1969, p. 25.

54. The planned level of production largely exceeded actual output, particularly for light sections and metal sheets:

	Planned Output	Output	Sales
Heavy sections	76,000	68,339	59,633
Light sections	65,000	23,022	21,674
Plates	28,000	31,198	23,688
Sheets	90,000	10,004	9,331
Total	259,000	122,563	114,326

55. Coopers International, as quoted in F. A. El Bahaï, *The Economics of the Iron and Steel Industry: The Egyptian Iron and Steel Company,* Institute of National Planning, Cairo, 1967, pp. 62–64.

56. Breakdowns or deficient performances are also reported for the limestone cracker, the raw material conveyor, the ventilator facilities, and the cooling unit of the blast furnaces. Ibid., pp. 34–60.

57. An efficient blast furnace should produce a minimum of 1,800 tons per day, and an efficient integrated plant producing flat products, 1.5 million tons per year. See UNIDO, *Iron and Steel Industry,* 1969, p. 24.

58. Ibid., p. 25.

59. The first LD installations in developing countries were in Argentina, Brazil, and India, all in 1960–61. See United Nations Economic Commission for Europe, *Long-Term Trends and Problems of the European Steel Industry,* 1959, p. 96, and *Principal Factors Affecting Labor Productivity Trends in the Iron and Steel Industry,* 1954, p. 15.

60. The value of the plant and equipment in 1963–1964 was put at £E15 million. See F. A. El Bahaï, op. cit.

61. The project is expected to realize a profit of 5.8 percent on invested capital. It is not specified how this figure was arrived at, nor is the domestic price structure known on which it is based. But if the forecast proves accurate and domestic prices remain at their present levels, it will certainly imply losses at international prices. See Federation of Industries, *Yearbook,* 1972, p. 31.

62. See L. Johnson, "A Case Study in Import Substitution: The Automobile Industry in Chile," *Economic Development and Cultural Change,* January 1967.

63. Otherwise, they had to pay the municipality the difference between domestic and foreign cost. Federation of Industries, *Yearbook,* 1955–1956, p. 113. The rationale of this arrangement is not clear to the authors; it amounted in effect to a production tax levied by the Cairo Municipality.

64. Federation of Industries, *Yearbook,* 1959.

65. GATT document, L1816; and Federation of Industries, *Yearbook,* 1960.

66. Federation of Industries, *Yearbook,* 1959–1960, p. 104.

67. *General Frame of the Five-Year Plan, July 1960–June 1965,* Ministry of Planning, Cairo, 1960, pp. 63 and 76.

68. See Hansen and Nashashibi, op. cit., Table 29.

69. In the 1970–1973 period a small Fiat 124 could be obtained in the black market for £E 2,000.

70. CAGMS, *The Manufacturing of Automobiles and Their Components,* June 1965, pp. 49–51.

71. Johnson, op. cit.

72. The official retail price of the car in Egypt was £E795 up to 1965 and £E1,140 thereafter.

73. *Middle East Economic Digest,* London, March 23 and March 30, 1973.

Chapter 10

Evaluation of Resource Use in Selected Manufacturing Industries, 1954-1970

Our estimates of effective rates of protection and resource costs are summarized in Tables 10–1 and 10–2. The sample of industries is not small (see Table 8–1) but biased—large, modern public industries are overrepresented, while private enterprises are grossly underrepresented (in fact, included solely in the cotton textile industry). Discriminated against by the government in regard to commodity input and credit and foreign exchange allocations, these private enterprises have had, at the same time, more freedom (or, at least, more possibilities of evasion) in pricing. By virtue of their labor-intensive technology, they are often competitive at international prices and have succeeded in exporting part of their production. Apart from the omission of such firms, the estimates in the tables are also very uncertain for some of the industries that are covered. Great caution should therefore be exercised in generalizing on the basis of our findings.

We note first that, with the exception of cement, all industries have at some time enjoyed protection to varying degrees. For some industries the effective rates of protection have been very high: iron and steel and automobile assembly are the extreme examples, but paper and yarn (the latter in 1970) had high effective rates of protection, too. In an institutional setup like that of Egypt, particularly after 1961, high rates of protection in themselves do not necessarily indicate either inefficiency and lack of competitiveness or resource pull and misallocation of resources. Protection may have accompanied the establishment of a domestic monopoly; in that case, a high measured rate of protection would indicate not high costs but high monopoly profits, and production could quite well be efficient and competitive in foreign markets

TABLE 10–1

Effective Rates of Protection (ERPs) in Ten Manufacturing Industries, Selected Years

(percent)

	1954	1957	1960	1962–63 to 1963–64	1964–65 to 1965–66	1969–70
Cement	−31	−45	−35	—	−28	—
Phosphates	15	34	—	—	7	—
Nitrates	25	48	—	—	12	—
Sugar	—	—	−5	—	—	14
Tires	—	—	240	262	—	—
Cotton						
Fabric	—	—	—	—	68	—
Yarn	—	31	62	—	—	213
Automobiles	—	—	—	305	—	—
Paper	—	—	—	240	—	—
Iron and steel	—	—	—	—	599	—

SOURCE: Hansen and Nashashibi, NBER Working Paper No. 48, 1975.

(the scale of production may even be too small). The tire industry offers an example of this kind of protection. In any case, since the beginning of the sixties, and to some extent even earlier, resource allocation has been determined by government decisions based on criteria other than private profitability. Hence, resource costs offer a better basis for discussing competitiveness and resource allocation.

The DRCs indicate a rather mixed situation at the end of the fifties. Two of the traditional industries—sugar and cement—were competitive or close to being so, while the important cotton textile industry was definitely noncompetitive at the then existing official exchange rate and given the ban on foreign cotton. But our estimates also indicate that, if foreign short staple cotton had been available as the raw material base, the production of yarn (and probably also of cloth) would have been almost competitive at the beginning of the sixties. If we add to these industries phosphate fertilizer, which was founded as a private venture prior to the Second World War, it could be said that all major industries established under the "ancien régime" had developed and maintained a comparative advantage and (with the above-mentioned qualification in regard to the cotton textile industry) were competitive at international prices. As could be expected, these industries are intensive in abundantly available domestic resources such as labor (sugar, textiles) or raw materials (cement, phosphate). In the case of textiles it was the compulsory use of

TABLE 10–2

Domestic Resource Costs (DRCs) in Ten
Manufacturing Industries, Selected Years

(piasters per U.S. dollar)

	1954	1957	1960	1962–63 to 1963–64	1964–65 to 1965–66	1969–70
Cement (f.o.b.)	20	21	28	—	31	—
Phosphates						
(c.i.f.)	38	36	—	—	33	—
(f.o.b)	—	—	—	—	36	50
Nitrates						
(c.i.f.)	52	61	—	—	52	—
(f.o.b.	—	—	—	—	62	—
Sugar, refined	—	—	34	—	—	54
Tires						
(c.i.f.)	—	—	59	59	—	—
(f.o.b.)	—	—	—	62	—	—
Cotton textiles						
Fabric (f.o.b.)	—	—	—	—	70	—
Yarn (f.o.b.)	—	47[a]	56	—	—	86
Yarn[b] based on foreign cotton (f.o.b.)	—	36[a]	38	—	—	54
Automobiles (c.i.f.)	—	—	—	113	—	—
Paper (c.i.f.)	—	—	—	208	—	—
Iron and steel (c.i.f.)	—	—	—	—	480	—
Exchange rates						
Official rate	35.2	35.2	35.2	43.5	43.5	43.5
"Realistic" rate (suggested by IMF, 1966)	—	—	—	—	61	—

Source: Hansen and Nashashibi, NBER Working Paper No. 48, 1975.
a. 1956.
b. Hypothetical.

domestic raw materials that made the industry noncompetitive; the real strength of the industry stems from its labor intensity.

After World War II, an attempt was made to go beyond the agriculture-based industries and manufacture basic intermediate products and consumer durables as import substitutes: paper, tires, nitrates, iron and steel, and automobiles. Some of these are highly capital-intensive (nitrate and paper) and most have a rather high import content. These industries were all founded under a highly protective regime, first via tariffs, later via quantitative restrictions. An evaluation of the DRCs of these industries during the 1960s shows that none achieved competitiveness at the then existing exchange rates, although both nitrates and rubber tires appear to be successful infant industries that would become competitive with the currency devalued to the "realistic" level advocated by the IMF.

It is also remarkable that a number of industries fared as well as they actually did after the devaluation of 1962, despite the nationalizations, employment drive, wage increase, and permanent foreign exchange crises. Phosphates, nitrates, and tires showed falling or unchanged DRCs, and cement continued to be competitive at the old exchange rate—albeit with a small increase in its DRC. In the first two industries important technological innovations were introduced at this time, and the latter two were able to improve their efficiency within the given technology. The strong increase in the DRC for phosphate in 1970 was due to a fall in the international price for this commodity.

But other industries—probably the majority—fared less well. The two big old industries which should have passed the infant industry stage a long time ago—sugar processing and cotton textiles—suffered a serious setback in competitiveness. These two are probably typical of manufacturing, apart from the "good" industries mentioned above. And then there were the entirely unsuccessful new industries—the Helwan iron and steel plant, the automobile assembly plant, and perhaps paper and pulp.

All industries of both relatively and absolutely deteriorating competitiveness suffered, of course, from the cost inflation and other problems of the period, particularly from falling or at best stagnant international prices. International competition in basic intermediate commodities is quite keen and technological innovations are rapid. The central administration has distorted the pattern of imports and domestic production. Apart from the paper work involved in the administration of these multiple price structures, production has been shifted from the underpriced commodities (for example, construction steel or popular types of textiles) toward more profitable products. This, in turn, has brought shortages to black markets and has distorted the pattern of imports.[1] Certainly, if prices for certain commodities or labor are to be used for attaining social targets, an alternative set of accounting prices should govern decisions of industrial firms as to production and use of resources. While resource flows have been diverted by the price structure, there are also instances where firms have suffered a distortion in their capital costs: some firms have reported paying higher prices than prevailing elsewhere for capital equipment imported from Eastern Europe, others have complained of being forced to finance the construction of social overhead (such as roads, electricity, water) in their location. But all this, along with the domestic inflation, affected the "good" industries as well.

The difference between the "good" and "bad" industries seems to be a matter of good or bad investment planning. For every one of the industries with declining competitiveness, it can be shown that inadequate investment planning by the authorities (i.e., the Ministry of Industry) was, if not the sole cause of the decline of competitiveness, certainly an important contributing factor.

The cotton textile industry was largely ignored by the Egyptian planners during a period when the developed countries and some underdeveloped ones modernized and rationalized this branch of manufacturing. Indeed, no overall modernization has taken place in the industry since the equipment replacement that occurred immediately after World War II. Moreover, the creation of additional capacity lagged behind demand, resulting in shortages and loss of exports. The sugar industry was expanded substantially during the sixties, and the immediate cause of the sharp decline in its competitiveness was the particularly strong increase of rural wages during the first half of the sixties. If the relative increase of rural wages turns out to be a temporary phenomenon that will be reversed once the armed forces are reduced again, the decline of competitiveness is also a temporary phenomenon. In that case, from a longer-term point of view, the sugar industry could be included among the "good" industries. But the prospect is different if the change in relative wages proves to be a permanent feature of the economy, which is quite possible since the gap between rural and urban wages usually diminishes during the process of development. From that standpoint, either the industry should not have been expanded at all, or a less labor-intensive technology should have been chosen (if it exists). The competitiveness of both the sugar and paper industries, incidentally, could have been somewhat improved had pulp production on the basis of bagasse been expanded. This technical process is relatively new, however, and it is not obvious that Egyptian planners lagged much behind on this score. The paper and pulp industry was clearly planned on a suboptimal scale, while the Helwan steel plant is ill-conceived in several other respects besides its obsolete technology. It is not clear, however, that steel production could not be a competitive activity if it were based on Western Desert ores, worked on the basis of up-to-date technology, and with more adequate planning in other respects. The new Soviet-built steel complex in Helwan will eventually have to deliver the proof.

The investments in the old Helwan steel plant and the automobile assembly plant were largely a waste of money (at least if any external learning effects are left out). They amounted to about one quarter of the investments made in the industries considered in this chapter. Thus, the losses from inadequate investment planning are very considerable. Apart from the automobile undertaking, there is no evidence to suggest that public investments were made in the wrong sectors. A better direction of the given volume of investments, with a more appropriate choice of technology in some sectors, could have probably saved the situation for those industries that actually suffered a loss of competitiveness. The wage increases would then have been an adjustment to increased labor productivity and not at all a cost inflation. In this indirect way, it may be argued that bad investment planning was the root cause of manufacturing industry's problems during the sixties.

There is an aspect of investment planning, generally neglected by the authorities, which has undoubtedly resulted in substantial losses in productivity: capital replacement. It is not so much a question of inadequate capital appropriations for replacement of equipment as reflected in the accounts of individual enterprises; indeed, these seem to conform with standard depreciation methods. Rather, it is the foreign exchange allocations and actual deliveries of equipment for this purpose that have fallen far short of demand from individual enterprises. The net profits realized in the fiscal year 1970–71 in industry by the public sector amounted to only 2.4 percent of the estimated value of invested capital.[2] Even if this is interpreted as retained earnings (after taxes, dividend payments, and debt servicing), it is much too low for self-financing and would place a heavy burden on the Treasury for financing capacity expansion. To be sure, industrial firms have no discretionary power over the disposal of their profits, which revert, in any case, to the state coffers.[3] Moreover, the Treasury favors the more profitable firms when considering requests for capacity expansion or replacement, which—given the distortion introduced in the distribution of profits by the price structure—biases investments away from enterprises that are socially "loaded." With a general foreign exchange shortage and pressure to start new projects as well as completing ongoing projects with costs exceeding original estimates, capital replacements tend to be ignored. We have already mentioned the example of cotton textiles, where modernization and expansion as well as ordinary replacement were postponed during the sixties. As a consequence, overutilization of partly obsolete machinery and equipment became a serious problem already in 1965, aggravated after the 1967 War. The share of gross investment in GDP was steadily shrinking, reaching 11 percent in 1970–71, and much of it went into new capacity, particularly the construction of the steel complex and the expansion and relocation of the fertilizer industry. Sugar offers another striking illustration of entirely inadequate replacement during the years from 1967 to

1973. A survey of cotton ginning mills, railroads, and printing plants revealed that much of the equipment in these industries was in an acute state of obsolescence, indeed, in many cases in a state of outright decay, causing severe declines in productivity. The stepmotherly treatment of replacement needs is beyond a reasonable doubt closely related to the monopolization of foreign exchange resources and the concentration of decision making concerning industrial investment in the hands of the Ministry of Industry. There is sufficient evidence to conclude that a general worsening has taken place since 1965 in the financial position of industrial firms in the public sector, together with (what is even more serious) a deterioration in the overall state of the country's capital stock as a result of insufficient capital replacement.

Inadequate investment planning also affected the good industries in other ways. Insufficient attention was given to linkages and to demand, particularly export demand. Lags in capacity expansion were noteworthy in the case of cement, but occurred also in the case of phosphate fertilizers, where failure to develop the necessary transportation facilities hampered the growth of output in the early 1960s and caused imports to rise. The automobile industry was left without reliable domestic sources of inputs (with the exception of tires), and both cement and fertilizers had to use imported packing material for a long time when it could have been supplied domestically.

But in regard to linkages the Egyptian authorities seem to have learned from their past mistakes. After the first five-year plan and the foreign exchange crisis, an increasing awareness seems to have grown out of the need to "rationalize" investments by supporting them with the necessary infrastructure, optimizing their location, and exploiting their potential linkages; the integration of the new steel complex with the chemicals and engineering industries and the utilization of bagasse for kraft paper bags can be cited as examples. Moreover, greater concern seems to be shown for exports, and a number of recent investments, particularly in the fields of cement and fertilizers, are export-oriented. In addition, a more favorable treatment is being afforded small private enterprises which have succeeded in exporting part of their production; they have been receiving increasing foreign exchange quotas and their export procedures have been simplified.

On the other hand, in the particular industries under review we have found little to indicate that the foreign exchange situation and the exchange regimes per se either damaged competitiveness or seriously disrupted current production. It is true that there have been instances of production disruptions directly related to raw materials and other shortages, but they have been mainly temporary, although the distortive effects of quantitative trade restrictions may have had a permanent and cumulative impact on other sectors through their normal linkages. Thus, we have shown how the 1916 ban on foreign cotton increased the costs of the textile industry and limited textile mills to using machinery adapted for long staple cotton, delaying the introduction of artificial fibers as well as short staple cotton. Another series of restrictions was necessary to ensure the textile mills of a sufficient supply of domestic cotton, which distorted the pattern of raw cotton production and exports. The ban on imports of phosphates in 1953, while increasing the capacity utilization of the industry, resulted in domestic excess demand that was satisfied neither by expansion of domestic capacity nor by imports. It was only after the effects of this measure were badly felt in agriculture that phosphate imports were resumed. In the post-1961 regime, with direct allocation of foreign exchange to various ministries, a more erratic pattern of trade developed, with wide fluctuations in the imports of certain commodities such as tires and paper. But these, as well as some abnormal inventory accumulations during the years 1964 to 1966, may be attributed as much to inadequate demand forecasting at the firm level as to inefficiency inherent in centralized trade administration. In any event, central planning did not improve the adjustment of supply to demand.

Finally, it is important to recall that the industries included in our study are mainly large public enterprises favored at the expense of small private enterprises. That the latter have suffered badly from shortages of raw materials, spare parts, capital goods, and credit is clear. Small private enterprises in industry and handicrafts, together with private consumers, were the main victims of the exchange regimes, but we have no data that can serve to measure, or even indicate, the loss of production in such enterprises or the loss of consumer satisfaction.

NOTES

1. "Report of the Committee on the Revelation of Truths on the Subject of the Rise in the Price of Steel and the Trade of Scrap Metal," and "The Public Sector . . . Where to?" *Al Talia,* August 1973, pp. 11–24 and pp. 66–72, respectively.

2. In the publicly owned industrial enterprises net profits were £E40.8 million on an estimated capital stock and circulating capital of £E1,700 million. It is not known how this figure has been estimated. Ibid., p. 67.

3. This is perhaps the most urgent area of reform, since it seems to affect even the smallest capital expenditures on technical progress. For example, the sugar industry requested from the Treasury £E1 million in foreign exchange to purchase equipment which would allow it to reduce the proportion of sugar left in the discarded bagasse. By its estimates such a measure would result in a net addition of 10,000 tons of sugar annually. The request was rejected by the Treasury, which stated that the priorities in foreign exchange allocation were determined by the Ministry of Industry. Ibid., pp. 56–57.

Appendix A

Acreage Response Functions for Eleven Egyptian Field Crops

As a basis for appraising the impact of agricultural cooperatives and government intervention in crop rotation and composition from around 1962–1963 onward, information about supply functions for major field crops was needed. For well-known reasons, our efforts were concentrated on estimating acreage response functions rather than supply functions. Misallocation is discussed in terms of factor input rather than in terms of output.

Reasonably good information about acreage, yields, and prices is available from 1913 onward; it stands to reason that the data are more reliable for later years than earlier ones. On the basis of data for the period 1913 to 1961, response functions are estimated showing cultivators' behavior undisturbed by government intervention. These are then used for predicting acreages for 1962–1968 at actual domestic and international prices. Comparison between predicted and actual acreages yields information on the impact of government interference with acreages. (See Chapter 7 for such comparisons.)

A MODEL FOR CROP ACREAGE RESPONSE

The model to be applied is, indeed, nothing but the production side of the standard foreign trade model under competitive conditions.

Assume that land, A, labor, L, and water, W, are the only inputs in agriculture. For crop i the production function is assumed to be

$$q_i = y_i(t)f_i(A_i, L_i, W_i), i = 1, \ldots, m \qquad (1)$$

317

where q_i is the quantity of crop i and $y_i(t)$ is a technical progress function.[1] Assume that the total supplies of land, labor, and water are given exogenously and are known. Thus we have:

$$\sum_{}^{m} A_i \leqq A$$

$$\sum_{}^{m} L_i \leqq L \qquad (2)$$

$$\sum_{}^{m} W_i \leqq W$$

The distribution of the inputs by crops is unknown except for land (see, however, [9, Tables 3.A, 3.B, and 3.C] on the list of references to Appendix A for the years 1961, 1963, and 1964); thus it is not possible to estimate the production functions (1) individually. Since our problem is one of the optimality of the individual crops we would get no help from an aggregate production function. The lack of information about the distribution of inputs by crops does not prevent us, however, from estimating individual supply functions or, as we prefer, individual acreage response functions.

We shall assume that all agricultural output prices are given exogenously, determined either from abroad or by the government. Both assumptions are reasonably good approximations in the Egyptian context (except perhaps for some of the small crops). Our model is then based on the maximization of total agricultural income,[2] and we have Max $\Sigma p_i q_i$ subject to the constraints (1) and (2).

With the inequality signs in (2) disregarded, maximization leads directly to the necessary conditions, in easily understood notation,

$$\frac{y_i p_i}{y_m p_m} = \frac{f'_{m,A_m}}{f'_{i,A_i}} = \frac{f'_{m,L_m}}{f'_{i,L_i}} = \frac{f'_{m,W_m}}{f'_{i,W_i}}, \ i = 1, \ldots, m-1, \qquad (3)$$

which with (2) gives us $3m$ equations to determine A_i, L_i and W_i. The q_is could then be determined from (1). The optimal inputs of land, A_i^*, are seen to be functions of the ratios of output prices times the technical progress function and of the total supplies of land, labor, and water, so that the acreage response functions can be written

$$A_i^* = A_i^* \left(\frac{y_j p_j}{y_m p_m}, A, L, W \right), \ \begin{cases} i = 1, \ldots, m \\ j = 1, \ldots, m \end{cases} \qquad (4)$$

and similarly for the optimal inputs of labor and water, which, however, we are not interested in here.[3]

All the arguments in (4) are directly observable and known, with the exception of the technical progress functions, y_i. As a proxy for $y_i(t)$ we shall use yield per acre of crop i. The optimal input of land for any crop is thus a function of all relative output values per acre and of the given total inputs of land, labor, and water; all the arguments are now observable and known. Yield per acre is, of course, influenced not only by technical progress but also by inputs of labor and water per acre and is, thus, strictly endogenous to our problem. It is clear, however, that for the individual crops in agriculture we cannot rely upon the conventional type of technical progress functions $y_i(t) = \exp(\rho_i t)$, where ρ_i is a constant rate of technical progress.[4] For individual crops, yields will tend to move in jumps at the introduction of new varieties, over and above the effects of other types of technological progress. For agriculture as a whole it may perhaps be true that new varieties are introduced in a more or less continuous stream (for underdeveloped countries even this assumption is certainly dubious), but for individual crops we cannot make such assumptions. Not only do new varieties only appear discretely, but yields may even fall between the appearance of new varieties because old varieties may degenerate. Thus, the yield of Egyptian cotton declined from about 1895 to about 1920 due to degeneration of varieties, soil exhaustion, and an increasing underground water table (an unexpected consequence of the old Aswan dam), and increased again from 1920 to 1940 due to new varieties and improved fertilization and drainage [5, in particular, Fig. 10].

Since the number of crops and thus of relative output values per acre is substantial (eleven) and the number of observations limited (at most forty-eight), we felt that we had to bring down the number of explanatory variables in the acreage response functions. We shall do that through constructing for each crop a *relative output-value-per-feddan index*, F_i, that is defined as

$$F_i = \frac{y_i p_i}{\sum\limits_{j=1}^{m} w_j y_j p_j}, \quad \sum_{j=1}^{m} w_j = 1, \tag{5}$$

where w_j is the weight given to crop j and y is interpreted as crop yield. As weights we shall use the relative crop acreages, averages for the period of estimation.[5] F_i may include all crops or only crops that are particularly competitive in regard to land (see below).

The acreage response function for crop i may then be formulated linearly as

$$A_i = a_{1i} + a_{2i}F_i + a_{3i}A + a_{4i}L + a_{5i}W \tag{6}$$

or as the corresponding log linear function. We used only the linear form in our estimates.[6]

Note, however, that for any arbitrary crop, say crop m, we have

$$A_m = A - \sum_{i=1}^{m-1} A_i$$

$$= -\sum_{i=1}^{m-1} a_{1i} - \sum_{i=1}^{m-1} a_{2i}F_i - A\left(\sum_{i=1}^{m-1} a_{3i} - 1\right) \qquad (7)$$

$$- L \sum_{i=1}^{m-1} a_{4i} - W \sum_{i=1}^{m-1} a_{5i},$$

so that, strictly speaking, (6) can apply to at most $m - 1$ crops. Our formulation of the acreage response functions thus implies an unpleasant lack of symmetry in the functional forms.

The next step is to introduce appropriate lags in the functions. We need a lag specification that will permit us to predict both short- and long-term responses or, to put it another way, to come out with both short- and long-term elasticities of acreage response. Various possibilities are open, but before we consider them a few comments upon the basic model may not be out of place.

For our purposes the present model has the great advantage of permitting us to predict acreages without having to consider possible effects on domestic factor prices; these are themselves endogenous to the problem. Thus, we can predict acreages on the basis of both domestic and international prices, in the short term as well as in the long term, without having to "solve the general equilibrium system," the usual headache in this problem. Identifying long-term response with optimal acreage, our response equations help us, in other words, to directly predict the optimum.

Strictly speaking, we have in fact solved that part of the general equilibrium system that is necessary for our purpose. The point is that the standard neoclassical trade model is dichotomized so that the supply (production) part can be solved without considering the demand side. It is this dichotomization we take advantage of. Its basic assumptions are perfect competition and the absence of nontraded outputs. There are problems with both of these assumptions but we do not consider them important (except for wheat).[7]

Another basic assumption for obtaining this neat result is that total supplies of domestic resources are exogenously given. For land and water this assumption is probably justified. The supply of cultivable land in the Nile Valley and the Delta is highly inelastic, and water supply is ultimately determined by the water flow of the Nile. Efforts to increase water supply for individual crops through a better distribution over the year and to increase the cultivated area have been governmental on the whole.[8] Some private investment in irrigation, drainage, and land reclamation did, of course, take place, particularly before the Great Depression, and the cultivated area did respond (downward) to the low relative profitability of agriculture during the Great Depression. By and large we feel, nonetheless, that it is justified to consider land and water as exogenously determined resources in the Egyptian context. For labor the assumption is less obvious. Until World War II, when urbanization was still slow, the assumption may not be too much out of line with reality. And during the sixties, the military draft may have been the most important determinant. With the rapid urbanization during and after World War II and the opportunities offered outside agriculture, however, labor supply to agriculture may not have been inelastic with respect to urban wages. Little evidence exists, unfortunately, as to the extent Egypt's agricultural labor supply depended upon urban wages, which is what matters in the present context.[9] The pull from the cities may have been of such a nature that urban wages made little difference to the flow of migration out of agriculture.[10] Lacking evidence to the contrary, we assume that the agricultural labor supply has been highly inelastic with respect to urban wages during the whole period.

The following considerations should also be noted:

1. Data for the total resources A, L, and W are of widely differing quality. Data for A are for acreage sown and are considered reliable, while those for L are shaky, to put it mildly; as a proxy for L only an index based on agricultural censuses of permanent labor taken every ten years, with interpolation on the basis of annual estimated rural population figures, is available. For W we have data for the monthly discharge of the Nile at Aswan, which may be fairly accurately measured itself but is at best a proxy for the use of irrigation water on the fields. It does not consider water storage below Aswan and this may be an important misspecification.

2. It is usual to divide Egyptian crops into three clearly distinguishable, though somewhat overlapping, groups of competing crops, with limited competition between groups 1 and 2:

Group 1 Summer (Autumn) Crops	Group 2 Winter Crops	Group 3 Perennial Crops
Cotton (lint and grain) Rice Corn Millet	Wheat Barley Beans Lentils Onions (winter) Helba	Sugar Cane

It is not obvious a priori whether for purposes of estimation we should consider groups 1 and 3 together and 2 and 3 together and calculate F_i correspondingly. We experimented with this division, but ended up by considering all crops as competing, so that F_i is defined in the same way for all crops. This may not be the best possible specification for crops like rice, barley, and cane.

3. Our model does not consider inputs of chemical fertilizers and this may be another serious misspecification. If included in the model, relative fertilizer price $p_{fert}/y_i(t)p_i$, $i = 1, \ldots, m$, would appear in equation (8). We would then have eleven relative prices as arguments. Our relative output-value index would now be inadequate because it is based on gross output values and does not deduct imported inputs. If we knew the fertilizer input per acre we could construct a *net* output value (i.e. value added) index for each crop corresponding to F; however, no back figures about fertilizer input per acre by crops are available. Another possibility would be to let the argument p_{fert}/y_ip_i appear in the response function for crop i. We do not have comparable fertilizer prices from 1913 to 1961, and the functional form may have changed over time [8]. In 1913 fertilizer input was negligible and over time a learning process has accompanied the increasing input of fertilizer. We have therefore not been able to include fertilizer prices as a determinant of land inputs. Fortunately, however, we may catch most of the impact of fertilizers through identifying the productivity factor, y_i, with yield.

4. Price information is not available for most of the years of the period of estimation—1913 to 1961—for the largest (by acreage) of all crops, clover (berseem), so that no estimates of the response function could be made for the area of clover. The interdependency of the area response functions expressed by equation (7) is therefore disregarded, and it is assumed that clover is a residual in this sense. This procedure is not very satisfactory, of course, but no other course seems to be open. More serious, perhaps is that the output value per acre for clover does not appear in the denominator of the relative output-value index, F, for the other crops. We have had to disregard clover entirely.[11]

5. No back data were available for output and prices of straw and stalks, important for some crops (wheat, in particular). For cotton, of course, both lint and seeds are included.

In regard to lag specification, we have chosen to follow the approach of an exponentially distributed lag attached to relative output-value. We assume that

$$A_i = a_{1i} + b \sum_{t=1}^{T} (a_{2i})^t (F_i)_{-t} + a_{3i}A_{-1} + a_{4i}L + a_{5i}W_\tau \qquad (8)$$

General reference is made to Koyck's original contribution [12] and Nerlove's contributions [15, 16, and 17], as well as Krishna's [14] and Behrman's [3] modified versions of Nerlove's model. Nerlove came out with prices, exponentially lagged, and the previous year's total acreage as the only explanatory variables. Krishna and later Behrman added relative yield as an independent explanatory variable (among other things). Our derivation implied that crop acreage should be made dependent upon relative output value, that is (relative) price times yield. It might be argued that expectations are formed quite differently for prices and yields [3, pp. 166–168]. A low price last year and a bad crop last year may not affect this year's sown acreage in the same way. A single crop failure may not change the cultivator's notions of what is the "normal" yield, and he may understand that crop failures are erratic events, although, of course, the notion of "normal" yield is subject to change.[12] At the time a new variety is introduced it is natural that yield expectations should shift upward autonomously; indeed, this is the reason for its introduction. Hence, a case can be made for separating prices and yields in the supply function or, at least, treating them differently from an expectations point of view. One way of handling this problem would be to define the yield variable in F, as, say, an average of the last five years and limit the exponential distribution to the price, although price and yield enter in a multiplicative way. Estimates were experimentally made on the basis of this hypothesis, but the results did not improve and the experiment was discarded.

The specification assumes that the present year's prices (and yields, of course) do not affect sown acreages. This is because the prices used in the estimates are those at which crops have actually been sold. For the major crops these tend to be the market prices ruling at the time of sowing next year's crop.

The total acreage, A, enters into (8) with a single lag in line with Nerlove's assumptions (which we keep although it is a bit difficult to see their precise rationale). Labor is naturally assumed to have its effects without lags, while water appears with the time indicator τ. For summer crops (see the list above) τ is taken to be an average of the months May and June, the critical time for rice. The rationale of this choice is that, whereas the other summer crops (cotton, in particular) have always got the water they require at zero prices for water, rice has traditionally (at least until the fifties) been treated by the irrigation authorities as a residual crop. For winter and perennial crops, τ is taken to be September last year (the peak of the flood), which is decisive for water supply at the time winter crops are sown (November and December).

Equation (8) then leads directly to

$$A_i = \alpha_{1i} + \alpha_{2i}(F_i)_{-1} + \alpha_{3i}A_{-1} + \alpha_{4i}A_{-2} + \alpha_{5i}L + \alpha_{6i}L_{-1}$$

$$+ \alpha_{7i}W\tau + \alpha_{8i}W_{\tau-1} + \alpha_{9i}(A_i)_{-1}. \tag{9}$$

In addition to the Nerlove specification, another one using Almon polynominally distributed lags and a third one with a simple two-lag structure were

tried out. However, both t and R^2 and—particularly important for our purpose
—standard errors of estimated values for these two specifications were so poor
that the Nerlove model was preferred despite its inherent bias at ordinary
least squares estimation. For our main purpose, prediction, the bias is a
secondary consideration, but for the elasticity values, calculated as a by-
product, it may be a serious matter, of course. To avoid the bias, estimation by
the instrumental variable method was therefore applied (see below).

So much for the general specifications. One further problem had to be
tackled. The government has at times imposed area restrictions for cotton,
sometimes accompanied by prescriptions to increase cereals (particularly
wheat) production. During the period studied here, cotton area restrictions
were imposed for the years 1915, 1918, 1921–1923, 1927–1929, 1931–1933,
1942–1947, and 1953–1960 [5, Table III]. It would be natural simply to exclude these years from the estimates. However, the loss of observations is
serious; also, the area restrictions may have merely imposed what the cultivators would have tended to do on their own; or, the restrictions may have
been evaded.

Two considerations usually guided successive governments in their area
restriction policies. In earlier years, it was always claimed by the Ministry of
Agriculture that peasants tended to cultivate more cotton than was socially
profitable in the long run (since cotton tends to exhaust the soil). Rightly or
wrongly, with this motivation the government has felt it necessary in years of
high profitability to hold back cotton cultivation, forcing peasants onto the
three-year rotation system. In other years, the government has ordered production to be cut down because the market abroad was considered to be
weak. This motivation was certainly behind the restrictions in 1931–1933. It is
difficult to know a priori whether such restrictions led the cultivators to cut
down the area more than they would have done otherwise, but they clearly
did not work "against the market" in such years. For the 1942–1947 period
much the same could be said. With European markets cut off, prices would
obviously have fallen sharply had everything been left to the market forces,
and a steep decline in cotton acreage would probably also have occurred without area restrictions. But there was the additional consideration that, cut off
from nitrate fertilizer supplies from abroad during several years, the risk for
soil exhaustion was great, even at a very low cotton acreage. And on top of all
that there were, of course, the food requirements of the Allied armies operating
from Egypt.

The restrictions from 1953 to 1960 are more difficult to rationalize. In
1953 they certainly tended to work in the same direction as the market forces,
considering the collapse of the Korean boom. But relative profitability was by
no means low, even after the cotton price drop in 1952 and despite the heavy
cotton export taxes levied in these years (see Chart A–1). The restrictions

were eased somewhat in 1954, but evasion must have become widespread, too; the cotton area increased despite a further decline in relative output value until 1956. After 1956, evasion was massive (see Chapter 6, p. 151). The increasing need for food grain imports, related to population growth, was one reason why the government tried to keep down the cotton area during these years; hence the simultaneous prescriptions for the wheat acreages from 1955 onward. It should be noticed, finally, that the optimum tariff argument has always played a role in policy debate in Egypt although opinions about its applicability have differed widely [4].

To keep the number of observations as large as possible (that is, forty-eight), an attempt was made to quantify the area restrictions rather than delete all years with controls. In a sense that is a relatively simple matter because the laws imposing the restrictions have always specified an upper limit, expressed as a percentage of his holdings, to the individual cultivator's cotton acreage. The laws were published in the *Journal Officiel du Gouvernement Egyptien*, from which the following details about the restrictions were compiled.

Until the end of the twenties the restrictions were simple. In each of the years 1915, 1918, 1921–1923, and 1927–1929, the upper limit was one-third, applying to any cultivator of land.[13]

During the period from 1931 to 1933 things became a bit more complicated. In 1931 the restrictions were directed exclusively toward the then leading long staple variety, Sakellarides. Prices on long staple cotton had fallen particularly sharply and the government tried to make cultivators keep long staple production below the private optimum. For that purpose a distinction was made between a "Zone Nord" of the Delta, including most districts in the governorates Behera, Gharbeya, and Daqhaleya, and the rest of the agricultural lands in the Delta and Upper Egypt. In the Zone Nord the upper limit for Sakel was 40 percent; in the rest of the country it was simply forbidden. For all other varieties there were no restrictions. The division between Zone Nord and the rest is interesting because it was in the former that the large cotton estates were situated. In 1932 restrictions were tightened. In Zone Nord the upper limit was 30 percent for all varieties, including Sakel. In the rest of the country the limit was 25 percent, with Sakel forbidden. In 1933 restrictions were relaxed again and limited to Sakel for Zone Nord, with an upper limit of 40 percent; for the rest of the country there was a general maximum of 50 percent, with Sakel forbidden.

The next period of restrictions was caused by World War II. For 1942 the upper limit in Zone Nord was 27 percent for all varieties; for the rest of the lands it was 23 percent. Cotton cultivation was entirely forbidden on basin-irrigated lands unless cotton had been grown there earlier. It was also prescribed that cotton must be preceded by clover, and that it was not permitted for two consecutive years on the same land. Certain long staple varieties (Zagora and Malaki) were forbidden or subject to special limits. This set of restrictions was in force for the years 1942, 1943, and 1944. For 1945 and 1946, the limits were unchanged at 27 percent for Zone Nord, but a further reduction to 18 percent was decreed for the rest of the country. A special limit of 14 percent was introduced for old basin lands that had been converted to summer irrigation and cotton cultivation was forbidden completely in the Aswan governorate. We were not able to find any law in the *Journal Officiel* for 1946 and 1947 applying to the 1947 crop or abrogating earlier laws, so we have assumed that the rigorous limits of 1946 applied here too (supported by [5, Table III]).

From the agricultural year 1942–43 (November–October) to 1945–46, there were area prescriptions for wheat and barley. For 1942–43, Zone Nord had a lower limit of 45 percent for wheat and barley (with at least 20 percent wheat) and the rest of the lands, 60 percent (with at least 50 percent wheat). These limits were applied also to 1944–45 and continued through 1945–46 with a minor modification.

For 1953 the upper limit for cotton was 30 percent for all cultivators and varieties. From 1954 to 1958 the upper limit of 30 percent remained in force for Zone Nord, but was increased to 37 percent for the rest of the Delta and Upper Egypt. For 1959 and 1960, finally, it was 33 percent for all cultivators and varieties.

Note, in addition, that from 1955 to 1959 there was a lower limit to wheat identical with the upper limit to cotton.

Although there have been restrictions for cotton and, for some years, also prescriptions for wheat and barley, we shall use only a single variable to express the impact of the controls on actual acreage. The rationale of this decision is mainly that the prescriptions for wheat have been highly correlated with those for cotton. We hope, therefore, that a variable based on the cotton acreage restrictions alone will capture the impact of all the controls on all the crops.

The question is now how to translate the upper limits for individual cultivators into a constraint on the total cotton acreage. What complicates matters is, of course, that cotton is cultivated by farmers who do not grow it exclusively but as one crop in rotation with others.

As an extreme case, assume first that half the total land in Egypt is on a three-year rotation and the other half, on a two-year rotation, and that all cultivators apply a simultaneous-consecutive rotation system, so that a cultivator grows cotton each year on one rotating part of his land. With a three-year rotation, a cultivator would thus always have one third of his land planted with cotton; on a two-year rotation, half his land would always be planted with cotton.

It is immediately clear that with this model an upper limit ≦50 percent would imply no reduction at all in the total cotton acreage, for no cultivator would at any time use more than 50 percent of his land for cotton.

At an upper limit ≦50 percent but ≧33⅓ percent, cultivators with a two-year rotation would be forced to cut down their cotton acreage, but cultivators with a three-year rotation would be unaffected. It is easily seen that in this interval each percentage point for which the maximum is below 50 will force a cultivator on a two-year rotation to limit his actual cotton acreage by two percent of the acreage he would choose were there no limitations. And since half the land is assumed to be on two-year rotation, the reduction of the total cotton acreage is simply 2 times 0.6 (because 60 percent of the cotton land at no restrictions is in two-year rotation), or equal to 1.2 percent. The total reduction caused by the maximum percent would thus be 50 *minus* the maximum percent times 1.2. At a maximum of 33⅓ percent, the reduction would be 20 percent of the free acreage.

At an upper limit ≦33⅓ percent, cultivators with three-year rotation will have to cut down their cotton acreages, too. A fall in the upper limit by one percentage point will now force cultivators on three-year rotation to cut down their cotton acreage by 3 percent of their cotton acreage at no restrictions. Cultivators with two-year rotation will have to reduce their cotton acreage, as before, by a further two percent measured upon their acreage at no restrictions. The combined effect is a reduction by 2.0 times 0.6 + 3.0 times 0.4, or by 2.4 percent of total cotton acreage without controls.

The relation between upper limit for the individual cultivator and reduction of total cotton acreage is thus nonlinear. It has a kink at 50 percent and another one at 33⅓ percent. In the intervals between 100 and 50, 50 and 33⅓, and 33⅓ and 0 it is linear as shown in Chart A–1 (the broken line OABC).

As another extreme model, we could imagine that all farmers, whether on two- or three-year rotation, rotate consecutively so that at any time they have only one crop on all their land. In any particular year we should then expect one third of the farmers on three-year rotation and half the farmers on two-year rotation to cultivate all their land with cotton and the remainder to have no cotton at all that year. In this case the total cotton acreage would simply be reduced to the upper limit and the area reduction would be represented in Chart A–1 by the 45° line through the origin, OC.

Our assumption that half the land of those who cultivate cotton at all is on three-year rotation and half on two-year rotation may not be entirely unrealistic (see Chapter 6, note 8).[14] Moreover, peasants usually follow the patterns of the first model with simultaneous-consecutive rotation. But big cultivators might, for reasons of large-scale economies, prefer the system with consecutive, nonsimultaneous rotation. It stands to reason, therefore, that the

CHART A–1
Limits to and Reduction of Cotton Acreage

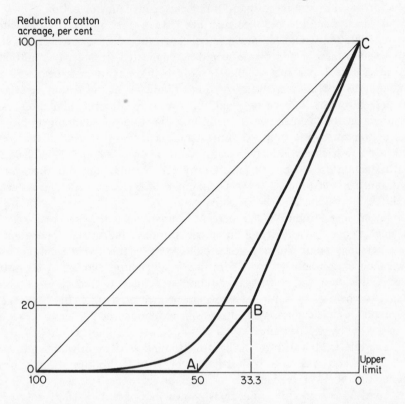

Reduction of cotton
acreage, per cent

aggregate relationship between individual maximum limit and total acreage reduction is a nonlinear relationship similar to the curve in Figure A–1 passing through the origin and the point C (0, 100) and running between the 45°-line and the broken line OABC. Calling the rate of acreage reduction K, and the maximum limit (expressed as a ratio) x, a relationship such as $K = (1 - x)^4$ might be reasonable, considering the actual maximal ratios and the actual reduction in cotton acreage in the years when limits are imposed. At $x = 0.5$, the cotton acreage reduction would be about 6 percent; at $x = 0.33$, about 20 percent; and at $x = 0.25$, about 35 percent.

Finally, we have to consider the evasion of controls. A glance at upper limits and actual cotton acreages (Chart A–1) reveals immediately what is confirmed by all observers and certainly should be expected in Egypt—that evasion at times has been considerable. It would appear that under "normal" conditions, restrictions are effective the first year after their introduction, but that thereafter, in a sequence of control years, evasion rapidly takes the upper hand. It may take the form of farmers with consecutive, nonsimultaneous rotation shifting to simultaneous rotation. With a three-year rotation, an upper limit of 33⅓ percent would then cut the acreage in the first year but have no effect whatever during the following year. This kind of evasion could even be legal. The years of World War II seem to have been an exception to this rule: not until the war was over did evasion become massive. We have assumed that for 1922 and 1923, 1928 and 1929, 1946 and 1947, and 1955 to 1960 evasion was so general that these years can be considered as having been without controls.

The construction of Table A–1 will now be readily understood. In column 1 we have, on the basis of the information given above, gauged an average figure for the individual cultivator's upper limit. For some years there was, indeed, only a single limit, but for most years an average had to be calculated. In doing so we tried particularly to gauge the importance of Zone Nord. The values for the control variable to be applied in the regressions appear in column 4. Needless to say, the table is based on a certain amount of subjective judgment.

To equation (9) we can now add a new term, $\alpha_{9i}K$, where K is the area reduction calculated in column (4) of Table A–1. We graft the controls variable K directly on (9) rather than on (8) because we have also considered "adaptation," or evasion. But it is not clear whether this is the best method of procedure.[15]

We should expect α_{9i} to be negative for cotton and positive for other crops. Equation (9) then becomes

$$A_i = \alpha_{1i} + \alpha_{2i}(F_i)_{-1} + \alpha_{3i}A_{-1} + \alpha_{4i}A_{-2} \tag{9'}$$

$$+ \alpha_{5i}L + \alpha_{6i}L_{-1} + \alpha_{7i}W_\tau + \alpha_{8i}W_{\tau-1} + \alpha_{9i}K + \alpha_{10i}(A_i)_{-1}$$

where the coefficients are related as follows:

$$
\begin{array}{lll}
\text{(i)} & \alpha_{1i} = a_{1i}(1 - a_{2i}) & \tag{10} \\
\text{(ii)} & \alpha_{2i} = ba_{2i} & \\
\text{(iii)} & \alpha_{3i} = a_{3i} & \\
\text{(iv)} & \alpha_{4i} = a_{3i}a_{2i} & \\
\text{(v)} & \alpha_{5i} = a_{4i} & \\
\text{(vi)} & \alpha_{6i} = -a_{4i}a_{2i} & \\
\text{(vii)} & \alpha_{7i} = a_{5i} & \\
\text{(viii)} & \alpha_{8i} = -a_{5i}a_{2i} & \\
\text{(ix)} & \alpha_{10i} = a_{2i} &
\end{array}
$$

Relations (iii) to (ix) may be used for testing the quality of the estimate.

For sources of data, see [7], [2], [1], [6], and Table A–1. The series used are presented in [9].

TABLE A–1
The Impact of Upper Limits to Cotton Cultivation

Year	Average Upper Limit to Cultivator's Acreage, x (%) (1)	$1 - x$ (2)	Prescribed Rate of Reduction of Total Acreage $(1 - x)^4$ (3)	Control Variable K (4)
1915	33⅓	0.67	0.20	0.20
1918	(33⅓)	0.67	0.20	0.20
1921	33⅓	0.67	0.20	0.20
1922[a]				0
1923[a]				0
1927	33⅓	0.67	0.20	0.20
1928[a]				0
1929[a]				0
1931	45	0.55	0.09	0.09
1932	25	0.75	0.32	0.32
1933	45	0.55	0.09	0.09
1942	24	0.76	0.33	0.33
1943	24	0.76	0.33	0.33
1944	24	0.76	0.33	0.33
1945	22	0.76	0.33	0.33
1946[a]	20	0.80	0.41	0
1947[a]	(20)	0.80	0.41	0
1953	30	0.70	0.24	0.24
1954	33	0.67	0.20	0.20
1955[a]	33	0.67	0.20	0
1956[a]	33	0.67	0.20	0
1957[a]	33	0.67	0.20	0
1958[a]	33	0.67	0.20	0
1959[a]	33	0.67	0.20	0
1960[a]	33	0.67	0.20	0
All other years	100	0	0	0

SOURCES: *Journal Officiel du Gouvernement Egyptien,* 1915, No. 85; 1921, Nos. 86 and 92; 1927, No. 5; 1931, Nos. 13 and 96; 1932, No. 100; 1941, No. 142; 1942, No. 174; 1942, No. 180; 1943, No. 92; 1944, No. 25; 1944, No. 107; 1946, No. 1; *Economic Bulletin,* N.B.E., various issues; Brown, op. cit., and Hansen and Marzouk, op. cit., pp. 98–99.

a. Characterized by evasion of controls.

METHOD OF ESTIMATION [16]

Multiple least squares regression tends to yield biased estimates of models like ours. This lagged variables model may, however, be considered as belonging to the class of general "noisy" or "errors in variables" model. It is known that the method of instrumental variables yields consistent estimates for general "noisy" models. This method has not found much application in econometrics because the approach has been to obtain the instrumental variables from outside the model, an impractical method that yields estimates with larger variances than those of least squares.

It can be shown, however, that instrumental variables may be obtained from within the model, and that the optimum instrumental variables matrix is the matrix of the noise-free variables of the model multiplied by the inverse variance covariance matrix of the error (disturbance) vector.[17] The term "optimum" is here used in the sense of yielding consistent estimates with the smallest variances. The latter can be shown to approach asymptotically those of the least squares' estimates. These desired properties of unbiasedness and least variances have been proven, theoretically, for the asymptotic case; yet, in all finite sample problems studied so far, the optimum instrumental variables method has, in fact, been always giving better results than least squares.[18]

Mathematically, our model is

$$y_t = \beta_0 + z_{1t}\beta_1 + z_{2t}\beta_2 + \cdots + y_{t-1}\beta_{n+1} + \cdots + y_{t-i}\beta_{n+i} + \epsilon_t$$

and for T observations we can write

$$Y = X\beta + \epsilon,$$

where Y is a T vector, X is a $T \times (n + i + 1)$ matrix, β is a $(n + i + 1)$ vector, and ϵ is a T vector.

Given the model, the optimum instrumental variables are obtained by adaptive, or recursive, estimation using the computer program ESTIMM as follows. First, the program yields the ordinary least squares estimate (L.S.). It then proceeds to obtain a so-called noise-free estimate of the endogenous variables, y_t. The noise-free estimate is obtained as the solution of the model with the y_ts as unknowns, and using the values of the coefficients, β, emerging from the least squares estimate together with the actually observed values of the exogenous variables, z. The lagged endogenous variables, y_{t-1} to y_{t-i}, appearing on the right hand side are, of course, unknown and obtained from the solution (with the exception of those with an earlier dating than 0 for which the actually observed values had to be used). The error term, ϵ, that is the "noise," is deleted (set equal to zero) to obtain a solution of y_t, "free of noise." The noise-free estimate of the endogenous variables is then used in the instrumental variables matrix to replace the "noisy," actually observed, values of the endogenous variables. For the other variables, the actually observed values were used as instrumental variables in this case. On this basis a new estimate of the model is made and this is the instrumental variable estimate, step 1 (I.V.1).

On the basis of the coefficient values obtained in I.V.1, the program then calculates a new noise-free estimate of the endogenous variables to obtain a new instrumental variables matrix in the same way as was done after the L.S. Thereafter, the program checks for first-order correlation among the errors, and estimates the inverse variance covariance matrix on the assumption that the errors follow a first-order autoregressive scheme. The inverse matrix (if obtained) is used with the new step 2 instrumental variables matrix to yield the instrumental variable estimate of the model, step 2 (I.V.2).

Summarizing, the least squares estimate (L.S.) is

$$\beta_{\text{L.S.}} = (X^T X)^{-1} X^T Y.$$

The instrumental variable estimate, step 1 (I.V.1) is

$$\beta_{\text{I.V.1}} = (\widetilde{X}_1{}^T X)^{-1} \widetilde{X}_1{}^T Y$$

where $\widetilde{X}_1$ is the first noise-free estimate of X.

The instrumental variable estimate, step 2 (I.V.2) is

$$\beta_{\text{I.V.2}} = (\widetilde{X}_2{}^T \Omega^{-1} \widetilde{X})^{-1} X_2{}^T \Omega^{-1} Y$$

where $\widetilde{X}_2$ is the second noise-free estimate of X and Ω is the variance covariance matrix of the errors.

For the present model some of the matrices to be inverted turned out to be almost singular because they contained both unlagged and lagged values of exogenous variables that change very slowly over time. In such cases, normal precision of the computer (IBM/360) was insufficient and double precision had to be used. Some matrices were, however, so close to singularity that even double precision did not prevent instability. These cases have been labeled "not applicable" in Table A–2.

In all estimates we used the standard formula for R^2

$$R^2 = (\Sigma y_t{}^2 - \Sigma e_t{}^2)/\Sigma y_t{}^2$$

where e_t are the residuals. This formula applies strictly to the L.S. and we have, of course, $0 \leqq R^2 \leqq 1$. Applying the same formula to the I.V., we can only be sure, however, that $R^2 \leqq 1$, so that the computations may yield negative values of R^2.

Durban-Watson statistics were not computed because the program corrects automatically for the presence of autocorrelated errors in I.V.2; in the case of L.S., the Durban-Watson statistic is uninteresting because L.S. of this model yields biased estimates in any case. It might have been useful, however, to use them for I.V.1 where I.V.2 failed.

RESULTS OF ESTIMATIONS

In most cases the three methods—L.S., I.V.1, and I.V.2—gave very similar results, implying that the bias involved in L.S. cannot be very serious in this particular case. For the lagged crop area there is, however, a substantial difference between the coefficients obtained for some crops (onions, beans, lentils); here the unbiased estimates give much larger coefficients than L.S.

For theoretical reasons we prefer to use the results of I.V.2 whenever available. For several crops the I.V.2 had to be abandoned, however, for computational reasons or because the coefficient of the lagged area variable was > 1, implying instability. In these cases I.V.1 was used. In one case I.V.1 also led to instability, and the L.S. results were used.

The findings are shown in Table A-2. Acreages are measured in thousands of feddans and water, in billions of cubic meters; labor is expressed as an index, with average labor force 1950–1955 = 100; F is a pure number defined by equation (5); and K is defined in Table A-1. Figures in brackets under the coefficient values are the corresponding t values. R^2 values and SER values (standard error of estimate) are given in columns 13 and 14, while column 15 indicates which estimate has been selected for calculating elasticities—shown in Table 6–3—and for the area predictions. Although our main interest is in the predictions, a few remarks about the details of the estimates are warranted. (We limit ourselves to the estimates selected for prediction.)

The R^2 values differ considerably, from 0.95 for cane to 0.39 for lentils. For five crops, R^2 exceeds 0.80. The standard error of regression, SER, is generally about 5–10 percent of the actual acreage at the end of the period of prediction; barley is an exception, with more than 35 percent. Thus, the fits cannot claim any high degree of accuracy, but compared with similar estimates for other countries they are not too bad.

Concerning coefficients, we note first that that of the control variable, K, has the expected sign for all summer crops and wheat—negative for cotton and positive for rice, corn, millet, and wheat—and is significantly different from zero at the 1 percent level. For other crops the sign of the coefficient of K is erratic and insignificant, as should be expected.

The coefficient of the relative output-value variable, F, has in all cases a positive sign, except for corn. The sign of the coefficient is significant at the 1 percent level for cotton, barley, onions, beans, lentils, and helba, and at the 5 percent level, for rice and cane. For the important food grains, corn, wheat, and millet, it is insignificant.

TABLE A–2
Results of Estimates of Acreage Response Functions

Crop (i) (1)	Estimation Method (2)	Coefficient of:				
		$F_{i,-1}$ (3)	$\bar{A}_{-1}$ (4)	$\bar{A}_{-2}$ (5)	L (6)	L_{-1} (7)
Cotton						
	L.S.	245.48	0.17	−0.02	2.31	−2.22
		(3.24)	(1.08)	(−0.12)	(0.85)	(−0.83)
	I.V.1	252.22	0.14	0.01	2.65	−2.54
		(3.39)	(0.89)	(0.08)	(0.96)	(−0.95)
	I.V.2	293.44	0.16	0.00	2.23	−2.13
		(4.02)	(1.08)	(0.00)	(1.15)	(−1.11)
Rice						
	L.S.	177.92	0.12	−0.09	−3.11	3.37
		(2.19)	(1.22)	(−1.00)	(−1.68)	(1.84)
	I.V.1	174.99	0.10	−0.08	−2.71	2.96
		(2.20)	(0.97)	(−0.83)	(−1.31)	(1.43)
	I.V.2	Not applicable				
Corn						
	L.S.	−136.69	0.04	0.19	4.64	−4.96
		(−0.77)	(0.21)	(1.30)	(1.70)	(−1.82)
	I.V.1	−78.48	0.40	0.13	7.33	−7.97
		(−0.42)	(1.81)	(1.09)	(2.31)	(−2.46)
	I.V.2	Not applicable				
Millet						
	L.S.	28.02	0.01	−0.05	−2.92	3.10
		(0.40)	(0.17)	(−0.69)	(−2.22)	(2.39)
	I.V.1	28.55	0.01	−0.05	−2.93	3.11
		(0.40)	(0.18)	(−0.67)	(−2.04)	(2.17)
	I.V.2	Not applicable				
Wheat						
	L.S.	75.44	0.09	−0.03	1.92	−1.41
		(0.63)	(0.73)	(−0.26)	(1.14)	(−0.88)
	I.V.1	78.80	0.05	−0.01	2.18	−1.67
		(0.68)	(0.36)	(−0.06)	(1.32)	(−1.06)
	I.V.2.	83.24	0.05	0.01	1.31	−0.86
		(0.80)	(0.47)	(0.06)	(0.83)	(−0.58)
Barley						
	L.S.	112.38	−0.05	0.03	1.08	−1.13
		(1.96)	(−1.24)	(0.65)	(1.53)	(−1.65)
	I.V.1	114.96	−0.05	0.03	0.85	−0.36
		(1.97)	(−1.17)	(0.65)	(1.16)	(−1.20)
	I.V.2	144.97	−0.02	0.02	−0.13	0.10
		(3.63)	(−0.74)	(0.69)	(−0.18)	(0.15)

(continued)

TABLE A–2 (continued)

		Coefficient of:			Statistics		Selected for the
W_τ (8)	$W_{\tau-1}$ (9)	K (10)	$A_{i,-1}$ (11)	Constant (12)	R^2 (13)	SER (14)	Predictions (15)
−73.11 (−1.71)	10.02 (0.23)	−1,901.50 (−9.21)	0.27 (3.67)	−37.00 (−0.07)	0.86	138.86	
−73.22 (−1.70)	6.66 (0.15)	−1,947.16 (−9.42)	0.22 (2.78)	−11.30 (−0.02)	0.86	139.54	
−67.29 (−1.87)	−4.37 (−0.11)	−1,910.95 (−10.01)	0.18 (2.41)	−19.46 (−0.03)	0.85	142.00	x
169.37 (6.54)	8.11 (0.24)	318.18 (2.85)	0.08 (0.52)	−742.50 (−2.08)	0.87	83.03	
167.87 (6.63)	−4.61 (−0.11)	327.14 (3.45)	0.16 (0.73)	−685.06 (−1.82)	0.87	83.18	x
−44.98 (−1.13)	34.72 (0.85)	658.69 (3.23)	0.29 (1.33)	77.00 (0.12)	0.64	129.29	
−51.31 (−1.23)	22.00 (0.51)	933.82 (4.76)	−0.24 (−0.63)	−700.15 (−1.11)	0.61	134.05	x
21.58 (1.16)	1.18 (0.06)	388.73 (2.89)	0.43 (3.47)	217.97 (0.97)	0.87	59.45	
21.64 (1.15)	1.34 (0.07)	390.20 (3.79)	0.43 (2.59)	217.01 (0.99)	0.87	59.45	x
−6.19 (−1.51)	−7.89 (−1.78)	576.43 (3.93)	0.14 (0.99)	593.00 (1.49)	0.69	96.47	
−6.24 (−1.53)	−7.40 (−1.66)	556.91 (3.74)	0.23 (1.16)	599.24 (1.52)	0.69	95.96	
−6.37 (−1.68)	−7.60 (−1.85)	529.94 (3.92)	0.25 (1.45)	534.38 (1.65)	0.69	96.67	x
−1.56 (−0.94)	−4.39 (−2.50)	12.87 (0.19)	0.74 (8.99)	328.31 (2.00)	0.88	39.05	
−1.66 (−0.99)	−4.30 (−2.40)	−8.56 (−0.13)	0.86 (8.57)	248.28 (1.44)	0.88	39.84	
−2.32 (−1.63)	−3.55 (−2.42)	−77.63 (−1.41)	0.95 (15.10)	102.14 (1.12)	0.86	43.38	x

(continued)

TABLE A–2 (concluded)

Crop (i) (1)	Estimation Method (2)	Coefficient of:				
		$F_{i,-1}$ (3)	$\overline{A}_{-1}$ (4)	$\overline{A}_{-2}$ (5)	L (6)	L_{-1} (7)
Onions						
	L.S.	2.31	0.01	0.00	0.11	−0.12
		(1.89)	(1.80)	(0.44)	(0.85)	(−1.00)
	I.V.1	4.41	0.02	−0.01	−0.08	0.07
		(3.12)	(1.99)	(−0.93)	(−0.45)	(0.38)
	I.V.2	Not applicable				
Beans						
	L.S.	48.99	−0.03	0.05	1.01	−1.18
		(0.74)	(−0.56)	(1.02)	(1.21)	(−1.49)
	I.V.1	109.00	−0.02	0.03	0.57	−0.68
		(1.57)	(−0.35)	(0.59)	(0.62)	(−0.75)
	I.V.2	Not applicable				
Lentils						
	L.S.	13.26	−0.02	0.02	0.39	−0.37
		(1.29)	(−1.64)	(1.71)	(2.37)	(−2.33)
	I.V.1	19.07	−0.02	0.02	0.35	−0.34
		(1.59)	(−1.70)	(1.71)	(1.75)	(−1.87)
	I.V.2	Not applicable				
Helba						
	L.S.	36.81	−0.04	0.04	0.56	−0.56
		(3.10)	(−3.16)	(3.00)	(2.13)	(−2.26)
	I.V.1	39.53	−0.04	0.04	0.49	−0.49
		(3.25)	(−2.92)	(3.08)	(1.43)	(−1.55)
	I.V.2	38.59	−0.04	0.04	0.12	−0.15
		(3.97)	(−2.76)	(3.95)	(0.28)	(−0.39)
Cane						
	L.S.	2.32	0.01	−0.00	−0.18	0.18
		(1.59)	(1.25)	(−0.88)	(−1.48)	(1.53)
	I.V.1	2.25	0.01	−0.00	−0.14	0.14
		(1.53)	(0.97)	(−0.78)	(−1.02)	(1.04)
	I.V.2	3.37	0.01	−0.00	−0.38	0.37
		(2.71)	(1.40)	(−0.41)	(−2.66)	(2.71)

NOTE: t-values are in parentheses.

TABLE A–2 (concluded)

		Coefficient of:			Statistics		Selected for the
W_τ (8)	$W_{\tau-1}$ (9)	K (10)	$A_{i,-1}$ (11)	Constant (12)	R^2 (13)	SER (14)	Predictions (15)
0.69 (2.41)	0.34 (1.07)	−11.70 (−1.11)	0.47 (2.83)	−112.95 (−3.69)	0.69	6.76	x
0.69 (1.96)	0.26 (0.66)	4.32 (0.28)	1.12 (3.13)	−64.52 (−1.43)	0.52	8.42	
1.26 (0.61)	−1.29 (−0.61)	83.01 (1.00)	0.39 (2.46)	215.50 (1.05)	0.60	47.11	
2.07 (0.99)	−1.01 (−0.46)	65.33 (0.75)	0.75 (2.49)	0.22 (0.00)	0.57	49.14	x
1.00 (2.68)	−0.42 (−1.00)	−4.87 (−0.36)	0.18 (1.06)	13.00 (0.38)	0.43	8.76	
0.91 (2.19)	−0.63 (−1.00)	−5.85 (−0.42)	0.44 (0.73)	8.87 (0.25)	0.39	9.01	x
0.73 (1.48)	−0.37 (−0.67)	−12.97 (−0.73)	0.64 (4.83)	19.75 (0.38)	0.70	11.74	
0.71 (1.42)	−0.47 (−0.80)	−16.10 (−1.03)	0.72 (3.05)	3.36 (0.05)	0.70	11.80	
0.63 (1.31)	−0.63 (−1.15)	−21.87 (−1.56)	0.91 (4.05)	−39.73 (−0.87)	0.66	12.51	x
−0.10 (−0.46)	0.18 (0.75)	18.19 (2.49)	0.90 (14.02)	−14.30 (−0.64)	0.95	5.13	
−0.14 (−0.61)	0.14 (0.59)	17.69 (2.42)	0.94 (12.55)	−9.25 (−0.43)	0.95	5.15	
−0.06 (−0.30)	0.20 (0.84)	16.72 (2.72)	0.87 (13.90)	−28.64 (−1.92)	0.95	5.36	x

The coefficients for the lagged and unlagged primary inputs, land, labor, and water, are generally insignificantly different from zero. Only in the case of water input in rice do we have definite expectations a priori with respect to sign, i.e., a positive sign for the unlagged water variable; the sign is, in fact, positive and highly significant. For the input coefficients a test was indicated on p. 329, according to which the product of the coefficient of the lagged variable and the coefficient of the lagged crop area should be equal to the coefficient of the unlagged variable with opposite sign. Since the coefficient of the lagged variable in all cases is positive, except corn, we should, as a minimum, require the lagged and the unlagged coefficients to have opposite signs (except for corn). According to this sign test, the estimates are satisfactory in 23 out of 33 cases.

The coefficient of the lagged crop area falls between 0 and 1 in most cases and is < 1 in all cases selected for predictions; only in one case (corn) is it negative. The significance of the sign of this coefficient is generally high. For seven crops it is significant at the 1 percent level, and only for three (rice, corn, and wheat) is it insignificant at the 5 percent level.

PREDICTIONS OF ACREAGES, 1962–1968

Three different predictions were made for the years 1962 to 1968.

Two were made on the basis of equation (9'), with estimated coefficient values inserted and $K = 0$.[19] In *prediction 1*, actual domestic ex-farm prices were used for calculating F, the relative profitability index; in *prediction 2*, actual international prices (f.o.b. or c.i.f., depending upon whether the commodity is exported or imported) were used for F. These predictions were sequential in the sense that the acreages forecast for one year were used for predicting acreages for the following year. *Prediction 3*, finally, was made on the basis of the stationary form of equation (9), with $K = 0$ for all years, and with actual international prices used for calculating F.

The data used for the predictions are presented in [9, tables], and the calculated F-values are shown in Table A–4. The results of the predictions appear in Table A–3 and are depicted, with the actual acreages, in Charts 7–1 to 7–11.

TABLE A–3
Acreage Predictions, 1962–1968
(000 feddan)

Crop (1)	Pre-diction (2)	1962 (3)	1963 (4)	1964 (5)	1965 (6)	1966 (7)	1967 (8)	1968 (9)
Cotton[a]	1	1595	1637	1691	1693	1551	1388	1376
	2	1677	1755	1792	1782	1626	1543	1585
	3	1796	1740	1800	1539	1495	1485	1539
Rice[b]	1	674	720	677	859	1126	1316	1458
	2	745	822	787	966	1242	1408	1557
	3	834	852	786	1111	1314	1432	1549
Corn[b]	1	1705	1725	1763	1783	1725	1662	1667
	2	1719	1752	1821	1850	1783	1735	1755
	3	1810	1765	1745	1607	1659	1613	1694
Millet[b]	1	438	433	415	400	462	548	597
	2	437	434	407	384	443	528	577
	3	453	464	460	547	581	612	616
Wheat[a]	1	1462	1456	1506	1523	1588	1706	1757
	2	1444	1444	1502	1526	1585	1696	1744
	3	1410	1486	1109	1434	1694	1700	1715
Barley[a]	1	148	138	155	159	154	207	257
	2	156	147	146	132	135	193	233
	3	(−108)	187	167	(−273)	1279	1089	961
Beans[b]	1	385	404	399	422	388	376	332
	2	352	335	312	312	277	268	223
	3	320	231	218	237	248	87	217
Onions[c]	1	53	50	47	50	48	40	39
	2	55	57	56	61	59	52	60
	3	70	54	49	55	36	42	36
Lentils[b]	1	87	89	87	89	72	64	58
	2	90	81	79	87	73	68	59
	3	78	73	70	78	71	63	71
Helba[a]	1	66	68	68	73	61	61	57
	2	(67)	(61)	(56)	(58)	(47)	(47)	(40)
	3	(92)	(61)	(39)	(51)	(75)	(42)	(1)
Cane[a]	1	107	102	94	82	79	82	86
	2	105	98	97	86	79	79	80
	3	88	133	89	52	46	35	44

NOTE: Prediction 1: Short-term, based on actual ex-farm prices.
Prediction 2: Short-term, based on actual international prices.
Prediction 3: Long-term, based on actual international prices and stationary form.
For Helba, predictions 2 and 3 were made at actual ex-farm prices (for Helba).
a. Estimation method: I.V.2.
b. Estimation method: I.V.1.
c. Estimation method: L.S.

TABLE A–4
Relative Value of Output per Feddan, F_i, 1961–1968
(at actual ex-farm and international prices)

Crop	Type of Price (1)	1961 (2)	1962 (3)	1963 (4)	1964 (5)	1965 (6)	1966 (7)	1967 (8)	1968 (9)
Cotton									
	Ex-farm	1.38	1.77	1.79	1.96	1.70	1.43	1.51	1.74
	International	1.66	2.06	1.97	2.11	1.84	1.86	2.04	2.20
Rice									
	Ex-farm	1.13	1.03	0.93	0.75	0.82	0.93	1.03	1.11
	International	1.53	1.48	1.42	1.25	1.38	1.34	1.46	1.54
Corn									
	Ex-farm	0.78	0.59	0.65	0.62	0.80	0.95	0.95	0.77
	International	0.68	0.45	0.51	0.53	0.76	0.72	0.64	0.55
Millet									
	Ex-farm	0.98	0.66	0.72	0.71	0.78	0.85	0.90	0.78
	International	0.94	0.65	0.57	0.49	0.58	0.60	0.59	0.57
Wheat									
	Ex-farm	0.87	0.73	0.71	0.65	0.68	0.72	0.70	0.63
	International	0.65	0.57	0.60	0.60	0.56	0.55	0.47	0.39
Barley									
	Ex-farm	0.65	0.56	0.65	0.63	0.48	0.52	0.48	0.39
	International	0.70	0.60	0.54	0.50	0.52	0.55	0.41	0.35
Beans									
	Ex-farm	0.74	0.98	0.78	0.87	0.79	0.90	0.56	0.75
	International	0.44	0.59	0.44	0.44	0.50	0.64	0.31	0.58
Onions									
	Ex-farm	2.59	2.96	2.52	2.15	3.08	2.46	2.63	2.20
	International	3.48	5.03	3.82	3.61	4.58	4.44	7.90	5.09
Lentils									
	Ex-farm	0.93	1.11	0.81	0.53	0.64	0.51	0.45	0.70
	International	1.04	0.75	0.64	0.56	0.72	0.69	0.47	0.72
Helba									
	Ex-farm	0.67	0.75	0.73	0.71	0.75	0.75	0.71	0.62
	International[a]	(0.70)	(0.65)	(0.60)	(0.57)	(0.65)	(0.68)	(0.64)	(0.50)
Cane									
	Ex-farm	2.57	2.17	2.07	1.71	1.99	2.03	1.92	1.99
	International	1.91	1.38	3.48	1.92	0.75	0.71	0.68	0.62

SOURCE: Our calculations. For definition of F_i, see p. 319.

a. In all calculations involving relationships between Helba and other crops values for Helba are at ex-farm prices. This, however, is of importance only for the "international" F_i-value of helba itself.

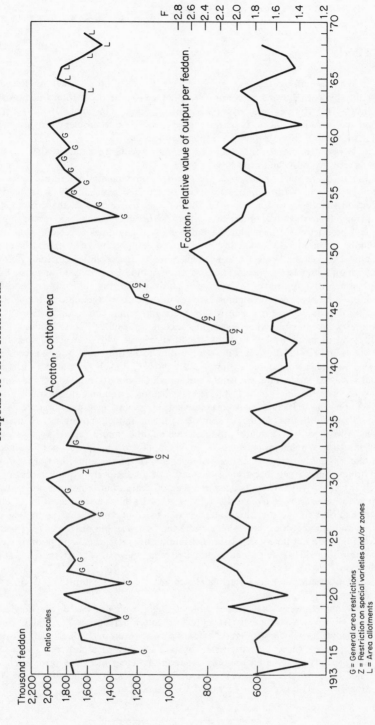

CHART A-2

Response to Area Restrictions

Thousand feddan

Ratio scales

A cotton, cotton area

F cotton, relative value of output per feddan.

G = General area restrictions
Z = Restriction on special varieties and/or zones
L = Area allotments

NOTES

1. With complementarities (externalities) between crops, such as the important externality between clover and cotton (see Chapter 6), the production function should be written as $y_i(t)f_i(A_i, L_i, W_i, A_j)$. This reformulation, important for the determination of land rentals, for instance, is of no consequence for our problem because it does not change the general form of the area response functions.

2. It would make no difference for our purpose if we assumed that maximization took place at the individual farm level.

3. Paul A. Samuelson [20, p. 5f] has made a fundamental point about models of the type applied here: With commodity prices determined exogenously, with homogeneous production functions, or long-term equilibrium (in the sense that there is no surplus or loss in any line of actual production when factors have been paid according to their marginal productivity), and with the number of commodities exceeding that of factors, the number of commodities actually produced in equilibrium (if it exists) cannot exceed the number of factors. We work in principle with 12 commodities (including clover) and 3 factors; on Samuelson's specifications, 3 crops should be cultivated at most. But the 12 crops we are studying have, in fact, been cultivated during the whole period.

From a purely theoretical point of view, in the case of agriculture, Samuelson's point is not terribly damaging. If we insist upon disaggregating commodities there is no good reason why we should not disaggregate factors as well. A classification of land by fertility and of labor by age and sex would supply us with a large number of factors; land prices and rentals do in fact differ according to fertility, and wages, according to age and sex. Indeed, going to the extreme and considering each person and each acre as a special factor of production, we would end up with about 10 million factors—much more than what even the finest actual market classification of commodities would produce (in 1961 cotton was marketed in 9 varieties and 13 grades, making altogether 117 cotton commodities). All this does not help the present model, however, because we have chosen to work with 12 actually produced commodities and 3 factors.

Samuelson's point, nonetheless, does not apply to our setup—not just because we have not explicitly assumed either homogeneity of production functions or long-term equilibrium, but, rather, because in our case not all factors are paid according to their marginal productivity. Water is delivered free of charge but is not generally available to the point where its marginal productivity is zero. In this sense agriculture is not in full market equilibrium and this circumstance saves us from Samuelson's point. The optimum that we are defining does, however, assume the best possible distribution of water; since market forces do not take care of the distribution of water, the assumption is clearly that the authorities distribute water optimally, and that is, of course, a rather bold assumption.

4. Our specification, that technical progress is Hicks-neutral, may, of course, be misleading.

5. Estimates were first made with variable weights, based on previous years' acreages. However, government restrictions on cotton acreages led to violent fluctuations in actual acreages which strongly affected the relative output value index. To make the index independent of such restrictions, constant weights were chosen.

6. In specifying the area response functions as linear in F_i we have, in effect, made them nonlinear in the (relative) prices. The nonlinearity follows directly from the definition of F_i. With two crops we would, for instance, have

$$F_1 = \frac{y_1 p_1}{w_1 y_1 p_1 + w_2 y_2 p_2} = \frac{1}{w_1 + w_2 y_2 p_2 / y_1 p_1}.$$

If the coefficient of F_1 is positive, the area, A_1, is an increasing function of p_1. As p_1 goes from 0 to $+\infty$, F_1 goes from 0 to $1/w_1$, which means that A_1 goes from a certain lower value to an upper limit. The area response curve, depicting the area as a function of its own crop price, is thus concave as seen from the price axis, which is in line with the traditional assumption of decreasing returns in agriculture. Furthermore, the existence of an upper limit to the crop area is consistent with traditional notions about the conditions of cotton and rice cultivation in Egypt (see Chapter 6, pp. 145–146).

7. Strictly speaking, a further assumption is that domestic prices are independent of whether commodities are exported or imported. Even without trade taxes, this assumption means disregarding the c.i.f.-f.o.b. gap, which, however, is relatively small for most agricultural products. The assumption is much more dubious in respect to trade taxes, since it implies that a given commodity is either taxed at import or subsidized at export at the same rate. It so happens that in our case this assumption is fulfilled to some extent because the government has kept ex-farm prices independent of whether export or import takes place. (A case in point is rice.) In any case, we assume that we know in advance whether a commodity will be exported or imported.

8. The possibility cannot be excluded, however, that in distributing water over the year, the government may actually have reacted to international prices; see Chapter 7, p. 176. Also, in its investment policies for agriculture the government may have taken into account private profitability.

9. If rural labor supply depends upon relative wage levels, we should replace L by the ratio between urban wage rate and agricultural output prices in our area response functions. The rural wage rate would be endogenous to our problem. Depending upon the nature of the labor supply function, other variables might have to be included in the response functions, such as time, prices of manufactured consumer goods, unemployment risks, et cetera.

10. A special study made in connection with the ILO-I.N.P. Rural Employment Survey did not single out wages as a particularly important motive for migration; see [19].

11. Since clover is complementary to cotton, it should have a negative weight in F_{cotton}; and vice versa for cotton in F_{clover}. Since we have used positive weights for all crops in all F, we have in fact assumed away all complementarities. Here is another possible misspecification of the model.

12. An experiment was made with predicting the 1962 cotton area on the basis of the actual yield in 1961 (which was about ⅔ of the "normal") and a "normal" yield. The actual yield predicted more accurately than the "normal" yield.

13. The *Journal Officiel* is not available in any U.S. library for the years 1917 and 1918. We have assumed that for 1918 the limit was one-third, as it actually was in all the other restriction years until 1929.

14. Note: our assumption that half the land is on two-year rotation and half on three-year rotation is of importance only for the ordinate of the kink at 33⅓ percent. At a higher proportion of land on three-year rotation the kinked curve would run a little lower, between 50 and 0.

15. If there were no problem of evasion of controls, the K variable should undoubtedly appear in equation (8) and thus appear in (9′) both lagged and unlagged like the other variables. For, assume that K appears unlagged in (9′), as is the case now, and that area restrictions were introduced for one single year and then removed. With (9′) there would then be a fall in the crop area in the period of control, as there should be; but there would also be a negative effect (diminishing over time) on the area during the following periods from the lagged crops area, $(A_i)_{-1}$. The actual reactions of the farmers might, in fact, even be the opposite: after a year of restriction they might tend to cultivate more cotton that they otherwise would. A lagged K variable would take care of that. To that extent (9′) is clearly misspecified.

We are, however, also confronted with the problem of evasion. We have "solved" that problem simply by deciding a priori that in a series of control years, evasion will be complete in all or at least some of the later years in the series. It stands to reason that evasion will increase gradually from year to year. The actual specification does take care of that problem: when we set the control variable at 0 despite its continued existence, its effects for the previous years will continue (at a diminishing rate) through the lagged crop area. Considering our assumptions about evasion years in Table A–1, it will be seen that the specification of (9') therefore makes sense for the control periods 1921–1923, 1927–1929, 1942–1947, and 1953–1960, but hardly for the single control years 1915, 1918, and the years 1931–1933. And there is always a problem with the years immediately following a series of control years.

For most of the control years our specification may thus be defended, but it is clearly not fully satisfactory. With a more complicated lag structure for the control variable the specification could perhaps be improved.

16. This section was written by Rabab A. Kreidieh.

17. For details, see [13].

18. Ibid.

19. It was not possible to use the K variable for the period of prediction because the controls here took on other forms. For the period of estimation the cotton area restriction always fixed an upper limit to the acreage and left it to the cultivators to decide the area below this limit. During the period of prediction the government imposed a certain acreage upon the cultivators.

REFERENCES TO APPENDIX A

[1] *Agricultural Economics [El iqtisad el zirai]*. Cairo: Ministry of Agriculture, various issues (in English and/or Arabic).

[2] *Annuaire Statistique de l'Egypte*. Cairo: Ministry of Finance, various issues.

[3] Behrman, J. R. *Supply Response in Underdeveloped Agriculture, A Case Study of Four Major Annual Crops in Thailand, 1937–1963*. Amsterdam: 1969.

[4] Bresciani-Turroni, C. "Relations entre la récolte et le prix du coton Egyptien." *L'Egypte Contemporaine,* Vol. 19, 1930.

[5] Brown, C. H. *Egyptian Cotton*. London: 2nd. ed., 1955 (1953).

[6] Clawson, M., Landsberg, H. H., and Alexander, L. T. *The Agricultural Potential of the Middle East*. New York: Elsevier, 1971.

[7] Hansen, Bent. "Cotton vs. Grain. On the Optimal Allocation of Land." Cairo: Ministry of Scientific Research, 1964.

[8] ———. "The Distributive Shares in Egyptian Agriculture, 1897–1961." *International Economic Review,* Vol. 9, No. 2, June 1968.

[9] ——— and K. Nashashibi. "Protection and Competitiveness in Egyptian Agriculture and Industry." NBER Working Paper No. 48, New York: 1975.

[10] Hansen, Bent and Marzouk, G. A. *Development and Economic Policy in the U.A.R. (Egypt)*. Amsterdam: 1965.

[11] El Imam, M. M. "A Production Function for Egyptian Agriculture, 1913–1955," Memo No. 259. Cairo: Institute of National Planning, December 31, 1962.

[12] Koyck, L. M. *Distributed Lags and Investment Analysis*. Amsterdam: 1954.

[13] Kreidieh, Rabab A. K. "Estimation of Economic Systems." Ph.D. dissertation, University of California, Berkeley, 1972.

[14] Khrishna, Raj. "Farm Supply Response in India-Pakistan: A Case Study of the Punjab Region." *Economic Journal*, Vol. 78, No. 291, September 1963.

[15] Nerlove, Marc. "Estimates of the Elasticities of Supply of Selected Agricultural Commodities." *Journal of Farm Economics*, Vol. 38, No. 2, May 1956.

[16] ———. *Dynamics of Supply*. Baltimore: 1958.

[17] ———. *Distributed Lags and Demand Analysis for Agricultural and Other Commodities*, Agriculture Handbook No. 114. Washington, D.C.: U.S. Department of Agriculture, 1958.

[18] Nour El Din, Soliman Soliman. "A Statistical Analysis of Some Aspects of Cotton Production and Marketing with Special Reference to USA and Egypt." Ph.D. dissertation, London University, 1958.

[19] "Research Report on Employment Problems in Rural U.A.R.," Report 13. Cairo: Institute of National Planning, 1965.

[20] Samuelson, P. A. "Prices of Factors and Goods in General Equilibrium." *Review of Economic Studies*, Vol. XXI (1), No. 54, 1953–54.

[21] Stern, Robert M. "The Price Responsiveness of Egyptian Cotton Producers." *Kyklos*, Vol. XII, Fasc. 3, 1959.

Appendix B

Definition of Concepts and Delineation of Phases

DEFINITION OF CONCEPTS USED IN THE PROJECT

Exchange Rates.

1. *Nominal exchange rate:* The official parity for a transaction. For countries maintaining a single exchange rate registered with the International Monetary Fund, the nominal exchange rate is the registered rate.

2. *Effective exchange rate (EER):* The number of units of local currency actually paid or received for a one-dollar international transaction. Surcharges, tariffs, the implicit interest forgone on guarantee deposits, and any other charges against purchases of goods and services abroad are included, as are rebates, the value of import replenishment rights, and other incentives to earn foreign exchange for sales of goods and services abroad.

3. *Price-level-deflated (PLD) nominal exchange rates:* The nominal exchange rate deflated in relation to some base period by the price level index of the country.

4. *Price-level-deflated EER (PLD-EER):* The EER deflated by the price level index of the country.

5. *Purchasing-power-parity adjusted exchange rates:* The relevant (nominal or effective) exchange rate multiplied by the ratio of the foreign price level to the domestic price level.

347

Devaluation.

1. *Gross devaluation:* The change in the parity registered with the IMF (or, synonymously in most cases, de jure devaluation).

2. *Net devaluation:* The weighted average of changes in EERs by classes of transactions (or, synonymously in most cases, de facto devaluation).

3. *Real gross devaluation:* The gross devaluation adjusted for the increase in the domestic price level over the relevant period.

4. *Real net devaluation:* The net devaluation similarly adjusted.

Protection Concepts.

1. *Explicit tariff:* The amount of tariff charged against the import of a good as a percentage of the import price (in local currency at the nominal exchange rate) of the good.

2. *Implicit tariff* (or, synonymously, tariff equivalent): The ratio of the domestic price (net of normal distribution costs) minus the c.i.f. import price to the c.i.f. import price in local currency.

3. *Premium:* The windfall profit accruing to the recipient of an import license per dollar of imports. It is the difference between the domestic selling price (net of normal distribution costs) and the landed cost of the item (including tariffs and other charges). The premium is thus the difference between the implicit and the explicit tariff (including other charges) multiplied by the nominal exchange rate.

4. *Nominal tariff:* The tariff—either explicit or implicit as specified—on a commodity.

5. *Effective tariff:* The explicit or implicit tariff on value added as distinct from the nominal tariff on a commodity. This concept is also expressed as the effective rate of protection (ERP) or as the effective protective rate (EPR).

6. *Domestic resource costs (DRC):* The value of domestic resources (evaluated at "shadow" or opportunity cost prices) employed in earning or saving a dollar of foreign exchange (in the value-added sense) when producing domestic goods.

DELINEATION OF PHASES USED IN TRACING THE EVOLUTION OF EXCHANGE CONTROL REGIMES

To achieve comparability of analysis among different countries, each author of a country study was asked to identify the chronological development of his country's payments regime through the following phases. There was no presumption that a country would necessarily pass through all the phases in chronological sequence.

Phase I: During this period, quantitative restrictions on international transactions are imposed and then intensified. They generally are initiated in response to an unsustainable payments deficit and then, for a period, are intensified. During the period when reliance upon quantitative restrictions as a means of controlling the balance of payments is increasing, the country is said to be in Phase I.

Phase II: During this phase, quantitative restrictions are still intense, but various price measures are taken to offset some of the undesired results of the system. Heightened tariffs, surcharges on imports, rebates for exports, special tourist exchange rates, and other price interventions are used in this phase. However, primary reliance continues to be placed on quantitative restrictions.

Phase III: This phase is characterized by an attempt to systematize the changes which take place during Phase II. It generally starts with a formal exchange-rate change and may be accompanied by removal of some of the surcharges, etc., imposed during Phase II and by reduced reliance upon quantitative restrictions. Phase III may be little more than a tidying-up operation (in which case the likelihood is that the country will re-enter Phase II), or it may signal the beginning of withdrawal from reliance upon quantitative restrictions.

Phase IV: If the changes in Phase III result in adjustments within the country, so that liberalization can continue, the country is said to enter Phase IV. The necessary adjustments generally include increased foreign-exchange earnings and gradual relaxation of quantitative restrictions. The latter relaxation may take the form of changes in the nature of quantitative restrictions or of increased foreign-exchange allocations, and thus reduced premiums, under the same administrative system.

Phase V: This is a period during which an exchange regime is fully liberalized. There is full convertibility on current account, and quantitative restrictions are not employed as a means of regulating the ex ante balance of payments.

Index

Index